VEDA AND LIVING LOGOS

Dedicated to the memory of

Hermann Beckh

(1875–1937)

VEDA

&

LIVING LOGOS

Anthroposophy
and
Integral Yoga

KLAUS J. BRACKER

LINDISFARNE BOOKS | 2018

Lindisfarne Books
An imprint of SteinerBooks /Anthroposophic Press, Inc.
610 Main St., Great Barrington, MA 01230
www.steinerbooks.org

Translated by Matthew Barton

Originally published in German as
Veda und lebendiger Logos:
Anthroposophie und Integraler Yoga im Dialog
(Info3-Verlagsgesellschaft Brüll & Heisterkamp,
Frankfurt am Main, 2014)
Design: Jens Jensen

Library of Congress Control Number: 2018909131

ISBN: 978-1-58420-938-6 (paperback)
ISBN: 978-1-58420-939-3 (ebook)

Printed in the United States of America

Contents

Foreword

In this book, Klaus J. Bracker has undertaken a monumental task. He has attempted a comparison, for the purpose of mutual illumination, of two esoteric traditions as presented by two authentic seers and representatives of those traditions—Rudolf Steiner and Sri Aurobindo, apparently as far removed from each other in terms of language and culture as West and East. Such an undertaking is without doubt both extraordinarily ambitious and courageous, since esoteric traditions, by definition, deny understanding and admittance into their mysteries to all but those most devout and capable of meeting their rigorous criteria, but more especially because, in our culture of materialistic and rationalistic science and technology, we are not likely to acknowledge the value of either the ambition or the courage that are implied.

Only the most advanced spiritual seekers, and perhaps a few of the most erudite philosophers, would even attempt to elaborate the meaning of the terms *Veda* and *Logos*, as they have come down to us veiled in the obscurity of ancient languages and cultures, much less attempt to enter meaningfully into their innermost sanctuaries of mystery and significance. Yet Steiner and Sri Aurobindo did exactly this in the early twentieth century. And because they did so, we actually have authoritative texts, written in the languages and under the circumstances of our time, through which those mysteries may be accessed. Nonetheless, even in the presence of initiates and seers, such access is confined to the elect who rise to the heights of devotion that such traditions have always demanded. Therefore, even to begin such a pursuit requires extraordinary determination.

It should not seem too startling, therefore, if the reader of this text of Klaus J. Bracker finds it challenging, for this knowledge has never been readily accessible to intellectual and rationalistic thought. In fact, the traditions that have been the purveyors of such knowledge have generally required the renunciation of such thinking by those who sincerely seek to enter the luminous realms to which these roads lead. As Sri Aurobindo once noted, no age has been further removed than ours from the ability to hear the truths conveyed by the speech of these esoteric traditions. There has been progress, however, since he wrote those words, as he himself acknowledged. By mid-century, as he predicted, the tides of Eastern wisdom had begun to break on Western shores, and since that time Hinduism and Buddhism in particular have become almost as prevalent in Western culture as its own religious traditions, and perhaps even more prevalent in the sense that they have inspired new study and research into the subjects of spiritual psychology and metaphysics, which had receded in relevance in the West since the Middle Ages, the Reformation, and the advent of modern science.

It is still helpful, however, for the pathfinders who have found a way to help us bridge the gap between our conventional ways of thinking and those that might still seem remote and mysterious. And Bracker's intention is clearly to provide such guidance and to bring somewhat closer to our range an awareness of that esoteric form of speech, and the luminous knowledge that it conveys. The words *Veda,* in Sanskrit, and *Logos,* in Greek, both mean "Truth." But by this is meant the highest truth of existence, which is not a concept with which we are likely to resonate in this age of multimedia stimulation, even if we find it seriously lacking in anything like "truth." The traditions of Veda and Logos, however, speak of the divine origin and meaning of our existence, and indicate that this can be known and experienced directly by an inspired and illumined mind. Such a mind—at one with that divine origin and truth—can also sometimes become the vehicle of its transmission through a revelatory power of speech. And because of this, it has been possible for such minds to convey this truth of experience in such a way that it is seen and felt by others. It is embodied in a form that reveals its substance to the soul that can hear.

As Sri Aurobindo put it in a volume on the form of sacred speech known as *mantra*, “The Mantra is a direct and most heightened, intense, and divinely burdened rhythmic word that embodies an intuitive and revelatory inspiration and ensouls the mind with the sight and presence of the very self, the inmost reality of things.” The “things” to which he refers here are spiritual things, beings, and states of inner experience. These are the realities that he wishes to be seen and known through the power of *mantra,* which he attributes to the goddess of illumined speech in Vedic literature, named *Savitri.*

In the thinking of the seers of Veda and Logos, the seeing and the power of speech that enables it are elevated by the understanding of this revelation to a mythological, cosmological, and psychological event in which the Seer, the Seen, and the Word that mediates them are a Unity—which is also a divine Trinity—the Absolute, its Force of creative expression, and its Embodiment in the luminous manifold forms of body, life, mind, and soul are experienced as one truth of being in the mind that is illumined by its presence. Thus there evolve, through the experience and understanding of the seers of this mystery through the ages of a tradition, systems of knowledge in which the Truth, the Word, and the Light are known as one creative force of existence and the supreme truth. This inspired knowledge is the substance of the Veda and Logos that have come down to us through the mystery teachings of the ages, which this book aspires to bring alive for us through the writings of Steiner and Sri Aurobindo.

May those who have an ear, hear this word, and enjoy its illumination!

Rod Hemsell
SALC (Sri Aurobindo Learning Center)
Crestone, Colorado, September 14, 2017

Preface

One of today's most vital tasks is to try to understand other cultures, and also their spirituality. Anyone who travels to another country can discover that our efforts to get inside the skin of what is "foreign" to us can at the same time lead to a deeper understanding of our own culture. In adolescence and youth it seems quite natural to find that the other reflects who we are back to us, gives us deeper insight into ourselves. In adulthood, this takes more conscious effort. The older we grow, the more fixed our point of view can become, and the more rooted we can become within it.

This book offers a wholesome remedy. After many years of study, the author, Klaus J. Bracker, who has been closely connected with Anthroposophy since the late 1970s, has brought together the approaches and ideas of two great questing minds—Rudolf Steiner (1861–1925) and Sri Aurobindo (1872–1950)—to create a kind of conversation between them. Given Western readers' greater familiarity with their own culture, it is helpful that reflections on Indian thought occupy more space here, and aid our deeper understanding of a culture and tradition that may be alien to us.

The concept of evolution is central to the thinking of both Rudolf Steiner and Sri Aurobindo. For both, the evolution of human consciousness means complementing the path of thinking and philosophy with that of the will, first by describing but then also pursuing this path. The final chapter on the concept of God in the work of both gives us a glimpse into the sublime heights that Sri Aurobindo was concerned with, and the dimensions that Steiner could likewise perceive. For Steiner, it was of outstanding importance to distinguish between different orders of spiritual being.

Anand Mandaiker
Berlin, August 29, 2013

Introduction

by Debashish Banerji and Robert McDermott

This book is an extraordinary accomplishment, a sure source of insight and inspiration for anyone interested in either Rudolf Steiner or Sri Aurobindo. It is insightful with respect to the ideas of these two spiritual teachers, one in the Christian esoteric tradition, one in the Indian-yogic tradition; it is inspiring with respect to the depth of appreciation that the author brings to each of these thinkers and the traditions from which they drew and that they revised. Most remarkably, the author is equally informed and positive about these vast, complex, profound, radically different teachers. Rudolf Steiner is devoted to Christ and to Christianity as well as having a deep spiritual and esoteric relationship to Krishna and Buddha. He also has a relationship to Madame Blavatsky, but unlike her he is steeped in esoteric Christianity and German idealist philosophy. Sri Aurobindo is steeped in the Veda, Upanishads, and the *Bhagavad Gita* as well as having a positive relationship to Western philosophy, especially the evolutionary philosophies of Hegel, Schelling, Nietzsche, and Bergson. There are countless books that compare thinkers but very few manage to enter into and bring forth both thinkers with equal insight and appreciation.

One of the great achievements of this book is the recognition that Rudolf Steiner and Sri Aurobindo each carries a task that was initiated and guided by specific spiritual beings and spiritual processes: Rudolf Steiner in response to Christ, the Archangel

Michael, and divine Sophia; Sri Aurobindo as the co-avatar with Mirra Alfassa in service of a supramental descent and transformation. Rudolf Steiner and Sri Aurobindo (always including the Mother) are as complementary as Krishna and Christ. Every page in this book is the result of careful scholarship, but not merely so; Bracker exhibits an intuitive understanding that is alive to the unbounded significance of these two spiritual teachers. His interpretations show the results of decades of sympathetic thinking. He places Rudolf Steiner and Sri Aurobindo in relation without loss, and thereby invites and enables the reader to reach a similarly elevated level of understanding, appreciation, and ultimately, imitation—specifically, the practice of Anthroposophy according to Rudolf Steiner and the practice of Integral Yoga according to Sri Aurobindo.

Because they carry and are carried by profound spiritual processes, an understanding of their karmic tasks and rich syntheses is essential and challenging. They are servants of spiritual, mysterious transformations affecting individuals, communities, civilizations, and ultimately, human capacities. Given *what* as well as *who* they were, their distinctively mystical–esoteric teachings cannot be understood and communicated adequately from an intellectual, scholarly, secondary level. Rather, their significance involves a consideration of distinctively spiritual categories: Steiner as high initiate and Sri Aurobindo as co-avatar. Thanks to Bracker's scholarly knowledge and spiritual discernment, the reader is invited to travel from biographies, writings, and teachings to mysteries and spiritual revelations.

1. Interpreting Early Vedic India

Bracker's first chapter concerns Rudolf Steiner's and Sri Aurobindo's interpretations of the Veda, the textual source of the Indian philosophical tradition. He explores whether the authors of these remarkable texts were Indo–European invaders who entered

India in approximately the fifteenth century BC or were an even earlier civilization. As most readers will lack sufficient knowledge to evaluate this scholarly dispute it will probably be useful to focus primarily on its relevance for an understanding of Rudolf Steiner's and Sri Aurobindo's respective interpretations of Vedic India. Here briefly is what is most at issue. For Professor Banerji's additional considerations see endnote.[1]

Sri Aurobindo did not detail or emphasize his views on the historical source of Veda. Rather, he made some incomplete researches into the historical and philological background of the Veda, but particularly in his public writings, was reluctant to publish his intuitions that had little support of scientific evidence. This reticence in claiming historical or natural facts based on subjective knowledge contrasts with Rudolf Steiner who was convinced of his clairvoyant reading of the akashic record and more willing to make them public. Rudolf Steiner offers details and emphasizes the importance of Vedic India, which he refers to both as ancient India and as the first post-Atlantean civilization. He assumed that historical scholarship would eventually confirm his descriptions of each period in the evolution of consciousness and many details within each evolutionary phase. Though both Rudolf Steiner and Sri Aurobindo fostered the acquisition of clairvoyant knowledge, they differed in their approaches to the dissemination of such knowledge. Steiner was more generous in his intuitive revelations, while Sri Aurobindo was more careful about matching his expression to his intended audiences, keeping in mind the potential of dogmatic cult formation and the enablement of spiritual bypassing.

2. Interpreting the Life of Sri Aurobindo

On the assumption that Western readers would likely have some knowledge of the life of Rudolf Steiner and little or no knowledge of the life of Sri Aurobindo, Bracker provides a full, fascinating, and insightful account of the evolution of Aravinda Ghose to Sri Aurobindo, and Sri Aurobindo's subsequent spiritual collaboration with his French-Egyptian-Turkish-Jewish spiritual companion, Mirra Alfassa, better known as the Mother of the Sri Aurobindo Ashram. This dramatic biography culminates with Sri Aurobindo's 1947 message on the independence of India on his seventy-fifth birthday and on his death in 1950. Sri Aurobindo said that his life was not lived on the surface for others to see, and Bracker respects this statement by neglecting ordinary events in favor of some of the inner realities of Sri Aurobindo's life, including his first major spiritual realization under the yoga teacher, Vishnu Bhaskar Lele, which he identified as a Nirvana experience; his vivid experience of Krishna in the Alipore Jail and beyond; and the descent of the Overmind, which he designated as the descent of Krishna into his body in November 24, 1926. Bracker emphasizes the remarkably positive consequence of Sri Aurobindo's Nirvana experience on his subsequent active life—namely, his ability to write and act out of the silence of the mind and his attainment of higher ranges of cosmic mind and what he subsequently termed *Supramind.*

Bracker relates Sri Aurobindo's ability to think and write from higher sources to Steiner's "active thinking and passive will." In a similar comparative vein and also with respect to human potential, Bracker discusses what it means to be a guru in relation to the post-Enlightenment view of the equality of all human beings widely affirmed in contemporary culture. Bracker also discusses the Overmind and its relations with the Supermind and the cosmos. Using some choice quotations from Sri Aurobindo's *Life Divine*, he introduces the central lines of Sri Aurobindo's Integral Yoga: (1) concentration on the "inner being" to bring about a more intimate relation between an individual and spiritual realities; and (2) opening to the cosmic ranges of mind above the ordinary mind through an increasing silencing of the mind. By "inner being," Sri Aurobindo refers to the subtle reality of the mind-life-body complex, and though living within the inner being is an important step in his yoga, it is more the "innermost being" or "psychic being" that brings the practitioner an intimate contact with spiritual reality, as described by Bracker.

3. Interpreting the Creative Word: Vac and Logos

The third chapter goes into the centrality of the Word as the Divine Logos in the works of Sri Aurobindo and Rudolf Steiner, including the possibility of the physical embodiment of the Logos. Bracker introduces Sri Aurobindo's interpretations of the Veda in terms of its solar mythos based in the goddess Aditi, whose sons are the suns. Bracker approaches Sri Aurobindo's discoveries concerning the Word in the Indian tradition from various sources including the Vedic *Vak*, Agni and Vishnu, Upanishadic *Om* and the Life-Breath, *Prana*, Tantric theory of *bijas* and Kashmir Shaiva/Tantric theory of *Vak*.

A key comparative convergence between Sri Aurobindo and Rudolf Steiner concerns the unity/synthesis of the forces of dynamism and wisdom in the Word/Logos. He also shows how Sri Aurobindo, due to his classical East-West scholarship, equated the Logos with the Supermind, *Vijnana* of the Upanishads. Bracker holds that the Source of cosmic manifestation was not merely affective and/or vitalistic, as modern Indian spiritual goals privilege, but equally included mind in the power of thinking and the body/material objects in the power of form. Sri Aurobindo carefully explained several levels of thinking, including sense-based, higher mind, mind of light, overmind, supramental. It would be a worthwhile endeavor to compare levels of higher knowledge according to Rudolf Steiner and Sri Aurobindo. Both Rudolf Steiner and Sri Aurobindo practiced and recommended a state of consciousness beyond ordinary thought. It may be better to redefine thought as a silent or concentrated opening to higher intuition, though Sri Aurobindo is more inclined to refer to the

Word as Real-Idea. The redefined thought then becomes receptivity to spiritual ideas that are available to structure all levels of the cosmos.

Readers would do well to consider whether Bracker sees the cosmos as a play of symbols, embodying Truths of the Logos or whether Logos is a free principle of Ideation that is present in laws and symbols but exceeds them. This is an important question, since the latter is Sri Aurobindo's view of the Logos, as a participatory co-evolutionary force. Bracker's equation of Christ with the embodied Logos, as based on Steiner seems, at least to the authors of this introduction, to need further elucidation. It is important to note that Bracker has written on this topic in his *Grail Initiation*, a book currently available only in German.

Bracker also traces in detail the Western sources and accounts of the concept of the Logos, beginning with Heraclitus, the Christology of St. John, and ending with Steiner's interpretations and "spiritual researches." In dealing with Heraclitus, Bracker draws on Sri Aurobindo's monograph on the pre-Socratic thinker, which becomes another Rosetta stone for his comparative study. Bracker has several fascinating insights concerning history based on Rudolf Steiner's clairvoyant researches—e.g., the relation of Aristotle and Alexander. While students of Steiner know that he expected his students to work toward "knowledge of higher worlds," readers unfamiliar with Steiner's instructions may wonder how his claims can be verified.

Readers will also want to evaluate the privilege that Christianity has accorded to the Word as Logos. As with the loss of the Idea in later Hindu spirituality, the Vedas gave equal creative power to Sight and Sound, Revelation and Inspiration, Ila and Saraswati, but from the Upanishads, Sound/Vibration stood at the head of the Divine Senses. The question is whether this conception of Logos as the Word may not be a phonocentric bias of the Indo–European language family, East Asian cultures offering expression of the Logos in pictographic/ideographic forms. This would not make a crucial difference to Bracker's theories, but would open other ways of understanding the Logos.

4. Psychic Entity and the "I" in Spiritual Evolution

This chapter reveals a profound similarity between Rudolf Steiner and Sri Aurobindo concerning the topic that they each considered of ultimate importance: The chapter begins with an account of Rudolf Steiner's and Sri Aurobindo's understanding of evolution and proceeds to an analysis of the nature of the human person within an evolving Universe. They offer similar accounts of evolution and share an opposition to the reductive aspect of the standard Darwinian view. This should be no surprise: the usual reading of Darwin emphasizes "the survival of the fittest" and other materialist claims whereas both Rudolf Steiner and Sri Aurobindo build on a spiritual view of evolution presaged by European thinkers such as Goethe, Hegel, Schelling, Nietzsche and Bergson. Decades before he wrote on evolution Rudolf Steiner was influenced by these thinkers, not by Darwin. While a student at Cambridge Sri Aurobindo absorbed Darwinian and neo-Darwinian philosophy of evolution but his spiritual insights and his deep study of the Upanishads led him to an exclusively spiritual reading of evolution. It would be difficult to separate the blend of intellectual from the spiritual content in Steiner's and Aurobindo's respective accounts of evolution, including the descent of the spiritual into matter, life, mind, and various levels of thinking above the intellect. As Bracker explains, both Rudolf Steiner and Sri Aurobindo affirm as well an upward direction from the human, especially at the upper levels of experience, to the divine. Both Steiner and Aurobindo affirm a dual direction of evolution—"from above and from below."

In his *Outline of Esoteric Science* (1909), and other writings and lectures on evolution, Steiner describes in sometimes astonishing detail the evolutionary process through three pre-earthly phases that he refers to as Old Saturn (warmth), Old Sun (air), and Old Moon (water), each of which contributed and continues to influence the evolution of Earth and humanity. Once materiality was achieved on Earth it was possible for mineral, plants, and animals to evolve further to human life, and thereby to human thinking. Steiner recounts that under the influence of adversarial beings certain "I" (human) beings identified too deeply with their corporeality, thereby setting in motion a battle for control of human consciousness. Steiner frequently indicates the subtle roles of two forms of anti-evolutionary forces: luciferic beings that work against human will and freedom and Ahrimanic beings that work against spirit in all of its manifestations. The incarnation of Christ had as its primary purpose the control of these anti-human tempters. Like Rudolf Steiner, Sri Aurobindo sees evolution as a struggle for the emergence of consciousness and psychic personhood, proceeding from the self-oblivion and self-fragmentation of the Divine, which he refers to as the Holocaust of the Divine Purusha and the Divine Mother. Both teachers agree that evolution is decisively aided by divine intervention: Logos according to Rudolf Steiner and a series of avatars according to Sri Aurobindo.

This chapter culminates in a compelling account of *Vak* or Logos that signal the eventual attainment of a divine life on Earth. Both Rudolf Steiner and Sri Aurobindo trace the series of ten avatars, or saviors, as described in the *Bhagavat Purana* (composed between fifth and tenth centuries AD. According to Sri Aurobindo, Krishna of the *Bhagavad Gita* is the eighth avatar, Buddha is the ninth, and the tenth, Kalki, "brings the Kingdom of the Divine upon Earth." Rudolf Steiner too traces these ten avatars and, following the Rosicrucian tradition, identifies the reappearance of Christ with the Kalki avatar. Bracker quotes Steiner's statement in this regard: "For the Rosicrucians, Christ was this one who was to come; Christ as the ever-evolving crystallization into the luminous exemplar of upwardly evolving humanity."

In his magisterial epic poem, *Savitri*, Sri Aurobindo traces the evolution of consciousness through ever-darker stages until the return of the Divine Consciousness: "A greater power must come, a larger light." Bracker compares Sri Aurobindo's vision of the end time with the identification of the human "I," the knowing of oneself, with the "Word of God" in the Book of Revelation.

In a profound and compelling exploration of the human "I," Bracker explains that both Rudolf Steiner and Sri Aurobindo identify the essential core of the human person—"I," or Spirit according to Rudolf Steiner and psychic entity according to Sri Aurobindo—with the warmth element. The warmth or fire nature of the "I" has a deep affinity with the will, and the will in turn is the capacity that communicates the soul's history to the immortal "I." In a similar way, Sri Aurobindo identifies the psychic entity, or "I," with Agni, the God of Fire. Bracker quotes from Sri Aurobindo's correspondence on poetry: "What you describe is the psychic fire, *agni pavaka*, which burns in the deeper heart and from there is lighted in the mind, the vital, and the physical body."

As Bracker explains, in Sri Aurobindo's view, the psychic being is "identical with our true, individual 'I'-hood." The "I" has many ways to evolve spiritually, most important being the yogas of knowledge, action, and love, especially "love for human beings and the world." Rudolf Steiner recommends the same disciplines: thinking, feeling, and willing. Both Rudolf Steiner and Sri Aurobindo see the human person striving toward full freedom made possible by love. Toward the end of this chapter Bracker attributes to Rudolf Steiner and Sri Aurobindo the same ideal of human life:

> It is by now perfectly clear that both Rudolf Steiner and Sri Aurobindo see evolution of the human being...ultimately as an ever more encompassing development of consciousness toward ever greater freedom. Both also see the evolutionary journey of the soul–spiritual human being as possible only through the realities of reincarnation and karma. (page 153)

5. The Second Coming of Christ and the Descent of Supermind

In the fifth chapter Bracker brings to conclusion his comparative synthesis of what Rudolf Steiner refers to as "new Christ consciousness," also referred to as the "return of Christ in the etheric," and supramental descent and manifestation that Sri Aurobindo and the Mother described as a new phase of earth evolution and a new spiritual species emerging from humanity. As in the previous chapters, Bracker presents each of these teacher's views independently, in their own right and significance, and then attempts to weave and synthesize convergent elements without forcing their respective components and perspectives into a unified position.

Bracker focuses on Steiner's affirmation of the transformative symbol of Christ in Earth history; its preparation before the incarnation of Christ at the baptism by John the Baptist; and its continuation since Christ's Crucifixion, Resurrection and Ascension. His account of Christ as avatar is accurate, subtle, and discerning. He recognizes that Rudolf Steiner often refers to Christ as the preeminent savior of humanity but he also recognizes that Steiner's account of Christ consciousness includes Krishna as the symbol of Shambhala, as "the promised land." According to Bracker, Steiner sees the action of the new Christ consciousness—again including Krishna—as dependent upon an increase in spiritual capacities realized by an increasing numbers of humans. Rudolf Steiner recognizes, as do Sri Aurobindo and the Mother, that divine working in the future will need receptivity and openness on the part of humans to accept the workings of the new forces that are transforming humanity and earth.

Klaus Bracker also weaves a fascinating tapestry of the dates of Steiner's predictions about the workings of the Christ consciousness in the present and future, and Sri Aurobindo's mystical experiences of Krishna and the transformation realized by the supramental consciousness. An essential question issuing from these correspondences is whether, or to what extent and in what ways, if any, the etheric Christ is involved in the supramental transformation announced in 1956 by the Mother of the Sri Aurobindo Ashram. Bracker notes Rudolf Steiner's warning in the early 1920s concerning the rise of a false Christ figure in the 1930s capable of impeding divine influence if human readiness and acceptance of the true Christ consciousness is wanting. This correspondence is all the more remarkable because Steiner did not live to see the rise of Hitler. Similarly, in the 1940s Sri Aurobindo warned that the rise of Hitler represented the capacity of demonic forces to retard human evolution.

Bracker quotes passages from Savitri that bring out the place of Christ as an avatar. Sri Aurobindo did not explicitly affirm the role of Christ in the supramental manifestation but wrote movingly of his place as an avatar of the Supreme, reenacting the mystery of the Divine Sacrifice. Bracker summarizes Sri Aurobindo's metaphysics of evolution involving the entire cosmos and its history and a yoga needed for humanity to precipitate the descent of the latent causal consciousness of supermind in the present age. In sum, Bracker shows the significance of Sri Aurobindo's references in his life and writings to Christ as well as to Krishna that reveal connections and convergences between Sri Aurobindo's vision of the supramental manifestation and Steiner's claims for the transformative power of Christ in the present and future. Bracker insightfully refers to the supramental manifestation as the fulfillment of the mission of Christ. Similarly, he emphasizes the apocalyptic vision of John of Patmos, author of the Book of Revelation, which depicts "a new heaven on earth," and convergence of these transformative events with the radically new consciousness to be wrought by Kalki, the tenth avatar of Vishnu.[2] In the subchapter "The Descent of the Supermind and the Second Coming of Christ," Klaus Bracker expresses a view, based on Sri Aurobindo's "The

Yoga and Its Objects," that Sri Aurobindo's reference to divine Ananda as the aim of yoga suggests "Christ's Kingdom of heaven" (pages 190, 211).

Bracker acknowledges but does not emphasize the centrality of the Divine Feminine in the teaching of Sri Aurobindo, and the decisive work of Mirra Alfassa, named by Sri Aurobindo The Mother, in the yoga of the supramental manifestation. In the second appendix, he describes the Mother's role as creator of Auroville, the utopian city she envisioned in Pondicherry, five miles from the Sri Aurobindo Ashram. Similarly, in this book he does not emphasize Steiner's strong statements on the role of Sophia in the entire evolution of human consciousness. Overall, Bracker neglects the divine feminine in the teaching and spiritual direction of both Rudolf Steiner and Sri Aurobindo. Steiner spoke more frequently of Christ and the Archangel Michael than he did of Sophia but his lectures on Sophia affirm the essential role of Sophia in the entire evolution of the cosmos, Earth, and humanity. Similarly, Sri Aurobindo insisted that the Mother was, and would remain, his equal partner, or co-avatar, in the transformation made possible by the supramental descent.[3]

Bracker ends this volume with a call for continuing research and synthesis between these remarkable modern spiritual teachers—Rudolf Steiner, an initiate of esoteric Christianity and Sri Aurobindo and the Mother, co-avatars of Integral Yoga and supramental transformation. Further reflection on this introduction and on the many esoteric assertions that this book offers has generated questions by the two authors of this essay.

We are left wondering about the best approach toward occult assertions that most human beings have not experienced. Specifically, Sri Aurobindo employs a layered approach; his public writings are cautiously metaphysical with few if any esoteric assertions. His communications to his disciples deal with occult matters but typically with a plurality of assertions (eg., concerning Overmind or Krishna); his diaries, however, are much more explicitly occult and include the names of deities and their actions. The Mother's talks are sometimes directly occult, ranging from references to spirits controlling plants or animals to vivid descriptions of the overmental gods. Interestingly, Christ is never featured in her assertions. Throughout his more than three hundred volumes of lectures and approximately thirty volumes written as books, Rudolf Steiner made countless esoteric disclosures and made more, and more profound, disclosures to private followers and to the priests of The Christian Community.

The authors of this introductory essay continue to hold as a question whether there is a single lineage affecting the whole of humanity or more likely (as we think) more than one, perhaps Krishna, Buddha, Christ and/or others—collaboratively or convergently affecting such an integral transformation. In his "Introduction" to this volume Bracker indicates that he intends his comparison of Rudolf Steiner and Sri Aurobindo to be an example of bridge building toward what he calls a "planetary spirituality." Readers of this book may gratefully note that there have been these two prophetic interpreters, Rudolf Steiner and Sri Aurobindo/Mother, who have presented similar visions of the future, using different symbolic and metaphysical systems, with some remarkable similarities.

6. Guru

This appendix contains two significant disclosures: the mission, incarnations, and spiritual contributions of Christian Rosenkreutz, and the shared conception of the inner teacher according to Rudolf Steiner and Sri Aurobindo.

It is worth contemplating the spiritual direction given to Rudolf Steiner by Christian Rosenkreutz and of the spiritual direction given to Sri Aurobindo by Krishna. As in so many of the comparisons that Bracker discerned between Rudolf Steiner and Sri Aurobindo, this comparison is also a contrast. Whereas Christian

Rosenkreutz is reported to have worked secretly in a series of incarnations, Krishna revealed himself to Arjuna in the *Bhagavad Gita* in a way that was intended for all humanity. According to Rudolf Steiner, the "I" of Christian Rosenkreutz incarnated in Lazarus who, after his initiation, was known as the Beloved Disciple who was at the crucifixion of Christ and subsequently wrote the Gospel of John and the Book of Revelation.

Rudolf Steiner explained that in order to be effective, and to be free of attention by disciples, Christian Rosenkreutz, who has been incarnating every century since the fourteenth century, needs to work undetected during his lifetime and for a century thereafter. Bracker mentions that Count of Saint Germain, the eighteenth-century Christian esotericist, was an incarnation of Christian Rosenkreutz. Rudolf Steiner was devoted to Christian Rosenkreutz and recommended that others should be as well. He did not disclose who gave him his life task, at least not in his *Autobiography: Chapters in the Course of My Life*, but it seems reasonable to assume that it was Christian Rosenkreutz, especially considering that Rudolf Steiner spent himself so tirelessly in practical work, exactly the quality for which Christian Rosenkreutz was known in his various incarnations.

Krishna, the incarnation of Vishnu, revealed himself to and communed intimately with Aurobindo Ghose while imprisoned in the Alipore Jail during 1908 and 1909. He later "descended" into Sri Aurobindo in 1926 in such a way that Sri Aurobindo referred to that event as the descent of Overmind. Following this descent, Sri Aurobindo announced the four attributes of the Mother and that his and the Mother's consciousness were "one and the same." Once again we are led to a similarity and a contrast: Christian Rosenkreutz and Rudolf Steiner were (and are) both initiators, i.e., Rudolf Steiner was (presumably) initiated by Christian Rosenkreutz and subsequently taught a path of Christian–Rosicrucian (or anthroposophic) initiation; Krishna was (and is) an avatar and Sri Aurobindo with the Mother are co-avatars who subsequently led followers to advance spiritually with the help of the yogas taught by Krishna of the *Bhagavad Gita*.

While Rosicrucianism is familiar to students of Western Christian esotericism, Rudolf Steiner seems to be rare, and perhaps alone, in his knowledge of the mission, incarnations, and modus operandi of Christian Rosenkreutz, the spiritually advanced individual at the source of the Rosicrucian tradition and its close relationship with esoteric Christianity. Students of Anthroposophy are likely to be familiar with the importance of Christian Rosenkreutz from parts of Steiner's lectures and from a comprehensive volume, *A Christian Rosenkreutz Anthology,* compiled and edited by Paul M. Allen (1968).

The second significant topic concerns the inner teacher. Christian Rosenkreutz influenced Rudolf Steiner as Krishna Sri influenced Aurobindo, and it is true that they each developed their own inner path and instructed their followers to do the same. Rudolf Steiner led his followers not to himself but to Christian Rosenkreutz, to the Archangel Michael, to Sophia, and ultimately to Christ as Sri Aurobindo led his followers not to himself but to the Mother. At the same time, both teachers encouraged their followers to develop their own individual inner paths or devotion to the universal teacher in accord with their individual karmic life task.

Such was the comparable ideal of each teacher, but in the end both had to compromise in response to the inadequate spiritual–esoteric development of their followers. Rudolf Steiner's followers created the Anthroposophical Society in 1912; he cooperated with this founding and gave a foundation stone for the Goetheanum; this was a physical stone. Steiner did not join this society devoted to his esoteric mission. Because his followers did not show sufficient evidence of independent spiritual development, in 1923 Rudolf Steiner refounded the General Anthroposophical Society and gave it a spiritual foundation stone called "The Foundation Stone Verse (Mantra)." Most dramatically Rudolf Steiner joined his own karma to this esoteric and exoteric community. In a similar way, as Bracker notes, Sri Aurobindo recognized that because few of his followers were able to depend solely on their inner teacher, Sri Aurobindo and the Mother had to serve as their guides. Because Rudolf Steiner was the sole teacher and organizer of the Anthroposophical Society, his task was more exhausting than the task assumed by Sri Aurobindo who was complemented by the Mother in realizing the practical application of his vision. Further, whereas Rudolf Steiner died at age sixty-five, Sri Aurobindo lived to seventy-eight, and the Mother lived to ninety-five.

7. THE MOTHER

The five core chapters of this book reveal its author to be a deep student of both Rudolf Steiner and Sri Aurobindo but not especially of the Mother. His account of Sri Aurobindo in this book focuses on a comparison of Rudolf Steiner and Sri Aurobindo almost to the exclusion of the Mother's role as co-avatar with Sri Aurobindo. It is important recall that Sri Aurobindo several times reminded his followers—especially the Bengalis who were strongly attached to Sri Aurobindo for cultural and political as well as spiritual reasons—that his "and the Mother's consciousness are one and the same." The reason for Bracker's neglect in the core chapters would seem to be his emphasis on the knowledge component of Integral Yoga, obviously highly developed by Sri Aurobindo and less systematically and explicitly by the Mother. In this appendix Bracker explains that the Mother, to whom he refers in quotation marks, is important as an exemplar of karma-yoga to the apparent neglect of Jnana Yoga. The Mother's commitment to karma-yoga is easy to observe—she created and directed the Ashram for twenty-five years while Sri Aurobindo was alive and for twenty-three years after his death, and presided over the creation of Auroville.

Sri Aurobindo's capacity for and devotion to Jnana Yoga, like that of Rudolf Steiner, is stupendous, surely greater than any twentieth-century spiritual teacher except Rudolf Steiner. Additionally, as followers of Rudolf Steiner emphasize, his practical works in the arts, sciences, medicine, agriculture, and education are without comparison. Sri Aurobindo's practical work is mostly invisible and done in collaboration with the Mother. The twenty volumes of her writings contain no works similar to Sri Aurobindo's *Life Divine, Synthesis of Yoga*, or *Savitri*, but as mentioned earlier, Sri Aurobindo attributed important changes in direction and understanding to the Mother. It is not easy to discern the specifics of her collaboration with Sri Aurobindo on his vast productivity, or whether she was at work on knowledge on her own, or whether her karma-yoga practice simply assumed the research and writing that came without cease during the quarter century that she collaborated with him. The Mother's deep understanding of the Integral Yoga is evidenced in her "Evening Talks" and in the compilation *The Mother's Vision*. Moreover, Sri Aurobindo credited the Mother with some features of the formulation of his yoga, which underwent significant changes after the Mother's final arrival in 1920 and after Sri Aurobindo's overmental realization in 1926.

8. Johannes Hohlenberg

Given the tendency of followers toward dogmatism, exclusivity, and presumption—as though their knowing, hearing, or reading their spiritual teacher entitled them to speak with the authority and eminence of their teacher—perhaps the most important disclosure in this appendix is Rudolf Steiner's advice to Johannes Hohlenberg that he apparently saw nothing in Integral Yoga practices "that would have stood in the way of Hohlenberg's anthroposophic orientation." The authors of this essay assume that Sri Aurobindo and the Mother would have offered similar advice on the compatibility of Integral Yoga and Anthroposophy. That Johannes Hohlenberg was a close friend and spiritual collaborator with Mirra Alfassa in Paris, and then in 1920 he met Rudolf Steiner and became the General Secretary of the Danish Anthroposophical Society, and then not only came to know Sri Aurobindo but painted his portrait, offers a vivid, even exciting, example of the positive relationship of Rudolf Steiner's Anthroposophy and the Integral Yoga of Sri Aurobindo and the Mother. It is surely inspiring that Klaus Bracker has followed the lead of Johannes Hohlenberg.[4]

Note: Most readers do not read a book's glossary or notes. With respect to this book such an omission would be a serious mistake. Klaus Bracker has poured his vast and careful scholarship into both the glossary and notes, a careful reading of which will provide the reader with valuable assistance and an intellectual treat.

ABOUT THE AUTHORS

Debashish Banerji, PhD (UCLA, Art History) is Haridas Chaudhuri Professor of Indian Philosophy and Culture at the California Institute of Integral Studies (CIIS) and chair of the CIIS East–West Psychology Program. His books include *The Alternate Nation of Abindranath Tagore* (Sage, 2008); *Seven Quartets of Becoming: A Transformative Yoga Psychology Based on the Diaries of Sri Aurobindo* (Nalanda University, 2012); and a book of poetry, *Half Aroma, Half Face* (Writers Workshop, 2017).

Robert McDermott, PhD (Boston University, Philosophy), is CIIS president emeritus and professor in the Philosophy, Cosmology, and Consciousness program. His books include *The Essential Aurobindo* (SteinerBooks, 1974/87), *The New Essential Steiner* (SteinerBooks, 2009), and *Steiner and Kindred Spirits* (SteinerBooks, 2015).

Author's Introduction

In the late twentieth and in the twenty-first century, the globalization of economics, technology, and communications has brought with it global awareness—not only of the enormous breadth of new, opening horizons, but also of deepening perspectives. Rudolf Steiner and Aurobindo Ghose, two great proponents of a spiritual and holistic perspective who meet in these pages, helped to prepare these developments with their innovative ideas and projects. This concerns nothing less than the grandiose endeavor to keep step inwardly with outward, material processes of increasing globalization. In many places today, we can discern an existential need to connect these external developments with inner, transcendental dimensions that encompass significant spiritual experiences both of the heights and depths of human nature.

Questions of absolute truth, absolute reality and the many countenances of God are also connected with this.[5]

The concept of an evolving spirituality is, as soon becomes apparent, one of the most important keys for understanding today's spiritual occurrences. Naturally this means a spirituality that regards the whole world—spiritual and physical—as an evolving entity, but equally one that encompasses a self-reflective capacity, an order of spiritual perceptions and realizations that is itself also gradually and continually evolving. As such, this outlook places itself with full awareness into the ongoing development of human spirituality through millennia. And from this arises the picture of an evolving organism of global wisdom and traditions developing through the ages, within which—increasingly from the twentieth century on—a spiritual self-awareness has begun to shine in humanity with an effulgence unknown to adherents of the diverse traditions of previous eras.

We can expect this evolving organism of spirituality to become increasingly, and more tangibly discernible in the near future, so that separate traditions across the Earth—and their concern with truth, beauty and goodness—grow ever more apparent and comprehensible as specific "organs" whose functions serve the whole. In this regard we can speak of the complementary and mutually supporting contributions of such traditions to the whole treasury of human wisdom, their increasingly apparent holism. Their mutual relevance has always been latent since the diverse traditions result from the totality of humanity's overall evolution. What is new here is a dawning global awareness of their deep connections and common roots.

Since material and spiritual evolution by no means develop in congruence, but show very different dynamics, the future cohesion between great spiritual traditions to create an evolving spirituality embracing all humanity can come to seem an urgent and existential need. If we miss this opportunity, the various strands of accelerated globalization threaten—given our subjugation to technocracy—to suppress authentic forms of spiritual life and, in the worst-case scenario, to make human spiritual freedom impossible.

Nor will the quest for a planetary spirituality that develops healthy forms ever lead to any sort of unifying doctrine. Its evolutionary and integral legitimacy will come, by contrast, from the meeting within its sphere of diverse spiritual streams, as plural, polycentric and subsidiary structures. Such encounters will be characterized by constructive critique and questioning from individual perspectives that support and do not seek to suppress other views in favour of one's own. These encounters between multiple perspectives will also require us to develop sympathy for their diverse terminologies, the "languages" that give expression to each tradition and its inner content. There will be a considerable need for translation between them all. This points to a process that will of course take a great deal of time and requires great persistence. But in the long term, if committed participants in this process of global spiritualization engage in such translation work, they will be able to avoid a situation where the common ground between them, the shared essence, is ignored or overlooked because of differing terminologies.

Openness to the different "languages" in which spiritual experiences are expressed also especially requires an openness to the different aspects of a single, comprehensive spiritual reality accessed by these diverse empirical routes. This is of great importance, and inevitably depends on the willingness of every serious participant to develop a capacity for inspiration that can engage with essentially new and unpredictable experiences when meeting a different tradition.

All who undertake this have to try to continually test and examine the truths involved. It certainly isn't a matter of finding a uniform common denominator in which all light and shade, everything positive and negative, are leveled out. At every fork in the path we must be able to perceive and dismiss distortions of the truth and the inevitable influx of bad or egoistic motives into the complex dialogic fabric of the new planetary spirituality. To ensure this, it will be necessary in future to practice a fundamental methodology of self-reflection,[6] that makes it possible for us to balance the multiplicity of our experiences, and the ideal conceptual form in which these are formulated, against a fruitful reality of perception and insight. On this same basis we will also be able to contextualize new, seriously tested, individual insights into spiritual reality. This present book, undertaken as an attempt to stimulate first efforts at such dialogue and help to further it, cannot yet achieve the full scope of such a methodology of reflection. One hopes that the greatest possible transparency and consistency in its line of thought can go some way toward compensating for this limitation.

In this context, our enquiry focuses on the Anthroposophy of Rudolf Steiner and the Integral Yoga of Aurobindo Ghose, or Sri Aurobindo;[7] and it is scarcely surprising, therefore, if this poses a considerable challenge. The difficulties that arise here are due first and foremost to the fact what while such relatively new forms of human spirituality testify to impulses of powerful renewal and great spiritual vitality, they are also associated with comparatively self-contained systems of understanding and modes of interpretation. Both schools of spiritual thinking are sustained, after all, by more or less clearly organized communities of teachers and pupils, whose core interest is, respectively, Anthroposophy or Integral Yoga. This is also unquestionably necessary given that the fund of wisdom in each case is of great scope, has multiple layers that can only gradually be penetrated, and an extensive, differentiated terminology. But a critical perspective here can highlight the fact that the modern spiritual schools that do not succeed in reaching beyond their own self-defined contexts and a merely internal discourse will have ever fewer prospects in the long term of participating in the process of an emerging planetary spiritualization. Once again, though, both Anthroposophy and Integral Yoga demonstrate almost ideal prerequisites for this active participation since both schools offer extraordinarily potent capacities of synthesis, both originated fairly recently, and both embody a very highly developed level of awareness. Based on all this, they both appear to be ideally positioned to play an especially important and possibly radical role in the future development of humanity's spirituality.

Integral Yoga and Anthroposophy are also, in the view of the author, apt for a dialogic encounter because Rudolf Steiner and Sri Aurobindo—each in his own distinctive way—made contributions to the perennial philosophy[8] that succeeded in characterizing the spiritual, cultural, and religious context in which they worked (the Indian East and Central European West respectively) in a grandiose synthesis, and at the same time spiritually opened up these sources anew. This relates especially to the Christianity in Anthroposophy and the roots of Integral Yoga in Sanatana Dharma.[9] One-dimensional, linear connections do not figure in either, though. Sri Aurobindo formulated Integral Yoga against the background of his outstanding knowledge of European culture, which he acquired in England; and Rudolf Steiner developed Anthroposophy in response to a rich tradition of Eastern wisdom that arrived in Western culture not least through the theosophical movement. Still more important, both Sri Aurobindo and Rudolf Steiner, with their gaze on humanity's future global spirituality, were concerned that their spiritual teachings and paths of practice and self-realization should go beyond various narrower confessions, denominations, and religious rituals. Because of this, the spiritual history of humanity will eventually affirm the innovative nature of both teachings all the more clearly.[10] The more differentiated and dynamic our view and understanding of past developments, the more precisely we can describe how the future will emerge.[11] The present comparative study, in line with the undertaking outlined above, and through a broadening of horizons that we hope will result, aims to elicit, from all who accord value to such things, this sense of the approaching future and the individual capacity for inspiration associated with it.

If we consider the course of humanity's spiritual and cultural evolution through the millennia up until our own era, an attempt to survey Integral Yoga and Anthroposophy together will seem all the more plausible since the Indian East and the European West, represented by each respectively, have as it were been joined at the hip from a very early stage. Naturally there are other connecting structures, too, between different loci on the globe and between other eras. The focus of our attention here on Anthroposophy and Integral Yoga is an expression also of the need for realistic self-limitation in the face of an enormous task. The author has in no way sought to arrive at some final meta-plane from which he might offer a full overview of the totality of all traditions.

Rudolf Steiner characterizes the Anthroposophy he founded as a "Path of knowledge that seeks to lead the spiritual in the human being to the spiritual in the cosmos."[12] The spirit in the cosmos must be seen not least as the divine from whose primordial revelation the world and the human being emerged. On the one hand, based on Rudolf Steiner's wide-ranging research, Anthroposophy offers us a wealth of spiritual-scientific insights that illumine the nature and development of human beings and the universe in terms of their physical, life, soul, and spiritual qualities. On the other, it gives us detailed information about ways and means by which we can increasingly take our own personal development and spiritual awakening in hand, so as to attain perception at higher levels of existence. Rudolf Steiner regards Anthroposophy as a necessity since, without spiritualizing the whole way we live by drawing energetically on anthroposophic practice, modern civilization will be in danger of falling far short of the higher destiny of humanity and the world.

Sri Aurobindo, meanwhile, says the following of the Integral Yoga he developed: "The object of yoga is to raise the human being from the consciousness of the ordinary mind...to the consciousness of the spirit."[13] This refers to spiritual consciousness as that "of our divine, immortal being." He says further: "It is God-realization and God-expression that is the object of our Yoga and more especially of its dynamic side."[14]

Since Integral Yoga starts very pointedly from our waking mind and consciousness, the practice it cultivates is—as in Anthroposophy—founded on extensive accounts of the various levels of human and cosmic existence: physical, vital, mental, psychic, and spiritual. Sri Aurobindo shows how the individual relates to God, and God to the individual, in this interwoven fabric. The paths of good works, illumined knowledge, dedication to the divine—and their integration—are something that the aspirant must pursue in individual freedom, and thus the requirements of the schools of Hatha Yoga, Raja Yoga or Tantra Yoga do not apply to Integral Yoga. The aim of realizing God and bringing him to expression—as the descent and influx of the supramental—is in addition not focused solely on the single individual as it is in those older forms of yoga. Instead it encompasses all humanity, and has in view the transformation of earthly consciousness.

The very title of this book indicates an encounter between the Indian Veda and Western Logos. From the Eastern perspective this is not a matter only of the Samhita of the Rid Veda in a narrower sense.[15] Rather, as understood in general, I use the term *Veda* to mean the whole tradition based on it. It has also become apparent to the author that the element of Veda can be authentically revived in Integral Yoga. The reader should therefore understand "Veda" in this broader sense. By reviewing the fundamental scope of the rich traditions on which Integral Yoga on the one hand, and Anthroposophy on the other are founded, I hope to illumine all the more clearly the significant future perspectives represented by each of these two spiritual schools. Here, over and above any merely cultural-historical perspective, both Veda and Logos will, I believe, reveal their living spiritual reality for the present and future.

This book aims to show, by explicitly slow and careful steps, why a focus on Integral Yoga and Anthroposophy, and the theme of building possible bridges between East and West that they facilitate, should by no means be seen as a limited or exclusive approach. It seeks rather to be one among many contributions to a globally uniting spirituality that has been emerging since the last century. It will have fulfilled its aim if it can awaken interest at diverse places in this bridge-building task. It is clear that this would mark only the very beginning of the work actually needed.

Here I would like to mention an episode from the middle of the twentieth century, one that seems significant as a prefiguring of future possibilities, and illustrates an early interplay of impulses from the anthroposophic and Integral Yoga schools. It played out between Germany and Jerusalem. In Stuttgart in the 1930s, Sophie

Kratt-Düvel was working as a Waldorf teacher. Soon after the twelve years of Nazi rule began, she warned her Jewish pupil Ruth Bender that her life might be at risk if she remained in Germany. In consequence, Bender immigrated to Palestine before it was too late, and remained very grateful to her teacher, to whom she felt she owed her life. In Jerusalem Ruth Bender became acquainted with the Protestant priest and theologian Heinz Kappes who had been prohibited from practising in Karlsruhe, in Baden, because of his socialist views. Soon afterward he left Germany, joining the circle around Martin Buber in Jerusalem, and giving lectures on mystical movements and schools. In a bookshop he came "by chance" upon Sri Aurobindo's major work *The Life Divine*, which grew to be of profound importance for him. For the rest of his life he was deeply connected with Integral Yoga, and he later translated all Sri Aurobindo's works into German. Prior to this, in the early postwar years, Ruth Bender started sending to Sophie Kratt-Düvel in Stuttgart small pamphlets written by Heinz Kappes, which included texts by Sri Aurobindo. And in consequence, Eckhard Karmasch, a nephew of this anthroposophist, became aware of Integral Yoga. A young man at the time, he once said that he owed Heinz Kappes a great debt of gratitude for taking him to visit Pondicherry for the first time, and introducing him to the "Sri Aurobindo Ashram." Later he generously supported the German theologian's translation work.

I hope that the friends and Sadhakas[16] of Integral Yoga will forgive me if this present study sometimes testifies to my fuller acquaintance with Anthroposophy. I cannot and will not conceal my own cultural and spiritual roots. I feel confident that future studies by others will enlarge and augment the perspectives offered here. My hope is that this book can help friends of Anthroposophy fathom the authentic nature of Indian spirituality and thus gradually come to critically question and review the reservations that, especially in anthroposophic circles, have led to a widespread lack of interest in India for many decades. From a more technical point of view, I would also like to make clear that I did not wish to "translate" every term in Integral Yoga immediately and directly into an anthroposophic one. The work of "translation" referred to earlier is more contextual. Rather than carefully matching terms, I hope that, in the course of my narrative account, they can mutually illumine each other, gradually coming into clearer focus in the light of each new aspect addressed[17] and, of course, vice versa.[18] Out of deep respect for his conversation partners in the East, the author has taken the greatest possible care in his account of Integral Yoga and in his selection of quotations from the works of Sri Aurobindo, doing this equally in relation to the works of Rudolf Steiner. This is the very least that should be expected of any attempt, as undertaken here, to contribute to a future culture of mutual engagement and encounter between humanity's great schools of spirituality.

I would like to give special thanks here to my sister Christine Böhm, whose deep familiarity and involvement with Rudolf Steiner's Anthroposophy was invaluable as the manuscript developed; and also to Wilfried Huchzermeyer, Nishtha Müller, Marianne Sörensen and Wolfgang Aurose, all of whom are fully versed in and deeply knowledgeable of Sri Aurobindo's Integral Yoga, and who supported this endeavor with friendly critique and advice. I would also like to thank the directors of the Sri Aurobindo Ashram Trust in Pondicherry, India, and the Rudolf Steiner Verlag in Basel for their kind permission to quote extensively from the works of Sri Aurobindo and those of Rudolf Steiner.

Sri Aurobindo (1872-1950) ca. 1915
and Rudolf Steiner (1861-1925) ca. 1900

Chapter 1

India in the Early Vedic Era

History and Spiritual Character

Anthroposophy and Integral Yoga both look back to a Vedic era of the ancient Rishis in India that, in broad terms, began millennia earlier than, for instance, the cultures of Mesopotamia. There are numerous passages in the works of Rudolf Steiner that speak of an early culture after the Great Flood, "many thousands of years old, and scarcely mentioned in exoteric documents." He continues:

> What the latter tell us dates to a time many millennia later. In those significant gatherings of wisdom, which we call the books of the Veda, in these ancient Vedas, we have in fact only a last echo of what had been preserved of a very early Indian culture, guided and governed by suprasensory beings and first established by the Holy Rishis.[19]

The founder of Anthroposophy sometimes speaks of this culture in very laudatory terms, for instance when speaking of "the primordial Indian culture...that preceded the Vedic era—a wonderful culture that awakens in us a *frisson* of awe, and that found its last reflection in the Vedas themselves."[20]

In relation to the origins of Vedic India, Sri Aurobindo likewise has an era in view compared with which the most ancient hymns of the *Rig Veda* appear as a late and "comparatively modern development or version of a more ancient lyric evangel." And he assesses the great wealth of the Vedic "litanies" as follows: "It is perhaps only the last testament of the Ages of Intuition, the luminous Dawns of the Forefathers, to their descendants, to a human race already turning in spirit toward the lower levels... of the physical life and of the intellect and the logical reason."[21]

In the further course of our enquiries, it will become apparent that the respective pictures of early Vedic India, drawn from the radical insights both of Sri Aurobindo and Rudolf Steiner, can be understood in a deeper sense as profoundly significant for the evolution of human spirituality.

Such comments about early Indian culture by both these spiritual teachers—somewhat more cautious in the case of Sri Aurobindo—are representative of their fundamental views, but—or so it initially appears—they contradict to no small degree what other commentators usually tell us.

Despite more than two hundred years of research in the field of Indology, modern scholars remain largely in the dark about the first beginnings of Vedic culture. It is generally agreed that the Vedas, and above all the most ancient of them, the *Rig Veda*, in the version passed down to us through the last three millennia in almost unaltered form,[22] originated at a somewhat earlier period. But academic Indology allows at the most a further millennium as the span during which accounts in the *Rig Veda* are said to have occurred, and during which the seers and poets, the Rishis, created over a thousand hymns that compose the ten Rig-Vedic song cycles, the mandalas. According to this view, the Vedic era of the Sapta Rishis, the "seven Holy Rishis"—the age ruled by the gods Indra, Agni, Mitra, Varun, the Maruts, and so forth—would have unfolded no earlier than the second millennium BC.

Currently, Western scholars assume that in this period (1800–1500 BC), nomadic tribes of Indo-European language and culture first set off from northwest Asia—a region said to have extended as far as southern Russia—and from the great steppes of central

Asia, and migrated southward in great treks. With herds of cattle, oxcarts and teams of horses, and equipped with bronze tools and weapons, they supposedly made their way gradually across the area of modern Afghanistan to reach the Punjab region. This "land of the five great rivers," the greatest of these being Sindhu, today's Indus, is said to have offered them the fertile grazing they needed for their herds, since it benefited from the seasonal rising of waters fed by the western Himalayas. On encountering the predominantly settled peoples of northwest India, these Indo–Europeans supposedly attacked and robbed them, and over centuries pushed them back into more southern and Eastern regions or subjugated them. In later centuries, in this view, as the lifestyles of the immigrants and the original population increasingly interpenetrated, the former likewise settled and adopted from the indigenous peoples various customs and linguistic forms (apparent from borrowed words), integrating these into their own way of life, language and world view. In social terms, this already led in early Vedic times to a situation where the Brahmins and Kshatriyas—as the ruling varnas or castes of priests and teachers, together with the princes and warriors—consisted largely of the light-skinned Indo–European population, while farmers and traders on the one hand, and servants on the other, came from the original populace, the Adivasi tribes or the Dravidian people, both of whom had darker skins.[23] This is said to highlight a division in the populace, a linguistic one too, that is still discernible today. Vedic Sanskrit and modern Indian languages such as Hindi and Bengali—the Indo–European languages of the descendants of the northwestern immigrants—are related to, for instance, ancient Persian, whereas the languages of the Dravidian group, including modern Tamil, Telugu and Malayalam, belong to the tribes and peoples who have settled in regions further to the South.

In the hymns of their most ancient song gatherings, the Rig-Vedic Rishis, who belonged to the varnas of the Brahmins or Kshatriyas, are believed to have expressed their ritualized worship of powerful natural forces, upon which depended the simple life of the Indo–Europeans settling in northwest India. Thus for instance Usha, Surya, Aditi, Indra, Agni, Sarasvati and Varuna are seen as divinities of the dawning day, the young, rising sun, the far reaches of space, of the weather approaching in lightning and thunder that brings longed-for rain, of fire, of the fertility-bringing waters of rivers, and of the cosmic order of sky, air and earth, encompassed by the universal ocean. In the naturalistic and academic mode of interpretation current today, the Soma so often celebrated in the *Rig Veda*, which Brahmins sacrificed to the gods, is seen only in connection with diverse intoxicating herbs and drinks by means of which worshippers entered into altered states of consciousness in order to feel closer to their natural divinities.

The Indus culture (Harappa and Mohenjo-Daro culture) that came to light through archaeological excavations in the past century, and that, at the time of the assumed Indo–European invasion (around 1800 BC) had already existed for over a millennium as a civilization with urban structures, is described in recent Indology as definitely pre-Vedic and, in line with the generally acknowledged ethnic divide, usually also as Dravidian in origin. At the time this civilization flowered, it was centered on a geographical territory more than three times larger than Germany.[24] But settlements of the Harappa and Mohenjo-Daro civilization have been found over a far wider territory, roughly speaking from the southern coast of modern Iran in the West to the northern Ganges valley in the East, and from the northern Afghanistan boundary river Amudarja in the North to the Godivari river in the South—an area therefore of between 1.5 and 2 million square kilometers.[25] Archaeological evidence has been found in Balochistan (the region southwest of Punjab) of precursor cultures with rectangular buildings of clay tiles, and agricultural cultivation, dating back to the sixth pre-Christian millennium.[26] In the prevailing view, such findings, supported by linguistic analyses, lead to the conclusion that Vedic culture by no means stood at early stages of cultural development on the south-Asian subcontinent. Vedic culture and language are thought to be of purely Indo–European origin, and to have only assimilated isolated older elements of a previous culture already present there. But given that the Veda indisputably forms the basis of the major parts of later religious literature on which the Sanatana Dharma, Hinduism, unfolded, assumption of this cultural-historical divide—between the Dravidian and other indigenous culture before 1800 BC, and Indo–European dominance since that time—at the same time means that the Sanatana Dharma could have developed only in India as the foreign fruit of non-Indian influences.

In India itself, and elsewhere, there are those who suspect that this view of the origins of Indian culture is characteristically Western, and has still not yet freed itself from the influence of colonialist thinking or even cultural imperialism. The theories and tenets of modern Indology have been formulated under the sway of major figures such as William Jones, Charles Wilkens, Wilhelm von Humboldt, Friedrich and August Wilhelm Schlegel, Friedrich Rückert and Max Müller, the latter having moved from Germany to England at a young age. During the nineteenth century, especially in the Anglo-Saxon world, hypotheses informed by an increasingly "Aryan" perspective became dominant in Indology. According to these ideas, all high cultures known at the time were "Aryan," or as they were later called, "Indo–Aryan" in origin. The affinity between Vedic Sanskrit and proto-Indo–Aryan, from which, for instance, Avestic developed,[27] became in this context an argument for the Indo–European influence that brought a new, civilizing principle with it from the northwest and implanted it on the subcontinent. The ongoing debate today about how properly to contextualize Indus or Harappa culture within the overall course of historical development shows, on the one hand, how the concept of Indo–European culture's primary influence on the past three and a half thousand years of Indian development is losing ground while at the same time—deduced, as it were, *a fortiori*—the validity of this stance is all the more passionately defended.

Critique of the Concept of the Indo–Aryan Invasion

In German-speaking countries, the international debate about the "Indo–Aryan invasion" seems so far to have awoken awareness of the issues involved only in isolated places. We can discern here only a negligible shift, for instance when people speak more recently of successive waves of "immigration" rather than of "invasion." In the Anglo-Saxon world, by contrast, things appear different: here the critique of this position is more often heard. Yet often one also hears Western scholars say, in a somewhat indifferent mode, that the theory previously outlined—of the Indo–European invasion of northwest India in the second century BC—is one that Indian patriots and nationalists primarily question and reject as inaccurate. In the interests of a balanced picture of early or proto-Vedic culture, therefore, it seems all the more necessary to attend especially to the controversial views that, in opposition to the Western mainstream, propose a continuity of cultural development in early India, and reject the idea of Indo–European influences entering so decisively from outside India in consequence of the supposed invasion. Increased attentiveness in this field is also advisable given that such clarifications can help position fundamental statements by Sri Aurobindo and Rudolf Steiner about the earliest Vedic culture within the context of other generally current theories.

One of the biggest problems for academics regarding possible connections between the Indus–Harappa civilization and the cultural origins of the hymns of the *Rig Veda*—as India's most ancient literary memorial—is presented by the fact that, despite a wealth of archaeological findings in locations such as Harappa and Mohenjo-Daro, the pictographic seals have not yet been deciphered, or at least are still generally regarded as undecoded. Indus archaeology and Vedic literature therefore remain disconnected from each other. In the mean time, however, the view of certain researchers that the Indus seals will not be deciphered unless we abandon the theory of minimum contact between Harappa and Mohenjo cultures on the one hand, and proto-Vedic culture on the other, has met with growing interest. These scholars suggest instead that one should attempt to interpret the seals in the light of the *Rig Veda*. The philosophy of religion author Egbert Richter-Ushanas is pursuing this, and for decades has been working to decipher the seals. He has apparently deciphered several hundred of the 3,200 pictographic seals and tablets with the aid of their correspondence to the *Rig Veda*, and speaks in this connection of a "fifth Veda," which "was said by Indian tradition to be lost, but supposedly preceded the four Vedas known to us."[28] In this context he clearly asserts a cultural continuity that—he suggests—would connect and unite the cultures of the Harappa peoples and the Vedic Aryans.

Here we must note in passing that the word *Aryas* was a self-designation by proto-Vedic ruling castes, the Brahmins and Kshatriyas.[29] An "Aryan" noble was someone who knew how to adhere to the customs and rites in the right order and in a way appropriate for the good of the community. The knowledge and ability required for this was what ennobled them. Sri Aurobindo usually translates the expression *Arya* as "one who seeks or strives for perfection." The "Aryas" were those who guided the people of their era in the right direction and acted as their exemplars. Thus the expressions *Arya* (singular), *Aryas* (plural), and *Aryan* originally had no relation to race or ethnicity.[30] In this study, therefore, I will usually refer to the leading group within proto-Vedic culture as the Aryas. Proponents of the "invasion theory," on the other hand, still use the term *Indo-Aryans,* or *Indo-Aryas,* to designate the Indo-European races that are said to have entered northwest India in the second millennium BC.[31]

In recent times, ideas have been put forward that go even further than those of Richter-Ushanas, and in fact turn the commonly accepted theory of an Aryan-led invasion on its head. The Belgian Sinologist and Indologist Koenraad Elst outlines his alternative to the invasion theory as follows:

> In the sixth millennium BC, the proto-Indo–Europeans were living in what is now Punjab, Haryana and western Uttar Pradesh, speaking a variety of mutually comprehensible dialects, and tending cattle as well as practising agriculture. Due to demographic growth, internal conflicts and the occasional economic crisis, some of them moved out through the Khyber pass to Margiana and Bactria, which was to remain a frontier zone of Indian culture for millennia.[32]

Elst speaks of other groups migrating toward the Caspian Sea or further eastward, and later figuring in historical records as the Tocharians. In these central Asian regions they adopted from the tribes they encountered there not only millet cultivation but above all horse breeding, and later brought this back with them to the Indian motherland. The argument, often cited to support the invasion theory that in pre-Aryan times, in Dravidian-dominated India, horses were unknown and must therefore be seen as arriving with the Indo–European influx, is therefore effectively relativized by Elst's conclusions.

One of the most important pieces of evidence for cultural continuity or even identity that connects periods before the decline of Harappa–Indus civilization with the Vedic era relates to the Sarasvati River. By far the majority of excavation sites where evidence of Harappa–Indus culture has come to light lay not to the west of, or along, the Indus, but to its east. Satellite photos have shown that in the Punjab and in Rajasthan there existed in early historical, or prehistorical times a huge river on whose former banks—unexpectedly—the greatest concentration of archaeological sites is to be found. There is much to support the idea that this is the dried-up bed of the Sarasvati River, regarded in the *Rig Veda* as the river of chief importance in the life of the early Aryas—due to which some scholars speak of Indus-Sarasvati culture. The US author David H. Osborn, who lives in southern India, writes:

> High resolution satellite images have verified descriptions in the *Rig Veda* of the descent of the ancient Sarasvati River from its source in the Himalayas to the Arabian Sea: "Pure in her course from the mountains to the ocean, alone of streams Sarasvati hath listened" (*Rig Veda* 07.095.01.1–2). The mighty Sarasvati River and its civilization are referred to in the *Rig Veda* more than fifty times, proving that the drying up of the Sarasvati River was subsequent to the origin of the *Rig Veda*, pushing this date of origin back into antiquity, casting further doubt on the imaginary date for the so-called Aryan Invasion.[33]

The foreword to Osborns book *Science of the Sacred* was written by David Frawley, likewise from the US, who is one of the West's highest-profile critics of the invasion theory and its implications. Based on rigorous comparisons between the Vedas, the Brahmanas, the Puranas, and so on in the Sanskrit original, he drew up genealogical lists of the early, middle, and late-Vedic kings. Along with the generally acknowledged drying up of the Sarasvati River and archaeological findings, this produces a timeline that he pointedly contrasts with the views of currently accepted Indology. In his work on the *Rig Veda* and Indian history, Frawley's archeologically focused timeline for early India, appears as follows:

> 7000–4500 BC: Early Agricultural Era: In this era, large villages like Mehrgarh existed with up to ten thousand people. We could also call these small towns or small cities. Groups of villages made up small kingdoms and had a ruling chief or king.
>
> 4500–3300 BC: Pre-Urban: Larger villages emerge leading to an urban culture along with more complex agriculture and crafts.
>
> 3300–2500 BC: Early Urban Phase: The urban phase of the Harappan (Sarasvati) culture has now been pushed to 3000 BC in Dholavira and Rakhigarhi and may go

back further. This was the height of early civilization in ancient India.

2500–1900 BC: Late Urban Phase: In the period, the Sarasvati already was in decline, with migrations beginning away from it.

1900–1300 BC: Post-Urban and Relocation Phase: The Sarasvats (Harappans) left their homeland for new regions mainly to the east, but also to the south and northwest.[34]

Frawley connects the list of Puranian Kings he has established with another list of Indian kings, referred to in the West by the Greek Megasthenes (around 350–290 BC). The latter's visits to India as diplomatic envoy enabled him to report that, from the first king Dionysus—as he called him following the custom of Mediterranean antiquity—to the arrival of Alexander the Great in northwest India, the royal line looked back to a succession of 153 kings. The whole period of their rule, according to Megasthenes, was said to have lasted 6,451 years. This timeline therefore dates Dionysus, the first Indian king in this succession, to 6776 BC. Frawley posits a "mythical era of Manu" preceding that date; and Manu—according to tradition—is the figure who saved himself and a small band of followers from the devastating flood that was visited upon the ancient world.[35] The Great Flood itself, which the biblical myth of Noah also recounts, can be connected in terms of the Earth's most recent history with the Great Floodwaters resulting from the end of the last Ice Age, the Vistulian glacial era, around ten to twelve thousand years ago.[36] Frawley's timeline, supported by archaeological evidence, suggests that the era of Manu thus falls at the beginning of what he calls the early agricultural period of ancient Indian culture.[37]

Spiritual insight into the Vedic world

Critiques by authors such as Richter-Ushanas, Elst, Osborn, or Frawley may have little impact on the premises of modern Indologists and cultural historians. Yet in the context of spiritual insight into the proto-Vedic era as embodied in comments, referred to at the outset, by Rudolf Steiner and Sri Aurobindo, we can regard these authors' views as innovative. Some reflections on methodology can help us to see why this is so.

Academic research into ancient cultures is a broad field involving a confluence of many separate disciplines. Geology, palaeontology, archaeology, anthropology, ethnology, linguistics, philology, the history of religion and philosophy and so on all make their contributions to a comprehensive overall picture. Specific findings, and their inclusion in a whole context, sometimes offer fascinating insights into long-lost cultures. But a whole picture of this kind will nevertheless always remain an approximation, since material evidence, when unearthed, is always somewhat random. For instance, discovery of the sites in modern Pakistan of Harappa and Mohenjo-Daro, in 1872 and 1922 respectively, was not inevitable.[38] The archaeological findings made there led to our currently established picture of Harappa and Indus civilization. But without these findings, our idea of the sixth to the third millennium BC in the northwest subcontinent of southern Asia would surely look very different.

Apart from the chance nature of such occurrences, historical methodology can only create an external reconstruction, from even the greatest wealth of data, of "how things actually were" and "what actually happened." This problem can be compared with the situation of someone who has lost his memory but otherwise retains all his faculties, and is compelled to reconstruct the story of his life from all sorts of outward evidence. However diverse and extensive, this evidence-based compilation of facts will always remain a very imperfect substitute. It seems probable that external data alone can never authentically recreate the missing dimension of his memory. Memory here represents the lost inner dimension of the past—its soul and spirit if you like. Since the latter is more subjectively tinged, and the external aspect more objective, it is clear that these two dimensions need to complement each other harmoniously to produce a real picture of someone's biography consisting of both outward facts and inner experience.

Applied to humanity's cultural history, this analogy begs the question of the possibility of an experiential dimension involving soul and spirit—one that would correspond to our own faculty of memory. If the external, "objective" but always fairly limited discoveries of modern research can be complemented by an inner, "subjective" yet self-like and therefore authentic experiential dimension, accessed through spiritual vision, genuine Spiritual Science or higher yogic knowledge, then "objectivity" and "subjectivity" could merge in a greater whole, a fuller and truer picture of the past.

Far-reaching spiritual knowledge, as embodied in Anthroposophy and Integral Yoga, points us beyond the limitations of external reconstruction of the past. Both traditions refer, in fact, to a comprehensive world mind or world memory—in Buddhist terminology called the *alaya vijnana* or "storehouse consciousness"—which human perception can discover, and to which we can gain conscious entry. If we do so, we become able to perceive past events: to understand the logic underlying their sequence and development, and to acknowledge, also, an enduring world beyond phenomena that arise and pass away. This world memory, according to both Rudolf Steiner and Sri Aurobindo, is founded on a higher, spiritual–etheric matrix referred to in the Indian tradition as the Akasha. In connection with a "supramental time vision," Sri Aurobindo speaks of reading in the "akasha lipi," or akashic script: "It [the psychic self] can gather on all hands all kinds of indications of happenings in past, present and future time. It can receive before its sight the etheric writing, *akasha lipi*, that keeps the record of all things past, transcribes all that is in process in the present, writes out the future."[39]

Although these words are clearly based on personal experience,[40] Sri Aurobindo gave little attention in his works to his reading of the *akasha lipi*, and the resulting findings. By contrast, Rudolf Steiner ascribed great importance in his works to spiritual research into the cosmic and human past. In 1904, at the beginning of his theosophical and anthroposophic activity, he first revealed details from his Akasha research in a series of articles on this theme. Characterizing his preoccupation with this research (the reading of the "akashic records") he refers to its subject as "enduring," or "imperishable," history in contrast to that of academic history, which concerns itself with "ephemeral" history, and is caught up in its transitory phenomena:

> Someone who acquires the ability to see into the world of spirit, perceives there all past occurrences in their eternal character. They stand before him not as dead historical testimonies but in their full *life*. In a sense what has occurred unfolds before him. Those initiated into the reading of this living script can look back into a much more ancient past than that depicted in outward history.[41]

This "living script" or cosmic memory can be more easily understood if we delve further into it. Rudolf Steiner speaks of the akashic sphere as the transitional realm between the formed or form-bearing world of spirit and the formless world of spirit (between lower and higher devachan). The spiritual–etheric akashic matrix, which here occupies an intermediate position, is distinguished by its capacity to receive an impress from both directions—from the higher, formless world of spirit and from the formed and created world. Thus it exists in the liminal realm between temporal occurrences on the one hand, and eternity on the other. The Akasha plays a key role in all creative acts in which cosmic-spiritual impulses—initially concentrated as it were in germinal points—seek to unfold and manifest in the physical world by first passing through the form-bearing world of spirit and then through the soul world.[42] In the reverse direction, however, the akashic sphere likewise receives the imprints of occurrences in the lower worlds, and these represent the spiritually enduring character of these occurrences. In the akashic sphere, therefore, are formed traces that the spiritual seer can follow so as eventually to decipher the akashic script and read its chronicles. And in this case too—comparable with the "germinal points" referred to above—we must conceive a quality of spiritual focus, of a point that can no longer be expressed in terms of the orders of space and time. To do so, the seer must have comprehended the eternal aspect of his being, his true self, and have realized the spiritual mode of perception of true intuition.[43]

In the context of the highest trinity in Indian spirituality of being, consciousness and bliss—the famous *sach-chid-ananda* of the Sanatana Dharma—Sri Aurobindo, like Steiner, accords the Self a deep affinity with the Akasha, specifically with the Akasha's *ananda,* or bliss nature. He writes of the core supramental sense, the organ of highest cognition and self-realization: "Its action is a result of the extension and vibration of being and consciousness in a supra-ethereal ether of light, ether of power, ether of bliss, the Ananda Akasha of the Upanishads, which is the matrix and continent of the universal expression of the Self... and the medium of its true experience."[44] This experience also includes the faculty of reading in the akasha lipi.

This research into our human past, which Steiner undertook by reading the akashic records, led him to present a wealth of perspectives on past eras of history, epochs of earthly evolution and in fact the whole evolution of the planet from spiritual beginnings through to today. The seership on which this was based enabled him to outline future evolutionary stages too. When he speaks in his major work *An Outline of Esoteric Science* of the planetary conditions of Saturn, Sun, Moon, Earth, Jupiter, Venus and Vulcan, he is referring to the panorama of the development of the whole cosmos, from its earliest beginnings through our present "embodiment" of the planet Earth and on into the furthest future of sublime evolutionary goals.[45] On one occasion, when he was still active within the Theosophical Society, Steiner spoke about the seven proto-Vedic "sacred Rishis" and related their order, as well as their connection with Manu (Manu Vaivashvata), to the sevenfold planetary conditions and the reflection of these in the seven planets.[46] These comments offer a telling instance of the knowledge he gained by reading in the akashic records.

According to Rudolf Steiner, Manu and the seven Rishis embodied comprehensive knowledge, comprehensive vision of the sustaining spiritual ground of the world. Back in the times before the Great Flood, in their earlier incarnations, they were leading proponents of the spirituality of the evolving cosmos. Whereas Manu encompassed the totality of this spirituality, according to Steiner the seven Rishis ("the chorus of the seven Rishis") each embodied one aspect of its sevenfold revelation, and were each connected with one of the seven planets:

> What the planets preserved as powers was concealed in the mysteries of the seven Rishis. Thus this chorus of the seven Rishis worked together, in complete unity with Manu, in the wonderful wisdom that they conveyed to their pupils. If we wish to characterize this, we must say that this primordial teaching contained roughly what we become acquainted with today as humanity's evolution through the planetary conditions of Saturn, Sun, Moon, Earth, Jupiter, Venus, and Vulcan. The mysteries of evolution were enshrined in the seven levels of the lodge, each of which signified a stage in humanity's progress.[47]

Rooted in the spiritual ground of the world, the Rishis, Steiner continues, attained the heights of knowledge necessary for reading the akashic records. They perceived the astral plane, both lower and higher devachan, and so the deep meaning of human existence lay open before them. They penetrated the secret of the "Word," the Vedic Vak, the "primordial Word of Creation," which embodies at the same time the inmost core of the Veda itself.[48] This in turn is related to the experience of *brahman*, within which the Rishi perceived the spiritual archetype of human beings and their "I."

Here it is characteristic that the most spiritually advanced of the ancient Indians experienced the "I" in such a spiritually sublime way. They came relatively late to an experience of the earthly "I," which we can see as lower in nature, long after having developed the rest of their soul (etheric and astral) structure to a very great degree with the aid of the devas. Millennia later when, for instance, the people of Europe awoke to their "I," their souls were still in a much rougher, coarser condition. The early Indians, by contrast, were very highly developed in terms of soul, morality, and spirit by the time they came to experience their own "I" in its more earthly incarnation. This is why, for long periods—albeit only with a dull sense of "I"—they felt their soul and the world's spirituality to be one, and lived with a sense that individual *atman* and universal *brahman* are in reality identical. In lectures in 1910, Rudolf Steiner described how such spiritual sublimity made it easy for them to read the akashic records, and to converse with spirit beings of a very high order, the Spirits of Movement and the Spirits of Wisdom (the name in Spiritual Science for the angelic beings Dynameis and Kyriotetes of Western tradition). The spirituality of other cultures came nowhere near this level. Steiner writes as follows of the most advanced of the early Indians (and here we should think too of the Aryas mentioned earlier):

> They awoke when their soul had already attained an extraordinary degree of maturity; they awoke in such a way that the most advanced of them were able, in a further, easy step of development, to read in the akashic records of what had occurred at an earlier stage of humanity's evolution. They could look out into their environment, into the world, and could read in the Akasha of what was occurring in the world of spirit.[49]

In this context Steiner also says that the early Indians' understanding of their own "I"-being was based on the lofty spiritual experiences they had in their intercourse with the Kyriotetes and Dynameis. The Rishis and Aryas, says Steiner, coined the terms *maha-purusha* and *mula-Prakriti* for these same spiritual realities. We will return in a later chapter to the question of these terms' spiritual significance, and also of the late-awakening "I" of these otherwise highly evolved Indian people.[50]

In Sri Aurobindo's philosophical account of Integral Yoga, he placed less emphasis on the cosmic, spiritual stages of evolution compared with Rudolf Steiner's Anthroposophy, where the participation of hierarchical beings in cosmic evolution is described in the greatest wealth of detail, and, in a sense, systematically. Set against the panorama of both the past and future evolution of the Earth, Sri Aurobindo's interest focuses more on the spiritual progress of the individual *sadhaka*—also in the accomplishment of "collective yoga." He seeks to access the world of the Vedas, and its significance for individual advancement. Vedic experience, for him, does not only embody something past, something completed, but is as it were the horizon that offers a prospect of the human being's spiritual future. From an anthroposophic perspective, this approach can be illuminating if we consider that the seventh of the seven cultural epochs that follow the Great Flood, will, in a certain way, reflect the first of these cultural epochs, that is, the ancient Indian, proto-Vedic culture, and enable it to flourish again at an entirely new level.[51]

Sri Aurobindo likewise focuses clearly on the sevenfold nature of, for instance, the most important Rishis, relating this to the seven stars of the Great Bear. According to him, their divine aspect fulfils and harmonizes consciousness in each of its seven principles, which together "superintend the evolution of the world."[52] In Sri Aurobindo's account, also, the seven Rishis in their human aspect—called the Angirasa Rishis in accordance with tradition—are embodied in the sevenfold stream that pours forth from the divine, spiritual realm into the world of human beings. He writes, "The Angiras Rishis are ordinarily described as seven in number: they are *sapta viprāḥ*, the seven sages who have come down to us in the Puranic tradition and are enthroned by Indian astronomy in the constellation of the Great Bear."[53] And he says of the Angirasa, that is, a Rishi belonging to the group of seven, that he embodies or possesses the power "of Brihaspati, the truth-thinking and seven-rayed, whose seven rays of the light hold the truth that he thinks (*ritadhītim*) and whose seven mouths repeat the word that expresses the truth."[54] But the sevenfold stream, the "seven rivers" in the Vedas springing from the very heart of Vedic pictorial language, is for Sri Aurobindo primarily a solar emanation. He speaks of them in the following quotation, which offers a striking example of his differentiated way of disclosing the spiritual dimension of ancient imagery:

> The seven Rivers of the Veda, the Waters, *āpah*, are usually designated in the figured Vedic language as the seven Mothers or the seven fostering Cows, *sapta dhenavaḥ*. The word *āpah* itself has, covertly, a double significance; for the root *ap* meant originally not only to move from which in all probability is derived the sense of waters, but to be or bring into being, as in *apatya*, a child, and the Southern Indian *appā*, father. The seven Waters are the waters of being; they are the Mothers from whom all forms of existence are born. But we meet also another expression, *sapta gāvaḥ*, the seven Cows or the seven Lights, and the epithet *saptagu*, that which has seven rays. *Gu* (*gavaḥ*) and *go* (*gāvaḥ*) bear throughout the Vedic hymns this double sense of cows and radiances. In the ancient Indian system of thought being and consciousness were aspects of each other, and Aditi, infinite existence from whom the gods are born, described as the Mother with her seven names and seven seats (*dhāmāni*), is also conceived as the infinite consciousness, the Cow, the primal Light manifest in seven Radiances, *sapta gāvaḥ*. The sevenfold principle of existence is therefore imaged from the one point of view in the figure of the Rivers that arise from the ocean, *sapta dhenavaḥ*, from the other in the figure of the Rays of the all-creating Father, Surya Savitri, *sapta gāvaḥ*.[55]

The seven Rishis stand within these seven rays. Like Rudolf Steiner, Sri Aurobindo also makes a connection between the seven waters or seven rays and Vak, the primal Word; as, for example, here: "They...lead to the Truth, they are themselves the source of the Truth, they flow in the unobstructed and shoreless Vast as well as here upon the Earth...they are called *sapta vānīh*, the seven Words of the creative goddess Vak—Speech, the expressive power of Aditi, of the supreme Prakriti."[56]

We should not let the differences of terminology obscure how close in essence are the findings of Sri Aurobindo and Rudolf Steiner. This study will seek to show, rather, that similar accords can repeatedly be found between Integral Yoga and Anthroposophy, despite the fact that these two great spiritual teachers, one in India and the other in Central Europe, employ different cognitive methodologies, and linguistic terms.

In later chapters of this book, as we continue to consider the spirituality of the Veda and its present and future actualization as expressed both in Integral Yoga and Anthroposophy, we will see that a useful and proper judgement of this spirituality's historical significance will necessarily take account, too, of the findings of higher cognition such as practised by Rudolf Steiner and Sri Aurobindo. The comments above on the akashic records and the seven Rishis offer instances, initially, of how fruitful such investigations can be. In chapter 2, focusing on a few salient features, I will introduce Sri Aurobindo as a human being and great yogi of India,[57] at the same time assuming that here in the West there is already sufficient knowledge of Rudolf Steiner's life and work[58] to render the same unnecessary in his case.

Chapter 2

Sri Aurobindo: The Life of a Great Yogi

Aravinda Acroyd Ghose[59] was born on August 15, 1872, the third of five children of a Bengali physician in Calcutta with enlightened, Western views. His siblings were two older brothers, then a younger sister, and a further brother.[60] His father had a love of all things British. English rather than the native Bengali, was the language spoken at home, though Hindustani was used for the servants. Dr. Ghose had acquired his medical title a year before Aravinda's birth in Aberdeen, Scotland, where he spent a year as a medical student and also showed a keen interest in the new tenets of Darwinism. In 1877 the father entrusted his three elder sons to the care of Irish nuns in the Himalayan region of Darjeeling, northwest Bengal, then later they were taken in by an English foster family so that they might benefit from European education and culture. At this point Aravinda was just seven years old. Soon after her sons had been sent to England, their mother Svarnalotta fell gravely ill—a seemingly incurable mental illness that had been emerging for many years—and the father separated from her. During his school days and his classical studies Aravinda lived successively in Manchester, London and Cambridge. In his foster family, strict and puritanical Christianity surrounded him, but despite his great interest in Western culture he did not generally adopt this outlook though he certainly became familiar with the basic ideas of Christianity. At the age of twenty-one, having achieved an outstanding degree, he returned to his native land as a young scholar. Besides excellent literary English he knew ancient Greek, Latin and French, as well as some Italian and German. Shortly before his ship docked in Bombay his father died in India of heart failure, tragically caused by the false news that the ship bringing his beloved son back to him had suffered shipwreck.

Thus, in February 1893 Aravinda A. Ghose stepped onto Indian soil for the first time as a conscious adult. His first seven years there appeared to him like a dream, and after fourteen years in Britain he was completely anglicized. He did not see his sick mother in Bengal until 1894. At first she did not believe that he was actually Aravinda because she only remembered him as a little boy. Only a scar that he had had since childhood finally helped her to recognize her son. Biographer Peter Heehs remarks that Aravinda was really an "orphan" when he returned home.[61] His own culture was so foreign to him that he did not even speak his northern Indian mother tongue, Bengali, and now had to set to work to learn it. He followed this with an entirely self-taught[62] study of Sanskrit and the reading of ancient sacred texts.

The moment he set foot on Indian soil, he had mighty spiritual experiences[63] that gradually give him original insights into the traditional Sanatana Dharma.[64] After a period as the Maharaja's private secretary in the northwestern principality of Baroda, during which he married the Bengali Mrinalini Bose in 1901 and taught at Baroda College, in 1906 he moved to his homeland of Bengal, where he took up a post as lecturer in English Literature at the Bengal National College of Calcutta. Besides this teaching work, the years up to 1908 were marked above all by his energetic political efforts on behalf of the Bengal movement for Svaraj, or self-rule, and independence from the British crown.[65] Unlike Mahatma Ghandi (1869–1948), a little later in the northwestern province of Gujarat,[66] Aurobindo Ghose (as he now called himself) still advocated the use of weapons. Primarily through the influence of the weekly journal *Bande Mataram*,[67] Aurobindo

Ghose became a brilliant proponent of the radical Bengali independence movement, and therefore much feared by the British.

Aurobindo's battle for "Bharata," or "Bhavani"—the "Mother India"—was certainly motivated by a strong religious inclination, and yet to begin with his political goals took precedence over personal spirituality and yoga exercises (chiefly Pranayama from 1904 onward). At the end of 1907 and the beginning of 1908, when he took yoga instruction in Baroda from the traditionally oriented Guru Vishnu Bhaskar Lele, he did so primarily with the aim, to start with, of becoming better fitted for his political campaigns.

But this experiment with Guru Lele took an entirely unexpected turn. Within three days, by repudiating all thoughts approaching him from without,[68] and in the spiritual stillness that thus ensued, Sri Aurobindo achieved realization of what he was later himself to call *Nirvana*. Something was initiated in him that would gradually lead to a change of emphasis from politics to spirituality.

> Now to reach Nirvana was the first radical result of my own Yoga. It threw me suddenly into a condition above and without thought, unstained by any mental or vital movement; there was no ego, no real world only when one looked through the immobile senses, something perceived or bore upon its sheer silence a world of empty forms, materialized shadows without true substance. There was no One or many even, only just absolutely That, featureless, relationless, sheer, indescribable, unthinkable, absolute, yet supremely real and solely real.[69]

His yoga teacher Guru Lele was much taken aback by the radicalism of Aurobindo's breakthrough, especially as he did not follow Advaitic Monism—to which Aurobindo's experience seemed most closely to correspond, if not even perhaps to Buddha Dharma. He relinquished his role and told his astonishing pupil that from now on he should unhesitatingly follow "the guide within him." But Sri Aurobindo himself went beyond this experience of Nirvana, subsequently attaining a further spiritual realization in which Nirvana as such was transcended.

> But meanwhile realization added itself to realization and fused itself with this original experience. At an early stage the aspect of an illusionary world gave place to one in which illusion is only a small surface phenomenon with an immense Divine Reality behind it and a supreme Divine Reality above it and an intense Divine Reality in the heart of everything that had seemed at first only a cinematic shape or shadow. And this was no re-imprisonment in the senses, no diminution or fall from supreme experience, it came rather as a constant heightening and widening of the Truth; it was the spirit that saw objects, not the senses, and the Peace, the Silence, the freedom in Infinity remained always with the world or all worlds only as a continuous incident in the timeless eternity of the Divine.[70]

After these experiences, Sri Aurobindo nevertheless continued his activities with undiminished energy, though his sublime state of awareness remained for many months afterward, and beyond. He had experienced the influx of a higher entity that now guided and governed everything else. "In the condition of absolute inner silence I was making speeches and conducting a newspaper, but all that got itself done without any thought entering my mind or the silence being in the least disturbed or diminished."[71]

To some extent this appears to resemble what Rudolf Steiner described about his own initiation, albeit from a different perspective. He commented that in awakening there is a reversal in the relationship between thinking and will, so that thinking becomes active while will becomes passive.[72] There is clearly a deep affinity between their two forms of expression here. When Sri Aurobindo says that he himself was not "doing this," it signifies nothing other than acting out of a receiving will.

Clearly it is not straightforward to speak of "transcending" Nirvana. This would strike readers familiar with the Buddha Dharma as wholly inappropriate, since the Buddhist term *Nirvana* (meaning "extinguished" or "scattered") refers to the complete dissolution of all ties with the contingent, empirical world. Whether as thought forms, memories and endeavors, and karmic conditioning or *samskaras*, in Nirvana consciousness is liberated from all these suffering-inducing factors, and awakens to the true reality of *Shunyata*, the emptiness of all existence—that is, empty of all ties and entanglements. In the inherently non-metaphysical Buddha Dharma there can be no "further realm" beyond this—no transcendence of it. For a pupil of the Buddha Dharma this would represent a source of renewed and undesirable *samskaras*, however spiritual its nature might be. But when Sri Aurobindo tells us that he did, nevertheless, experience this, he touches on profound differences between the Buddha Dharma and the Sanatana Dharma, to which he henceforth felt ever more deeply committed.[73]

Alipur

Through the realizations arising from his meeting with Guru Lele, a transformation occurred for Sri Aurobindo with which he kept faith despite his initial uncertainty about his further course. He now experienced his actions as increasingly guided by the divine. Outwardly things changed also and—paradoxically enough—seemingly very unfavorably for him. He was arrested on May 4, 1908, and detained by the British Indian authorities in the wake of an attack, attributed to him as leader, which left two English women dead on a public road. After a short time spent at the police station of Lal Bazar Hajat, he was transferred to the state prison of Alipur, which at that time still lay outside the city of Calcutta, and two weeks after his arrest a trial began against him and his codefendants that was to last almost a year.

On his release a year later, on May 6, 1909, radical changes had occurred in Aurobindo within the prison walls.[74] What had happened?

Three weeks after regaining his freedom, Sri Aurobindo addressed the annual general meeting of the "Society for the

Protection of Religion"[75] to which he had been invited. Instead of a political speech that the audience of around 600 people was expecting from him, he gave them an account, in places very intimate, of what had happened for him while in prison, which had led to his transformation. His address was given as if in a conversation with the divine being—Shri Krishna—whom he had personally encountered, and to whom he had come ever closer since his yogic break-through. Known as the *Uttarpara Speech,* this was the only occasion when he spoke openly in public about his spiritual experiences. It is so striking and informative about his spiritual development—from freedom fighter to vocational yogi—that I would like to reproduce lengthier passages and summaries from it here.

> When I was arrested and hurried to the Lal Bazar Hajat, I was shaken in faith for a while, for I could not look into the heart of His intention. Therefore I faltered for a moment and cried out in my heart to Him, "What is this that has happened to me? I believed that I had a mission to work for the people of my country and until that work was done, I should have Thy protection. Why then am I here and on such a charge?" A day passed and a second day and a third, when a voice came to me from within, "Wait and see."[76]

Sri Aurobindo now grew completely tranquil. He was transferred to solitary confinement at Alipur Prison, and awaited what God—Shri Krishna, as it becomes apparent—would tell him.[77]

> In this seclusion the earliest realization, the first lesson came to me. I remembered then that a month or more before my arrest, a call had come to me to put aside all activity, to go into seclusion and to look into myself, so that I might enter into closer communion with Him. I was weak and could not accept the call. My work was very dear to me and in the pride of my heart I thought that unless I was there, it would suffer or even fail and cease; therefore I would not leave it. It seemed to me that He spoke to me again and said, "The bonds you

> had not strength to break, I have broken for you, because it is not my will, nor was it ever my intention that that should continue. I have another thing for you to do and it is for that I have brought you here, to teach you what you could not learn for yourself and to train you for my work." Then He placed the Gita in my hands. His strength entered into me and I was able to do the *sadhan* of the Gita. I was not only to understand intellectually but to realize what Sri Krishna demanded of Arjuna and what He demands of those who aspire to do His work, to be free from repulsion and desire, to do work for Him without the demand for fruit, to renounce self-will and become a passive and faithful instrument in His hands, to have an equal heart for high and low, friend and opponent, success and failure, yet not to do His work negligently.[78]

Thus it seemed to Sri Aurobindo that Shri Krishna was intervening in the external conditions of his imprisonment. The strict isolation of solitary confinement was lifted and he was now allowed to walk in the prison yard at least twice a day for half an hour. During one of these walks the power of Shri Krishna once again entered him and he perceived—in accord with the Sanatana Dharma—that the Highest indwells all beings and things.

> I looked at the jail that secluded me from men and it was no longer by its high walls that I was imprisoned; no, it was Vasudeva who surrounded me. I walked under the branches of the tree in front of my cell, but it was not the tree, I knew it was Vasudeva, it was Srikrishna whom I saw standing there and holding over me His shade. I looked at the bars of my cell, the very grating that did duty for a door and again I saw Vasudeva. It was Narayana who was guarding and standing sentry over me. Or I lay on the coarse blankets that were given me for a couch and felt the arms of Sri Krishna around me, the arms of my Friend and Lover.[79]

To begin with, nevertheless, Sri Aurobindo was still preoccupied with formulating instructions to his lawyers for his defense, and thus still remained "politically" or at least "juristically" active.

But "divine intervention" was soon to extend to this domain too. Unexpectedly a new lawyer, but one by no means unknown to him, appeared on the scene.

> You have all heard the name of the man who put away from him all other thoughts and abandoned all his practice, who sat up half the night day after day for months and broke his health to save me,—Srijut Chittaranjan Das. When I saw him, I was satisfied, but I still thought it necessary to write instructions. Then all that was put from me and I had the message from within, "This is the man who will save you from the snares put around your feet. Put aside those papers. It is not you who will instruct him. I will instruct him."[80]

Henceforth Sri Aurobindo surrendered entirely to his divine friend—and, as we know, was set free. And once again he heard the inner voice:

> I am guiding; therefore fear not. Turn to your own work for which I have brought you to jail and when you come out, remember never to fear, never to hesitate. Remember that it is I who am doing this, not you or any other. Therefore whatever clouds may come, whatever dangers and sufferings, whatever difficulties, whatever impossibilities, there is nothing impossible, nothing difficult. I am in the nation and its uprising and I am Vasudeva, I am Narayana, and what I will, shall be, not what others will. What I choose to bring about, no human power can stay.[81]

However, Sri Aurobindo did not yet know what his specific task would be. He assured Shri Krishna with firm resolve that he was not seeking Mukti, redemption, through yoga—a word we must now understand in its full scope as expanded practice, as used in the *Bhagavad Gita*. Instead he wished to serve the spiritual ennoblement of India. To understand more clearly what he should do, he asked for "Adesha"—for a clear spiritual task bestowed on him from Krishna's mouth.[82] In answer he received two messages. The first was this:

> I have given you a work and it is to help to uplift this nation. Before long the time will come when you will have to go out of jail; for it is not my will that this time either you should be convicted or that you should pass the time as others have to do, in suffering for their country. I have called you to work, and that is the *adesh* for which you have asked. I give you the *adesh* to go forth and do my work.[83]

And the second message:

> Something has been shown to you in this year of seclusion, something about which you had your doubts and it is the truth of the Hindu religion. It is this religion that I am raising before the world, it is this that I have perfected and developed through the *rishis*, saints and *avatars*, and now it is going forth to do my work among the nations. I am raising this nation to send forth my word. This is the Sanatana Dharma, this is the eternal religion that you did not really know before, but that I have now revealed to you. The agnostic and the sceptic in you have been answered, for I have given you proofs within and without you, physical and subjective, which have satisfied you. When you go forth, speak to your nation always this word that it is for the Sanatana Dharma that they arise, it is for the world and not for themselves that they arise.[84]

Peter Heehs, Sri Aurobindo's biographer, has traced the great impact of the *Uttarpara Speech,* which was severely criticized by left-wingers for its supposed nationalism, especially as Sri Aurobindo was said to have encouraged particularistic nationalism in India by means of it. Right-wingers, meanwhile, exploited it to justify their nationalistic Hinduism, using phrases and sentences from it out of context in rabble-rousing fashion. Heehs by contrast emphasizes that with this Sanatana Dharma Sri Aurobindo is always only concerned with the eternal religion that stands timelessly behind all the chance phenomena of different sects and confessions, and also lies at the core of non-Hindu holy texts such as the Bible or the Qur'an. Here he cites a comment by Sri Aurobindo, about his understanding of the Sanatana Dharma, reproduced in the June 1909 issue of the weekly journal *Karmayogin.* According to this, "its real, most authoritative scripture is in the heart in which the Eternal has His dwelling."[85] And Heehs adds in relation to Sri Aurobindo: "The true *sanatana dharma* was not a matter of belief but of spiritual experience and inner communion with the Divine."[86]

So at this point Sri Aurobindo had been set free, although the British authorities continued to keep him under observation and were determined to arrest him again and bring him to trial at the next opportunity. But another inner call came to him—a new Adesha—and in consequence he stopped working for the Bengal independence movement and, after an interim period in French-speaking Chandernagore, arrived in April 1910 by ship, the "Dupleix" in Pondicherry, which was also under French rule. There he was to live until his death in 1950. Since his arrest in May 1908, Sri Aurobindo had been separated from his wife Mrinalini, who had fled back to her father's house in the wake of the brutal police campaign. Until 1915 continual efforts were made by the authorities in Bengal to induce Sri Aurobindo, by fair means or foul, to return to British India. He consistently rejected all of these. Only two decades later, the British finally relinquished the idea of fetching him back to northeast India. To begin with, various old friends from the liberation movement also continued to seek his collaboration, until he eventually made it clear in the Madras-based newspaper *Hindu* that he had completely renounced politics.[87]

Pondicherry: Mirra, the Arya, and the Ashram

Compared with most of what had preceded this, life in Pondicherry acquired a new and decidedly spiritual orientation. Looking back later, Aurobindo divided his biography into the time in Pondicherry and the time before it, up to his arrival there on April 4, 1910. What now began in initially extremely impoverished circumstances,[88] with the help of first two, then four, followers and pupils who had come with him from Bengal, had the potency—also in its outer form—to grow and expand into one of modern India's greatest spiritual ashrams. To begin with, Sri Aurobindo had thought that the stay in Pondicherry might only be temporary, but as time went on this view changed, and not only because of renewed political persecution in British India.[89] The importance of his future task grew ever clearer to him. A quarter of a century later he described this situation as one in which "the magnitude of the spiritual work he had taken up appeared to him and he saw that it would need the exclusive concentration of all his energies."[90]

Henceforth, Sri Aurobindo instructed the small group of sadhakas in a wholly unconventional way, developing the new, future yoga. All actions were oriented entirely to this yoga, with scarcely any outward rules about their communal living. In the early phase, yoga instruction of his pupils unfolded solely through the manner of their shared life together, and through informal evening discussions. Nevertheless this yoga work did not go unnoticed by the outside world. In the Tamil surroundings of Pondicherry, Aurobindo came to the attention of K. V. Rangaswami Iyengar, who belonged to a family of landowners. His grandfather, the owner of estates in the Kaveri-Deltas region, supported a house guru, Shri Vasudeva, who died around 1880. Asked shortly before his death who the sons of the family could find to be another guru, Shri Vasudeva is said to have replied that a yogi would come as a refugee from the North in thirty years time, and would practice a Purna Yoga—which means an integral yoga. This would be a sign that India was close to liberation. When K. V. Rangaswami Iyengar heard of Sri Aurobindo's arrival in Pondicherry, he was immediately certain that this must be the Uttara Yogi, the yogi from the North, and subsequently made contact with him through a friend.[91]

As early as April 1910, a French man, Paul Richard, had arrived at the house of the benefactor Shankara Chettiar, where

Sri Aurobindo first found shelter. He was visiting southern India with political aims in mind, but was at the same time very interested in spirituality. He was so struck by his first encounter and his discussions with Sri Aurobindo that on his return to France he gave a vivid and detailed account of this to his wife Mirra Alfassa Richard. A lively correspondence soon developed between Paris and the French enclave in the Tamil India of the South. In Pondicherry itself, in the first years after Sri Aurobindo settled there, streams of pilgrims started to flow from all over India: people who hoped that by merely looking upon the face of the Mukti they would find liberation. Sri Aurobindo however felt hard pressed and besieged by these throngs.

Mirra Alfassa (1878–1973), the wife of Frenchman Paul Richard, was an artistically gifted woman thoroughly versed in many schools of esotericism and occultism. She had had her own spiritual experiences from childhood on. Of Turkish-Egyptian origins, she was related to the Jewish Alfassa family. In fin-de-siècle Paris, she had, for instance, hosted Alexandra David-Néel,[92] who later journeyed through Tibet, and spiritual teachers such as Abdu'l Baha Abbas and Hazrat Inayat Khan, someone who would later spread knowledge of Sufism in the Western world. In 1906 and 1907, she spent two periods of several months as the guest and pupil of a little known but nevertheless highly influential occultist Aia Aziz in Tlemcen, Algeria, receiving personal instruction from him. Aziz (1848–1927) who called himself Max Théon, also came from a Jewish family and had undergone a Cabbalistic initiation when still a youth. In the 1870s, in his mid-twenties, he was said to have helped found the legendary "Hermetic Brotherhood of Luxor," which in turn led to the founding of the Theosophical Society under H. P. Blavatsky and Henry Steel Olcott.[93] Mirra Alfassa was therefore thoroughly conversant with such esoteric contexts, and with "secret doctrines" such as those that fed into Blavatsky's Theosophy. It would not however be accurate to call her a follower of the theosophical movement.

Mirra Alfassa listened intently to her husband's account of meeting Sri Aurobindo, and knew immediately that she too would meet him. The Richards set off for Pondicherry at the beginning of 1914, and at the end of that March Mirra Alfassa—later called the "Mother"—first met Sri Aurobindo. This encounter would be of lasting importance for both of them and for Integral Yoga altogether.

Since her youth, Mirra would have "nightly encounters" with diverse spiritual guides who instructed her while she was lying—outwardly—asleep. At the age of twenty-six in 1904, she had a vision in a dream of a dark-skinned Asian figure who henceforth led her on her "inner journeys" and to whom she spontaneously gave the name *Krishna*. The significance of this meeting stayed with her when she awoke, and she hoped eventually to stand before him in reality. Later she wrote as follows about her first encounter with Sri Aurobindo on March 29, 1914, in Pondicherry: "My vision exactly! Dressed in the same manner, with the same stance, in profile, his head erect. He turned his face toward me, and I saw in his eyes that this was he!" And, "The moment I saw Sri Aurobindo, I recognized in him the familiar being whom I called Krishna."[94]

Paul and Mirra Richard remained in Pondicherry for almost eleven months, and in May 1914, already, encouraged Sri Aurobindo to start a monthly journal of philosophy through which he could impart his insights and the foundations of his yoga work to an interested public. The first issue of *The Arya* appeared on Sri Aurobindo's birthday on August 15, 1914.[95] Alongside the English edition, a French version, entitled *Revue de la Grande Synthèse*, was also published. Each monthly issue was sixty-four pages in length and consisted largely of articles written by Sri Aurobindo: wide-ranging essay series in installments, which would later be published in book form following some revision and additions, and would become known as the most important theoretical works of Integral Yoga: *The Life Divine; The Ideal of*

Human Unity; The Human Cycle; Essays on the Gita; The Synthesis of Yoga; The Secret of the Veda; and *The Foundations of Indian Culture,* to name only the most important titles.[96] In these books, spiritual conceptions are formulated and developed in a highly compressed diction. It is therefore all the more astonishing to note that Sri Aurobindo wrote several of the extensive texts referred to here almost simultaneously, issuing them chapter by chapter alongside numerous other smaller works.[97] *The Synthesis of Yoga* is a mighty undertaking on its own, since it endeavors nothing less than to interrelate three primary branches of Indian yoga, whose higher unity had long since been lost so that, for the past millennium and a half, their traditions had lived on in separate and distinct forms. These three are Karma Yoga (the yoga of works), Jnana Yoga (the yoga of knowledge) and Bhakti Yoga (the yoga of loving dedication to the divine). The three were now embraced in the new synthesis produced by Sri Aurobindo in his Purna Yoga, or the Integral Yoga of self-realization.[98]

Mirra Richard, who later reported that Sri Aurobindo always wrote with a mind completely stilled and tranquil, supported him energetically with translation. Various editorial tasks now fell to her, first and foremost translation of the essays into French. This personal collaboration had to cease in February 1915 since Paul Richard was obliged to return to France because of the outbreak of war in Europe. His wife went with him, and later also followed him to Japan (1916–1920). In the renewed correspondence that began, one of the topics concerned ongoing spiritual support of the Richards couple,[99] as well as experiences and difficulties encountered with the yoga development she had embarked on under Sri Aurobindo's tutelage. The journal *The Arya* continued to appear. The project increasingly became financially successful, too, which was of great help in assuring the survival of the little yoga community in Pondicherry. Sri Aurobindo's intense writing activity for *The Arya* can seem to us like the creation of a spiritual counterweight to World War I, then raging in Europe, accomplished in great quiet and seclusion in a far-flung corner of the world. In January 1921, eight months after Mirra Alfassa returned to India for good, *The Arya* ceased publication altogether. Over its lifetime of six-and-a-half years, a great spiritual organism of ideas had been brought into being.

It is important to add that at least two years previously, in December 1918, Aurobindo's wife Mrinalini Ghose, who had been living apart from him but had always hoped he would return to Bengal, had died during a severe flu epidemic that was raging across large parts of Asia. Mirra Alfassa fell ill with what appears to have been the same disease, in Tokyo in January 1919, but was able to gather her inner strength to overcome it and recover.[100] The Richards finally left Japan by ship in March 1920, and traveled to Sri Lanka and India. After a one-week stay in Colombo, Mirra Alfassa thus returned to southern India in the company of her husband Paul, and on April 24 they arrived in Pondicherry. In a verbal account of these last sea miles she said:

> I was on the boat, at sea, not expecting anything (I was of course busy with the inner life, but I was living physically on the boat), when all of a sudden, abruptly, about two nautical miles from Pondicherry, the quality, I may even say the physical quality of the atmosphere, of the air, changed so much that I knew we were entering the aura of Sri Aurobindo.[101]

From now on, Sri Aurobindo and Mirra were to collaborate on yoga and spiritual work in a way that testified to great accord and harmony between them. This work provided the foundations for the ongoing outward growth and development of the small yoga community in Pondicherry, which was organized and structured to meet the needs of the sadhakas. However, Paul Richard felt increasingly alienated, and after about a year he separated from his wife and went to northern India as a sannyasin. Later he divorced her. The continuing development of the community now lay chiefly in Mirra Alfassa's hands, whereas Sri Aurobindo withdrew into the inner sanctum of his work, focusing exclusively on sadhana. After *The Arya* ceased publication, scarcely any of his writings are extant for the period between 1921 and 1926. Peter Heehs comments, "In 1926, toward the end of his six-year furlough from writing, Aurobindo remarked that if he had continued to bring out *The Arya*, he would not have been able to advance in *sadhana* to the extent he did during those years."[102] In relation to these years of consolidation and yogic community from which the ashram was later to emerge, Sri Aurobindo said of Mirra Alfassa, later always addressed as "the Mother":

> It was only some time after the Mother came from Japan that it took the form of the Ashram, more from the wish of the sadhaks who desired to entrust their whole inner and outer life to the Mother than from any intention or plan of hers or of Sri Aurobindo.[103]

The year 1926 is regarded as the official year of the founding of the Sri Aurobindo Ashram in Pondicherry. Toward the end of that year, the community numbered only twenty-four members, accommodated in two houses. But three years later, in 1929, there were eighty-five community members living in sixteen houses belonging to the ashram. When Sri Aurobindo died at the end of 1950, there were around 800 members. From 1926 onward, the outer, and inner, spiritual guidance of the sadhakas, and the management of the ashram, was expressly entrusted to the "Mother," Mirra Alfassa. Sadhana, the spiritual practice of the sadhakas, was left so free and open that there were no required rituals or meditations or any systematic instruction in particular types of yoga. The sadhaka was urged to find, through self-knowledge, the spiritual practice that best accorded with his own nature. The one ruling principle for all was that the pupil of the new yoga should develop an enduring aspiration toward the divine, opening himself to the influx of divine, spiritual forces so that these could bring about his ongoing transformation toward Supermind.

In later years, though, many sadhakas reported that they had received very helpful inner guidance from the "Mother."

At the same time, the impressive outward development work undertaken by Mirra Alfassa from the 1920s onward testifies to the marked focus of Sri Aurobindo's yoga on *this* world and all its demands. From the outset the ashramites were urged to accompany the freedom of their inner path with productive outer work. Over the course of the decades, with Mirra Alfassa's encouragement and supervision, the ashram developed numerous "departments": agricultural operations and gardens, bakeries, diverse factories and manufacturing enterprises, a big community kitchen with dining room, guest houses, sports facilities, medical centers, later on a library that now houses 80,000 volumes in twenty-five languages, printing works, photography labs and an art gallery. Musical offerings, featuring Indian and Western music equally, and theatrical performances, became a firm part of cultural life at the ashram from an early stage. The ashram school, the International Center of Education, was founded in 1952, two years after Sri Aurobindo's death, and now educates children and students from kindergarten age through to university degree level.[104]

Overmind

The year 1926 is significant for aspirants of Integral Yoga not least because of a lasting spiritual watershed that occurred through, with, and in Sri Aurobindo, and represented a new stage of his self-realization.

From the early days in Pondicherry, a tradition had arisen in which the yoga community gathered on the veranda each evening for quiet meditation and conversations with Sri Aurobindo. He had always dismissed regular courses or lecture series on questions relating to Integral Yoga as too inflexible for the requirements of sadhana practice. Initially he did not want to take on the role of guru either, since in his view it was more appropriate for his yoga to develop and unfold freely in the community of sadhakas.

Nevertheless he took up this task in 1923 when it became apparent that arbitrary re-interpretations of the new yoga were starting to spread among his students.[105] During these evening gatherings Sri Aurobindo had the opportunity to oversee his pupils' progress in yoga in quiet, subtle yet intensive and enduring ways. The conversations were not always the most important aspect of this. Despite all intimacy between them, he always kept the sadhakas at a certain distance. Ambalal B. Purani, for instance, an important sadhaka who joined the community on 1923, describes gatherings during which Sri Aurobindo remained completely silent for three-quarters of the time, "without any outer suggestion from him, or there was only an abrupt Yes or No to all attempts at drawing him out in conversation." And further: "And even when he participated in the talk one always felt that his voice was that of one who does not let his whole being flow into his words; there was a reserve and what was left unsaid was perhaps more than what was spoken."[106]

On the other hand there were evenings when Sri Aurobindo spoke of key matters concerning yoga, and of details relating to his own progress in it.

These accounts were primarily to do with his teachings on what, from that period on, he called the overmind. Ambalal B. Purani writes that toward 1926 and during that year, Sri Aurobindo spoke increasingly in the evening gatherings about the need to integrate more strongly into yoga work, into sadhana practice, the sphere of the spiritual world that mediates between the most sublime world, the *sachchidananda,*[107] the supermind, on the one hand, and the lower, created world of the mental, vital and physical realms on the other. Aurobindo calls the upper sphere, which contains the true essence of all creatures and beings in a potential, purely spiritual germinal state, the *supermind,* whereas, from 1927 onward, in written accounts, too, he refers to this other, mediating realm as the *overmind.* He also speaks of it on occasion as the sphere of maya, since within it mental consciousness can, in unfavorable circumstances, experience illusion, and confusion. While the perfect unity and harmony of all divine reality holds sway in the supermind, in sublime being, consciousness, and bliss, this realm initiates the first germinal elaborations of developmental impulses in the world of the "original cosmic maya," in the overmind. Accordingly, in this maya of the overmind there exist an endless wealth of spiritual forms, all of which contain within them the potential to develop into distinct worlds in ongoing descent into lower realms of creation: into the mental, vital and physical realms. Essentially, the overmind can thus be understood as the "configuring maya." We should note that Sri Aurobindo's use of the term *maya* is always clearly distinct from any sense of illusion or nihilism, as is widespread for instance in the Advaita Vedanta and in many schools of the Buddha Dharma. For him, by contrast, the original or archetypal maya plays an important role in the creation of the real, tangible universe.[108] The "cosmic game," or "play," it indicates, also called Lila in Hinduism, arises primarily from this overmind, the transitional realm between the upper and lower hemispheres of all-embracing existence.

> Overmind takes all Truth that comes down to it from the Supermind, but sets up each Truth as a separate force and idea capable of conflicting with the others as well as cooperating with them. Each overmental being has his own world, each force has its own play and throws itself out to realize its own fulfilment in the cosmic play. All is possible; and from this separative seat of conflicting and even mutually negating possibilities comes too, as soon as mind, life and matter are thrown out into play, the possibility of ignorance, unconsciousness, falsehood, death, and suffering.[109]

The "overmental beings" referred to here are, according to Sri Aurobindo, to be understood as actual spiritual entities. However, in the sphere of the "original cosmic maya," their existence is not as separate and distinct as are creatures in the physical, material world. These overmental beings, rather, known as devas (heavenly or luminous ones) in the Sanatana Dharma, are much more permeable by one another and far more easily imbued with higher truths. In regard to Indian religion and spirituality, this explains a curious idiosyncrasy of super-earthly, overmental beings: in the ancient texts, many of them appear as devas that represent, especially, the highest transcendental divine nature, or *parabrahman*, whereas elsewhere they figure as subordinate demi-gods.[110] It is this idiosyncrasy, not least, that can make the Hindu pantheon appear so confusingly complex to a Western reader.[111] Before we deal specifically with the special occurrences of 1926, it will be necessary to first characterize the overmind in somewhat broader and more extensive detail.

In approaching this initially supraconscious realm, Sri Aurobindo was guided by the question as to how the human being, as he evolves divine qualities slumbering within him that are originally of supramental nature, but are hidden to begin with, can establish a conscious connection with these same supramental origins, and thus with truth-consciousness, or divine gnosis. In his experience, after all, there exists in the sphere of the overmind, with all the elements that both illumine and can sow confusion, an almost overwhelming hindrance impeding all striving for conscious union with the supramental. The sphere of the overmind can thus be seen equally as a mediating realm and an obstacle.

According to Sri Aurobindo, the reality and experience of intuition offers the sadhaka an assurance that we can connect with higher spiritual worlds. This holds true even when intuition only flashes up occasionally, to be immediately enveloped by "imitative," "mental motions" and dragged back down to the level of ordinary waking consciousness. Through conscious sadhana practice, however, we can experience the reality of intuition and what it reveals to us in ever more comprehensive and complete ways. With this aim in view, conscious sadhana is accomplished, in principle, by two complementary paths: first by concentration on the inner being who dwells behind the external personality.

Experienced first in the heart region, this inner being facilitates a more feeling connection with cosmic qualities active behind form, life, and mental consciousness. Second, conscious opening of oneself to the realities dwelling above the mental realm enables the sadhaka to discover a "vast static and silent Self... which we feel to be our real or our basic existence, the foundation of all else that we are."[112] This experience can in turn easily pass over into that of Nirvana, and lead to the desire to remain in that state or to seek it repeatedly. In response to this danger, Sri Aurobindo offers a "less negative path" to those who open themselves continually to greater realities, of light, knowledge, power, and bliss, which descend most dynamically into that silent self. He describes a four-stage ascent into this descent of realities, and ultimately this allows the sadhaka to reach the "source of this intuition,"[113] a "superconscient cosmic Mind in direct contact with the Supramental Truth-Consciousness,"[114] which acts as a "determinant of all movements below it and all mental energies."[115] It is the overmind that, "with the wide wings of some creative Oversoul, [links] this whole lower hemisphere of Knowledge–Ignorance... with that greater Truth-Consciousness."[116] These wings are for him at the same time *hiranmayena patrena*, the "golden lid" of the *Isha Upanishad*,[117] which the sadhaka seeks to open because—unopened—it conceals our vision of supramental truth consciousness.

In the descent and transition from Vijnana, the supramental, to the original maya, the overmental, the unity of being, of consciousness, is fragmented into a multiplicity of independent spiritual forms and forces, each of which pursues its own "right to fulfil itself."

> The one total and many-sided Real-Idea is split up into its many sides; each becomes an independent Idea-force with the power to realize itself. The one Consciousness-Force is liberated into its million forces, and each of these forces has the right to fulfil itself or to assume, if needed, hegemony and take

> up for its own utility the other forces. So too the Delight of Existence is loosed out into all manner of delights.... Overmind thus gives to the One Existence-Consciousness-Bliss the character of a teeming of infinite possibilities that can be developed into a multitude of worlds or thrown together into one world in which the endlessly variable outcome of their play is the determinant of the creation, of its process, its course and its consequence.[118]

In the overmind, certainly, there are conflicting realities, which however only appear to be irreconcilable opposites of our ordinary mind. For an overmental intelligence they are complementary, or "coexistent correlates." The forces and realities in the world of original maya are, as mentioned earlier, tangible spiritual beings and none other than the devas, the divinities celebrated in countless rites in human religions. And thus Sri Aurobindo says of these overmental gods:

> Each God knows all the Gods and their place in existence; each Idea admits all other ideas and their right to be; each Force concedes a place to all other forces and their truth and consequences; no delight of separate fulfilled existence or separate experience denies or condemns the delight of other existence or other experience. The Overmind is a principle of cosmic Truth and a vast and endless catholicity is its very spirit.[119]

We must however add here that the divinities in the overmind are manifest, but that at the same time they possess still higher, that is supramental, modes of existence. Elsewhere Sri Aurobindo writes, "The Gods, who in their highest secret entity are powers of this Supermind, born of it, seated in it as in their proper home, are in their knowledge 'truth-conscious' and in their action possessed of the 'seer-will.'"[120]

When the lines of activity of beings manifesting in the overmind penetrate into the world of ordinary mind, this inevitably leads to the distinctions existing there becoming isolated and often apparently irreconcilable single ideas devoid of any linking or unifying spirituality. Due to this tendency, the overmind becomes a hindrance on the path to experiencing the supramental Vijnana. Increasingly from 1926 onward Sri Aurobindo was concerned to cast light on the overmind and bring it to conscious experience, so as to open the "golden lid," referred to above, to vision of Vijnana. It is characteristic of his yoga that it never sought a one-sided ascent to vision but instead considered every ascent, even the most sublime, merely as preparation for the descent of the reality he strove for—an influx into the reality of earthly life.

The evening discussions of 1926, therefore, were ever more concerned with the question of a tangible descent of the overmind. According to accounts by Ambalal B. Purani, expectation grew among the sadhakas that something extraordinary would soon occur. Sri Aurobindo came later and later to the evening discussions, and the sadhakas interpreted this as being due to his ever-greater exertions in yoga work.

Then finally on November 24, 1926, toward sundown, Mirra Alfassa summoned all the ashramites to a gathering. Ambalal B. Purani noticed a Chinese tapestry hanging on the back wall of the veranda, of black silk with gold braid, and embroidered with three dragons in a circle, each of which was biting the other's tail. Looking back later he connected this with a prophecy according to which truth will manifest on Earth when the three worlds (*Bhur–Bhuvar–Svar*)[121]—are united. The sadhakas sensed something like the pressure of an imminent manifestation descending from above, and an energetic charge to the atmosphere. Many of them saw an "oceanic flood of light" falling from above, and the moment Sri Aurobindo appeared with Mirra Alfassa, a sustained, resonant stillness held sway in which a meditation lasting three-quarters of an hour took place. Subsequently the ashramites passed before Sri Aurobindo and the "Mother," as she was henceforth known, bowing before them in devotion and receiving a blessing from both.

Once Sri Aurobindo and the "Mother" had withdrawn again, Datta,[122] a Western ashramite, was inspired to cry out: "Today the Lord has descended into the physical!"[123]

By "the Lord," Shri Krishna was meant—Vasudeva, Narayana—who had given Adesha to Sri Aurobindo in Alipur jail, and whom Mirra Alfassa had regarded from a young age already as her spiritual leader: Krishna in the form of an overmental being. This is how everyone at the ashram understood Datta's outcry; and for his part Sri Aurobindo was later to confirm it:

> It [November 24, 1926] was the descent of Krishna into the physical... Krishna is not the supramental light. The descent of Krishna would mean the descent of the Overmind Godhead preparing, though not itself actually bringing, the descent of supermind and ananda. Krishna is the anandamaya, he supports the evolution through the Overmind leading it toward his ananda.[124]

In this account, the marked gesture of devotional reverence toward Sri Aurobindo, and also already toward the "Mother," may give us pause for thought. As we saw previously, Sri Aurobindo originally did not wish to be a guru for others. If we look back to the first ten years in Pondicherry, up to the point when Mirra Alfassa arrived from Japan, we find, rather, a yogi who forms a loose yoga community with a few other sadhakas to whom he, as by far the most advanced and experienced, offers friendly advice and guidance. However free the ashramites were left later on in their sadhana practice, too, *guru shishya* (the traditional teacher–pupil relationship in the Sanatana Dharma) is questionable from the perspective of modern Western spirituality because of the risk of subtle, unconscious dependencies. The fact that Sri Aurobindo accepted it is only partly explained by the expectations of the predominantly Indian members of the ashram and their Hindu background. Mirra Alfassa, the "Mother" no doubt also played a not insignificant role here.[125]

That a higher principle can descend upon, or unite in a descending movement with the spiritual seeker in an initiation experience, is not unknown in Western, Christian spirituality. Rudolf Steiner points out that this significant occurrence is termed *rebirth* within contemporary Grail mysteries.[126] Elsewhere I have written in detail[127] of how this is connected particularly with Shri Krishna or the innocent Jesus soul, and of its great importance in Rudolf Steiner's own spiritual development.

Vijnana: Outlook on the Supermind

Above and beyond the unique nature of the manifestation on November 24, 1926, this day, later known as the "Siddhi Day," was also connected with a radical change of circumstances at the ashram: henceforth Sri Aurobindo withdrew completely from active participation in the life of the community. He spent the next twenty-four years in rooms on the first floor of the ashram building in Rue de la Marine. Only the "Mother" and later on certain selected pupils of his were allowed access to him. In general the sahakas were required to address any questions they had to the "Mother." This withdrawal of Sri Aurobindo was for the purpose of intensifying his sadhana practice.

The manifestation on November 24 had telling reverberations during the period immediately following it, insofar as Mirra Alfassa and the sadhakas began to take Sri Aurobindo's realization of the overmind as the model and example for their meditation. During these weeks and months, there were numerous manifestations among the ashramites of lofty figures and forms of light, and this was seen as a sign of the arrival of a new phase in their sadhana practice. But the way in which Sri Aurobindo responded to Mirra's enthusiastic report of these occurrences is characteristic of him. Decades later she herself recounted their conversation, which Wilfried Huchzermeyer recorded in his biography:

> Then Sri Aurobindo looked at me...and said: "Yes, this is an Overmind creation. It is very interesting, very well done. You

> will perform miracles that will make you famous throughout the world, you will be able to turn all events on Earth topsy-turvy, indeed," and then he smiled and said: "It will be a *great* success. But it is an Overmind creation. And it is not success that we want; we want to establish the Supermind on Earth. One must know how to renounce immediate success."[128]

This led Mirra Alfassa to urge that all exertions leading to such manifestations should cease.

Not until the early 1930s were the ashramites encouraged to send messages and questions to Sri Aurobindo in writing. This led to a hugely swelling correspondence, a task that Sri Aurobindo largely undertook during the night. Letters soon started arriving from all over India, and also from Europe and America. The volumes of correspondence later published are extensive.[129] Sri Aurobindo also began to revise the essays first published in *The Arya,* to prepare them for book publication; and tireless work on his poetic magnum opus, *Savitri,*[130] was to absorb him for the next twenty years. However, his greatest and hardest work was accomplished in the invisible realm: the descent of overmind was to be followed by that of supermind. In his own words, Sri Aurobindo was not striving here on his own behalf, but this work was accomplished for earth consciousness, which, despite its intellectual, cultural, and technological brilliance, he experienced as being hopelessly obscured. In a letter, somewhat personal in tone, written in 1935, he says:

> I am seeking to bring some principle of inner Truth, Light, Harmony, Peace into the earth consciousness—I see it above and know what it is—I feel it overgleaming my consciousness from above and I am seeking to make it possible for it to take up the whole being into its own native power, instead of the nature of man continuing to remain in half-light, half-darkness. I believe the descent of this Truth opening the way to a development of divine consciousness here to be the final sense of the Earth evolution.[131]

This work in the invisible realm was often not recognized, let alone understood by those around him. Replying to a written question about his sadhana practice, and whether he invariably dwelt in higher realms, he replied, "No, it is not with the Empyrean that I am busy, I wish it were. It is rather with the opposite end of things—in the Abyss that I have to plunge to build a bridge between the two. But that, too, is necessary for my work and one has to face it."[132] And when his trusted pupil Nirodbaran asked him whether there was anyone with whom he could ever share his ascent into supermind, since all the sadhakas continually faltered, he replied only: "Romantic one! I am not soaring and soaring—I am digging and digging."[133] In this context we should mention a particular practice that Sri Aurobindo had taken up already a long time before 1920: walking. At certain times he would walk up and down for eight hours at a time, leaving traces in the quicklime floor of his rooms. At other times he walked for six hours a day, though perhaps less in the 1930s.[134] This "digging" of which Sri Aurobindo speaks signifies a continuous delving into the physical body, the unconscious, in order to bring down the higher qualities of overmind, and of supermind, and thus to transform earthly existence. This is a theme that Mirra Alfassa would also take up again decades later in her practice. It clearly shows Integral Yoga to be a yoga that sought to bring down spiritual reality into Earth conditions.

This outward motion, albeit in a very confined space, sparingly extended three times a year for the "darshans" when Sri Aurobindo, with the "Mother," showed himself to the ashramites and ashram guests, was limited still further in 1938 when he had an accident and suffered a complex fracture of the upper thigh. This occurred on the eve of the darshan of November 24—that is, exactly twelve years after the descent of the overmind. From then on his strict withdrawal was at an end since Sri Aurobindo was now reliant on a number of helpers. They included Nirodbaran whom we have already mentioned, the physician and personal secretary of Sri Aurobindo. He was to accompany the great yogi over the remaining twelve years[135] of his life.[136]

After World War II began, Sri Aurobindo took a keener interest in world politics again, also in his correspondence, speaking of the dangers attendant on German National Socialism, and proposing support for England and the Allies. He also kept a sharp eye on events within India in the last years before it gained independence. He harbored some frail hopes about the possibility of a union that might prevent the rupture between India and Pakistan, but history took another course through the policies of the Congress Party led by Ghandi.[137]

The day that India secured its independence from the British Empire, a goal that Sri Aurobindo had once fought for in Bengal, fell on his seventy-fifth birthday: August 15, 1947. At the request of *All India Radio*, Sri Aurobindo issued a message that was broadcast on the eve of the great day. It began with these words:

> August 15, 1947, is the birthday of free India. It marks for her the end of an old era, the beginning of a new age. But we can also make it by our life and acts as a free nation an important date in a new age opening for the whole world, for the political, social, cultural and spiritual future of humanity. August 15 is my own birthday and it is naturally gratifying to me that it should have assumed this vast significance. I take this coincidence, not as a fortuitous accident, but as the sanction and seal of the Divine Force that guides my steps on the work with which I began life, the beginning of its full fruition. Indeed, on this day I can watch almost all the world movements I hoped to see fulfilled in my lifetime, though then they looked like impracticable dreams, arriving at fruition or on their way to achievement. In all these movements free India may well play a large part and take a leading position.[138]

The idea underlying these words by Sri Aurobindo is one he had invariably pursued since he adopted his conscious sadhana practice. He reformulated this anew at the end of 1948 as his view of inner development toward supramental realization began to strongly accentuate the transformation of physical corporeality also. This wide-ranging essay is the last thing Sri Aurobindo wrote, and was published just two years before he departed from his physical body in the rooms of the ashram on December 5, 1950. I would therefore like to conclude this outline of Sri Aurobindo's biography with words from the same essay, which characterize the humanitarian scope of his vision:

> A new humanity would...be a race of mental beings on the Earth and in the earthly body, but delivered from its present conditions in the reign of the cosmic Ignorance so far as to be possessed of a perfected mind, a mind of light that could even be a subordinate action of the supermind or Truth-consciousness, and in any case capable of the full possibilities of mind acting as a recipient of that truth and at least a secondary action of it in thought and life. It could even be a part of what could be described as a divine life upon Earth and at least the beginnings of an evolution in the knowledge and no longer entirely or predominantly in the Ignorance. How far this would go, whether it would eventually embrace the whole of humanity or only an advanced portion of it, would depend upon the intention in the evolution itself, on the intention in whatever cosmic or transcendent Will is guiding the movements of the universe. We have supposed not only the descent of the supermind upon the Earth but its embodiment in a supramental race with all its natural consequences and a new total action in which the new humanity would find its complete development and its assured place in the new order.[139]

Chapter 3

The Creative Word

From 1901 onward, Rudolf Steiner—supported by Marie von Sivers who was later to become Marie Steiner, his wife—formulated and developed his Western-oriented Spiritual Science. The connection of both of them to the Alsatian poet and esotericist Édouard Schuré (1841–1929) was, from then on, of an importance that should not be underestimated. Steiner and von Sivers translated the former's mystery plays, *The Sacred Drama of Eleusis*[140] and *The Children of Lucifer*[141] from French into German, and, in these versions, first organized performances of the plays in 1907 and 1909 in the context of the Theosophical Society. Among other things, this undertaking can be seen as an important preparation for both the writing and performing of Rudolf Steiner's own four mystery plays,[142] which trace the lives of his protagonists in scenes depicting inner processes and meditative content.[143] Not least through this collaboration with Schuré, and in close cooperation with Marie von Sivers, Rudolf Steiner also developed a new approach to artistic and spirit-expressive "speech formation," as a means of conveying the living, ensouled and spirit-sustaining Word. Édouard Schuré, though older than Steiner, became his pupil, and also wrote the much-read text *The Great Initiates*.[144] During the years of World War I, Rudolf Steiner would say of this content of this book, that it "surely belongs to the universal human spiritual values that stand above all that divides nations."[145]

Schuré included Shri Krishna among the ranks of these "great initiates," notwithstanding his status as a divine incarnation, the eighth Avatar manifestation of Vishnu.[146] In his great survey of the secret doctrines of religions emerging in the post-Atlantean era—from India through Persia[147] and Egypt to the ancient Hellenic world—culminating finally in the life, suffering and death of Christ Jesus, Schuré accords Shri Krishna a central and outstanding role. In line with Puranic sources, Schuré sees him as the incarnation of the "Solar Word" and refers to his mighty emanation as this can later be discerned "in the temples of Asia, Africa and Europe":

> In Persia he appears as Mithras, who reconciles luminous Ormuzd and dark Ahriman; in Egypt as Horus, the son of Osiris and Isis; in Greece as Apollo, the god of the Sun and Lyra, and as Dionysus, who reawakens souls. Everywhere the Sun god is a mediator, and light is also the Word of Life.[148]

In Schuré's motive of the Solar Word we can find, as if summarized and encapsulated, much of what this present volume is concerned with. In accord once again with Rudolf Steiner we can also discover Shri Krishna to be the epitome, the most radiant incarnation, of ancient India's former, brighter spirituality, prior to the beginning of the "dark age," or Kali Yuga.[149] In saying that Shri Krishna pervaded Asia, Africa, and Europe, Schuré is speaking of this same radiant emanation.

As embodied in the *Vishnu Purana*, to which Schuré refers in *The Great Initiates*, we can see Krishna as the bearer of the Solar Word in especially poetic form where Devaki, the virginal daughter of the king, appears in Book V. Finding safety, in a sacred Brahmin grove, from persecution by her dark brother, King Kamsa, she is spiritually impregnated with the being of Krishna by the highest Sun God. The relevant passage, however exuberant the language of the Puranas, shows the Vedic spirituality we referred to earlier reappearing as if immanent both in Krishna and also, already, in his virginal mother Devaki. The text describes how no one in her vicinity can endure the radiant light surrounding her from this moment of conception onward. And henceforth, it is said, the invisible gods sing their continuous hymn of praise:

> "Thou," said the divinities, "art that Prakriti, infinite and subtile, which formerly bore Brahma in its womb: then wast thou the goddess of speech, the energy of the creator of the universe, and the parent of the Vedas. Thou, eternal being, comprising in thy substance the essence of all created things, wast identical with creation: thou wast the parent of the triform sacrifice, becoming the germ of all things: thou art sacrifice, whence all fruit proceeds: thou art the wood, whose attrition engenders fire. As Adití, thou art the parent of the gods; as Diti, thou art the mother of the Daityas, their foes. Thou art light, whence day is begotten: thou art humility, the mother of true wisdom.... O mother of the universe. The whole Earth, decorated with oceans, rivers, continents, cities, villages...; all the fires, waters, and winds; the stars, asterisms, and planets; the sky, crowded with the variegated chariots of the gods, and ether, that provides space for all substance; the several spheres of earth, sky, and heaven; of saints, sages, ascetics, and of Brahmá; the whole egg of Brahma, with all its population of gods, demons, spirits,... men and animals, and whatever creatures have life, comprised in him who is their eternal lord, and the object of all apprehension; whose real form, nature, name, and dimensions are not within human apprehension—are now with that Vishnu in thee.... Thou art wisdom, ambrosia, light, and heaven. Thou hast descended upon Earth for the preservation of the world. Have compassion upon us, O goddess, and do good unto the world. Be proud to bear that deity by whom the universe is upheld."[150]

In Devaki, Vishnu the sustainer, the *maha-purusha*, is here distinguished from Aditi as the all-embracing *mula-Prakriti*,[151] whose child he himself becomes in his incarnation as Krishna.

Thus the father element corresponds to the eternal, unchanging, highest self, and the mother element to the subtlest *ur*-substance of the universe, with its infinite germinal capacity. Speech in the original Vedic concept of it as the "Solar Word," which the Purana here conveys in the words "the goddess of speech, the energy of the creator of the universe," in tension between *Purusha* and *Prakriti*, and in the context of the mysterious Aditi, is at the same time the mediating element between eternal self and human self. Below we will examine this in closer detail from the perspective of Rudolf Steiner's Anthroposophy and of Sri Aurobindo's yogic philosophy.

OM: The Pranava

One of the most important mantras of the Sanatana Dharma comes from the *Rig Veda* and is still regarded to this day as sacred throughout India. Chanted especially at sunrise and sunset,[152] this is the famous Gayatri, the Gayatri Mantra from the third mandala of the *Rig Veda*, ascribed to Rishi Vishvamitra, whose name means "the friend of all":

tat savitur varenyam
bhargo devasya dhimahi
dhiyo yo nah pracodayat[153]

In the hymnal Gayatri, the Rishi invokes Surya, the divine being in the Sun, as *Savitur.* Given that the distinctive verse form of the Gayatri both addresses and at the same manifests Savitur, it is possible in the context of our current observations that this "sun mantra" contains indications of what the "Solar Word" may signify in the Vedic context. Hermann Beckh, the anthroposophic Indologist and later priest of the Movement for Religious Renewal translated the relevant verse in the *Rig Veda*, the "sun mantra," as follows: "Let us receive the love-awakening light of the enlivening, divine Sun being, so that it may give a forward impetus to our thinking."[154]

As Beckh elaborates, the human being here receives through the Word an impetus or impulse from the sphere of the Sun's spirituality, which has a close affinity to Christ, to encompass spiritual truths increasingly through the individual power of thinking. He also notes that this intrinsically future-oriented, early Vedic impulse, was unable to make later headway in India, and that only very isolated schools of yoga continued to cultivate it in their practice. This relates to the path, prompted by Vak, the "Solar Word," yet rarely pursued, of developing the meditant's individual thinking capacity. As word and thought separated from each other from the age of the Upanishads onward, many yogic schools in India, in Beckh's view, adopted instead the practice of breath-borne meditation.[155] We will return to this important theme in the next section. First, however, we must examine in detail how the Vedas regard and understand the Word.

If one uses the Gayatri as a single mantra, it is usually preceded by invocation of the three worlds: OM—*Bhur–Bhuvar–Svar.* This is *vyahriti*, the great speech, or great Word. Here *bhur* stands for the earth—the material, sense-perceptible world, *bhuvar* for the air or the elemental world, the astral plane, and *svar* for the broad, expansive solar world, the heavens in the sense of lower devachan. The invocation is intended to resound through all these worlds of the lower hemisphere—the worlds of creatures and cosmic beings. But the opening OM, or AUM,[156] is the *pranava*, the sound at the beginning of all things,[157] which pervades all planes and worlds through to the sphere of the *turiya*, the unutterable Fourth, which is far superior to the three lower worlds.

Through their mantric practice, the Rishi and Brahmin create the closest possible connection, for our human form of existence, between the highest spiritual worlds and this world. This is founded on the reciprocity that is always implicit in Vedic practice. In one direction, naturally, it takes effect in an invocation in which—as it rises—the human voice, the Vedic phrase intoned by human beings, is borne up toward the eternal spirit. In the other, descending direction, the highest comes down into manifestation, in the wealth of forms in which it desires to show itself to the human spirit. This continuing reciprocity constitutes the closely interwoven fabric of Vedic reality. Divine revelation of the Word—Vak—in the hymnic Veda, is what then enables the Brahmin to send his word, as offering, toward God; and this in turn endows specific divinities with the power to continue to manifest. It becomes apparent that this close-woven tissue of offering and revelation is "life" in the higher sense. Thus the Gayatri mantra, the Solar Word, is at the same time the "Word of Life" of which Schuré also speaks, for the name *Savitur* hymned in the Gayatri means, in the Vedic context, "the one who gives an impulse that awakens and enlivens." He is the great impulse-giver, both of individual thinking and of universal life, these two being a single higher unity within him. This spiritually vital fabric of reciprocity also, not least, gives rise to the incomparably enduring, complex, and all-embracing hymns, whose forms and figures of words became an unbroken tradition admired throughout the world. Articulation, rhythm, tonal qualities, and speech melos have remained very largely constant through three thousand years of oral tradition, due to reverence for the sacredness of the Veda felt by pious Indians.[158] But the sacred *pranava*—OM—conceals within it the subtlest essence of this reciprocal Vedic process, the inmost life principle of Vedic tradition, *rik*, as this is intimated in the *Chandogya Upanishad*:

> The essence of these beings is the earth.
> The essence of the earth is water.
> The essence of water is plants.
> The essence of plants is a person.
> The essence of a person is speech.
> The essence of speech is the Rik (hymn).
> The essence of the Rik (hymn) is the Sāman (chant).
> The essence of the Sāman (chant) is the Udgītha.[159]

Udgitha is identical with *OM*. *Vedanta* means "the end of the Vedas." In the classical sense only the Upanishads—which arose toward the end of the Vedic period, and essentially summarize its spiritual and mystical philosophy—constitute the text of the Vedanta. However in later centuries the *Bhagavad Gita*, that precious inner jewel of the mighty Mahabharata epic, also came to be included in the Vedanta, since it offers a brilliant spiritual extract of Vedic truth. In the *Bhagavad Gita*, Krishna homes in on the reality of increasingly subtle essences of the Vedic Solar Word—as the *Upanishad* also does—for instance when, in the *Vibhuti Yoga* or the "yoga of powerful manifestation" he says of himself on the one hand: "I am *Vishnu* among the *Adityas*, radiant Sun among lights and slendors"; and on the other: "*Gayatri* among the poetic meters I am"; or, shortly before this: "...among words am I the single-syllabled *OM*."[160]

The fourfold structure of the *pranava* ॐ—OM—AUM—is explained in the brief discourse of the *Mandoukya Upanishad*. As we have seen, it is the essence of essences: "The past, the present and the future, all that was, all that is, all that will be, is OM. Likewise all else that may exist beyond the bounds of Time, that too is OM."[161] The fourth aspect is what raises the three modes of time into eternity, transcending them. The same *Upanishad* is therefore concerned with four levels of consciousness that the meditant is directed to penetrate and possess with the AUM, such that he always remains entirely wakeful within them. These states are: ordinary, sense-sustained waking consciousness; the dream state; the state of deep sleep; and so-called "trance consciousness." The first level is that of ordinary human awareness, the second is one we share with the higher animals, the third with plants, and the fourth with minerals. At the first level, the "A" corresponds to our modern waking "I"-consciousness; at the second level, the "U" corresponds to the Kama principle as the bearer of our dreaming state, and of animals' soul body; at the third level, the "M" is connected with the Prana principle as the bearer of deep sleep consciousness, the life body of plants; and the fourth element of AUM, finally, always present in the full OM, in its fading into the infinite, its unutterability and inaudibility beyond all phenomena, is capable also of irresistibly penetrating with its light and power of consciousness the lifeless physical level of the mineral.[162] This is *turiya*, the fourth principle, which—identical with *brahman*—transcends the finite worlds of the temporal realm. The fully realized OM, or AUM, thus brings what Rudolf Steiner called "continuity of consciousness,"[163] which at the same time signifies mastery of all requirements that arise during the ascent of knowledge to the highest realms of upper devachan. According to Sri Aurobindo, this is the path toward awakening in supermental atman consciousness, Vijnana, which is capable of entering those spheres of the absolute that are continuously unmanifested (*tat*) and encompass all power of manifestation (*sat*).[164] Human "I"-consciousness in the modern sense realizes itself on the earthly or physical plane, whereas the true center of consciousness of groups and species of animals—comparable to an "I"—resides on the astral plane, that of plant beings in the world of lower devachan, while the center of consciousness of minerals has its existence in upper devachan.[165] In our physical organization we possess the mineral element, in our life or ether organization an element that resembles the plant, in our soul body, or astral organization, an element similar to that of the animal, and only in our "I"-organization do we appear as intrinsically and essentially human in the narrower sense. For the aspirant, penetrating all four levels of his individual being in full consciousness therefore signifies awakening in the three higher worlds referred to, and at the same time full realization or mastery of self.

When addressing the AUM during lessons he gave in his Esoteric School, Rudolf Steiner also highlighted its connections with the three modes of time. Here he was concerned with insight gained through the phenomenology of the sounds contained in the ॐ:

- **A** is the past, sounds clear and defined.
- **U** is a dull vowel and signifies the present. It encompasses both the clarity of the past and freedom of action in the present.
- **M** is the uncertainty of the future, which can lead on to any further vowel and any as yet undefined action.[166]

Rudolf Steiner also connects the three first elements of the ॐ with a threefold action of the Logos unfolding during the evolution of the Earth and humanity from the most distant past through our current epoch to the furthest future.[167] This prefigures an important motif in the later development of Anthroposophy, and enables us to understand that we bear within us, in our soul and spirit, the key to comprehending all cosmic evolution. This is because the three modes of time are, very specifically, also what constitute our soul life, in the distinct faculties of thinking, feeling, and will. Thinking, or more precisely the ideational capacity based on the neurosensory system, is an expression of the forces of the past, whereas the will relates to what is still to come, to the future. In feeling, we experience ourselves inwardly and intensively in the present. This accords precisely with the states of consciousness we have described, and of which the *Mandoukya Upanishad* speaks: full wakefulness is, initially, bound up with thinking, feeling has an affinity with dream, and will possesses the same degree of consciousness as exists in deep sleep.[168] The true human "I"—in its affinity with the eternal—transcends these three levels and by nature corresponds ultimately to the *turiya*.

In its inner dynamic, the OM prefigures the path of awakening through all four levels, and thus signifies this unerring realization of the higher self. The *Mandoukya Upanishad* then also says of the AUM and its four aspects that they are nothing other than the four limbs of atman, of the Self. "Now this the Self, as to the imperishable Word, is OM; and as to the letters, His parts are the letters and the letters are His parts, namely, AUM." And: "Letterless is the fourth, the Incommunicable, the end of phenomena, the Good, the One than Whom there is no other; thus is OM. He that knoweth is the Self and entereth by his self into the Self, he that knoweth, he that knoweth."[169] This is entirely in accord with what was stated above about word and thinking, and the two divided paths. Through the *pranava*, the Word of Words, and the most intense internalization of consciousness possible through it, it becomes apparent that both paths are essentially one in the Vedic worlds.

Vak: The Word of the Rishis

As the evolution of Word and Thinking—or Vak and Manas—generally grew apart, this was founded in the inevitable advance of humanity and yet was not unproblematic. It was, literally, a *critical* development. In the *Shatapatha Brahmana* there is a tale according to which Manas and Word both contested with each other for predominance. Manas asserted that the Word could only express what it, Manas, had already previously thought, whereas Word objected that it was superior to Manas because it conveyed and communicated what Manas merely thought. Since they could reach no agreement, they turned to Prajapati, the Lord of Creatures, a form of manifestation of the All-Creator and All-enacter Vishvakaman. The latter gave Word a clear answer: "The Mind is certainly better, because you only imitate and follow what the Mind is doing."[170] Already in this early text, which is included in the narrower Vedic canon, a division is made between word and thinking. But the answer shows that the "word" is now only seen as the human word, even among Rishis or Brahmins. Vak, the speech of the Rishis, and of the divine, is no longer seen in its universal creative dimension. This distinction had become necessary, according to Steiner, to allow the principle of freedom, of individual thinking, to grow stronger within humanity.

Anthroposophic Spiritual Science acknowledges two powerful groups of spirit beings who endanger human and earthly evolution in the long term; the ahrimanic beings, who wish to fetter human consciousness to the Earth and to matter, and to prevent it freely finding its way to the spirit; and the luciferic, who try to divert human consciousness from earthly tasks and requirements, and give us a taste for a bodiless and only seemingly spiritual[171] form of existence. Luciferic and ahrimanic spirits[172] act in diverse realms, in different ways, to pursue their respective interests. In lectures he gave in 1915, Rudolf Steiner described how the Vedic Rishis, in their work in the fields of speech and thinking, came into dangerous conflict with certain luciferic spirits. The latter sought to bring about developments that would prematurely sunder thinking from speech, and place it at the service of a wise but entirely abstract dogmatism across the whole globe. Steiner speaks of the threat at that time of a fanatically pursued "luciferic Monism."[173] The Vedic Rishis were at risk of succumbing to this tendency, and in a sense to become "possessed" by these luciferic beings. However, their spiritual strength was greater, and they succeeded in wresting from the luciferic beings a form of evolution that ultimately accorded with fitting evolutionary goals.

In later reflections, in November 1919, Steiner described how, nevertheless, the Rishis allowed themselves to be taught by these wise luciferic beings, whose spiritual and cosmic truths were originally no different from those underlying evolution's true aims. The difference lay in the intention, in the manner in which these wisdoms should be handled. The luciferic beings wanted to hinder earthly human beings from their tasks here on Earth, whereas the Rishis endeavored to acquire these same wisdoms in a way that they could fruitfully employ within earthly conditions. When asked what the Rishis of the early Vedic period had won through this conflict that benefited humanity's overall evolution, Rudolf Steiner replied, "...everything that humankind has developed throughout evolution as capacities of speech and capacities of thinking."[174] And he adds that while the luciferic element is connected with the standardization of thinking, the ahrimanic element is active in the differentiation and fragmentation between languages. The most beneficial, wholesome thing today, he suggests, is to practice a spiritual thinking that can rein in the tendency to fragmentation in the different languages, so as to guide both thinking and speech in a future-oriented evolutionary direction.[175,176] It is characteristic of Steiner that he does not categorically condemn the adversarial spiritual–cosmic powers, but shows how their dynamic could be transformed in a positive sense. The field of work, or conflict, within which the Rishis accomplished this was that of language, more specifically the Vedic Sanskrit in which they sang their hymns.

Sri Aurobindo wrote of classical Sanskrit that it is

> ...perhaps the most remarkably finished and capable instrument of thought yet fashioned...lucid with the utmost possible clarity, precise to the farthest limit of precision, always compact and at its best sparing in its formation of phrase, but yet with all this never poor or bare: there is no sacrifice of depth to lucidity, but rather a pregnant opulence of meaning, a capacity of high richness and beauty, a natural grandeur of sound and diction inherited from the ancient days.[177]

Elsewhere, however, he sets this against the ancient Vedic Sanskrit of the Rishis:

> The Vedic Sanskrit represents a still earlier stratum in the development of language. Even in its outward features it is less fixed than any classical tongue; it abounds in a variety of forms and inflexions; it is fluid and vague, yet richly subtle in its use of cases and tenses. And on its psychological side it has not yet crystallised, is not entirely hardened into the rigid forms of intellectual precision. The word for the Vedic Rishi is still a living thing, a thing of power, creative, formative. It is not yet a conventional symbol for an idea, but itself the parent and former of ideas. It carries within it the memory of its roots, is still conscient of its own history. The Rishis' use of language was governed by this ancient psychology of the Word.[178]

The contrast appearing here between the living word of the Rishis and the later, intellectualized Sanskrit of India's late Vedic philosophers is a direct expression of the above mentioned subordination of Vak to Manas that occurred at the time of the Upanishads and initiated Vedanta, or the end of the Vedas. The Word emanating into the world became abstract and theoretical, thinking became intellectual, or had to cease in *samadhi*. Yogic breathing exercises increasingly sought to compensate for the loss of life force and the resulting separation of spiritual practice from the world of earthly life.

Nevertheless, Rudolf Steiner had the same high regard for Sanskrit as Sri Aurobindo, and spoke extensively about the spiritual sources from which this unique language of the Rishis emerged. He connected this with his wide-ranging accounts of the post-Atlantean cultural epochs, which began with the dawning of ancient Indian culture.[179] He was thus unquestionably speaking of early Vedic Sanskrit. Like Sri Aurobindo in a different context, Rudolf Steiner also spoke of "folk souls," or "folk spirits"—spiritual beings active in the qualities of temperament or sensibility of different peoples, which, through their inspiration, help to develop these qualities into an encompassing soul-spiritual milieu. Other spirit beings collaborate with these folk souls, working to form the language of a people right into elaboration of their larynx and other organs of speech and articulation. Finally he describes beings that inspire development of the mode of thinking that develops in a people or nation. We will call these three groups of beings folk souls, spirits of language, and spirits of thinking. It should be noted in passing that at all times and in every cultural milieu it is a matter of developing a balanced relationship between the spiritual influence of higher powers, and the freedom we need for our individual development. In long-gone times, however, such influence was doubtless hugely greater than in our modern age, when the impulse of freedom is coming ever more strongly to the fore.

In respect of ancient Indian culture, Rudolf Steiner describes a point in humanity's cultural evolution when folk soul, spirit of language, and spirit of thinking were united in the greatest possible harmony in a particular people, a very specific culture. "This," he said, "is the Indian nation, the people who initiated post-Atlantean culture in the first post-Atlantean era." And his account continues as follows:

> During this Indian culture a configuration arose in which those three beings were working together most harmoniously. From this resulted what we can call the historical role of the Indian people.... This was why the ancient, sacred language of the Indians could work so powerfully, exerting its mighty cultural influences both then and in subsequent periods of history.... And on this in turn is founded the unique Indian philosophy, a thinking active and creative from within outward, that no other people of the world has ever yet attained. On this rests the inner consistency of thinking in Indian culture. In all other regions we observe different conditions and circumstances. What arose there was unique and distinct.[180]

Based on all that has been said so far, it is clear that this harmonious interplay in early India contributed substantially to reception and mediation of the "Solar Word," enabling Rishis and Brahmins to experience the divinity of this Word (*Vak*) and profoundly absorb the wealth of its inspiration.

In relation to the language of poetry, Sri Aurobindo asks what constitutes speech and lends it "its life and appeal and significance," what subtle power fills "the body of the sound" and lives as its "soul." And he speaks of a superconscious power in us that, beginning from above, takes hold of its "material" of subconscious realms and from there raises itself into human awareness, coming to expression both fundamentally and in manifold ways in our overall evolution. Taking a closer look at this latter, inner ascent, which follows upon a prior descent of divine inspiration, Sri Aurobindo also speaks in this context of the tantric[181] doctrine of the Word:

> It is this Force, this Shakti to which the old Vedic thinkers gave the name of Vak, the goddess of creative Speech, and the Tantric psychists supposed that this Power acts in us . . . on higher and higher levels . . . and that thus the word has a graduation of its expressive powers of truth and vision. One may accept as a clue of great utility this idea of different degrees of the force of speech . . . and recognise one of the grades of the Tantric classification, Pashyanti the seeing word, as the description of that degree of power to which the poetic mind is called to elevate itself and which is original and native to its manner of expression.[182]

Based on the concept of the "seeing word," the common translation of the "Rishi" as the "poet seer" appears all the more illuminating. Sri Aurobindo's reference here to tantric *pashyanti* signifies the third degree of a fourfold ascending series, expressing the heights or depths of the spiritually experienced word: *para vak*, the highest word—at the level of the non-dual *turiya*—corresponds to the loftiest realm; *pashyanti*, the seeing word, is revealed to inspired, imaginative consciousness, and to attain this the Rishi must concentrate his awareness within his causal body; *madhyama*, the mediating word, acts in the realm of etheric formative forces, and in this sense is on the way to becoming incorporated within the bodily human being;[183] finally *vaikhari*, the physical word, is the means whereby people ordinarily communicate, the most externalized expression of Vak.[184] This four-level model of the word, which can be aligned with the above four stages of the *pranava* OM, is mentioned here because it can quite clearly be traced back to profound rigvedic reflections. We find the corresponding source in the first mandala of the *Rig Veda*:

> *chatvari vak parimita padani / tani vidur brahmana ye manishinah*
> *guha trini nihita nengayanti / turiyam vaco manushya vadanti*

A recent translation of this verse by Nishtha Müller, an Integral Yoga sadhak from Germany, runs:

> The word was formed on four planes. The singers of the soul word, who possess intuitive thought, know of these. Three are concealed in the secret cave and give no (outer) sign of themselves. The fourth (material) plane of the word is spoken by human beings.[185]

This leads us back to Sri Aurobindo. In a later passage of the above essay, he again refers to the spiritual origin, inspirational descent, and human reception of the Vak:

> The inspired word comes, as said of old the Vedic seers, from the home of Truth, *sadanad ritasya*, the high and native level of a superior self that holds the light of a reality that is hidden by the lesser truth of the normal sense and intelligence.[186]

And:

> The word comes secretly from above the mind, but it is plunged first into our intuitive depths and emerges imperfectly to be shaped by the poetic feeling and intelligence, *hrida tashtam manisha*. An intuitive self in the depth of each of our parts of being, hid in sense, life, heart, mind, is the transmitting agent, a subliminal power concealed in some secret cavern within of which the curtained and crystal doors disclose only occasional and partial transparencies or are sometimes half open or ajar—*nihitam guhayam guhahitam gahvareshtham*.[187]

Where the "I" is awake to this initially hidden process, the outwardly expressed word will be all the more enlightened and intuitive. Where by contrast the "I" is inwardly distant from this, the word will be informed far more by lower vitality and mere intellect.

It can astonish us to find how closely this description corresponds to and complements Rudolf Steiner's spiritual-scientific account of the process of inspiration at work in the Vedic seer poets of ancient India. In this context Steiner accentuates the importance of the Vedic Soma cult and, in harmony with Sri Aurobindo's account, characterizes, from below upward, the opening of the deeper levels of being, in which the will principle is at work, to the spirituality of the cosmos. In this will nature, which is not least also bound up with our metabolism, we find a reflection, surely, of the "intuitive self" referred to by Sri Aurobindo, which is "hid in sense, life, heart, mind." The founder of Anthroposophy puts it like this:

> You see, I am pointing you to the inner, soul-corporeal experience of human beings in ancient times who, precisely by virtue of this soul-corporeal-physical manner of experience, experienced the cosmos, had their cosmic and suprasensory perception by this means. And when people drank the Soma drink in the Orient, they knew the sublime spirit. This Soma drink, which permeated, pervaded and wove through their inner being became active in their blood. And when they fell asleep, the "I" and astral body that had been weaving in their blood took with it the forms that had arisen through assimilation of the Soma drink; and then their being unfolded and spread out in breadths of space, and they felt themselves united with the spiritual realities of the cosmos in their nightly experience.[188]

The influence of the Soma drink right into the blood of the poet seer[189] corresponds clearly to the effects of the Vak, of the word, which in Sri Aurobindo's view above lends speech "its life and appeal and significance." And here is Steiner once again, in a different passage, reflecting on the Vedic Rishis:

> And when they did not wish to express what they experienced on Earth, but instead to express in speech what the soul experienced when it felt itself removed from the Earth and transported out into the cosmos, their speech became what poetry was in ancient times.[190]

We will conclude this series of quotations with a last one by Sri Aurobindo, which concerns the more heavenly Soma, and affirms its connection with the "creative Word." Sri Aurobindo is speaking of a hymn in the *Rig Veda* addressed to the divinity Soma, which tells of a straining cloth and the jug for the Soma drink: the finely woven cheesecloth stands for thinking but the jug into which the Soma is poured is the "human system." In this hymn, Soma is identified as the Vedic godhead Brahmanaspati. Aurobindo remarks:

> Soma is addressed here as Brahmanaspati, a word sometimes applied to other gods, but usually reserved for Brihaspati, Master of the creative Word.[191]

Though approaching from different perspectives, Sri Aurobindo and Rudolf Steiner are in mutual accord that Vak, the Word of the Veda, entirely pervades and penetrates the human being. We should not be distracted by the fact that Rudolf Steiner gives more emphasis to the soul's ascent, and Sri Aurobindo to the descending aspect of the creative Word's manifestation in and through the human being. This appears to be only an expression of the reciprocity of the Vedic process, which we spoke of in the previous section. At all events, the words by Sri Aurobindo just quoted can be understood to mean that, in accordance with the Veda, pupils should seek to acquire mastery of the creative Word through their relationship to Vak in all strata of their own being. In the next chapter of this book, we study more closely the strong "I" quality that can be discerned in this endeavor.[192]

The Indian spiritual teacher lets the Word, the mantra, develop through the totality of the human being's nature, in modern times also, to culminate in a connection between heart and mind. The reflections in this section now conclude with incisive words from an apposite passage in *The Secret of the Veda:*

> The mantra, though it expresses thought in mind, is not in its essential part a creation of the intellect. To be the sacred and effective word, it must have come as an inspiration from the supra-mental plane, termed in Veda, Ritam, the Truth, and have been received into the superficial consciousness either through

> the heart or by the luminous intelligence, *manisha*. The heart in Vedic psychology is not restricted to the seat of the emotions; it includes all that large tract of spontaneous mentality, nearest to the subconscient in us, out of which rise the sensations, emotions, instincts, impulses and all those intuitions and inspirations that travel through these agencies before they arrive at form in the intelligence. This is the "heart" of Veda and Vedanta, *hridaya*, *hrid*, or *brahman*. There in the present state of mankind the Purusha is supposed to be seated centrally.[193]

Vak: The Word of the Sublime

According to Sri Aurobindo, the *brahman* hidden within the human being and connected with the human heart corresponds to the original Vedic understanding of this term. Only later did *brahman* come to assume the one-sided, abstract meaning of the eternal and absolute. As we turn in our reflections to the Word as divine, spiritual creative power, this motif of the *brahman* in the heart can become a key for gaining deeper insight into the intimate, Vedic interplay between human and divine word. In one Vedic offering ritual, for instance, passed down to us in the *Brahmanas*, we read, "May fire (*Agni*) be placed in my speech (*Vak*), my speech in the heart (*hridaya*), the heart in me (*mayi*), the 'I' (*aham*) in the immortal (*amritam*), the immortal in Brahman."[194]

The divine Vak, through which the universe came into being and development, speaks these words through the female seer Vag-Ambhrini, turning our gaze from the microcosmic into the macrocosmic realm; and yet it still remains the same Vak:

> At the world's summit, I bring forth the Father.
> My origin is in the Waters, in the ocean.
> Thence I am spread through all existing worlds
> and even touch the heaven with my forehead. (7)
> I breathe out strongly like the wind while clasping
> unto myself all worlds, all things that are.
> I tower above the Earth, above the heavens,
> so mighty am I in my power and splendor. (8)[195]

Raimundo Panikaar encapsulates his study of these words of the Vedic hymns as follows: "*Vāk* was before all creation, preexisting before any being came to be. It was she who initiated the creative process."[196] And Sri Aurobindo, for his part, states that "the Word is a power, the Word creates":

> Certain schools of Vedic thought (even) suppose the worlds to have been created by the goddess Word and sound as first etheric vibration to have preceded formation. In the Veda itself there are passages that treat the poetic measures of the sacred mantras—*anushtubh*, *trishtubh*, *jagati*, *gayatri*—as symbolic of the rhythms in which the universal movement of things is cast.[197]

Since the time of the Upanishads, the "tone as first, configuring etheric vibration" has most commonly been seen as identical with the *pranava*, the OM, which we considered above. In the last section we saw in connection with the Soma that Brihaspati—or Brahmanaspati—is named the "Lord of the creative Word." In the later development of Hinduism, Brihaspati became Brahma, the creator god of the classical *trimurti* of Brahma, Vishnu and Shiva. In the female seer's hymn above we hear that Vak "brings forth" the "Father." Once again there is an intensive reciprocal interplay also between the "Word" and the "Lord of the Word."

It is characteristic of Vedic spirituality that names and concepts have a very dynamic, mobile, and almost flowing relationship to one another, so that (since all schemas are inevitably inadequate here) pupils must use the filtering cloth of the Vedas—that is manas, and thus their thinking—to repeatedly bring the underlying processes and spiritual laws anew to their awareness. This interrelationship of dynamic reciprocity (here between the "Word" and the "Lord of the Word") is expressed as follows in another Yajur-vedic text that concerns Prajapati, the "Father of Beings": "Prajāpati was there; *vāk* was his companion. He united with her. Then she parted from him and bore all these creatures. Afterward she came back into Prajāpati."[198]

This wealth of seemingly divergent relationships between the Vedic divinities and the feminine goddess of the Word, Vak, should not confuse us: Soma, Brihaspati, Prajapati—and even the connection we have shown to the *brahman.* What can trouble the often linear thinking of Westerners should be taken, rather, as indication that the sacredness of the Word is due to the creative, spiritual activity of a multiplicity of beings at work in it. The following reflections, once again drawing strongly also on Anthroposophy, aim to help summarize within a somewhat more general orientation these interrelationships within which Vak appears.

The *brahman* that resides in the inmost heart and at the same time enables the whole universe to manifest, stands, in Sri Aurobindo's view, behind everything he calls the supermind. For him, therefore, the tangible and abstract aspects of *brahman* are one. In the original *ishvara* or in the Purusha, which stands distinct from the manifest world of Creation, *brahman* is intimated as the highest and most sublime, as the one who consciously intends this whole world. In its most subtle, most spiritual condition the evolving world of Creation, on the other hand, is addressed as the *Mula-Prakrikti*—in a sense the *ur*-substance, which lends finest, suprasensory materiality to cosmic forms and developments. These differentiate themselves according to the three *gunas,* or states of this Prakritic *ur*-substance, *tamas, rajas* and *sattva.* Here *tamas* refers to everything that tends toward weight, dullness and darkness; *rajas* to all that displays fiery dynamism and passion, agitation, excitation and movement; and *sattva*, finally, to qualities favoring peace, calm and bright clarity, and leading through the opening of created beings to pure spirit that shines from the supramental world of the Purusha or *ishvara* into the Prakriti.[199] The sphere in Prakriti, or Mula-Prakriti, that is always turned in utter openness toward the Purusha—in direct proximity to its world—and can receive and assimilate everything from it and that, in addition, offers the potential for all developments, configurations and forms, is referred to in the language of the Rishis as the goddess Aditi, the mother of the gods. Aditi, whose twelve children, the Adityas, include among others Vishnu, Mitra, Varuna, Surya, and Savitar, fills that furthest and most all-embracing sphere[200] as infinite consciousness, and was experienced by the Vedic seers as boundless expanse, and infinity *per se*. From it, from Aditi, Vak resounds, the language of the most sublime divinity. Indeed, the fact that this conscious world intention that the Purusha bears within it, can conjure forth—in seven chief streams—the infinite multiplicity of beings in the world of Prakriti, is first and foremost founded in the reality of speech and its capacity. The sphere of Aditi, spread out at the threshold of the universe, forms as it were the membrane that can enable the Word of the Sublime to resound. In Vak, the potential for this resounding—made possible by Aditi—becomes living, creative reality. This cosmos, this universe is continually created by it. But the Rishis perceived the sevenfold principles of existence appearing in the Veda, according to which this whole Creation is ordered, and which enliven it, in the "seven rivers," or "seven streams," we mentioned earlier, that pour into this world.

Sri Aurobindo takes up the pictorial language of the Veda, and its close affinity with nature, when he says that water of these "seven rivers" can lead to truth. If we follow them to their sources, they lead to the truth consciousness of the supermind, vouchsafed to the Rishis as the primordial Word, the language of the highest. And the seven Rishis themselves were the divinely inspired human representatives of this sevenfold order of the universe:

> [The Seven Waters] lead to the Truth, they are themselves the source of the Truth, they flow in the unobstructed and shoreless Vast as well as here upon the Earth. They are figured as fostering cows (*dhenavah*), mares (*ashvah*), they are called *sapta vanih*, the seven Words of the creative goddess Vak,—Speech, the expressive power of Aditi, of the supreme Prakriti, who is spoken of as the Cow just as the Deva or Purusha is described

> in the Veda as Vrishabha or Vrishan, the Bull. They are therefore the seven strands of all being, the seven streams or currents or forms of movement of the one conscious existence.[201]

Earlier we suggested that Rudolf Steiner regarded the seven Rishis especially also as early Indian representatives of awakening human "I"-being.[202] It was likewise suggested that his vision perceived this "I"-awakening to have occurred in the spiritual intercourse of the proto-Vedic human being with very lofty spiritual beings, who in the Western tradition are known as the spirits of movement and the spirits of wisdom.[203] They belong to the second hierarchy of spiritual beings and gave the impulse for humanity's evolution already during the two earlier planetary embodiments preceding the "Earth" stage—ancient Moon and ancient Sun.[204] In addition, Rudolf Steiner points elsewhere to a still higher, twelvefold origin of the universal Logos, encompassed or united in the governing Sun Spirit, a lofty being from the hierarchy of the Kyriotetes, from whom it shines out sun-like into the cosmos. The same high spirit is called Christ in the language of esoteric Christianity. Indian spirituality knows him as Vishnu, whose avatar appears as Krishna.[205] His presence and origin must be assumed as being beyond that of Aditi, beyond the Mula-Prakriti. The revelation of his being is supramental in nature.[206]

In his Oslo lectures on *The Mission of the Folk Souls,* Rudolf Steiner considers characteristic differences in the way people in diverse cultures of the post-Atlantean period found their way to an awakening of "I"-being. Whereas in earlier periods the Europeans, say, experienced their own "I" within a comparatively little developed soul culture, and with a level of emotional wildness, urge, and drive that rode roughshod over personal freedoms, strongly obscuring the conscious "I," something entirely different held sway in early Indian culture. These peoples, by contrast, had undergone intensive inner development according to Rudolf Steiner, achieving a high level of soul culture and spiritual capacities that, already before they awoke to their "I"-being, were much "richer" than those of the Europeans; and in the process they had developed the tendency to devote themselves reverently to the world of spirit, and open themselves to it. At the time they awoke to the "I," far higher ranks than beings of the angelic and archangelic orders—as in the case of the peoples of northern, central and western Europe—were involved in the inner elaboration of their elevated soul culture: the Dynameis and Kyriotetes we have mentioned. The angelic beings of lesser orders had worked upon them in still earlier periods of evolution that they had long grown beyond at the time of their "I"-awakening. In the following passage from these same lectures by Steiner, relating to these matters, we approach again the question of Vak, the loftiest and most sublime Word:

> And so they [the early Indian peoples] looked up to what they later called the entirety of all spirits of movement and all spirits of wisdom: to what were later referred to, in the Greek expressions, as Dynameis and Kyriotetes. They looked up to these and said of them: Mula-Prakriti, that is the sum of the spirits of movement, and Maha-Purusha, the entire sum of the spirits of wisdom, living as it were in a whole spiritual unity.[207]

If we assume that Sri Aurobindo and Rudolf Steiner were enquiring into the single reality of the spirit, albeit from different angles, and if, in addition, we give serious credence to their findings as steps upon the long path of humanity toward ever more comprehensive insight and knowledge, then it seems to be of considerable significance that the two meet and agree when it comes to speaking of Purusha and Mula-Prakriti. If we consider both perspectives and their implications together we can discover how profoundly the divine-human mystery of speech, the Word, is related to the mystery of the true human "I." We must regard the development of speech and thinking among the Rishis as integral to their awakening to true "I"-being. Everything seems to confirm this. And to better appraise what is at work here, let us remember that, in Steiner's view, one of the Rishis' most important missions—and seminal for all bearers of the early Indian evolution of consciousness—was to pave the way for the development of human speech and then also human thinking. The reciprocal process at work in the Vedic Word, in which divine speech and human speech interpenetrate, must, as we have seen in detail in the previous section, surely be connected with fulfilment of this mission.

Accordingly, as the Rishis, and after them their pupils, raise their spirit to Mula-Prakriti and the Purusha, gaining the living, Vedic Word from inner dialog with these, that is, with Dynameis and Kyriotetes in the sphere of Vak, and themselves in turn bring forth this living Word in which Manas, thinking, is still fully comprehended, they awaken to their own true "I"-being. The "I" of the Rishis comes to itself in dialog with its divine counterpart. And the Maha-Purusha thus finds in the human being the one who, in the terms of the Vedas, answers him as *chaitya purusha*, as the individual spirit–soul awakening to itself, whereas the nature of Vak, of the Word, becomes individual reality in the spirit–soul itself. What constitutes Vak in the universal orders of existence will thus also be rediscovered—in miniature—in human speech.

One example from the fund of human speech can illustrate the correspondence between human language and the language of the highest. The "seven rivers" of the Veda mentioned earlier, which we must understand as the "seven Words of the Vak," and which, according to Sri Aurobindo, flow both "in unhindered and shoreless immensity," and here on Earth, will meet also at the end of the long path of evolution from divine to human speech. The streaming, flowing element is of course present in the vowels of human speech. They flow from the speaker's inner being and give expression to it, brought forth upon the stream of air from the "I"-nature of his spirit–soul. Inner here is made outwardly manifest. In his continual effort for a living, creative speech, Rudolf

Steiner presents the sevenfold cosmic affinity of the vowels, speaking of their correspondence with the seven visible planets. Sun and Moon, traditionally counted among the planets, correspond here to the diphthongs *au* and *ai*. In simple, accurate words, Steiner states at one point that "the vowels allow what is inward to stream outward."[208]

But this means nothing other than that the principle made manifest in speech through outstreaming from within—as Purusha accomplishes through the Vak—is also present in human beings, and can equally manifest through them as the *chaitya purusha*. It could be objected that Sanskrit does not really have seven vowels. In fact its alphabet contains thirteen vowels. But if we study this more closely we find that apart from the free-flowing seven long vowels and diphthongs in Sanskrit, *ah, ee, oo, eh, ai, oh,* and *au,* six further sounds are counted as vowels: the short *a, i, u* (derived from the above) along with three so-called consonantal vowels: the short and long voiced "R" and the short voiced "L."[209] All this can show us that in speech an inner essence—of the most sublime being and of the human being equally—is made outwardly manifest. Through the mutually spoken and heard word, the human being's true "I"-being can intimate its inner affinity with the divine.

The Vedic image of the "seven rivers" ought not to mislead us into interpreting human speech or language as "watery" in nature, in the sense suggested by the Rishis. The active power—especially in the human being—that brings the word to expression, is, rather, fiery. Agni, the Lord of Fire, a divinity to whom roughly two hundred hymns of the *Rig Veda* are dedicated, is a figure whose energy enflames and configures the spoken word. In his lengthy introduction to the *Kena Upanishad,* Sri Aurobindo speaks of how the word in the human being "is formed by Agni, the secret will-force and fiery shaping energy in the mind and body."[210] David Frawley, who has a close affinity with Sri Aurobindo's Integral Yoga, describes as follows the connection between

Agni, the divine, cosmic fire, speech, and the Jivatman—i.e., the inner nature or essence of the human being:

> Agni has three main internal (*adhyatmic*) forms as speech (*vak*), *prana,* and intelligence (*buddhi*), which are the ruling forces in the three aspects of our being as body, life and mind. They are the three lights of our internal nature and the three manifestations of the Soul or Jivatman, the consciousness or light principle within us.[211]

In the next section our perspective will shift from the Vedic world to an outlook that became spiritually available in the Mediterranean and European region around two and a half millennia ago through the idea of the Logos. In the next chapter we will take up again the question of, especially, human inner being and its fire or warmth-relatedness; but first we conclude this section on Vak, the "*Word of the Sublime,*" with accounts by Sri Aurobindo from his aforementioned introduction to the *Kena Upanishad.* In these passages the Indian spiritual teacher enquires into how human beings continually engender the creative word, transposing thought vibrations into emotional and vital ones, then ultimately into physical resonances. Accordingly, he says, we keep invoking movements and forms tirelessly within our natural surroundings. But, as already suggested, unschooled persons mostly remain unaware of the scope of this creative activity through the word. By contrast, says Sri Aurobindo, the Vedic mantric tradition is based on an entirely conscious cultivation of the otherwise hidden power of speech. Musical and speech sounds are observed and enacted as they rise into mental and supramental worlds, ultimately reaching the "true root of things and beings"—in accordance with the four levels of the word or of the *pranava* OM, of which we spoke earlier.

It is sometimes said that the Indian tradition is aware of creation from *sound* but not from the Word. Sri Aurobindo's analysis leads him to a different finding. He, like the former Vedic seer-poet, discovers that at the highest planes the vibrations of musical and speech sound are incessantly filled and penetrated by immediate, conscious experience of the supramental nature of truth underlying all things and beings; and he perceives that these vibrations continually give expression to the truth of existence. Thus for Sri Aurobindo, creation through etheric sound vibrations and through the Word or Logos are one and the same thing, as the "two logical poles of the same idea." He writes:

> Both [theories] belong to the same ancient Vedic system. This, then, is the supreme Word, Speech of our speech. It is vibration of pure Existence, instinct with the perceptive and originative power of infinite and omnipotent consciousness, shaped by the Mind behind mind into the inevitable word of the Truth of things; out of whatever substance on whatever plane, the form or physical expression emerges by its creative agency. The Supermind using the Word is the creative Logos.[212]

The Logos

In the eastern Mediterranean, the Logos first arose in human awareness in Hellenic philosophy—in the works of Heraclitus and the Stoics—and over the next five hundred years it paved the way for Christian understanding of the Son of God as the Logos who became a human being in Christ Jesus. Rudolf Steiner says of early Christian mystery schools that the cultivation of human speech there served to reveal to pupils the workings of the divine Logos. Just as the divine Word precedes all temporal and spatial creation, so pupils were to recognize that they could likewise conceive of everything in dissolved form as "tone vibrations of the divine cosmic Word." And then, characterizing the understanding of a pupil in the early Christian mysteries, he continues:

> In a certain respect he distinguished between the "Father in the hidden realm" who had not yet given utterance, the "Word," or the "Son," resounding through space; and then the Word becomes fixed or solid, as "manifestation." This offers

> us a deeper understanding of the beginning of the Gospel of St. John: "In the beginning was the Word, and the Word was with God, and a God was the Word. The same was in the beginning with God. Through Him all things were made and without Him was not anything made that was made." Everything that arose came forth from the Word. We have to take these things very literally, and then we can also easily perceive the creative nature of the Word, or Logos. In the Christian sense, what comes second is the Word or Logos. *Logos* should not be translated by anything other than "Word," for what is meant is that all that exists as outward creation is founded on the unspoken, creative Word; that this sounded forth as Word, and that therein lies the origin of all existence.[213]

We will now trace the broad developments that led to this Christian view of the Logos. Its Western origins in Heraclitus were connected with the Ionian mysteries of Artemis at Ephesus, close to the western coast of Asia Minor.[214] During the lifetime of Heraclitus (ca. 535–475 BC) the flourishing of Ephesus came to expression above all in building works on the mighty temple of Artemis. After it was completed this was counted among the "seven wonders" of the ancient world, but was destroyed by fire in 356 BC, supposedly on the very night that Alexander the Great was born in Macedonia. It is said of Heraclitus—by no means a friend of ordinary folk—that he lived mostly in seclusion within the sacred grove of the Artemision. After writing his magnum opus, entitled *Peri Physeos,* or *On Nature,* he is said to have laid it on the temple's altar as an offering to the goddess. Only fragments of this work are still extant, some reconstructed from later authors. The goddess Artemis, daughter of Zeus and sister of Apollo, was revered in Asia Minor particularly as lunar divinity, as an instance of the "Great Mother" archetype. Besides being a goddess of the hunt—called Diana by the Romans—she also stood for fertility and good fortune in birth, for all germination and sprouting, growth, and proliferation. To summarize, we can say she represented the elicitation of all creative life.[215]

Heraclitus sees in the "ever-living fire"—both in the world and in the soul—the primal quality from which all phenomena emerge and into which they repeatedly return in eternal alternation. At the same time he sees forms developing via air and ocean through to earthly substance.[216] But for its realization in the cosmos and human being, the Logos draws especially on the forces of warmth or of fire. As Karl-Martin Dietz puts it: "Passing through the cosmic substance of fire, whose purest form is also called *ether,* the Logos manifests in the world."[217] Heraclitus says, at the very beginning of his work, that this Logos is "eternal" and that "everything arose in accordance with it."[218] But then he continues, "This world, which is the same for all, no one of gods or men has made; but it was ever, is now and ever shall be an ever-living fire, and kindles and extinguishes at need."[219] Lightning is regarded as the concentrated power of fire, and thus: "Lightning governs all things."[220]

The connection indwelling it between the cosmic fire and Logos and—by extension—the human soul, is illumined in the following fragments: "Fire is endowed with reason."[221] And in the same way that lightning corresponds to fire, so fire, in which spirit and insight are implicit, corresponds to the "dry ray of light": a renewed concentration and inward intensification of fire—the soul. Heraclitus writes, "A dry soul is wisest and best. The best and wisest soul is a dry beam of light."[222]

The "ever-living fire" of Heraclitus stands between "fullness" and "want."[223] Here we encounter the two aspects of fire or heat, and of the warmth ether, which are also related to the dual aspect of time. Fire destroys what exists, puts an end to what has come from the past; but through fire as life-giving warmth, as brood warmth in a nest for example, a new beginning arises and develops into the future. "Fullness" follows the latter, and "want" the former. But the fire nature of the spirit–soul as it increasingly awakens to its true "I"-being, establishes and expresses itself—via the dual aspect indicated—between past and future in verticality, balance, and presence of mind, thus relating itself to eternity.

Lightning and *ray of light* no doubt refer to this higher fire quality of the soul.

Even if Heraclitus represents a comparatively elitist ethos, the individual's participation in the Logos is for him a quality intrinsic to all human beings, and one that connects them. He believes one must hearken to this common characteristic. Many however cannot see this connecting quality, and therefore he writes, "Whereas the Logos is common to all, the many live as if they had their own private reason."[224] Nevertheless he also says, "If you were to follow every path you would still not discover the limits of the soul. This is the depth of its Logos."[225]

Following detailed analysis, Karl-Martin Dietz came to regard the connection, as Heraclitus sees it, between the Logos, the cosmic and individual fire, and the single soul, in terms of three aspects of the Logos: its common or shared quality, its eternal quality and its indivisible unity. In its shared characteristic the Logos overcomes the soul's isolation and expresses itself in the individual's thinking and knowing, but ultimately as world spirit. In its eternal aspect the Logos overcomes all that is transient, and in fire embodies world substance and its continual changes and fluctuations. As single unity, finally, it represents God as the world's essence and intrinsic being.[226]

Rudolf Steiner seems to be thinking of Heraclitus' present and future significance when he summarizes his view: "And the force that is physically active in fire lives at a higher plane in the human soul, which melts down sensory knowledge in its crucibles and brings forth from this knowledge a vision of eternity."[227] Then he goes more deeply into the question of human existence, constituted of both eternal and temporal aspects:

> Through the eternal aspect [human beings] have become something quite specific; and from this specific nature they should create a higher nature. They are dependent and independent. They can participate in only the eternal spirit, which they perceive in accordance with the mingled state that the eternal

> spirit has brought about in them. And precisely for that reason they are called upon to shape the eternal from the temporal.[228]

The development of the idea of the Logos can look back on a magnificent history spanning two and a half millennia. In his book *Die Logoslehre* (the Logos teaching), Wilhelm Kelber summarized this history from the time of Heraclitus to Origenes in a work of lasting importance and relevance. His book is one we can scarcely overlook if we are concerned to understand what, in terms of spiritual history, is meant by the Logos becoming human. It is an excellent complement to this book especially because Kelber carefully unfolds the many inner connections between the Logos idea and Anthroposophy. For the purposes of this study, we will now briefly examine three stages in the development of the Logos idea that draw on Heraclitus: the Stoics, the Logos as it figures in the work of Philo of Alexandria, and finally the Logos in the Gospel of St. John.

In the school of the Stoics, which originated with Zeno of Citium (around 333 to 264 BC), the prime emphasis is on living a virtuous life, and not allowing one's thinking and way of living to be disturbed by emotions and feelings. One is meant always to meet one's fate with as much sovereign composure as possible—and thus "stoically." The pupil develops wisdom through *apatheia*, the absence of emotions. The stoics took up Heraclitus' Logos idea keenly and developed it further. In this philosophical outlook the Logos continued to be regarded as cosmic in nature, and active through the primordial fire. An important new stage of understanding arose with the stoic concept of the many *logoi spermatikoi*, that is, words with "seed potency." The one, eternal Logos that utters and sustains the whole cosmos through the primordial fire differentiates itself into the many diverse *logoi*, the manifold formative gestures and forms of influence of the Logos, in a sense as its distinct sounds or syllables. Accordingly, the diverse *logoi* are the living developmental principles that stand behind each being and thing in the created world. The Church Father Eusebius of Caesarea wrote as follows in relation to the stoic teaching on fire and the *logoi spermatikoi*: "The first is the fire that contains the logoi, as it were as seeds of the universe, the causes of all that has arisen, that arises and will arise."[229]

Wilhelm Kelber regards the development of the concept of *logoi spermatikoi* as possibly "a completely unique event in the history of human ideas." But this view may well be based on Kelber's lack of familiarity with the testimonies of Indian spirituality. I would point here only to what was said in the previous section about the "seven rivers" of the divine Aditi as the "seven words of the Vak," and the analogy of this to the seven vowels in human speech. The ancient Vedic perspective was further developed in Kashmiri tantrism into the concept of *bija mantras*, the seed syllables, based especially on the germinal potency of the vowels. Every student of tantra sees the *pranava* OM (AUM), which we examined earlier, as the first of all these *bija mantras*.[230] If we take the Vedic roots of authentic tantra as our point of departure, we find there an early teaching of the sacred power of the Word that long precedes the development of the Logos idea in the Mediterranean region from the six to fifth centuries BC.

But we should note another point Kelber makes—that, strikingly, the most important representatives of Stoicism did not come from the Greco-European mainland but, like Heraclitus at Ephesus, from Asia Minor or the eastern islands of the Mediterranean. He sees this as an expression of something alive in the Logos idea that is a last gift of Asia to European culture, and contrasts with the philosophical outlooks of the triumvirate of Socrates, Plato, and Aristotle.

Philo of Alexandria (ca. 20 BC–AD 50), who saw himself, like the Stoics, as following in the footsteps of Heraclitus, was of Jewish descent and at the same time entirely committed to Hellenism. His works, written in Greek, are primarily philosophical exegeses of the Jewish Torah. Philo is exemplary of the increasing synthesis at that time between Judaism and Greek culture. For Philo, the transcendental God, the God of the *Pentateuch,* or five books of Moses, is in sharp contrast to the world of matter.[231] He sees the Logos, the Word, through which God created the world, as the essential mediator. The creative Logos, *logos poietikos,* for its part, comprises countless Dynameis: living powers that must be seen as attributes of God, both as his thoughts and as the servants who fulfill his will. These include angels and demons equally. In Creation they embody structural formulae thanks to which the cosmos can emerge from the chaos of matter. These Dynameis are certainly comparable to the *logoi spermatikoi* of the Stoics. Philo addresses the Logos as the "second God," or the *hyios theou*, the "Son of God" who is suspended in a sense between a personally embodied and impersonal cosmic existence. The Alexandrine sees him as having become flesh in all God's Creation. For Philo, sensory, fleshly existence is, though, a sinful condition: although the human being is the bearer of a Logos whose archetype is the divine Logos, earthly, material existence is initially pernicious for this reflected Logos. To put it another way, "the flesh is the grave of the soul."

Redemption from this condition is something Philo thinks the soul can attain in ecstasy, through liberation from the body. By this means, mediated by the Logos as eternal wisdom, the soul becomes one with God. Finally we should emphasize one aspect of Philo's Logos teaching that is significant for understanding of the creative word in general. Philo distinguishes two sides of the Logos, entirely in keeping with the meaning of *Logos* as the Word: the spiritual and the uttered word. The latter belongs to the sense world because it can be spoken and heard while the first remains latent—it holds itself back in itself, as it were in the ideas of God.[232] As Philo sees it, the Logos in these two aspects connects the divine-spiritual with the material world.

Philo was contemporary with Christ Jesus, who, not so far from Alexandria, in Palestine, taught, healed, underwent crucifixion and resurrection—but it seems he paid no attention to the one whose apostles and disciples soon began to proclaim him as the Word of God become human as God's Son. Nevertheless, Philo's work supplied orientation of the first order to a series of Church Fathers in the first centuries of the Christian era, clarifying the idea implicit in the Logos. Later this led to questions in certain quarters as to whether the Logos Christianity of, say, Clement of Alexandria or Origenes, in fact derived from the non-Christian works of Philo.

St. John and the Prologue

The old Christian tradition according to which the Apostle John is also the Evangelist, and the same disciple the Gospel of St. John refers to as the one "whom Jesus loved" (John 13:23),[233] was not disputed by later theologians. Despite overwhelming skepticism about this, the matter is still considered to be unresolved. But Rudolf Steiner confirmed it anew through his spiritual research. The founder of Anthroposophy even goes a step further in his enquiries into the question of John, by identifying the disciple "whom Jesus loved" with Lazarus—who, with his sisters Martha and Mary Magdalene kept a household in Bethany that supported Christ Jesus and his disciples in their journeys on foot, providing them also with provisions. Lazarus is also said to be loved by the Lord (cf. John 11:3 and 11:36). After an illness from which he died, a unique initiation occurred, performed on Lazarus by Christ Jesus when—according to the Gospel—he awoke him from the dead (John 11:1–46). This awakening initiation made Lazarus into John. Rudolf Steiner established the Logos connection of this initiation by asking who this Christ is who brought it about; why the sickness is described as being "not unto death, but for the glory of God" (John 11:4); and what Christ's words "I am the resurrection and the life" (John 11:25) actually mean, also questioning exactly what occurred with Lazarus. Rudolf Steiner then replies as follows to these questions:

> [Jesus] is the "Word become flesh." He is the eternal that was in the beginning. If he is truly the resurrection then the "eternal that was in the beginning" was resurrected in Lazarus. We are therefore concerned here with a resurrection of the eternal "Word." And this "Word" is the life to which Lazarus is awoken. We are presented here with a "sickness," yet one that does not lead to death but is instead for the "glory of God," thus serving to manifest God. If the "eternal Word" was resurrected in Lazarus, then the whole occurrence really serves to make God manifest in Lazarus, for through it he became a different person. Previously the "Word" of the spirit did not live in him; now this spirit lives in him. This spirit has been born in him.[234]

John, imbued in this way by the divine Logos, is therefore also the same person who leaned upon the breast of the Master at the Last Supper (cf. John 13:25), and who stood beneath the Cross on the hill of Golgotha together with Mary, mother of Jesus, another Mary, and Mary Magdalene, his sister. Shortly before his death, the Crucified One said to his mother, pointing to John: "Woman, behold thy son" (John 19:26), and then to John, "Behold thy mother"—after which "the disciple took her unto his own home" (John 19:27).

John, the disciple whom Jesus loved, also makes himself known, finally, in the last verses of the Gospel of St. John, as the one who "testifieth of these things, and wrote these things" (John 21:24).

From the earliest documents on the history of the Christian Church we see that John remained true to his Master's instructions until the end, housing the mother of Jesus until she died at Ephesus. The pupil of Paul, Dionysius the Areopagite, hinted that he himself had seen Mary, the mother of the resurrected Christ, at Ephesus.[235] John was banished from Ephesus to Patmos, where he received *The Secret Book of John*, or *Apocalypse*. He also returned here and wrote his Gospel, dying here, too, according to Eusebius of Caesarea (ca. AD 260–340).[236] Already in the first years of Christianity, it was suspected that, whereas John recorded in his writings a good deal of what he witnessed (including in the Epistles of St. John and the New Testament), much relating to his deeper encounter was passed on in oral form to only a few. Authorities who cited this more esoteric teaching included Clement of Alexandria (ca. AD 150–215), the great Christian teacher of the divine Logos who became human in Christ Jesus.[237] Clemens characterized this developing Johannine Logos tradition in relation to the Parable of the Sower (see Matt. 13:3–23) and with reference to the living seed-power of the Word:

> For when a word is sown, so that a soul connects with another soul, and a spirit with another spirit, then, as it seems to me, they bring the scattered seed to growth and let it come to life.[238]

And here follow the timeless words of the first verse of the Prologue of the Gospel of St. John:

> In the beginning was the Word, and the Word was with God, and the Word was God. The same was in the beginning with God. All things were made by him; and without him was not anything made that was made. In him was life; and the life was the light of men. And the light shineth in darkness and the darkness comprehended it not (John 1:1–5).

Because of the lofty nature of his vision, Johannes was symbolized as eagle among the four evangelists. John Scotus Eriugena (around 815 to 877), a later bearer of the Logos mystery, heard the call of the Johannine eagle and translated it with the words,

> The blessed theologian John therefore flies [as spiritual eagle] beyond not only what may be thought and spoken, but also beyond all mind and meaning. Exalted by the ineffable flight of his spirit beyond all things, he enters into the very arcanum of the one principle of all.[239]

But John also connects this sublimity with the deepest inwardness. His unique spiritual closeness to the Logos-become-human comes to expression particularly in his capacity to reconcile in his vision of Christ Jesus the mighty cosmic dimension with the inwardness of the mystery of the Word. He is able to hear the inmost nature—as it were listening intently at his breast, his heart—of the one who is himself the Word, who created this whole cosmos. And John understands that he, the Logos, encompasses the greatest cosmic breadth and the most intimate inwardness as "eternal life": that he embodies this and wishes to enable all who hearken to him to partake fully of it. Thus, in his Gospel, John also reproduces the sayings, the "words of eternal life" (John 6:68) in which Christ Jesus himself reveals his divine "I"-being, the "I AM," and his living connection with the world of humankind: "I am the bread of life" (John 6:35); "I am the light of the world" (John 8:12); "I am the door" (John 10:9); "I am the good shepherd" (John 10:11); "I am the resurrection and the life" (John 11:25); "I am the way, the truth and the life" (John 14:6); and "I am the true vine" (John 15:1).[240]

Here we see once again how Word and true "I"-being are one and the same: the Word-nature of the "I am," of the Logos. Through his or her "I" evolution, the human being who gains access to, and participation in, these mysteries will come to reply to the one who is his or her source and origin, doing so through this same Word-nature with which he or she has been endowed.[241]

The Ephesian Logos Mystery in the Works of Rudolf Steiner and Sri Aurobindo

In certain early Christian mystery schools, as already mentioned, there was intense cultivation and practice of the spoken word, in the quest to trace it back to its origins in the divine Logos.[242] According to Rudolf Steiner's akashic research, a similar practice existed already at the time of the Artemis mysteries at Ephesus. Here the pupils sought a powerful experience of the creative potency of the Logos. In particular it was intended that they should experience the Logos both in its micro- and macro-influence in the sphere corresponding to Artemis, the bringer of life and fertility. A significant observation of the pupil's own speech related to the stream of air that makes the word sound forth. In their experience, the stream of air was the middle and mediating element of speech, from which rises a fiery motion of warmth into the head region where it connects with the thoughts that words seek to express. Through warmth, thoughts are taken up into speech. By contrast, as Rudolf Steiner puts it, a "watery" element "trickles down" into the region of circulation and metabolism from the stream of air, comparable to the secretion of a gland, and "by this means the pupil gains an inner sense of the word. The word trickles down as fluid element."[243] In this way the thought from above, and feeling from below, both connect with the spoken word.[244] Just as here, at a microcosmic level, words are formed between air, fire (warmth), and fluid, so the Logos acts in the same way at the macrocosmic level. The Logos pupils of Artemis enquired into this correspondence. And Rudolf Steiner recounts the very mysterious processes that they discovered here in relation to the terrestrial, planetary actions of the creative Logos.

This concerned processes at a period of the Earth, when its watery envelope was still to a large degree permeated by "fluid proteins" and by finely dissolved calcium substances. Rudolf Steiner describes how in evaporation, in the mist rising into the atmosphere from the watery element, some of these protein substances were carried aloft and there assimilated cosmic configuring forces from the starry universe, which subsequently enabled them to coagulate into particular organic forms. He is speaking here of the creation of animal forms. In the watery stratum, these primordial organic forms now imbued themselves with calciferous substances ascending in the watery element, and became the first foundation for later skeleton forms.

As a result of their exercises in uttered speech, says Steiner, these pupils at Ephesus in the first millennium BC were led forth from the confines of their corporeality through a mighty expansion of their memory to a kind of planetary recall of the whole Earth, thus gaining a form of experience that encompassed the whole planet. And in this ecstatic state, the development of animal forms became something they were able to spiritually hear. And what these pupils heard was in fact nothing other than the "Word of the World, the Logos."[245]

Both processes (microcosmic speech and the macrocosmic action of the Logos) correspond to each other: in the first instance occurring between air, fire (warmth), and fluid, and in the second—at a planetary level, in calcium—between the watery sphere, the atmosphere, and solid substance. Thus one process, compared to the other, is shifted by one level in the order of its elements. Steiner describes a very similar, qualitatively related action of the planetary Logos in relation to silica and plant development. He goes on to say that John's spiritual vision of the realities he describes played into his composition of the prologue of his Gospel, and that there he was at the same time pointing "to this macrocosmic mystery and its transposition into maya."[246] But we would seriously misunderstand Rudolf Steiner's view of the Gospel of St. John if we thought he was tracing the content of the prologue back to the mysteries of Ephesus only, without encompassing the unique nature of the Christ event. Nothing would be further from the truth. Instead he sees the deep connections between both spiritual realities:

> That is the reality at the beginning of the Gospel of John: initially we have returned there to a primordial beginning of what now exists. The Word lived in this primordial beginning, in this principle. And a God was the Word, for it was the creative principle at work in all. We can truly say that in the teachings of the primordial Word imparted to the mystery pupils at Ephesus lies what later led to the beginning of the Gospel of John.[247]

In the last year of his lecturing activity, the founder of Anthroposophy went on to accord great significance to the mysteries of the Logos once again, when he refounded the stricken Anthroposophical Society. During the "Christmas Foundation Meeting 1923/24" organized for this purpose, he spoke in a series of evening lectures about *World History in the Light of Anthroposophy.* There he considers diverse mysteries that he had also referred to in the weeks and months previously, and centrally also the Artemis mysteries at Ephesus. The context for these accounts by Steiner can be found especially in his intense spiritual encounter and collaboration with his companion in medical work, Ita Wegman (1876–1943).[248] Once again he now considers the practice of spiritually experiencing the macrocosmic Logos within microcosmic human speech. But this time Steiner places special emphasis on the fact that at Ephesus, situated on the mainland of Asia Minor, the ancient, Asiatic mystery wisdom shines out again for the last time. By means of their expanded faculty of memory, at least, the pupils here gain once more a tangible experience of the mighty divine forces that hold sway through the cosmos and configure it. West of the Aegean, by contrast, in Greece, wisdom assumes a far smaller, almost merely "human" form in the gods of Olympus, in whom the macrocosmic dimension became scarcely recognizable.

In these lectures Steiner characterizes the relationship to Ephesus of two great historical figures: Aristotle (384–322 BC) and his royal pupil Alexander (356–323 BC). In the lectures Steiner speaks of a number of incarnations in which the two knew each other. They were, he says, both directly connected with the Artemis mystery at Ephesus in an earlier incarnation at the time of Heraclitus. This past is conjured in the fact that, in the night of Alexander's birth in Macedonia, as already mentioned, the arsonist Herostat set fire to the temple of Artemis at Ephesus, which was destroyed. It must be emphasized that Rudolf Steiner relates this incident to the—similarly fateful—arson attack on the first Goetheanum in Dornach a year previously, which destroyed his architectural masterwork, also called the "St. John Building" and the "House of Speech."[249] Rudolf Steiner vividly describes how the instruction by Alexander's teacher Aristotle on the four elements and the four directions of the compass gave Alexander—whose birth was heralded by fire—an irrepressible urge to journey southeastward, to India, a region ruled by fire. And it is also important to mention that during his military campaign, which some may see as an expression of megalomania, he tarried for a while in Egypt and founded the Hellenic metropolis of Alexandria not far from the Nile delta, only afterward setting off properly for the southeast. He did eventually reach the borderlands of India, the realm of Agni and Indra.

One can feel strangely moved by Alexander's efforts at recreating in India, the world region of fire, a connection to the fire of Heraclitus' Logos: India, where knowledge of the fiery nature of the sublime creative Word had been at home for many millennia. It was an attempt. And it is also remarkable to see that, by founding the city of Alexandria, he created the conditions at least for the future Christian metamorphosis of the Ephesian Logos mysteries there—their resurrection if you like—several centuries after him in the Alexandria of Clement and Origenes.

Rudolf Steiner's account of Heraclitus and his Logos teaching as a later reflection of primordial Asiatic mysteries, is clearly and vividly confirmed also by Sri Aurobindo. His words below connect in a way with the passage by him last cited, in which he speaks of the Logos as "the Supermind using the Word." Sri Aurobindo dedicates a great, seven-part essay to Heraclitus, establishing at the beginning that the founder of the Western teaching of the Logos possessed, like almost no other, the power of intellectual stimulus of the later Greek philosophers, but at the same time also the intuitive vision, the intuitive Word of the ancient mystics. Moreover, he says of the Ephesian, "Heraclitus is using the old language of the Mysteries." Then he goes on to describe the Heraclitean view of the Logos less in terms of its Word nature and more in relation to consciousness:

> We get very near the Indian conception of Brahman, the cause, origin and substance of all things, an absolute Existence whose nature is consciousness (*Chit*) manifesting itself as Force (*Tapas, Shakti*) and moving in the world of his own being as the Seer and Thinker, *kavir manīshī*, an immanent Knowledge–Will in all, *vijñānamaya purusha*, who is the Lord or Godhead, *īsha, īshvara, deva*, and has ordained all things according to their nature from years sempiternal, Heraclitus "measures," which the Sun is forced to observe, his "things are utterly determined." This Knowledge–Will is the Logos.[250]

In relation to fire in the fragments of Heraclitus, Sri Aurobindo also asks, "What... is the 'ever-living Fire' in which [Heraclitus] finds the primary and imperishable substance of the universe and identifies it in succession with Zeus and with eternity? Or what should we understand by 'the thunderbolt that steers all things'?" He answers forthwith, saying of the kinship between Vedic teachings and the Logos doctrine of Heraclitus:

> To interpret this fire as merely a material force of heat and flame or simply a metaphor for being that is eternal becoming is, it seems to me, to miss the character of Heraclitus' utterances.... But then we get back at once to the Vedic language and turn of thought; we are reminded of the Vedic Fire that is hymned as the upbuilder of the worlds, the secret Immortal in men and things, the periphery of the gods, Agni who "becomes" all around the other immortals, himself becomes and contains all the gods; we are reminded of the Vedic thunderbolt, that electric Fire, of the Sun who is the true Light, the Eye, the wonderful weapon of the divine pathfinders Mitra and Varuna. It is the same cryptic form of language, the same brief and abundant method of thought even; though the conceptions are not identical, there is a clear kinship.[251]

But this deep and detailed analysis leads Sri Aurobindo to the view that Heraclitus was not, ultimately, able to attain the sublime height of the Vedic Rishis.

Ephesus and Eurythmy

In our observations so far on the creative Word, both as it figures in Indian spirituality and in the Western Logos tradition, we can notice, on comparing the accounts of Sri Aurobindo with those of Rudolf Steiner that the latter, in relation to this action of the Logos—knowledge of which spread through Europe from Ephesus—focuses more on tangible creation in the realm of life processes whereas Sri Aurobindo adopts a more transcendental perspective. As we have shown at various places, he invariably traces the action of the Logos to its origin in the Supermind. This present book is founded on the conviction that these differing perspectives of the two great spiritual teachers need not divide them but can, rather, be seen as mutually enhancing.

Following the first of a series of early lectures that Rudolf Steiner gave to members of the Theosophical Society, *The Gospel of St. John,*[252] he approached the Russian painter Margarita Woloschin (1882–1973) to ask her if she could "dance" what he had said about the prologue to the St. John Gospel. She did not perhaps immediately understand what he meant, or at least did not immediately assent. A while later he came to her again and spoke to her about the "ancient temple dances through which the profoundest secrets of the world were revealed."[253] Only later, as Woloschin relates, did she understand that this—completely unpressured—information and question about finding expressive movement for the mystery of the Logos concerned the possible founding of eurythmy, which, after 1911, was to be initiated not by her but by Lory Smits (1893–1971).[254]

Rudolf Steiner spoke of the speech and tone eurythmy he inaugurated as "visible speech" and "visible song." His suprasensory vision had shown him that the creative powers of the Word—right into the configuration of each vowel and consonant—deeply penetrate our whole bodily organism, creating the form of our diverse organs. In their totality they constitute our etheric body of formative forces, the dynamic structure of the *pranamayakosha* in the Indian tradition. These etheric formative forces—following the archetype of the divine Logos—are of cosmic origin and constitute the microcosm of the human being, expressed in the wise ordering of our corporeality's life processes and formative principles. And this Logos-bearing etheric body also forms the matrix that configures the development, growth, and health of the physical body. When we speak the words of our language we produce—as shown above—sounds, syllables, and words through our air, warmth, and fluid organism. The manifold formative principles of our etheric body correspond here to the forms of articulated, exhaled air in speech, and have a reciprocal dynamic resonance and relationship with one another. Rudolf Steiner once put it like this:

> That we speak, that we produce words in the ordinary way, is due to the fact that we hold back the movements of the body of formative forces, localizing them in the chest region, the larynx and neighboring organs, the tongue and so forth. Through this localization of movement processes that encompass the whole organism, the etheric body brings the larynx and its neighboring organs into motions that produce words and speech. The movement of the larynx is an organic movement of our whole etheric body. But we can re-assimilate this again into the whole body.[255]

He concretized his research in collaboration with his spiritual companion Marie von Sivers, later Marie Steiner (1867–1948), elaborating with the first eurythmists how these Logos-borne formative forces and developmental movements could be expressed in bodily movement in gestures and spatial forms. Thus eurythmy was born. In the last year of his work, Rudolf Steiner gave a course for eurythmists entitled "Eurythmy as Visible Speech," in which he characterized in great detail each speech sound and the movement corresponding to it. Taking the sound "f" as an example, he shows in these lectures how he saw the Ephesian mysteries—though he does not mention them by name—and those of southern Asia—i.e., India, in a larger, interrelated context. The Egyptian Isis mysteries also belong to this:

> In ancient mysteries where "In the beginning was the Word, and the Word was with God" was living experience, when...people really sensed the creative nature of the Word, the Logos—for you see Logos cannot be translated as "wisdom," though modern scholars sometimes show their lack of understanding for ancient things by assuming this; Logos has to be translated as "verb," or "word."... In those times, in the ancient mysteries, people said roughly the following about the "f," especially in the mysteries of the Near or Middle East, Africa, southern Asia; they said that when people speak the "f," they expel their whole breath; but it is through the breath that the gods created humankind, and thus the whole of human wisdom is contained in the wind, in the air, in a breath of wind. Therefore, by mastering the breath and all that people can learn by doing so in yoga philosophy, the Indians felt the inner wisdom with which they filled themselves when uttering the "f." And this is how it was experienced in more ancient yoga practice in India; one performed yoga exercises, the technique of which involved inwardly feeling the human organism and the wealth and wisdom it contained. And by uttering the "f," one felt the wisdom in the Word coming to consciousness.[256]

In performing the eurythmy gesture of "f," it was to be accordingly enlivened and ensouled in tone and color experiences. This example can illumine for us the inner intensity with which Rudolf Steiner wished eurythmy to be practiced. Since the speech sound "f" does not figure in Sanskrit, we can ask what other speech sound might be referred to here. *Va* is probably closest to it, the "v" of which was widely uttered in the same way as "v" in the English *vast* and as the "w" in the German word *Wasser.* This is illuminating since in Sanskrit *Va* is seen as a so-called semivowel. In some regions of India, the *Va* is indeed spoken with a softer sound, close to "w" in English (as in *wafting*). This leads us on to the Vak itself, but also to the Sanskrit word *vayu* (air, or wind) and to the Vedic divinity Vayu—the god of the wind, the universal deva who, as "the master of life" inspires both breathing and the dynamic energies connected with it.[257] This is in agreement with Rudolf Steiner's words above about yoga and mastery of the breath. And from this position of *Va* in the Sanskrit alphabet, a path now leads us back one last time to the realm of the mysteries at Ephesus in which, according to Steiner, the relationship of the vowels to the consonants was established from the heights to the depths.

Earlier we mentioned that the vowels manifest interiority of soul and spirit. The consonants on the other hand represent the things and creatures of the outer world.[258] This can easily be shown, for instance in the "b" in *burrow* or *building,* also in the Hebrew for house, *bet;* all these convey safety, enclosure, and protection. The eurythmy gesture of "b" thus also resembles the movement and stance of a mother protecting her infant in her arms. According to Rudolf Steiner, the inner nature of the vowels, and the outward affinity of the consonants played in to the Ephesian Logos mysteries. The suggestions by Steiner below, perhaps seemingly mysterious, are invariably also intended for eurythmy, although this is not explicitly stated. By elaborating eurythmy movements, Rudolf Steiner enabled modern people to model the processes described in stance, gesture, and motion. Here too we might ask about the status of eurythmy and its deeper relationship to Indian culture's great past and great future.[259]

From a certain degree of attainment onward, the pupils at Ephesus learned to perceive the lunar sphere of Artemis, connected with all ether-borne and ether-permeated development, growth, and flourishing, and also with the secrets of human conception and birth, and beyond it the forces and powers of the spiritual sun at work behind this sphere. According to Rudolf Steiner, they learned how the developing human etheric body (*pranamayakosha*) forms before birth in the Moon sphere surrounding the Earth by uniting within it the light influences of the rest of the planetary cosmos that endow it with requisite differentiations. There forms what we can call a "light ether body." Above and beyond this, though, an individual spirit–soul—that is, an astral sheath and an "I"-being—prepares for incarnation in this developing human entity, and as it does so these aspects or bodies approach the light ether body from the spiritual sun. All this dawned on the adept in spiritual tones that were entirely vowel-like in character: the Sun Word in which he heard the inner being of the one seeking incarnation in a new life. But this was met, as if rising from the Earth toward it, by another sound element, which was consonantal in nature.

> And at Ephesus, things were arranged like this: the one who was able to let this influence work upon him at the place of initiation was really transported entirely into what thus emerged from the Moon-transformative sunlight. There resounded toward him as if from the Sun: *"J O A."* He knew that *J O A* activates his "I," his astral body. *J O*—"I," astral body; and the approaching light ether body in the *A* [*ah*]. *"J O A";* as this resonated in him, he felt himself as an "I," as astral body, and as etheric body. And then, since he was transported into the cosmic realm, it was as if the sound eh-v, permeating the *J O A*, sounded upward from the Earth; these were the earthly forces rising in this *eh-v* sound.[260]

This, in very concentrated form, conveys the initiate's experience of human incarnation. As the higher cosmic powers interpenetrate with the earth element, this ultimately reveals, at Ephesus, the one who, as the God of the people of Israel, served to prepare the incarnation of the Sun Word, the Christ. Known in India as Ishvara, or Vishnu, this was Yahweh, *JHVH,* or Jehovah. We will end this chapter on the "creative Word" with the passage that directly follows the one above, and names Jehova explicitly—as an interweaving of the vowel and consonant character of the Ephesian pupil's spiritual experience:[261]

> And now he [the initiate] felt in the *JehOvA* the whole human being. He had a premonition, an intimation, of the physical

body only to be acquired on Earth, in the consonants that belonged with the vowel qualities that, in the *J O A*, point to "I," astral body and etheric body. This immersion in the *JehOvA* enabled the pupil at Ephesus to sense the last steps or stages leading to a descent from the world of spirit. But at the same time this inner experience of the *J O A* was such that one felt oneself resonating in it within the light. And then one was a human being: resonant "I," resonant astral body, within a shining etheric body of light. Then one was sound within light. And this is our nature as cosmic human being.[262]

To Nature (excerpt)
Friedrich Hölderlin[263]

That I still played around your veiling garment
And still around you, like a blossom, hung...
Who felt your heart in my heart tender-warming,
In every sound of yours that round me rung.
That I, with trust, with longing, stood before you
Still, enriched as you, before your face,
To find there endless solace for my weeping,
And for my love, a world to hold in place.

That to the Sun my heart still warmly tended,
As though its tones in her she deep-imbibed,
Who named the stars as brothers, new-befriended,
And called the Spring the melody of God...
That in the breath that stirred the grove, your
Spirit, Spirit of Joy, still in the heart held sway
With quiet ripples wellingly outspreading, O
So you nourished me with golden days.

Down the valley, where the stream could cool me,
Where the youthful bushes sported green
Among the silent cliff-walls danced so gaily,
Sky-blue through their branches showed its sheen.
When, by flowers surrounded, stood I, quietly
And deep into my soul their fragrance drank,
To me, who stood embraced by light and glory,
From out the heights the golden cloud now sank—

When far across the naked heath I rambled,
Where from the twilit grooves of sturdy cliff
The Titan-song of waters rushed and rumbled
And night of clouds hung over like a roof...
When the storm with surging weather-pattern
Forth before me in the mountains bore,
And heaven's lightnings flashed their arrows at me,
There did You appear, O Soul of Nature!

(Translation by Charles Lawrie)

Chapter 4

Evolution and True "I"-being

Earlier in this book we saw that, in Great Britain in 1870 to 1871, the father of Aurobindo Ghose had been keenly involved in the debates raging around Charles Darwin's theory of evolution.[264] This was because Krishna Dhun Ghose had been forbidden from finishing his medical studies in India and thus from obtaining his license to practice as a physician. For this reason he went instead to Scotland and was admitted to King's College in Aberdeen, where he eventually qualified in 1871. On his return to northern India, Dr. Ghose was a convinced adherent of Darwin's ideas. We can see how great was the influence of these ideas at the University of Aberdeen, in particular, from the fact that in 1872, the year after Dr. Ghose qualified and returned to India, the author of *On the Origin of Species* (1859) and *The Descent of Man* (1871) was invited to take up the post of Rector at the university—though he turned this down due to the health problems from which he had been suffering for many years.[265]

In retrospect, Sri Aurobindo summed up his father's thinking with the often repeated, critical remark that he had been a "terrible atheist." It seems very probable, as Sri Aurobindo's biographer, Peter Heehs, highlights, that this choice of words refers particularly to Dr. Ghose's time in Scotland, and to the Darwinism that he assimilated and accepted then.[266] Let us recall here that Darwinian evolutionary ideas led to the originator of these ideas himself, who had once studied theology, gradually distancing himself in the course of his life from the possibility that life had any divine or spiritual source. The agnosticism of Krishna Dhun Ghose appears to mirror in miniature this trajectory of Darwin's own life. It can strike us as significant that Aurobindo Ghose incarnated into a milieu informed by such a worldview, given that after 1910, in stark contrast to Darwinism, he was to give the idea of evolution a very markedly spiritual nuance and orientation.

The writings of Sri Aurobindo are pervaded by all kinds of comments about involution and evolution; indeed, his view of evolution is central to Integral Yoga. Sri Aurobindo seeks to enlarge the Western concept of evolution with his own viewpoint, incorporating into it also, at great length, the tradition of Sanatana Dharma, or knowledge of the greater reality of the spirit. He intentionally sets this new outlook against the Western one. However, it seems as if his understanding of the evolutionary ideas of the "modern Western world" and his critique of them, were based primarily on Anglo-Saxon sources and their strictly materialistic perspective, and that in his works he takes only marginal account of the Central European view of evolution, with its different philosophical accent.

Through into the nineteenth century, elaboration of this Central European outlook, which, in the wake of German Idealism in the broader sense, took account of a spiritual influence acting on all that develops and evolves, gave Rudolf Steiner one of the most important foundations for his science of the spirit. It was not by chance that his formulation of Anthroposophy from 1900 onward was based on his extensive engagement with the philosophy of Idealism and what he had learned from studying Goethe, including very particularly the latter's scientific writings. Below, as we trace the most important aspects of both Western and Central Europe's developing concept of evolution, this highlights the point of departure for, respectively, Sri Aurobindo and Rudolf Steiner.[267]

The Idea of Evolution in the Eighteenth and Nineteenth Centuries

Rejection by Enlightenment philosophers of the picture of a craftsman-like Creator God—who "makes" all creatures,[268] and who, despite all dogmatic caveats, resembled the Platonic Demiurge—underpinned parallel development of a concept of evolution in both Western and Central Europe. This primarily encompassed the world of living organisms as a great, lawfully structured whole, within which later forms emerge organically from earlier ones, and at the same time sought to trace and interpret manifold changes of form from simpler to more complex ones.

Charles Darwin's theory of evolution was founded on earlier phases of the concept's development, as formulated in the English-speaking world by, among others, William Paley and Richard Owen.[269]

The philosopher and theologian William Paley (1743–1805) endeavored to formulate a natural theology that could plausibly relate detailed investigation of natural forms with traditional Biblical beliefs about the Creation. His interest was focused on the purposefulness of anatomy and the functions of living organisms, in particular of individual organs such as the eye. Just as one could derive from each part of a clock the purposefulness according to which its whole mechanism is produced and organized, the same held true, thought Paley, for specific organs, for instance the eye. Paley became famous for this analogy between the clockmaker who realizes his purposes in the created clock and the creator God manifesting his various purposes in created beings and their diverse parts. While Paley's view remained, really, a static and non-evolutionary one, it nevertheless formed one of the foundations on which Darwin based his theories. It is generally known that the aim and purpose of the evolution of species as Darwin saw it was adaptation for survival, or the "survival of the fittest."[270]

Rigorous Darwinism does not acknowledge higher aims than survival as an end in itself. In the battle for survival, creatures multiply more if they develop species variants that are better adapted to prevailing conditions than earlier variants. In this way "natural selection" occurs. Here, therefore, mere survival is seen as the meager purpose governing and driving evolution, rather than any higher, future-oriented aim.

The zoologist Richard Owen (1804–1892), like Paley, sought to acknowledge a divine power at work within the hierarchies of manifest species. Through extensive anatomical studies—based on a large number of animal skeletons—he discovered a kind of model structure or template found in the limbs of all quadruped vertebrates: one bone in the upper arm, two in the lower forearm, several small ones in the wrist, five bones in the palm and, finally, five fingers. These and further observations led Owen to attempt to describe not only the type of a single species but an *ur*-idea underlying all vertebrates: the archetype: "He saw the archetype as a matrix originating in the mind of God that preceded the diverse forms and realized itself in them in manifold ways."[271] The realization of this, he thought, had begun long before the animal species that nowadays inhabit the Earth began to evolve;[272] since the first manifestation of the archetype in fish-like forms, it had gradually acquired forms of ever more consummate embodiment and finally come to highest expression so far in the human being—as the "glorious raiment" of this archetype. As Christoph Hueck points out, Owen was clearly seeking the spirit in nature and in the human form. While Darwin, as Hueck shows, also based his work on Owen, he replaced the idea of the archetype as the origin of species with another idea—that of species descending from common physical ancestors. According to Darwin, this physical descent is the only originating and determining factor from the past.

Building on his valuable empirical research, Charles Darwin formulated important aspects of his concept of evolution by reinterpreting his predecessors (e.g., Paley and Owen) in such a way that eventually he believed he no longer had any need to resort to metaphysical ideas such as the "purpose" and "aim" of a superordinate Creator or of an archetype as originating divine thought. Darwin shifted the origin of the forms of species, and the divine purposefulness that Owen saw in the archetype, into the laws of physical heredity and the battle for survival. Dismissing higher principles of any spiritual or divine kind eventually led to the situation we find ourselves in today, in which the evolutionary theory he conceived, updated in diverse ways, has become the prevailing modern outlook with its inevitably and entirely materialistic and mechanistic impetus.

Whereas Sri Aurobindo's spiritual vision of evolution clearly takes issue with, and sets itself apart from Darwinian naturalism primarily, Rudolf Steiner's spiritual view of the evolution of the world, of life and of the human being happily takes up the thread of the Central European idea of evolution we spoke of earlier, which is connected with the names of Herder, Goethe, Hegel and Schelling. How does this idea differ from the evolutionary theory informed by an Anglo-Saxon outlook?

Baruch Spinoza (1632–1677) sought to unite the world and God in his phrase "God or: substance or: nature." In his concept of nature, God, *Natura naturans*, and the world of creatures, *Natura naturata*, are combined in a greater whole; and he sees no external divinity above and beyond this. Gottfried Wilhelm Leibnitz (1646–1716) tried to understand how the divine could work on through natural beings and, while preserving the unity of all, bring forth such diverse changes of form. He came to regard the Aristotelian concept of "entelechy" (what bears its *telos*, its goal, within itself) as being of decisive importance: for him this was the indwelling, ensouling and formative power that brings forth involutionary and evolutionary changes. Johann Gottfried Herder (1744–1803) traced the history of human ideas and found the "evolution" principle predominant there; he made initial attempts ("my great theme!") to transpose this onto the development of natural creatures and—in his account—the way they evolve under both spiritual and corporeal influences. Previous philosophical ideas of this kind came to be of great significance for Johann Wolfgang von Goethe (1749–1832) in the context of his scientific investigations. In dialogue with Herder, he picked up the latter's idea of evolution and energetically pursued and developed it.

Quite specifically in his investigations of nature, Goethe, with his encompassing, and even universal outlook, was invariably concerned with tangible detail and reality. While philosophical minds such as Spinoza, Leibniz, and Herder acted as a powerful stimulus in his own enquiries, his efforts were focused on discovering ideas that, in his own perception and experience, accorded with reality. Inspired by his encounter with Herder, his Italian journey (1786–1788) unexpectedly became an opportunity for him to reconfigure the inner cosmos of his views and set them in tumultuous motion. Besides his studies of ancient buildings, artworks, and artefacts, Goethe's interest in Italy came to focus especially on botany, given that known plant species appeared so markedly different in the Mediterranean climate from north of the Alps. In addition, there were also numerous unknown species that he wished to investigate. At Padua and Palermo, and later when he returned to Weimar, he developed his view of the "archetypal plant," which he had also sought previously. The archetypal plant—the *Urpflanze*—taught him to see how nature "develops in manifold ways from simplicity."[273]

His discovery was of a fundamental form that appears in countless variants in the diversity of flowering plants, and became for him a certain and tangible perception.[274] Goethe methodically elaborated this perception, presenting and describing it in his book *The Metamorphosis of Plants* (1790), much of which was probably recorded in aphoristic form already during his Italian journey. Thus even before 1800, the idea of evolution as applied to the realms of nature had taken hold in Central Europe.

Plant metamorphosis (or in other words lawful developments and changes of form) becomes apparent within even a single specimen in configurations that emerge from one another and undergo continual change. Goethe himself, in his introductory words on his basic discovery, offers a first example to make clear what he means:

> 1. Anyone who observes the growth of plants with even a little care will easily see that certain of their external parts sometimes change form and pass over soon more or less entirely into the shape of the next-adjoining parts.
> 2. Thus, for example, the simple blossom usually changes into a double flower when, instead of stamens and anthers, petals develop that are either identical in shape and color to the other petals of the corolla or at least bear clear signs of their origin.[275]

This led him to the view that even in the ordinary development of a single specimen, through metamorphosis, the various parts of the plant emerge lawfully from the originating form, which is blastodermic or germinal in nature (cotyledon). This Goethean concept of metamorphosis was later taken up by Rudolf Steiner and employed to develop deeper understanding of a universe in continual evolution. Goethe, for his part, also investigated the animal world in accordance with these ideas, for instance the metamorphosis of vertebrae, and then also their reconfiguration into the various bones of the skull. His search for a metamorphosis of animal forms led him to the concept of the *type*, as Richard Owen also later—and similarly—used it:

> In the meanwhile I had devoted my studies fully to a theory of bones; for in the skeleton the marked character of every form is preserved safely and for all times.... Here I soon felt the need to establish a typus with which to compare all mammals in terms of their accord with or deviation from it; and as I had

> previously sought the archetypal plant, so I now tried to find the archetypal animal or in other words, ultimately, the very concept and idea of the animal.[276]

These excerpts are sufficient to show that ideas of evolution as Goethe formulated them make great demands on a mobile and at the same time plastic, inner capacity of perception. Goethe was very well aware of this, as attested by Frank Teichmann, an anthroposophically oriented Goethean. He cites this passage from Goethe:

> But if we examine all forms, especially organic ones, we find that nowhere does there exist anything permanent, at rest, anything that is finally concluded, but that, rather, everything is in continual and volatile motion.... What has been formed is immediately reconfigured, and, if we wish to some degree to come to a living perception of nature, we must ourselves remain as mobile and pliable as the example nature offers us.[277]

Teichman is quoting this passage to point, like other Goethe connoisseurs, to the fact that the evolution of living beings and organisms occurs not just outside and separate from human beings. Rather than having a merely external part in this process insofar as we ourselves embody a particular stage of evolution, we only really experience evolution if we consciously participate in it by making our thinking adaptable and mobile enough to inwardly and dynamically grasp continual changes of form between growth and decay, expansion and contraction. The quality of awareness that Goethe is invariably concerned to invoke makes all of his observations and perceptions seem close to artistic creation.

Goethe's evolutionary thinking, with its equally scientific and artistic qualities, drew on previous philosophical outlooks and was later taken up again, and systematized, in turn, by representatives of German Idealism.[278] I will refer here, by way of example, only to Schelling.

Friedrich Wilhelm Schelling (1775–1854) took issue with traditional, static ideas of "involution" and "evolution" that proposed the "preformation" of each entity. In this view, the form of every creature was already contained in miniature in its germinal condition, "involved" (wrapped within) the seed. As the organism grows after fertilization, and develops its prior potential, it is thus only evolving its preformed, involved shape. Schelling stated that this concept was inadequate because it offered no possibility of conceiving the development of anything new. He countered such ideas with the Goethean concept of metamorphosis, in a way that enabled him to overcome anything static in his natural philosophy, and favor instead the idea of what he called "dynamic evolution." Schelling's point of departure was the reality of ideas, whose *a priori* nature precedes all empiricism. In the realm of this *a priori* reality of ideas he discovered the "subject of nature," its "producing productivity," *Natura naturans*, in contrast to all empirical enquiry that is always concerned only with the objective properties of nature as its product, *Natura naturata.*[279] In the subject, nature, discerned *a priori*, Schelling saw the guarantee of its unity, whereas in the cognitively necessary transition to its object, he saw the step into the endless diversity of forms and their apparently infinite changes. It is clear here that Schelling, too, never regarded evolution as a solely external natural process but that he saw its reality primarily in the realm of ideas and the continual motion of its acts of consciousness. In this context his concept of evolution has been termed "logogenesis" by various authors. Schelling himself asserts that there cannot be a fixed concept of the subject nature, the principle at work in natural existence, "for since it [the principle] is engaged in continual movement, progress, intensification, any concept can only momentarily apply; as living being it is in fact not One thing but infinitely many.[280] And, "from this it can be seen that in no living whole in scientific art is there any point that one could as it were hold fast or fix, but rather that the development of the whole must be awaited before the full concept of the developing subject can be given."[281]

Both the Goethean and the Idealist concept of evolution make high demands on those who seek to grasp it, since their thinking must come into appropriate motion to be able to assimilate consciously[282] what constitutes the evolution of the nature of the evolving being. A metamorphosis of thinking, perceiving consciousness is needed—a development from logical reason, which tends only to grasp static, dead properties, to a living thinking that can immerse itself in the stream of actual life without losing itself there.

Rudolf Steiner was to take up this theme again in a very decisive way, founding anthroposophic Spiritual Science upon mastery of such capacities. Yet the prevailing mode of cognition of the Western world continued to seek the one-sided certainties of the world of objects (failing to understand the Idealist concept of the subject as instigator of knowledge, and discrediting it as a merely private interiority). The Positivism arising from this outlook saw and still sees in Darwinism and neo-Darwinism[283] the best means of understanding evolution. In the first half of the twentieth century both Rudolf Steiner and Sri Aurobindo inevitably rejected such views as inadequate.

Cosmic Evolution I

Around the turn of the century, Rudolf Steiner had elaborated an outline of the evolution of ideas in Western culture, which he published in 1901 as *Worldviews and Outlooks in the Nineteenth Century.*[284] During these years he had engaged with the Darwinian theory of evolution, especially in the form in which Ernst Haeckel[285] publicized it in the German-speaking world. In his *Autobiography*, Steiner suggests that he gained a "*true organic evolution* from primordial times until today" only after he had concluded these studies, but that, nevertheless, Haeckel's Darwinism only provided him with the material for this, and amounted only to a "series of sense-perceptible facts in nature." And:

> For me, within this series of facts, *spiritual impulses* were at work, as these hovered before Goethe in his idea of metamorphosis. The scientific evolutionary series as represented by Haeckel, never stood before me as something in which mechanical or merely organic laws held sway, but rather in which the spirit leads living creatures from simple through complex forms until it arrives at the human being.[286]

The following words by Sri Aurobindo seem to have been written in a closely related spirit:

> The Western idea of evolution is the statement of a process of formation, not an explanation of our being. Limited to the physical and biological data of Nature, it does not attempt except in a summary or a superficial fashion to discover its own meaning, but is content to announce itself as the general law of a quite mysterious and inexplicable energy. [287]

In his day, Sri Aurobindo—also when considering Europe—already saw the end of the Darwinian idea of evolution approaching. Attempts at the time to describe the vital force (e.g., Hans Driesch, Henri Bergson) or also the discovery of the unconscious, especially the Collective Unconscious (C. G. Jung), confirmed him in his views. (From a modern perspective this must however appear as the expression of a premature hope, since neo-Darwinism today still remains unquestioned and firmly rooted in the public mind).

In our reflections we are primarily concerned here with the contributions of Sri Aurobindo, and later equally of Rudolf Steiner, to a spiritual understanding of evolution. The yogi philosopher takes issue with current evolutionary theory, objecting that it is saddled with two paradoxes: first that everything it describes is said to unfold entirely independently of a self-reflexive and intentional mind, and indeed denies the existence of this, but that such a mind or consciousness must in fact be seen as the superior antecedent of such evolution; and second, that all phenomena of life and consciousness are only epiphenomena of matter[288] in the Darwinian view, which therefore fails to grasp the principle distinction between matter and consciousness. Furthermore, Sri Aurobindo urges that the principle of "battle for survival" as the prime instigator of life should be replaced or at least complemented by the principle of "love."[289] In his essay "Evolution," he outlines a new picture of evolution, drawing once again on fundamental themes in traditional Sankhya teachings—the Purusha as eternal consciousness contrasts with Prakriti, nature, within which beings evolve mentally, vitally, and materially. In nature, Prakriti, evolutionary impulses are initiated from the mental plane, and thence encompass the vital and then the material realm. Like the material plane, the vital and mental levels embody realms of reality whose elements and entities are themselves also evolving. Accordingly we can speak of at least three worlds in which parallel processes of evolution are unfolding, with processes from the mental realm always acting on the vital level, and in turn from the vital on the material realm. In this view, evolution occurs in such a dynamic way that it has always led, and always will, to new, qualitative leaps—for instance in the hierarchy of species—through the fact that evolutionary tendencies or intentions work out of higher realms of reality into the material world, or indeed, as we can say, erupt into them. Sri Aurobindo puts it as follows:

> Instead of slow, steady, minute gradations it is now suggested that new steps in evolution are rather effected by rapid and sudden outbursts, outbreaks, as it were, of manifestation from the unmanifest. Shall we say that Nature preparing slowly behind the veil, working a little backward, working a little forward, one day arrives at the combination of outward things that makes it possible for her to throw her new idea into a realized formation, suddenly, with violence, with a glorious dawning, with a grandiose stride? And that would explain the economy of her relapses and her reappearances of things long dead. She aims at a certain immediate result and to arrive at it more quickly and entirely she sacrifices many of her manifestations and throws them back into the latent, the

> unmanifest, the subconscient. But she has not finished with them; she will need them at another stage for a farther result. Therefore she brings them forward again and they reappear in new forms and other combinations and act toward new ends. So evolution advances.[290]

The unmanifest and unconscious should not here be too simply equated with processes that act "below" the threshold of awareness—i.e., outside the compass of individual consciousness, but one-sidedly assigned only to the pole of matter. Rather, Sri Aurobindo has two things in view; what acts "below" is, in his vision, complemented by the "upper" level of what indwells and acts within ordinary consciousness, which is the primary agency and is "localized" more toward the pole of absolute spirit. Otherwise his characteristic references to involution and evolution could be seriously misunderstood. What are we concerned with here?

Sri Aurobindo never tires of telling us that a modern yogic view of God, the world, and human beings must help bridge or close the gulf that yawns between the sublime or absolute, and nature, within which creatures evolve: the abyss between Purusha and Prakriti.[291] Sri Aurobindo's idea of evolution aims to convey a tangible sense of how reality consists of a web woven from both poles, arising through the dual interaction of involution and evolution. To put it very simply, we can say that all evolution unfolding from undifferentiated matter and from this substrate gradually producing the vital, mental, psychic, and finally supramental spiritual realities, is founded on an involution of mighty, cosmic dimensions. Descending from the loftiest spiritual levels, in an unimaginable process of densification, the supramental, psychic, mental, and vital levels involve or integrate themselves into matter and here, in pure latency and potential, hold ready the seeds for future evolutionary processes. But complete involution at the same time leads to complete loss of awareness of self and its sublime origins. The subsequent emergence of vital, emotional–mental, psychic, and spiritual qualities, is in turn tantamount to a continual growth of conscious awareness[292]—an ever more encompassing capacity and process within which, for instance, our modern intellectual consciousness is ultimately only an imperfect transitional stage.

In an account of the concept of evolution in Integral Yoga that is as simplified as this, there is a certain and not inconsiderable danger. It might seem reasonable in consequence—and supposedly in accord with Sri Aurobindo himself—to attach this general view of evolution to Darwinian or neo-Darwinian theories, merely enlarging these by adding to them the concept of the involutionary processes of higher potencies. This would however be too easy a route toward a spiritual view of evolution. Such a view is also problematic in that it would suggest that nothing qualitatively new can emerge within the whole cosmic process since only what first involved may then evolve.

Such shortcuts in a supposedly spiritual view of involution and evolution do certainly arise on occasion.[293] Such accounts, which assume an original condition of complete involution with full absorption of the higher levels of existence (as if they had been lost), cannot however be reconciled with Sri Aurobindo's comments above about the continual influx of vital, mental, or even higher agencies, which ultimately descend right into the physical–material world of evolution. Here, after all, we must allow for "new" involutionary processes that occur in order to prepare "new" evolutionary ones. Such influxes only remain plausible if we regard all those higher levels of existence as real worlds in which real evolutions are accomplished.[294] They cannot have been completely and entirely lost in an ultimate involution. In fact, Sri Aurobindo has in mind a complex web of involutive and evolutive processes that overlay each other temporally. Indeed, he speaks of reciprocal involution in the material and the spiritual realm: "In a sense, the whole of creation may be said to be a movement between two involutions, Spirit in which all is involved and out of which all evolves downward to the other pole of Matter, Matter in which also all is involved and out of which all evolves upward to the other pole of Spirit."[295]

From this dual, reciprocal motion, what we can call "patterns of interference" will arise, explaining how, in ongoing evolution that occurs in the physical–material world, progressive impulses can come to effect repeatedly anew from the higher realms to which belong the vital, mental, and still further spiritual aspects. Human existence is likewise embedded in this dual, reciprocal pattern of involutionary and evolutionary processes. As human beings our basic situation is this: "Man himself is a doubly involved being; most of himself in mind and below is involved in a subliminal conscience or a subconscience; most of himself above mind is involved in a spiritual superconscience."[296] Elsewhere, in relation to the development of the spiritual human being, Sri Aurobindo also speaks of a "double evolution":

> In fact, the creative Consciousness-Force in our Earth existence has to lead forward, in an almost simultaneous process...a double evolution. There is an evolution of our outward nature, the nature of the mental being in the life and body, and there is within it, pressing forward for self-revelation because with the emergence of mind that revelation is becoming possible, a preparation at least, even the beginning of an evolution of our inner being, our occult subliminal and spiritual nature.[297]

Between the material and spiritual pole, however, the soul, which is the very meaning of evolution, lives and acts. Possibly it, rather than higher levels, creates the locus where anything really new can enter the world. In the essay mentioned above on "Involution and Evolution," Sri Aurobindo summarizes the ideal intent of the whole process as follows:

> The soul fulfils itself in Nature when it possesses in her the consciousness of that eternity and its power and joy and transfigures the natural becoming with the fullness of the spiritual being. The constant self-creation that we call birth finds there

> the perfect evolution of all that it held in its own nature and reveals its own utmost significance. The complete soul possesses all its self and all Nature.[298]

Whereas, in the accounts Sri Aurobindo published during his lifetime—such as in the monthly journal *The Arya*[299]—a more abstract style predominates, focused entirely on the spiritual essence of his content, in his diary entries, *Record of Yoga*, and similar, posthumously published writings, we find very specific and detailed spiritual research questions and corresponding findings. These materials, for instance, testify to a series of imaginative visions, *chitra-drishti*, of very early stages of the Earth's evolution, and historical circumstances in which Sri Aurobindo perceives what certain representatives of early humanity underwent at the time. In one case he relates a scenario of banishment and flight, of conflict between the inhabitants of an ancient land, and its usurpers, then of a great, fortified city in which, in later times, the original inhabitants and colonizers eventually live together and mingle.[300]

In connection with these visions, Sri Aurobindo wrote a text intended to help survey the great trajectory of the evolution of humanity and the Earth, and to locate his various visions in an overall temporal context. These passages describe evolution largely in terms used in traditional Sanatana Dharma, and are of particular interest here because they strikingly testify to the dual nature of evolution—from "above" and from "below"—and in some respects correspond with accounts by Rudolf Steiner.

In this text, *The Evolutionary Scale*, Sri Aurobindo shows how divine thought takes effect in the life of the cosmos. He sees the beginning of this activity in the forming of the material world with the Sun as its center. The Sun itself is for him the manifestation of the being of great Agni, the god of fire, who is the same as Maha-Vishnu, the conscious universal divine being behind the material cosmos, the Virat-Purusha. Maha-Vishnu differentiates himself into diverse divinities—into Agni Tvashta, the shaping fire, Vishvakarman, the architect of the universe, Prajapati, the lord of creatures, and Matarishvan, who grows and breathes in the Earth mother's realm.[301] Prajapati then acts as Surya Savitri, the creative Sun God, who for his part gives rise to numerous solar divinities, the many single Purushas of an equal number of feminine sun energies. Later, Prajapati creates from the cosmic substance of the Sun the planets that successively form one Bhumi, or "earth," upon another, as the scene of material development, the respective sites of Manu's manifestation. Manu, whose fourteen-fold cycle creates one world epoch, a *Manvantara*, is "...the mental being, who is the nodus of manifest life-existence and the link between the life and the spirit."[302] We should regard today's planet Mars as the former arena of evolution,[303] but the fiery Agni Tvashta still always as the governing principle of today's Earth. Agni Tvashta manifests through Prajapati, and he in turn again ultimately through Manu in the earthly world. However, "not in the physical world at first, but in the mental world that stands behind the earthly life; for Earth has seven planes of being, the material of which the scenes and events are alone normally visible to the material senses."[304]

Above the material plane are six further planes from which are created the human being's life sheath, consciousness sheath, knowledge sheath, and bliss sheath. The two highest of the seven planes, the "dynamic" and the "essential," do not correspond to anything currently existing in the human being's potential corporeality.[305] But from the beginning, as plant and animal forms begin to populate the Earth in "lower evolution," "Man already exists but as a god or demigod in Bhuvarloka of Bhu [the Earth], not as a human on Earth."[306]

The human being is termed a "Son of Manu." Initial animal-human evolution, which precedes the actual appearance of the human being, is to be seen as a preparation that unfolds until the appearance of the typus best suited for the human being to incarnate into. "When the human body is ready, then he [the son of Manu] descends upon Earth and occupies it. He is not a native of Earth, nor does he evolve out of the animal. His manifestation in animal form is always [only] a partial incarnation."[307]

Evolution from which the human being emerges is connected with a tenfold, increasingly intensifying influx of qualities that Manu prepared in *bhuvarloka*, the elemental world. Through ten epochs these formative impulses of Manu, termed the ten "types," manifest in the evolving human being, and constitute ten evolutionary stages within him: "Man…progresses through the ten types which have been fixed for human evolution in the Kalpa. In this Kalpa [the present world age] the types, *dashagu* [ten light-rays], are the ten forms of consciousness."[308]

In the next but one section of this chapter, we will again encounter a tenfold quality—Sri Aurobindo and Rudolf Steiner are in accord about this—in the tenfold Avatar manifestations. It must for now remain an open question, though, whether these two tenfold contexts should be related to each other.

Sri Aurobindo's evolutionary thinking naturally also encompasses the realms of the human individuality's evolution through rebirths, as well as the detailed question about the relationship between evolving reality and the highest godhead. The first of these themes will be taken up again later in the present chapter, while the second question will be examined in the following chapter.

Cosmic Evolution II

While Sri Aurobindo tends in his numerous published works to speak, from ever new perspectives, of the principle significance of the cosmic dimensions of involution and evolution, and their relationship to past and future, Rudolf' Steiner generally focuses more on the specific evolutionary realization of manifold entities—the human being, natural creatures, the beings of the world of spirit—through the great cycles and epochs of cosmic development. Below we will first offer a brief outline of this.

But before we do so the following should be considered. In Goethe, too, we find signs of an alternation between an outlook that accentuates strict immanence on the one hand—that is, seeing the divine as subsumed entirely in the visible world—and on the other looks up to a higher divine, spiritual reality that has certainly not been completely absorbed by the material pole in an original process of involution. We encountered a similar question in the previous section when considering, in contrast to Sri Aurobindo's true position, the tendency toward an over-simplifying view of involution and evolution. In his introduction to Goethe's scientific writings, Rudolf Steiner summarizes Spinoza's view of *scientia intuitiva* or "beholding knowledge," and thus at the same time points as follows to the latter's important influence on Goethe in the 1770s and 1780s: "The God of Spinoza is the content of the world's ideas, the driving force and all-sustaining principle."

One could, says Steiner, conceive of this principle as governing finite things from without. Spinoza, on the other hand—and with him the younger Goethe—conceives of this entity, God, the originating principle "as merged in finite things so that it no longer exists above and alongside them, but henceforth only *within* them." And: "This view by no means denies that originating *ur* principle; it acknowledges it fully, but regards it as *poured out* into the world."[309]

At the end of his life, Goethe himself came to hold a different view however, according to which a greater, higher remainder existed that his observation could by no means access: "No organic creature corresponds entirely with the idea that underlies it; behind each one the higher idea is hidden: that is my God; that is the God we all eternally seek and hope to behold, but we can only intimate and not see him!"[310]

In his major philosophical work, *Intuitive Thinking as a Spiritual Path: A Philosophy of Freedom*, Rudolf Steiner for his own part formulated a monism that encompasses both the sense-perceptible world and the world of ideas. This outlook, he said, draws its principles for explaining the world from human experience alone, likewise seeking sources of action only within the observable world. The human being's relationship to God must, in accordance with this monism, be seen as follows:

> Every human being encompasses with his thinking only a part of the totality of the world of ideas, and to this extent individuals differ also through the actual content of their thinking. But these contents exist within a self-contained totality comprising the content of all human thinking. Thus in our thinking we apprehend the common primal being that penetrates all human beings. To live in reality filled with thought content is at the same time to live in God.[311]

Here we should remember that such monism encompasses both the visible world and the world of ideas. But in his autobiography, which he wrote toward the end of his life, it becomes apparent—despite accentuation of this monist outlook—that the agency of the world of ideas, or, rather, the world of spirit, is a reality for Steiner that he invariably experiences as primary by contrast to, let us say, realities evolving upward "from below." Thus he writes of the 1880s and 1890s:

> Wherever I could engage with them, I found the sciences of organic nature to be pervaded by Darwinian ideas. At the time, Darwinism's highest ideas appeared to me a scientific impossibility. I had gradually come to form a picture of human interiority that was spiritual in nature, conceived as an integral part of a world of spirit. I thought of it as submerging itself from this world of spirit in natural existence, incorporating itself into the natural organism so as to perceive and act through this in the sense world. Despite having a certain respect for the doctrines of organic evolution, I could not allow them in any way to detract from this picture I had formed. I regarded the emergence of higher organisms from lower ones as a fruitful

idea, but thought it immeasurably difficult to reconcile this with my knowledge of the world of spirit.[312]

Rudolf Steiner's early efforts to overcome this difficulty led many years later to his major anthroposophic work *An Outline of Esoteric Science.*[313] There—and complementing it in numerous public and internal lectures—he described cosmic evolution in terms of manifold specific developments in actual beings and entities. To do so he starts from the four elements surrounding us today in nature—fire or heat, air, water and earth—and highlights their significance in Europe from ancient times through to the Rosicrucian tradition. Fire or heat are the most volatile of the elements, earth creates solidity, and water and air—rising from the earth realm—in turn increase in mobility and volatility.

Cosmic evolution emerges from divine, spiritual will when very sublime spirit beings intentionally and consciously densify their substance to a state of warmth and surrender it to the world process within which—as if germinally—the first matrices of creatures develop, having in this warmth nothing but their quasi mineral-physical corporeality.[314] These creatures are the human being's earliest ancestors, emerging involutively from the very sublime spirituality of the primal cosmic substance, but condensing only as far as the very initial physical stage of pure warmth. Rudolf Steiner calls this cosmic condition the planetary embodiment of "Old Saturn." Everything that manifests here corresponds to a mighty, divine-spiritual outbreath, followed by an equally mighty inbreath so that this cosmic condition of Old Saturn ultimately withdraws again from manifestation. This can be compared with the breaths of Maha–Vishnu and the "days and nights of Brahma." Drawing terms from the Sanatana Dharma, Rudolf Steiner calls the emergence of a cosmic manifestation, of a planetary condition, *manvantara,* and the withdrawal from manifestation again, *pralaya.*

Cosmic evolution continues with a new manifestation following a first *pralaya*. This new emergence first recapitulates the forms of the previous *manvantara*, but then brings forth something new. Through the influence of a further group of lofty spirit beings, a further densification of spiritual substance occurs within the field of remanifesting warmth, now reaching a gaseous condition, that of air. Subsequently the evolutive field of this planetary condition is further enhanced by the emergence of light that, as etheric quality, as light ether, augments the element of air. Within this environment of air, warmth, and light, the remanifesting earliest matrices of the human being condense to the level of air, and into these gaseous forms light and warmth are now also incorporated, corresponding to a first enlivenment of these human germs. Like today's plants they have a physical body enlivened by the etheric, albeit at a far more rarefied level. In terms of consciousness they are at a level comparable to a state of deep sleep. But meanwhile, in forms not yet enlivened by an etheric element, we find the earliest precursors of our animals. The wealth of this manifestation or *manvantara*, called "Old Sun," again returns to a state of cosmic latency, into *pralaya*.

According to Rudolf Steiner's vision, the third condition, "Old Moon," again recapitulates everything that has so far evolved. A further group of lofty spirit beings now help to densify the substantiality of this state to the watery level, and accordingly also to the early corporeality of human ancestors. The reality of Old Moon is now filled with tones and resonant sounds as the sound ether emerges to augment the fluid element. Thus the physical corporeality of human precursors is composed of fluid, air, and warmth; it is etherically enlivened and—a new stage of realization—permeated with astrality as a very early quality of sentient consciousness. The level of consciousness of these human precursors is comparable to dream consciousness today. During this planetary stage they experience rhythmically alternating phases of stronger, brighter with weaker, duller awareness. The precursors of the animals, which arose already on Old Sun, now have the etheric element incorporated into them and are enlivened. Forms that, as yet remain without this, become the forerunners of our plant kingdom. Eventually this manifestation again withdraws into *pralaya*.

The fourth condition, the "Earth" stage, finally, constitutes our present planet Earth, likewise successively recapitulating the levels of warmth, air, and water, and condensing to solid minerality. This mineral state is however initially as subtle as, say, airborne aromas that nowadays, through our sense of smell, tell us of the substance from which they evaporate. Through the agency of a further group of lofty spirit beings,[315] the human being is first provided with a physical, etheric, and astral corporeality, and endowed with the spiritual spark of his "I"-being from the fiery, spiritual warmth substance of the same spirit beings. After prior involution, the beings of the animal and plant kingdom also evolve further, and the mineral kingdom as such arises, developing through stages intrinsic to it of dust, liquefaction, congealment, and crystallization. A further etheric quality emerges to augment the solid mineral realm—that of the life ether, the strength of which makes it possible to inform with spiritually intended, living configurations a physical substance that has densified to the mineral level.

The spiritual warmth entelechy of the human "I" represents a first great evolutionary milestone insofar as here, for the first time, a spiritual being within cosmic manifestation becomes embodied as far as the physical level. Previously it was only present above the manifested realms of the cosmos, in a state of latency and pre-existence in the lap of the high spirit beings, the "spirits of form" or Exousiai, from whom it emerged. Human "I"-being constitutes itself now in a first, merely sentient, self-reflective consciousness, growing in the course of the evolutionary process now initiated, through development of object awareness to ever-greater self-responsibility and freedom. To be embodied in a physical–etheric–astral corporeality is in turn the necessary precondition for developing this free self-awareness. In a subsequent section of this chapter we will examine in more detail the evolution of the human being's self-aware "I"-being.

Comparable to the pre-existent latency of each human being's individual "I"-being before coming to Earthly birth, the "group souls" of animals, plants, and minerals exist at various planes of the world of spirit. The lower the degree of consciousness of these natural entities here on Earth, the higher the locus, says Rudolf Steiner, of their group soul in the world of spirit. Accordingly, the group souls of the higher animals are closest to earthly manifestation since their dreaming sentience has most affinity with waking human consciousness. Each group soul represents the type of one species.

Actual human development in the course of the planet Earth's manifestation was preceded by long periods of time in which, from the sphere of the spirits of form (Exousiai), specific influences were acting on the still very soft and plastic bodies of animal-like human precursors, the inheritors of Old Moon evolution. By this means these physical–etheric–astral bodies were rendered capable of permanent assimilation of the spiritual-fiery "I"-being. This spiritually instigated influence was intent on bringing forth a protohuman *Urbild*, the human archetype, which was initially embodied in a still animal-like corporeality. As a result of this agency of the spirits of form, pre-human soul beings on the one hand differentiated themselves as bearers of that archetype, and on the other, fish-, reptile-, bird- and mammal-type forms developed but invariably solidified too soon to be able to lastingly assimilate spiritual "I"-being. These organic forms survived but were now as it were indirectly ensouled from without or above by the animal group souls we spoke of, and in this way began to unfold their specific series in animal evolution. Variants and specializations of the various types of vertebrates (broadly fish, reptiles, birds, and mammals) eventually emerged in accordance with the model of metamorphosis that Goethe first described. Only the life forms that retained the subtlest materiality and greatest plasticity were fitted to take up and physically embody the pre-human soul beings who, in something like a breathing process, organized themselves in accord with the human archetype.

Anthroposophic Spiritual Science tells us that then, during the Earth's early evolution, an event of great significance occurred that was to have a lasting effect on human existence. Under the influence of certain adversarial beings, at a time when life forms were already more strongly materialized, early "I"-endowed humans bound up their soul-spiritual being more deeply with their corporeality than they had been archetypally predisposed to do in accordance with the conscious aims of the spirits of form. In particular, the "I" bound itself too greatly with astrality and the desire nature concealed in it. This gave rise to lower egoity, the ego, which we must not confuse with true "I"-being. This occurrence led in turn to deep-seated changes in the whole body, soul, and spirit configuration of early human beings, and meant that they were no longer uninterruptedly able to realize the archetype shining before them. As a result they became at the same time subject to death. The periodic alternation now began between earthly incarnations and body-free sojourns in various planes of the spiritual world after death: a recurring rhythm of incarnation and excarnation, or reincarnation, henceforth governed these evolving "I"-beings. From now on the succession of incarnations was to determine the long path—long stretches of which still lie ahead of us today—whereby human beings might eventually attain the divine likeness of their archetype.

In this mighty evolutionary panorama, which Rudolf Steiner elaborated, he repeatedly describes processes and occurrences in the physical, life, soul, and spiritual environment of developing humankind that issue from lofty spirit beings and call forth new, progressive configurations in us. Such incisive influences first encompass the realm of organic human development, then later also cultural and finally spiritual development. We internalize these in turn, thereby developing ever-new capacities that become the foundation for our own, autonomous actions. Rudolf Steiner summarizes this recurring process as follows in his *Esoteric Science*:

> On this is based all evolution: that an autonomous entity must first separate itself out from the life of its surroundings, whereupon its surroundings inform this distinct, separate being as in a reflection, after which the separate entity continues to evolve independently.[316]

Avatar and Evolution

In chapter 3 of this book we looked extensively at the creative Word—the Vak, or Logos, along with the emergence of the world of living creatures out of the creative wealth of this divine Word. Here once again are some words of Sri Aurobindo on this theme: "Out of whatever substance on whatever plane, the form or physical expression emerges by its creative agency. The Supermind using the Word is the creative Logos."[317]

In light of our previous descriptions of cosmic evolution, it might seem as if there were a yawning, irreconcilable gulf here. How can we bring together Rudolf Steiner's account of the development of the animal kingdom, from the perspective of the Ephesian mysteries for instance, with the evolutionary "emergence of higher organisms from lower ones," which he spoke of elsewhere as a "fruitful idea." Or, in the case of Sri Aurobindo, how can the "creative agency" of the Logos accord with the evolution he describes as ascending out of involution? Both teachers have clearly wrestled hard with this problem, and, surprisingly, both have found the same powerful motif that can bridge this gulf.

The motif I refer to—Avatara—originates in the Sanatana Dharma, and is initially a pictorial and mythological idea. By using it both Sri Aurobindo and Rudolf Steiner demonstrate how the ideas bound up with this theme can be rendered fruitful and available for modern consciousness, precisely by relating them carefully to the realities of evolution. In the classical sense, India regards the Avatar Shri Krishna or his form as the super-earthly, cosmic divinity Shri Vishnu. The Sanskrit word *avatāra* means roughly "descent," and points to the "manifestation of divine consciousness on Earth." Shri Krishna is the central figure in the *Bhagavad Gita*,[318] the superlative *Song of the Sublime*, probably the most significant revelation of him in written form.[319] Relating in turn to the *Bhagavad Gita*, and entirely in the same spirit, the extensive *Bhagavata Purana*[320] was composed between AD 500 and 1000. This work goes into much detail about Krishna and positions him as the eighth in a series of ten Vishnu avatars.

Below we quote two important passages from the work of Sri Aurobindo and Rudolf Steiner alongside each other, and will then highlight the commonalities between them. Both Steiner and Sri Aurobindo here base what they say on the Puranic tradition referred to of the ten avatars. In one of his *Letters on Yoga*, Sri Aurobindo writes:

> Avatarhood would have little meaning if it were not connected with evolution. The Hindu procession of the ten Avatars is itself, as it were, a parable of evolution. First the Fish Avatar, then the amphibious animal between land and water, then the land animal, then the Man–Lion Avatar, bridging man and animal, then man as dwarf, small and undeveloped and physical but containing in himself the godhead and taking possession of existence, then the rajasic, sattwic, nirguna Avatars, leading the human development from the vital rajasic to the sattwic mental man and again the overmental superman. Krishna, Buddha and Kalki depict the last three stages, the stages of the spiritual development—Krishna opens the possibility of Overmind, Buddha tries to shoot beyond to the supreme liberation but that liberation is still negative, not returning upon Earth to complete positively the evolution;

> Kalki is to correct this by bringing the Kingdom of the Divine upon Earth.[321]

He also says of the "Vibhutis," who are partial divine manifestations as opposed to full avatar realizations (*pūrnāvatāra*) and far more common than the latter, that within evolution these are responsible for smaller transitions, whereas the great evolutionary steps (or we might say, those of macroevolution) can only be governed by full avatars. Moreover, beginning with the Dwarf Avatar, it is apparent here, too, that evolution gradually shifts from the organic, biological process to the field of cultural development—and ultimately spiritual development instigated by Krishna, Buddha, and Kalki.

Rudolf Steiner illumines the same context in an internal esoteric lesson given to a small group of pupils in Berlin in the summer of 1903. It is noteworthy here that he introduces the Eastern theme of avatars as a content of the Rosicrucian tradition, which at first glance appears a genuinely Western tradition:

> The outward forms of the world of phenomena have an inner significance beside their outward one: they are as it were symbols of a former evolutionary phase. "Everything transient is but a metaphor" to those who look deeper. For the psychograph whose astral perception enables him to gain vision of inner development, of the soul of the world, the things of the manifest world reveal their inner history. The eye of the Dangma sees in an evolutionary series the metamorphoses of the Logos. The sacred books of the Vedas and the chronicles of the Rosicrucians speak of ten such avatars or metamorphoses of our present Sun Logos. To the clairvoyant organ, our modern lancelet fish (Amphioxus lanceolatus) indicates and recalls an incarnation of the Sun Logos, and is analogous with vertebrate precursors. We can imagine this if we think of the symbols of sickle, scorpion, fish and so on in the calendar, which symbolize processes in the cosmos of planets and stars. Vertebrae, from which[322] the fish, amphibians, birds and mammals evolved successively, were only a first potential in their early

> precursors, in the same way that in today's lancelet the organ of feeling is hinted at only in a single nerve strand, from which, in later developments, the brain of water creatures, the fish, emerged and organized itself.[323]

Rudolf Steiner then describes all ten levels, rising from the Fish Avatar up, and accords each separate stage its own mantric verse, arriving finally at the Kalki Avatar. At this point it becomes clear, when he says that the Rosicrucians identify the Kalki Avatar with Jesus Christ, that all he has been presenting emerges from the esoteric outlook of the *Rosicrucian Chronicle*[324] mentioned above, and its Christian esotericism:

> The tenth avatar is the one who is still to come; Kalki, in the Indian tradition. The Rosicrucian Chronicle states: But when the times are fulfilled, the eye opens and human destiny is inwardly illumined, choose the luminous figure for your guide: then destiny itself will be your law and loving will. Whosoever's eye is opened, sees living roses grow upon the cross. For the Rosicrucians, Christ was this one who was to come; Christ as the ever-evolving crystallization into the luminous exemplar of upward-evolving humanity.[325]

If we compile these accounts, and those we referred to earlier about cosmic evolution through states of manifestation in warmth, air, water, and earth, as given in Steiner's *Outline of Esoteric Science*, we can try to understand the whole picture in terms of the manifold actions of hierarchical beings that culminate, no later than the fourth planetary embodiment of Earth, in the potency of repeatedly manifesting avatars.

We might approach what both have in view, Rudolf Steiner and Sri Aurobindo, in the following outline: a high, divine-spiritual being, the avatar, acts periodically at long intervals upon evolving organic creatures. Attention focuses here particularly on the evolutionary series of vertebrates. The organic substrate, upon which the influence of the avatars takes hold, has to be imagined in the earliest times as highly soft and plastic, comparable to an embryonic or fetal condition. In the late stages it becomes apparent that the avatar entity focused his configuring impulses principally on the human form. Initially, therefore, only very simple forms arise, into which the soul–spiritual human being as it were seeks to penetrate, but in which it cannot take up permanent dwelling: fish- and amphibian-like creatures, or something resembling warm-blooded mammals. From these initial forms, when it becomes clear that human souls cannot incarnate in them, various animal species develop further in micro-evolutionary stages. Partial manifestation of the avatar being, in the Vibhutis, also accompanies these evolutionary series. By contrast the central line in the world of evolving organisms gathers and unites around it the individuals that continue to preserve the greatest, softest plasticity, and are always most open to the great evolutionary impulses emanating from successive avatar manifestations.[326] From this quasi-fetal "center" of living creatures the human form then at last emerges, as the original goal of the evolution of vertebrates. Accordingly, if rightly understood, the vertebrate animals do not give rise to the human being but rather the reverse: the soft, pliable configuration that seeks continually to realize the human form, gives rise at various stages of its unfolding to the diverse animals species, as it were separating them out from itself as species-typical, consolidating forms that live on alongside the central development and are unable to assimilate the soul-spiritual human entity.[327] Kalki, finally, the tenth avatar manifestation, is, at the other end of the scale, the one who points humanity toward its future—in terms of Christ, as Rudolf Steiner and the Rosicrucians express it, or of the Kalki Avatar, in the language of Sri Aurobindo. This tenth avatar's descent most strikingly demonstrates how natural and later cultural evolution will culminate in a greater, spiritual evolution.

We can see how close the views of Sri Aurobindo and Rudolf Steiner come to one another in respect of evolution and the avatars—especially the Kalki Avatar—if we examine the concordances existing in the future image of "Kalki" and his Western counterpart between Sanatana Dharma and Christianity. To illustrate this I would like to offer a brief comparison here between Puranic and biblical sources.

We can see from the *Bhagavad Purana*, mentioned earlier, that the Kalki Avatar is to be born as the son of famed Brahmin Vishnuyasha and his wife Sumati in the city of Shambhala, at the time of the transition from Kali Yuga to the new Satya Yuga. This is the time when those who rule the Earth will have degenerated into thieves and exploiters.[328] According to the *Agni Purana*, Kalki, together with his teacher and priest Yajnavalkya, will destroy with his weapons those dishonorable ones who wrongly govern; he will re-establish truth and the thirst for truth, and found a new, just kingdom. But in general he comes to purify the world rather than to teach, since at that time human understanding will be very impaired. Kalki will appear on his white horse Devadatta, a sword in his hand, and furnished with eight mystic gifts and eight divine qualities. He will come to punish those robbers and thieves who dared to present themselves as kings. But when it is said that such a person will be killed by the sublime avatar, we must remember that in the Puranic view he undergoes complete purification at the moment of death, comparable to the self-realization of a yogi who has meditated all his life and leaves his body while focused entirely upon the highest sublimity. Thus the *Bhagavad Purana*. But according to the *Vishnu Purana*, those who receive complete purification from Kalki and acquire a mind as clear as crystal, will give rise to a new race that will establish the future civilization of the dawning Satya Yuga, or also Krita Yuga.[329]

The question of why humanity needs such violent intervention in order to advance arises not only in relation to the *Puranas*, but also the Book of Revelation, the last book of the Bible, with its account of the end time. However mysterious this may seem, it suggests that evolution cannot occur without passing through grave crises. First we will simply place these great pictures side by side, for in the Book of Revelation, the Apocalypse, a rider likewise appears on a white horse: on one occasion when the "Lamb" opens the first seal, followed by further riders, on, respectively, a fire-red, black and ashen horse (Rev. 6:1–8). But later—after the "Beast" and "Dragon" have appeared, "Babylon" has been vanquished and immediately after a jubilant, exuberant outbreak of joy among countless pure saints at annunciation of the marriage of the "Lamb"—the rider on the white horse bursts forth, this time to initiate the first eschatological battle:

> And I saw heaven opened, and behold a white horse; and he that sat upon him was called Faithful and True,[330] and in righteousness he doth judge and make war. His eyes were as a flame of fire, and on his head were many crowns; and he had a name written, that no man knew, but he himself. And he was clothed with a vesture dipped in blood: and his name is called The Word of God. And the armies which were in heaven followed him upon white horses, clothed in fine linen, white and clean. And out of his mouth goeth a sharp sword, that with it he should smite the nations: and he shall rule them with a rod of iron: and he treadeth the winepress of the fierceness and wrath of Almighty God. And he hath on his vesture and on his thigh a name written, King Of Kings, And Lord Of Lords. (Rev. 19:11–16)

The Revelation of Saint John also tells us something about the origin of this white rider. A few chapters earlier, we hear of the childhood of the one who is to "rule with a rod of iron": he is the son of the cosmic woman whose raiment is the Sun, who has the Moon under her feet and on her head a crown of twelve stars. She will bring forth her son in great travail, but he will be at threat from the great red "Dragon" with seven heads, ten horns and a crown on each of his seven heads, and will seek to destroy the boy immediately he is born (Rev. 12:1–4). "And she brought forth a man-child, who was to rule all nations with a rod of iron: and her child was caught up unto God, and to his throne" (Rev. 12:5).

The first apocalyptic battle indicated in the above quote from the Book of Revelation leads to the conquest of the "Beast" who is cast into the fiery lake with his "Prophet," while the "Dragon" is bound and banished to the abyss for a thousand years. And just as, in the *Puranas*, the Satya Yuga arrives with the Kalki Avatar, so the victory of the white horseman in Revelation is followed by the "thousand-year reign." In the period of this reign, all those will be elevated who previously suffered persecution and death because they testified to the Word of God. But already as the white horseman breaks forth, he is followed by whole armies, likewise on white horses and dressed in pure, shining white linen, referred to by the Evangelist with the words, "for fine linen is the righteousness of saints" (Rev. 19:8). Kalki, too, establishes the civilization of the new age together with those who, thanks to the purity they achieved, survived the tumultuous crisis. In their hearts will live pure goodness; they will raise their children in the light of this pure goodness, and their spirit will be self-illuminating. And finally the *Kalki Purana* speaks of how Kalki's regency—in Shambhala—will last a thousand years, like that of the white horseman in the Christian tradition.

In his *Essays on the Gita*, Sri Aurobindo speaks of Jesus Christ as the avatar following Krishna and Buddha, and is strict in his correction of all those who mock him by saying, "Save thyself. If thou be the Son of God, come down from the cross" (Matt. 27:40), and disparage him as not being divine since he died such a dishonorable death. Sri Aurobindo states that the divine must indeed take on human suffering and death: "...the human limitation must be assumed in order to show how it can be overcome."[331] Sri Aurobindo sees Kalki, in turn, in the line of future continuation of what was begun through Christ Jesus. In his mystery drama *Savitri*, he also concerns himself with the dynamic arc from "Gethsemane and Golgotha" to the coming avatar. That the age of darkness has grown deeper since Golgotha, and that upward evolution seems, despite everything, to have stumbled and stalled, could tempt seekers of truth to take flight from the Earth. But this would never help to redeem life, which would merely be "left behind on a fallen earth." Sri Aurobindo expresses in the following words in *Savitri* his expectation of Kalki's appearance, and humanity's task in accompanying him:

> A greater power must come, a larger light.
> Although Light grows on Earth and Night recedes,
> Yet till the evil is slain in its own home
> And Light invades the world's inconscient base
> And perished has the adversary Force,
> He still must labour on, his work half done.[332]

Again, in the *Essays on the Gita*, Sri Aurobindo puts it vividly and succinctly: "Even, the Avatar of sorrow and suffering must come before there can be the Avatar of divine joy."[333] This phrase, "Avatar of joy," reflects the great outbreak of joy among the saints in the Book of Revelation, at the annunciation of the marriage of the "Lamb," just before the appearance of the white horseman. These examples may suffice. There is a whole series of striking affinities between the "white riders" in the two traditions, and this allows us to ask whether at least some sections of the *Puranas* contain messages from the same future realm of the spirit as the Book of Revelation.

In Revelation, the second and third names of the "white horseman" are referred to as follows: "...and he had a name written, that no man knew, but he himself." And shortly after this: "...and his name is called The Word of God" (Rev. 19:12–13). This touches on the themes of the present chapter and our discussion of "true 'I'-being," since the "name that no man knew" is connected with the name that only individuals can use for themselves: "I." Emil Bock, an esoteric pupil of Rudolf Steiner, priest of The Christian Community and cofounder of the Movement for Religious Renewal, follows this trail and discovers in the "name that no man knew but he himself" an intensification of the name "I," by which people, as individuals alone, can call themselves. The white horseman, for him, is the one who knows the deepest secret of true "I"-being, and its origin and fulfilment in the evolution of the Earth and humanity. The origin and goal of the "I" are both divine in nature; its origin is hinted at in the Old Testament words "I will be the one that I will be" (Ex. 3:14),[334] while the goal and fulfilment is announced in the words of the apostle Paul, "I live; yet not I, but Christ liveth in me" (Gal. 2:20). The divine and the human "I" thus enter into inward correspondence with the white horseman: the first lends the second its substance in the loftiest sense. From here Emil Bock makes a connection between the second and the third name of the white horseman, who becomes for him a luminous, divine exemplar or precursor for the further evolution of every human being endowed with true "I"-being:

> We learn to say "I" in such a way that another says "I" through us; that is the mystery of the "I," which also encompasses the second name of the white rider. This name refers not merely to the natural but to the God-filled, "I"-endowed human being, who bears the divine "I" within his human "I."[335]

Thus as Bock sees it, the second name of the white rider becomes a seed and bud of the third, which is "the Word of God." This is the name that is inscribed on the garment of white linen of the white horseman, although this raiment is also "dipped in blood."

> On this raiment stands the name "The Logos of God."... Through the indwelling of Christ, not only does the human being receive a power working inward, but a new power also radiates from him. In human speech there also speaks Christ, who is himself the "Logos of God."[336]

I would like to round off this section with these accounts by Emil Bock.[337] They can probably best be understood in the context of the interplay between avatar and evolution, given that the avatar stands for the divine-spiritual immanence that, through its respective manifestation gives decisive stimulus to the evolution of earthly beings, leading us toward sublime spiritual heights of which, as yet, we can have only faint inklings.

"I"-being and Psychic Being

The cosmos, within which evolution is accomplished and the human being progressively awakens to his "I"-being, arose through a primary manifestation of fiery warmth substance. Anthroposophy and Integral Yoga are of one accord on this, as we saw in the last section of this chapter. Below we will consider also the origins of our inner soul being, the "I," out of warmth or fire.

Let us first recall that in Rudolf Steiner's account not only did the whole cosmos develop from this fiery warmth substance, as the earliest etheric–physical manifestation, but so also did the planetary condition of our present Earth. Rudolf Steiner speaks of the "earth-fire sphere" in which, from the very earliest beginnings, manifold soul-spiritual entities appear. At a very early stage the soul forms that will later become human beings as yet bind themselves least of all with this earth-fire.[338] They touch into the fire-earth only, as it were, at an outermost point.

Later, there arise what can be described as vessel-like mantles of fire and heat in which pre-human soul forms partly immerse themselves. Later Steiner speaks of "fire bodies" into which an airy or gaseous element is now incorporated. Through further stages of manifestation of the fire and warmth condition, the soul or astral body and the life or etheric body initially also penetrate these first physical forms, whereupon life becomes more independent in these early forms of human precursors, which remain still subject to the influence of the spirits of form mentioned previously, the Exousiai; and these forms continue to exist when the soul-spirit nature of the pre-human being withdraws again from the early Earth, and from these bodies. Thus bodies are available for souls that once again immerse themselves in earthly forms; these bodies are offered them as from ancestors so that something like a sequence of generations arises and, under the sway of the spirits of form, a first type of memory emerges, a consciousness connecting the generations. The embodied soul acquires a first sense of "I" through this memory, which is strengthened by the fiery quality of the etheric through which the human being feels connected with the "external fire of the earth." As this inner warmth experience intensifies further, the early human being on Earth comes to feel the actions of the spirits of form as Rudolf Steiner expresses it for them in modern words: "Now the spirit beings irradiate and glow through the Earth's circumference, and from it a spark has separated and warms through my inner being."[339]

In association with this, an early faculty of memory is further internalized and individualized. After the soul element has become more finely structured through diverse ways of connecting with the physical, etheric, and astral bodies—that is, after the first matrices of sentient soul, mind soul, and consciousness soul have developed—the human being is eventually endowed by the spirits of form with a spark from their fire, with the "I": "The 'I' was kindled in him."[340]

All this precedes the fateful occurrence intimated in the section "Cosmic Evolution II," which resulted in the human being connecting too strongly through the "I" with astral desire nature, so that a lower egoism arises. (We should never confuse the "I" with the ego.) Consequently, with the fire spark we bear within us, human beings engage too strongly with the earth-fire, in a wilful manner that runs counter to the intentions of the beings of the Sun, the Exousiai. All this is connected with the "Fall" of the human being.

It is clear that to Steiner's spiritual perception the "I" appears thoroughly fiery in nature. This continues to hold true in us today, in that warmth, especially that of the blood, is the decisive element within our bodily organization and enables the "I" to connect with the latter. "I"-governed activity warms us through and penetrates us; those with "I"-initiative can also enthuse, inspire and "enflame" others with their ideals. In human beings today, however, the lower ego almost always plays a part, too. True "I"-filled initiative, so often invoked in an anthroposophic context, should ultimately "burn up" and consume our lower egoity.

The consciousness soul we referred to remains throughout earth time the specific organization in which the consciousness we initially owe to our astral body[341] is concentrated in self-awareness. What was described above relates to the very early Earth period. In those eras of evolution we must conceive of the soul elements only as very early predispositions. The actual birth and unfolding of the sentient soul falls at the time of Egyptian culture, that of the mind soul at the time of Greco-Roman culture, and of the consciousness soul only during our present epoch,[342] starting with the Renaissance and Humanism.

In modern humanity, the consciousness soul occupies the realm of relatively brightest, clearest awareness. In its light, the self-reflexive "I" indwelling it is to a high degree self-aware in its cognition and actions. At all other levels of our being, the "I" appears only in veiled guise. But the consciousness soul bears within it the mental inheritance of the mind soul as modern intellectuality, which initially makes its light a cold one: the "I" is embedded in a very lonely isolation, and from this starting point must recreate connection with deeper, purer heart qualities so as to be able to unfold its warmth or fire nature again freely and in clear awareness. The "I" warmth or fire nature, however, has a deeper affinity with the soul potency of the will[343] than with mental consciousness. What the "I" that survives beyond birth and death can regard as the fruits of its development, acquired in earthly incarnation, it owes to the impulses and deeds that it has accomplished through the will, and continues to accomplish.[344] In future-oriented will actions, through its series of earthly lives also, the "I" continually rejuvenates itself. It is the ever-youngest aspect in us, which is also why Steiner calls it the "baby" in human evolution.[345]

But nevertheless the "I"—in incarnation—comes to itself most in the consciousness soul. The will warmth of the "I" is already activated as it gives itself up to self-reflection. And the inner locus where it exercises this function can be experienced as an inner sanctum. Here the "I," which at lower levels lives in a more concealed way, experiences itself unveiled. "We might say that at each stage we ascend through, a further veil falls away from around what is hidden within. And in what fills the consciousness soul, this hidden being enters unveiled into the inmost temple of the soul."[346]

I would like to add to this passage from *An Outline of Esoteric Science* another from another foundational text by Steiner, *Theosophy*. There he speaks of the fact that, whereas suprasensory sheaths (such as the etheric and astral) are visible to the clairvoyant, the "I" is not. "Our 'I'...remains invisible... veiled in [the] human holiest of holies,"[347]

We should remember that for Rudolf Steiner, however interior the concept of the "I" may be, its fiery nature comes to expression especially in will activity. While psychic being, in Sri Aurobindo's work, is in many respects comparable to the "I" as described by Steiner, at first glance it seems doubtful whether they share this characteristic.

In the view and vision of Integral Yoga, the Vedic divinity Agni brings forth the universe from his fire nature.[348] And Sri Aurobindo likewise sees our inner pychic being as intrinsically related to this fire god, of whom it is also said that he is "ever young" and continually rejuvenates himself in fire.[349] In conversation with close pupils, he once touched on the thought that a psychic being guides the evolution of the human being upward from birth to birth. This led to one of his pupils, Ambalal B. Purani whom we cited previously, conjecturing: "Then it seems that the function of the psychic being is the same as that of Vedic

Agni who is the God of Fire, who is the leader of the journey." At which Sri Aurobindo replied: "Yes. Agni is the God of the psychic and, among other things that it does, it also leads the upward journey."[350] And in a correspondence about poetry and poetics, he noted, "What you describe is the psychic fire, *agni pavaka*, which burns in the deeper heart and from there is lighted in the mind, the vital and the physical body."[351]

In Integral Yoga, the psychic being is, one can say, the pivot of the scales where evolution either ascends or the whole adventure comes to naught. Human beings, as transitional beings on the path to a new species, can take only a first step toward effecting the transformation they seek—that is, developing the Supermind—through the indwelling psychic, or soul, being. In his major work, *The Life Divine*, Sri Aurobindo shows that the soul entity is initially largely concealed under the veils of human nature. But, unlike these veils, it is imperishable and not the result of former manifestations, nor limited by these; rather, it contains within it the possibilities for all future manifestations. It is not impaired or polluted by the invariably imperfect nature of each successive manifestation within these sheaths or veils.

> It is an ever-pure flame of the divinity in things and nothing that comes to it, nothing that enters into our experience can pollute its purity or extinguish the flame. This spiritual stuff is immaculate and luminous and, because it is perfectly luminous, it is immediately, intimately, directly aware of truth of being and truth of nature; it is deeply conscious of truth and good and beauty because truth and good and beauty are akin to its own native character, forms of something that is inherent in its own substance.[352]

At the same time everything that runs counter to truth, goodness, and beauty will be unmistakably perceived and rejected by the psychic being. Body, life, and mind are its tools, and it accepts the limitations these bring with them. The psychic being itself, however, is something different and greater. The fact that it must gradually penetrate its tools or organs, successively making its veils more permeable, leads to development that is, though, not free of delays and distortions. The mind can also for long periods fail to perceive and acknowledge the psychic being:

> But the veil is thick and we know not the secret Light within us, the light in the hidden crypt of the heart's innermost sanctuary. Intimations rise to our surface from the psyche, but our mind does not detect their source; it takes them for its own activities because, before even they come to the surface, they are clothed in mental substance...[353]

The mind can also be conquered by the influences of the vital Ego, giving scope to its impulses, and thus considerably impeding the Sadhana, or spiritual practice, that cultivates the psychic being. The soul or psyche will then withdraw temporarily, and await the mind's further evolution.[354] But ultimately the psyche seeks to support and continue natural evolution, through which the fields of body, life, and mind must first be developed. "The soul gathers the essence of all our mental, vital and bodily experience and assimilates it for the farther evolution of our existence in Nature; but this action is occult and not obtruded on the surface."[355]

Only gradually can the hidden aspects emerge more clearly; and in the reciprocal interpenetration of the psychic being with mental and vital aspects, a "psychic personality" develops, and fosters communication between the surface and the psychic being. The process now propels us toward awakening to our own psyche, and from this point on our further "psychic transformation" can be initiated in more rapid development. Further on, I give a more extensive quotation from *The Life Divine*, which summarizes much of what we have been discussing, and also clearly shows that without doubt the psychic being is, in Sri Aurobindo's view, identical with our true, individual "I"-being. Here it might seem as if this does influence and affect our other sheaths, yet is not so much regarded as the source of action and initiative in the outer world. The *psychization* of human nature, as transformation through this influence is called elsewhere,[356] culminates in human beings opening to God. The actual state of affairs in respect of our actions in the world is shown further.

> The true soul secret in us . . . this veiled psychic entity is the flame of the Godhead always alight within us, inextinguishable even by that dense unconsciousness of any spiritual self within which obscures our outward nature. It is a flame born out of the Divine and, luminous inhabitant of the Ignorance, grows in it till it is able to turn it toward the Knowledge. It is the concealed Witness and Control, the hidden Guide, the Daemon of Socrates, the inner light or inner voice of the mystic. It is that which endures and is imperishable in us from birth to birth, untouched by death, decay or corruption, an indestructible spark of the Divine. Not the unborn Self, or atman, for the Self even in presiding over the existence of the individual is aware always of its universality and transcendence, it is yet its deputy in the forms of Nature, the individual soul, *caitya purusha*, supporting mind, life and body, standing behind the mental, the vital, the subtle–physical being in us and watching and profiting by their development and experience. . . .
>
> It is this secret psychic entity which is the true original Conscience in us deeper than the constructed and conventional conscience of the moralist, for it is this which points always toward Truth and Right and Beauty, toward Love and Harmony and all that is a divine possibility in us, and persists till these things become the major need of our nature. It is the psychic personality in us that flowers as the saint, the sage, the seer; when it reaches its full strength, it turns the being toward the Knowledge of Self and the Divine, toward the supreme Truth, the supreme Good, the supreme Beauty, Love and Bliss, the divine heights and largenesses, and opens us to the touch of spiritual sympathy, universality, oneness.[357]

Sri Aurobindo locates the true soul in the "true, invisible heart"—as "... the little spark of the Divine which supports the obscure mass of our nature."

And he says of this "spark": "Around it grows the psychic being, the formed soul or the real Man within us."[358]

We must remember this key role of the "psychic being"—comparable to the "I" in the works of Rudolf Steiner—as we now study how, for Sri Aurobindo, opening to the divine and active engagement with earthly challenges are two gestures that most definitely augment each other, and are both of equal importance for Integral Yoga.

But first, in passing, a comment is required on the concept of synthesis in Integral Yoga. Sri Aurobindo's extensive work *The Synthesis of Yoga,* from which the last passage was taken, is divided into four parts from which the synthesis he intends can be derived. These are: Karma Yoga, the Yoga of Works, Jnana Yoga, the Yoga of Integral Knowledge, Bhakti Yoga, the Yoga of Divine Love, and finally the Yoga of Self-Perfection, in which integration of the three previously named yoga paths[359] is to be accomplished. Earlier we suggested[360] that three yoga fields, connected with will, thinking, and feeling, must be integrated at a higher level, that of the true "I," or self. Whereas the somewhat longer passage above (quoted last but one) concerns the psychic being within the yoga fields of Knowledge and Divine Love, we see below how necessary it is for this soul being to work also in the field of Integral Karma Yoga.

Active, willed engagement with the world—including in its darker, more problematic and spirit-remote regions—is usually governed in human life by a vital and lower-mental will that knows no striving for the spirit or the divine. According to Sri Aurobindo, many spiritual disciplines avoid such engagement and, wary of simply becoming mired in lower realms, regard it as irreconcilable with their goals. Instead they focus on otherworldly paradises, on ending the cycle of rebirths, on Nirvana. By contrast Integral Yoga accepts the challenge of earthly engagement, knowing that this path of Karma Yoga is among the most difficult and laborious. The Sadhaka tackles the works of "will and power, possession and acquisition, production and fruitful expense of capacity, battle and victory and mastery." In other words, we should grasp hold of life and actively shape it, since "the spirit needs it [the life force] to give an outer force and form to its manifested possibilities and arrive at a complete self-expression incarnated in matter."[361]

What makes the Yoga of Works so very arduous is not only the dull resistance and often chaotic confusion of earthly-material and vital conditions, but also the fact that the human being has become deeply entangled in them unknowingly and as it were narcissistically through a "false soul of desire." But for the Sadhaka of Integral Yoga this is no reason whatsoever not to work and seek to be active: he affirms work in and upon the world. His striving is therefore directed to ensuring the gradual ascendancy of his true psychic being over that desire soul.

> If the curse of disquiet and disharmony and perversion is to be lifted from Life, the true soul, the psychic being, must be given its leading place and there must be a dissolution of the false soul of desire and ego. But this does not mean that life itself must be coerced and denied its native line of fulfilment; for behind this outer life soul of desire there is in us an inner and true vital being which has not to be dissolved but brought out into prominence and released to its true working as a power of the Divine Nature.[362]

In time the whole trajectory becomes an ascending sacrifice so as to realize divine nature upon Earth through life's works, and achieve progressive transformation. Development of individual consciousness, its spiritual growth into an increasingly universal dimension, is accomplished in the field of the Yoga of Knowledge. The Yoga of Loving Devotion, however, also—and chiefly—supports the whole process of the interplay between the Yoga of Works and the Yoga of Knowledge. This is because the psychic being draws the strength to follow these paths not least through its loving connection with the highest realm of the divine, as embodied in an especially pure form in Bhakti. Sri Aurobindo distinguishes vital and mental modes of loving, as well as divine love, from *psychic* or *soul love.* He says that this is unsullied by the effects of the ego. Soul love is a flame of intense warmth, the only pure fire, one that burns without consuming any fuel—a white and not a red flame. It can live and come to expression most fully and easily in devotion to the highest divine. And thus psychic love—in self-surrender—must increasingly come to master and transform all other aspects of our being so that, as psychic love always endeavors to achieve, a perfected being comes to be an expression of union with the godhead. Ultimately also, love between people will become free of merely physical, vital, and mental stirrings.[363] We may say that soul being is most itself in the ego-free condition of psychic love in which it goes beyond itself.

What significance should be accorded to conscious, love-borne working in the world? Toward the end of his life Rudolf Steiner observed that an innate receptivity to the spirit and a broader scope of capacities for relating to the world with which many of his pupils found their way to Anthroposophy, was also associated with a certain reserve toward outward life and reluctance to engage actively with it. It is possible that this went hand-in-hand with something Sri Aurobindo likewise characterized in connection with many spiritual disciplines as wariness toward the "lower regions" of life. Many pupils of Anthroposophy, said Steiner, showed a tendency to "hold back fully from entering the physical body," and "to enter with less intensity into outward corporeality as they descended from the spiritual into the physical world than others do." This, he said, could certainly lead them to "coping less easily with life."[364] But he went on to say that this situation could be positively addressed by developing what he called "soul initiative," in love for human beings and the world: "Through finding soul initiative in life, a capacity to initiate something out of one's inmost core of being, to judge and form resolves."[365]

In the light of what we have just discussed, it is valid to assume that this might apply equally to the Sadhakas of Integral Yoga, for such soul initiative must, surely, proceed primarily from our psychic being.

Recurring Lives on Earth

The question about what existed before birth and what will be after death is something, said Sri Aurobindo, that the human intellect can never give a satisfactory answer to. In an extended yogic philosophical enquiry into the riddle of rebirth,[366] he examines various approaches to an answer presented by Western materialism and the Judeo-Christian tradition, or by schools of the Buddha Dharma and the Mayavadins.[367] None of these traditions regard it as essential to assume the principle of a soul-spiritual individuality continuing through many lives. Whereas the ancient schools of the East teach reincarnation, this is rejected by modern, Western cultures, which are predicated entirely on material reality and see no reason to acknowledge the soul's suprasensory origins. Nevertheless, says Sri Aurobindo, it is possible to pursue certain scientific ideas in such a way that we can, with their help, escape from the prison of materialism. Science can show that capacities and qualities possessed by the human individual can never be fully explained in terms of the physical, organic foundations of evolution; and thus, even within modern paradigms, it is possible to open up a prospect of higher modes of existence of the human soul and spirit. From there it is only a further step to approach the idea of an evolving soul being which, in a body-free state, is capable of ascending into other worlds and later returning to birth on Earth.

The Buddha Dharma does not acknowledge any self-sustaining individuality but emphasizes that all "I" experience is always only illusory. Rebirth in this sense, therefore, is only the renewed manifestation of a karmic complex originating in past causes, a new illusory personality.[368] The followers of Advaita Vedanta or Mayavada, do affirm the existence of an eternal self, but assert that this is in reality only one, not many; and that one can, at most say, that this Self is able to ensoul the mentalized body that seemingly exists in maya, with the "idea of an 'I,'" as Sri Aurobindo puts it when describing the view of Advaita Vedanta. Yet this strict Vedantic doctrine also sees the idea of a continuing soul-spiritual entity passing through a succession of lives on Earth as nothing but an illusion that should be relinquished. For the Mayavadin, individual development has no reality.

But if, as in Integral Yoga, it is assumed that the overall process of cosmic involution and evolution concerns the path of a real, individual entity in developing ever more encompassing consciousness, the true meaning of the individuality who pursues this path can only be grasped if we find in the spiritual self and psychic being realities of an eternal nature such as belong equally to the highest divinity. Only this context makes it plausible that an authentic soul-spirit can eventually itself discover the cosmic Self and the highest, divine reality. But the path from unconsciousness to awakening to divine consciousness renders rebirth—as an evolution through a long series of earthly lives—an indispensable necessity. "Then, secure behind all the changings of our personality, upholding the stream of its mutations, there must be a true Person, a real spiritual Individual, a true Purusha."[369]

Sri Aurobindo points here to the need for a whole, slow, gradual evolution through a succession of stages in which the universal spirit can gradually realize his intentions, "...through the enlarging and ascending individual soul-consciousness in the body."[370] And: "This ascent can only take place by rebirth within the ascending order."[371]

In relation to this evolutionary ascent, Sri Aurobindo now distinguishes (within the spiritual nature of the human being) between the eternal being, or unalterable spiritual self, on the one hand, and on the other the "soul of personality," one's "cosmic and mutable being," which, albeit of eternal origin, can nevertheless develop and evolve by passing through long periods of soul experience within the configurations of nature, and in doing so must also follow the baseline of evolution. In one's spiritual self, by contrast, we are "one with the Transcendence which is immanent in the world and comprehensive of it."[372] The immortal spirit has always held sway over every level of evolutionary realization—of mineral, plant, and animal forms. But only when the mind has evolved far enough to facilitate self-awareness, does the evolving entity assume human form, and the individual soul awaken to itself within it. The latter has always also accompanied past stages of evolution in a latent, not yet emerging condition.

In relation to the future, Sri Aurobindo opens up a prospect in which the soul—evolving through a series of earthly lives—is also to release and develop the higher and highest capacities of its being that were also initially hidden.

> Man is there to move from the ignorance and from the little life which he is in his mind and body to the knowledge and the large divine life which he can compass by the unfolding of the spirit. At least the opening out of the spirit in him, the knowledge of his real self and the leading of the spiritual life must be attained before he can go definitively and for ever otherwhere. There may too be beyond this initial culmination a greater flowering of the spirit in the human life of which we have as yet only the first intimations.[373]

The ascending line of rebirths, in other words, will not cease when we reach Supermind and its realization by the human being.

For those who acknowledge rebirth as a spiritually substantiated reality, an insistent question now arises about the states we pass through between two embodiments. Does one earthly life follow immediately on the previous one, or are there intervening phases of assimilation between them, during which the immortal soul and spirit dwells in other worlds? Sri Aurobindo offers a simple, clear answer.

Earthly death is followed by necessary states whereby the soul, or psychic being—the "traveler between death and birth"—works through the outcomes of one's previous life in, first, the vital world, and then the mental world. Insofar as these fruits have informed the vital element, laying aside the old vital "mantle" and passing to a new level concludes this assimilative work. Something comparable occurs in the mental world. Here, too, old mental habits and forms are processed, so that the previous mental sheath can be laid aside. The soul now ascends higher, to its "final resort," its "true home," coming to "a plane of pure psychic existence in which the soul would await rebirth."[374]

And, after dispensing with the mantles or sheaths bearing, and corresponding to, experiences preserved in the subtle–physical, the vital, and the mental, the soul takes with it in this ascent only extracts, only the essence of these experiences. These essences of a life concluded in turn, after a new birth, make it possible to take up again the evolutionary thread that the individuality had previously been following. At the same time they form the basis for possible subliminal memories of former lives on Earth, although these only enter ordinary awareness very occasionally, in children with a special predisposition for this or as the consequence of advanced yogic development. Such memories nevertheless show something like active resonance with the "subliminal being," which even during life on Earth remains in lasting connection with the higher worlds, and the "place of resort." Usually, people do not recall their previous lives, and this is also fully in accord with an evolution of one's being, which is all the freer as a result.

At this "place of resort" in pure psychic existence, which the ascent leads us to, and from where we embark toward a new birth, consciousness can only be maintained by highly evolved souls who, in their last earthly existence, were not primarily determined by the physical and vital-mental planes. But whether they can or not, "alignment" occurs for all souls in this place of refuge: after old characteristics and motivations have been laid aside, or also strengthened and reorganized, the individual past is reappraised and new orientation found for the future.

The generally valid law of karma, according to which the deeds of one life decisively inform the conditions prevailing in the next, should not however be misunderstood as a rigid mechanism in Integral Yoga—as some kind of cosmic computation or moral accounting, with fixed recompense for achievements and failures. It is true to say that "each being reaps the harvest of his works and deeds, the returns of the action put forth by the energies of his nature."[375] Nevertheless, karmic consequences correspond here to the energy specifically activated rather than to a model of reward and punishment; we can say of the human being that "he is what he has made himself; the past man was the father of the man that now is, the present man is the father of the man that will be. Each being reaps what he sows; from what he does he profits, for what he does he suffers. This is the law and chain of Karma, of Action, of the work of Nature-Energy."[376]

For Sri Aurobindo, however, no law can ever compel the spirit, the self; a greater spiritual freedom exists that goes beyond karma. Accordingly, karmic laws work most consistently in the physical realm, and have an already more flexible correspondence with the vital and mental realms. But the intervention of higher laws and influences can cancel karmic obligations at any of these levels. By its very nature, the psychic being enjoys greater freedom in relation to them.

> If a certain amount of results of past Karma is formulated in the present life, it must be with the consent of the psychic being which presides over the new formation of its earthly experience and assents not merely to an outward compulsory process, but to a secret Will and Guidance. That secret Will is not mechanical, but spiritual.[377]

Karma serves ultimately as the "instrument" of the eternal self for realizing aims and evolutionary goals it has set the individual being.

Rudolf Steiner also regards it as a wise dispensation that in our present age—in general—we do not have active memories of our former lives on Earth. At the same time, the facts of remembering and forgetting, like those of falling asleep and waking up, are a significant focus of his enquiries into the connection between different earthly lives of one and the same individuality. In his early essay "The Workings of Karma," he first describes how memory enables us to maintain consistency of awareness between the days of our life, which is repeatedly at risk of interruption by loss of consciousness during sleep.[378] Memory allows us to connect yesterday's actions with today's and likewise to understand our specific present surroundings—both geographical and social—as the consequence and expression of our life hitherto. Through our purposeful actions and deeds in the past we have defined or even created our surroundings ourselves, and in the intentional action of new day we reconnect with them again. "My memory connects my logical actions of today with my logical actions of yesterday."[379] Rudolf Steiner regards memory as a core inner function that must primarily be assigned to the "I" as the central entity of the human soul.[380] It mediates between the condition of bodily existence that is always only here and now, and the eternal home and dwelling of the human being's spirit being. This applies likewise to the passage from one earthly life to the next.

The nature of memory as an inner quality of the soul must be grasped in a deeper way than as mere recall in ordinary waking consciousness. Rather, it encompasses also the whole realm of the development of habits and abilities, and can be encountered even at the level of organic life. The functions of separate organs, and even biological heredity, can be conceived as a physiological manifestation of "habits," as an ongoing, biological memory function.[381] At the other end of the spectrum, toward spirit, a type of subliminal memory also exists, which, as an essence of the fruits of this life, is as it were passed on in a kind of heredity to our being in a next incarnation. In this new life, the reborn being now realizes this essence in one's gifts and capabilities, which, although prefigured in that being from the past, emerge fully only now. Starting from these deeper, inner memory functions and the soul's mediation between eternal spirit and new corporeality, Rudolf Steiner finally arrives at a picture of the threefold nature of the human being as body, soul, and spirit:

> In each new incarnation, the human being finds himself in a physical organism that is subject to the laws of external nature. And in each incarnation it is the same human spirit. As such, then, this is the *eternal* in manifold embodiments. *Body* and *spirit* stand opposite one another. Between them must be something like the memory I have connecting my deeds of yesterday with those of today. And this is the *soul*. This preserves the workings of my actions in former lives. It enables the spirit to appear in a new incarnation as the sum of what my previous life made of it. *Thus body, soul, and spirit are connected.*[382]

In each incarnation, the soul brings the eternal spirit together anew with the earthly corporeality that must always obey physical laws, weaving former deeds into new destiny by means of the continuum of its deep memory. In this new incarnation, the tangible qualities of our spirit–soul lead us into our new surroundings. But these qualities are the outcome of our actions in former lives, which imbued the spirit–soul. Thus they are the "...real cause of my being born into particular circumstances and conditions": "And what I do today will become *part* of the cause of my encountering particular circumstances in a subsequent life. In this way the human being does indeed create his own destiny."[383]

We should not think of karma as a court of law passing judgment on our actions, for it is our own being itself that has arranged the interplay of conditions of a new incarnation. And in this light, common perplexity at why "Good must often suffer while Evil enjoys good fortune"[384] finds its own self-evident answer.

In regard to the intervening existence between two incarnations, Rudolf Steiner distinguishes "memory residues" which the "I" takes with it on its path after death. If we also take account of later publications by him,[385] we discover such "residues" to be of three kinds: those of the etheric, astral and "I"-sheath relating to the previous life, with which the spirit–soul is initially surrounded. As we lay aside our etheric mantle very soon after death, the spirit–soul experiences a magnificent pictorial "panorama" of the phases of our life. Then, on laying aside the astral mantle, we experience a passage—in reverse—through all joys, fears, pain, and so on that we experienced in life, especially those that we caused in others. Everything we did out of our lower instincts, our drives, and desire nature echoes on in this astral mantle, the "body of cravings," *kama rupa*, and must be worked through as the spirit–soul now—no doubt often painfully—experiences the aftereffect of what this meant for its former surroundings. Even the subtlest egotism, as may, for instance, inform cultural and religious activities, will figure here. And only after this will the spirit–soul have laid aside its astral sheath entirely.[386] But in its "I"-sheath, by contrast, it takes with it all the fruits it gathered of spiritual striving and spirit-related experience, and whatever contributed to the lasting enhancement of its capacities. Only this third "residue" of a former life has future potential. In relation to this enduring essence, people will reach different evolutionary levels, of a higher or lower nature. The greater the scope of this essential, spiritual store of experience in an individual—acquired through the whole sequence of lives on Earth—the wider, more significant and more multifaceted will be the spirit–soul's potential in a new incarnation. Ultimately, in a higher world of spirit, the spirit–soul will turn decisively toward the future and as it were "design" a new life. In *Devachan*, the "place of bliss," its former experiences will be transformed into seeds, predispositions, and capacities for the future. And the richer the essences thus recast into new qualities, the more consciously will the spirit–soul be able to help in configuring these processes. In this way, the human being's higher development will at the same time become a path toward ever-greater spiritual freedom: "The store of experiences gathered in his spirit will grow ever richer; and in consequence he comes to meet his surroundings, his destiny, with ever greater maturity. Increasingly this makes him master of his fate."[387] With each incarnation, things grow brighter around the spirit, the spirit–soul, and freedom dawns with ever more irrefutable reality.

> The compulsions of the environment become ever less; increasingly the spirit can be self-determining. But the self-determining mind or spirit is the *free spirit.* Acting in the full, bright light of consciousness is free action.... The full freedom of the human spirit is the *ideal* of his evolution.[388, 389]

In accord with this ideal, a far-distant future prospect then arises in which new light falls on the question of the importance that individual memory of former lives can have:

> Higher evolution of the human spirit signifies progression through ever new incarnations. This higher evolution comes to expression in that the spirit increasingly understands the world in which its incarnations occur. But the incarnations belong to this world itself. In relation to them, too, the spirit emerges from a state of unconsciousness into that of conscious awareness. On the path of evolution lies the point in which the human being is able to look back with full awareness on his incarnations.[390]

Evolution of our whole cosmic past toward the acquisition of human freedom is an evolution sustained by the gift of wisdom's light. For this reason Steiner summarizes the cosmic past as "Cosmos of Wisdom." But the goal of everything human beings accomplish out of their conscious and free deeds lies in doing this, in the future, increasingly out of love. "This power of love must begin in the human being on Earth. And the 'Cosmos of Wisdom' then evolves into a *'Cosmos of Love.'* From everything the 'I' can unfold within itself, love is to emerge."[391]

As we look to the future, then, ever greater freedom and ever greater love must unite within us. It should also be noted here that, as Steiner's work developed, he found it ever more important to emphasize that deeds and actions arising in willed exertion through "I"-initiative—best of all if these flow from love for humankind and the world—give rise to "experiences" that sustain developmental progress from life to life.

By now, it is perfectly clear that both Rudolf Steiner and Sri Aurobindo see the evolution of human beings—from their earliest physical manifestations through stages of organic and ensouled life—ultimately as an evermore encompassing development of consciousness toward ever greater freedom. Both also see the evolutionary journey of the soul–spiritual human being as possible only through the realities of reincarnation and karma.

Besides the numerous parallels we have pointed to in accounts by Sri Aurobindo[392] and Rudolf Steiner,[393] however, in some important points and questions we find marked differences, too. These appear, for instance, in regard to the place of higher spiritual beings and their workings within cosmic and human evolution. Sri Aurobindo describes the state of existence between death and rebirth as a path upon which the old is transformed into the new purely in accord with spiritual laws. Here it is possible to experience some degree of closeness with the souls of relatives or good friends. And in this state, soul-and-spirit beings can continue their devotion to the highest divine as they already practiced this during earthly life. However, we scarcely find in the works of Sri Aurobindo accounts of diverse spiritual beings—such as the Devas—accompanying the spirit–soul on this journey, or collaborating with it to bring about future transformations. There seems to be no room for this. The devas or divinities are for Sri Aurobindo "permanent emanations" of the divine with particular tasks and functions within the supermental and "threefold world"—the physical, vital, and mental world. He calls them "cosmic personalities," who represent defined, circumscribed emanations and are very different from one another. The higher of these beings belong to the overmental plane; and all of them can manifest as far down as the physical, intensively uniting with those with whom they have an affinity, so that the latter become the bearers of the former. But the Devas themselves undergo no transformation, for they are "typal and not evolutionary beings"—that is, as personally constituted cosmic beings they do not follow an evolutionary path. The attribute "typal" means here roughly perhaps "archetypal," if we do not regard this in terms of a single, general, all-preceding archetype, but as the manifold coexistence of a whole number of "archetypal beings" each with a different character.[394] And since the Devas are non-evolving beings, they possess no psychic being either, but are constituted, rather, through a specific kind of Purusha of divine origin, and the Prakriti corresponding to it.[395] In Integral Yoga they do not seem to engage in "communication" with the human spirit–soul in its existence between death and rebirth.

As fundamentally apparent, by contrast, in Steiner's *Outline of Esoteric Science*, it would be inconceivable in an evolving universe for countless spiritual beings above the human realm not also to be participating in all-encompassing cosmic evolution. In *Esoteric Science*, for instance, we hear of diverse hierarchical beings who passed through their "humanity stage" during earlier planetary conditions. Or we learn of beings whose proper course of evolution is retarded, so that they relinquish possible evolutionary progress for certain purposes. In a late lecture, Steiner says: "...that the world is in a sense built up by 'stages,'" and that at a level higher than human beings and nations, one can perceive processes of evolution "not undergone by human beings but by spirit beings, albeit ones who stand in a particular connection with humanity's evolution."[396]

In this context it is important to consider all of Rudolf Steiner's descriptions of how the angelic orders support the diverse conditions of human existence, and its proper evolution in manifold ways. He offers accounts that vividly illumine the post-mortem ascent of the human spirit–soul in connection with the beings of the three hierarchies.[397] In brief outline—for there is no scope here for more than that—the beings of the third hierarchy receive the "web of destiny" of the deceased after they have experienced the great retrospective panorama of their life; then, after shedding the astral sheath, the beings of the second hierarchy incorporate the consequences of those deeds into the astrality of the cosmos. Finally, the beings of the first hierarchy enable the due "configurations of earthly life" to "be resurrected" for future realization from what has thus been assimilated.[398]

It seems likely that not insignificant differences of view such as these are directly connected with how Rudolf Steiner and Sri Aurobindo each approach the next great question, culminating in Integral Yoga on the one hand, and Anthroposophy on the other: that of the highest, divine nature which not only precedes and sustains the whole cosmos, but is also its evolutionary goal.

Chapter 5

The Divine: The Second Coming of Christ and the Descent of Supermind

To study the question about—first—Rudolf Steiner's view of the divine in the way I intend[399] necessitates a few preliminary remarks relating to the last year of his work, in which we can distinguish two six-month periods: first the time from April to the end of September 1924, a period of simply unbelievable activity even if we only consider the lecture cycles he gave;[400] then the half year of his illness, from October 1924 to his death on March 30, 1925. During these last six months of his life he nevertheless produced some highly significant written works,[401] including texts relating to the divine realm.

In the first of these two periods, his last half year of work as a lecturer in the spring and summer of 1924, Rudolf Steiner unfolded before members of the Anthroposophical Society—newly refounded at Christmas 1923—a kind of spiritual history, and prehistory, of the different cultural streams that had found their way together within this Anthroposophical Society or would do so in future. In his esoteric reflections on karmic relationships (*Karmic Relationships*) he discoursed on the spiritual and cultural identities of these streams as such, each of which had arisen from its own karmic conditions and trajectories that are characteristically embodied, in particular, in the leading representatives of these streams.[402] Two significant currents of this kind are those of the Platonists and Aristotelians, whose spiritual and historical developments were informed by polar opposite stances toward knowledge of the human being, the world, and the divine.

Those belonging to the Aristotelian stream prepared themselves in previous incarnations through centuries to encompass and illumine conceptually precise thinking—which underpinned the scientifically oriented, positivist, and materialist views of the last two centuries—in such a way that, through self-reflecting inner observation, they could fashion this into a new means to experience the spirit in an individually free and self-responsible manner. Rudolf Steiner himself, in his works on epistemology and *Intuitive Thinking as a Spiritual Path: A Philosophy of Freedom,* mentioned previously,[403] had made outstanding contributions to this kind of self-founded thinking, intended to support pupils of Anthroposophy from the early twentieth century onward in accessing the first levels of higher knowledge. There are strong and coherent grounds that demonstrate why Rudolf Steiner himself took up this Aristotelian outlook at an early stage. For him it pointed beyond even the legacy of German Idealism and Goetheanism, which he nevertheless also highly prized, and corresponded to complex biographical necessities of his own, as well as cultural and spiritual–historical imperatives.[404] It therefore seems apparent that the paths to knowledge of higher worlds and realities, as Rudolf Steiner described these in subsequent writings,[405] are ones that trace an upward ascent of knowledge: modern sense-based knowledge grows beyond itself to rise through the three levels of imaginative, inspired, and intuitive consciousness.

In his sequence of studies on karma in 1924, it now became increasingly apparent that Rudolf Steiner was addressing his listeners primarily as souls possessing an affinity with the aforenamed Aristotelian outlook. In the medieval period, one of the leading figures and exponents of this school had been incarnated as Thomas Aquinas. Individualities belonging to the Aristotelian stream had come together at the beginning of the twentieth century around Rudolf Steiner and the development of Anthroposophy. Initially however, it was not possible to join forces with the other great karmic group, the Platonists. In 1924, Rudolf Steiner offered a prospect in which this would come about toward the end of the twentieth century: when the souls of the Aristotelian stream would be reincarnating again, and alongside them, for the first time in several centuries, the souls of the Platonist stream. This, said Steiner, would in fact be the first occasion ever when these two groups will have worked together at the same time in earthly incarnation.[406]

As to the spiritual disposition of the souls with an affinity to Platonism, Rudolf Steiner identified the most important teachers and leading representatives of the School of Chartres Cathedral at the end of the twelfth century as figures such as Alanus ab Insulis or Bernardus Silvestris. This outlook can be roughly understood in terms of Plato's *anamnesis*—often a "sudden" awakening of a deep memory of the soul's origin. Thus anamnesis can encompass pre-birth and cosmic experiences, alongside a profound inner knowledge of the origin of the human soul in the divine realm. It can arise in a flash of intuitive illumination,[407] conveying inspired understanding and illumining whole worlds of imaginative pictures. In this context, Steiner characterizes the insights and perception of the teachers in Chartres as largely pictorial in nature. The inner character of this experience and mode of Platonic cognition is primarily one gained as a descent or influx of knowledge from above.[408] And this descent of knowledge is in polar contrast to the mode of rising or elevating knowledge that is characteristic of the Aristotelian disposition.

Without the prior history of an Aristotelian orientation that can enable modern consciousness to re-access the possibility of attaining higher stages of knowledge, in the form of Rudolf Steiner's Anthroposophy and its, as it were, "self-elevation from below," souls with a Platonic affinity would scarcely find an opportunity to introduce into their incarnation and the modern world the living impulse of their "spirituality and wisdom from above"—or at least could attempt this only under most difficult conditions. What can, however, make progress possible here is the preparatory convergence throughout a century of souls with a Platonist and Aristotelian affinity (from "above" and from "below"), albeit initially without being simultaneously incarnated. And then—only a few decades later—when their collaboration takes effect in modern civilization through both groups incarnating on Earth, this is meant, according to Rudolf Steiner, to produce the real "culmination" of the anthroposophic movement. In a synthesis of both outlooks and approaches—rising and descending knowledge—synergies will arise between the two groups that have never previously been possible.

In view of the Aristotelian accent in the first phase of the anthroposophic movement's development, it seems understandable, as already intimated, that Steiner, in his developing role as teacher, strongly accentuated cosmology and anthropology, remaining by contrast somewhat cautious in relation to questions about the divine. Within his Christology, aspects of cosmology and humanity's evolution likewise predominate, while the purely divine origins of Christ are kept more in the background. It is because of this that the recent study *Metaphysics of World Evolution,*[409] which considers Steiner's *Outline of Esoteric Science* in extensive detail, arrives at the view that the founder of Anthroposophy, at least in this, his major work, neglected or excluded themes such as the transcendent nature of the divine Trinity or the divine origins from which all cosmic emanations proceeded; and that Rudolf Steiner's living Spiritual Science still requires its future fulfillment in the form of "true, re-enlivened theosophy."[410]

But how do we gain access to Rudolf Steiner's deeper intuitions about divine nature, to which too little consideration may be given though they might contribute to this "re-enlivening"? The spiritual being who governs the karmic streams mentioned above, in a way that simultaneously inspires yet leaves human beings free, is the archangel and time spirit Michael. Under his aegis, those who belong to these streams assimilated the spiritual impulses underlying Anthroposophy already half a millennium before their earthly work and activities in the twentieth century.

According to Steiner, Michael has ever been the custodian of the original "cosmic intelligence," which, since the beginning of the modern era, departed from its cosmic home on the Sun and took up habitation in the earthly world; here it increasingly became our merely terrestrial intelligence, and is now at risk of degenerating into cold, dead intellect. One of the most important tasks of the anthroposophic movement, therefore, is to re-enliven and spiritualize human intellectualism, in free collaboration with the intentions of Michael and in resistance to the tendencies of that cosmic spirit of "cold, frosty," and dead intellectualism—known otherwise as Ahriman.[411] It must be remembered that Michael preserves human freedom by never intervening directly in human concerns. Rather, he is an exemplar demonstrating to us how, in accord with him, we can relate to our fellow human beings, to the world as a whole, and not least to the true nature of the divine. He awaits the initiative and actions of us earthly human beings. The spiritual activity of the individual is therefore indispensable if we are to see Michael as our guide and exemplar.

In the last six months of his life, Rudolf Steiner sent from his sickbed to the members of the Anthroposophical Society letters that continue the karma reflections referred to above. They appeared in weekly instalments under the title of *The Michael Mystery.* Here, alongside illuminating accounts of the workings of Michael, he also makes fundamental statements about the relationship of truly divine nature to the whole cosmos and to the human being, elaborating an outlook that could provide a possible basis for discovery and formulation of the genuine, spiritual-scientific theosophy that has been the subject and question of more recent enquiries (see above). Below we will examine these communications in more detail.

The Divine in the Intuition of Rudolf Steiner

The earliest, purely spiritual origins of humanity's evolution were such that human precursors were completely and directly interwoven with the divine, although their consciousness was dim and they were largely unfree. At that time the universe was nothing but the unclouded expression of this undistorted, unobscured unity of the pre-earthly human being with the godhead. But this original oneness now began to undergo immense changes. As evolution proceeded, and human beings acquired ever-denser corporeality, and became subject to the law of birth, death, and rebirth, human perception of the presence of divine being in the cosmos increasingly waned. Descending into the terrestrial world, through into our own times, humanity experienced four stages of decreasing and eventually lost connection with the godhead: originally this godhead directly and fully enveloped and permeated early human ancestors; later, when the stars first shone forth, the cosmos and all existence became a "revelation" of the divine—as yet, though, in a way that allowed its nature and being to remain in living connection with such revelation; subsequently the cosmos no longer appeared as the living manifestation of divine nature but a mere reflection of it in terms of "agencies" perceived to be at work there; at the fourth stage, finally, where we find ourselves today, humanity lives in the world as the "work" of God, but no longer recognizing or perceiving the cosmic and natural agencies that underlie all life and its configurations, let alone the original revelation of the divine or divine beings as such. This life of ours in the "world of effects" or "works," founded on sensory perception and the rational thinking that accords with it, is at the same time a life in a "world become empty of God."[412] These four stages, down to the last one, are thus designated as follows:

Essence
Revelation
Agency
Works

How, in a first step, can we understand the meaning of "works" and "agency"? The archangel and time spirit Michael, as suggested above, wishes the intellect that was once cosmic and has now grown human to be re-enlivened and spiritualized. The individual must accomplish both. But if, even in only a first, tentative way, we reach an experience of body-free thinking and can ourselves testify to the way in which knowledge creates reality, at the same time we reach the sphere in which Michael points us toward the progressive development of thinking. This is already something that occurs in the suprasensory domain, since Michael does not work on the physical plane. Though, from the Sun, he surely observed the descent of cosmic intelligence to the Earth, he did not himself pursue this same path to its end. Instead, in the last third of the nineteenth century, according to Rudolf Steiner, "he chose the world of rhythm for his dwelling place,"[413] thus not the physical realm. In this too he has an especially close connection and affinity with Christ, as we will see more clearly below.

To bring thinking into accord with the laws of the "world of rhythm"[414] means to begin to enliven and spiritualize it, and is tantamount to the step from the "world of works" back to the realm of cosmic "agency." Here the pupil learns to experience and perceive the etheric, on which all living processes and forms depend. Rudolf Steiner's labor in the field of Goetheanism over many years at the end of the nineteenth century was valuable and wide-ranging preparatory work here. It must be said though that, at our contemporary stage of evolution, this cosmic-etheric agency or potency is no longer directly connected with divine nature and its manifest reality.

To approach—in a second step—what Rudolf Steiner might mean by "essence" and "revelation" of the divine, we can draw on helpful passages from two public lectures that he gave in 1916 and 1920, which focus on this question of "revelation." These lectures, which are concerned in particular with the ecclesiastical teacher and representative of high Scholasticism Thomas Aquinas, bear a strong inner relationship to the letters on the *Michael Mystery* mentioned earlier.

The core idea—of paramount interest here—in the first of these two lectures (given in Liestal on October 16, 1916), concerns the distinction between two truths: those discovered by employing human reason, and those that can dawn on people solely through divine revelation. Since the latter constitute the traditional contents of religious faith, they are also called articles or truths of faith; the former, on the other hand, insofar as the employment of reason touches on these articles of faith, and can effectively support and sustain them, are called by both Rudolf Steiner and Thomas Aquinas "*Praeambula fidei*" (the rational conditions for faith). In the lecture referred to, Steiner fully affirms this distinction made by Aquinas, and ascertains that anthroposophic Spiritual Science, which he, Steiner, represents, falls entirely into the realm "...of what is accessible to self-reliant human powers of cognition,"[415] and thus into the sphere of *Praeambula fidei*. In addition he emphasizes that this science of the spirit therefore does not conflict with the teachings of the Church.

Examples of *Praeambula fidei* as Thomas Aquinas regards it can be seen, for instance, in the spiritual nature of the human soul, and the reality of the Creation, which everywhere reveal signs of the Creating God to whom they owe their existence. Revealed truths, by contrast, in Thomas's view, tell of the Trinity and the incarnation of Christ in Jesus of Nazareth. Without questioning these latter truths, Rudolf Steiner now moves on—in modern times—from Thomas's position, by claiming that human progress in knowledge has now led to the possibility of considerably extending and widening the domain of *Praeambula fidei* into—as we can conclude—the sphere of the spiritual cosmos, with which the awoken human soul can henceforth enter into living interaction. And he confirms this about anthroposophic Spiritual Science. By extending rational knowledge, "Spiritual Science thereby acquires truths that support the articles of faith still more strongly than truths gained merely through the intellect."[416]

The second of these two lectures, given in Dornach on May 24, 1920, concerns the philosophy of Thomas Aquinas—in particular the importance of Thomism today—and picks up the thread of the Liestal lecture again. In citing it here I would like to emphasize that it does not relativize or refute that earlier lecture, but adds an additional aspect. In Dornach, Steiner elaborated further on the idea of broadening the *Praeambula fidei* (although now, in 1920, he no longer uses that term). This new aspect can help us build a bridge with the letters referred to earlier, on *The Michael Mystery*, to which we will then subsequently return. This new perspective proposes that the world of ideas of human beings, their "soul-spiritual content," can assimilate something that "redeems" cognition: the "Christ principle."[417] From the perspective of this lecture in May 1920, this signifies first that our capacity to penetrate into the world of spirit issues from Christ: "Redeemed human reason, which has a true relationship with Christ, penetrates into the world of spirit."[418]

In fact it seems that Rudolf Steiner had an early intimation of this "redemption of reason" already toward the end of his time in Weimar. In the year of his great "inner reorientation" (1896/97),[419] he concluded work on his edition of Goethe's scientific writings which—in the Stuttgart Kürschner edition—also contains the *Proverbs in Prose*, annotated with Rudolf Steiner's detailed commentaries. The same footnotes state tellingly, albeit not entirely in accord with the doctrine of immanence, and without any reference to the role of Christ:

> The divine in the universe can be found only by those who discover it within their self. But what announces itself within as divine is the same as the divine without. When the divine dawns upon us, the distinction between inner and outer ceases; we merge with the outer world and live our way into the *single unity* of divine being.[420]

The key motif above, of the "redemption of human reason" is taken up again in significant fashion in the letters on *The Michael Mystery,* with reflections on Michael as such and his departure from the Sun toward the Earth. The Christ deed however preceded this descent of cosmic intelligence into the realm of earthly humanity, accompanied by Michael on his way down from the Sun into the "world of rhythm." "What began five centuries ago for human consciousness was already enacted in the wider scope of its overall nature at the time the Mystery of Golgotha was accomplished on Earth."[421]

The divine-spiritual beings of origin, as this letter continues, "sent the Christ from the Sun to Earth." And in another letter, from the perspective of Michael himself, he says, "Michael sees the greatest earthly event occur. From the realm that Michael himself served, the Christ being descends into the earthly realm, in order to be present when intelligence should arrive entirely with the human individuality."[422]

That the human being—in freedom—should find access again to the spiritual–cosmic world, is inconceivable for Rudolf Steiner other than through relationship with Christ's sojourn on Earth, the Mystery of Golgotha. And there will be significance not only for knowledge but for morality when we allow our loving actions to shine out into the world and into the whole cosmos. Since Christ's deed on Earth, we bear deep within us something which must be awoken with the aid of Michael, and which "...preserves our connection as human being with the nature of the divine spirit"[423]—or in other words with the one divine-spiritual origin of all. Out of this connection humanity will, through its moral deeds, introduce into the universe something illumined and full of reality that never previously existed.

> The divine spirit from which we originate can, as cosmically unfolding human entity, illumine the cosmos that only otherwise exists as a reflection of the divine spirit. Through humanity there will dawn a being no longer the same as once existed as cosmos. In passing through human nature, the divine spirit will experience a reality of being that it did not previously manifest.[424]

Michael, as witness to the pre-cosmic origin of the world and human being, seeks to awaken the aspirant to this reality. Only by this means will we, in the "passage through human nature," become able to lead the divine spirit, from which we and everything else arose toward a completely new revelation or cosmic manifestation. The ahrimanic adversaries, the forces of obstruction, are however doing all in their power to prevent this future revelation at last shining forth from the human being. Human beings can, in turn, defend themselves steadfastly against the suggestion of these spirits that they should confine their capacities to acting solely on the physical–material plane by spiritualizing intelligence and, as a result, connecting with Christ. "For he [the Christ] entered the world with an intellectuality that is wholly of a kind that lived once in the divine-spiritual realm when this, in its *essence*, still constituted the cosmos."[425]

We should not take offence here at the word "intellectuality." "Intelligence," "wisdom" or even "Logos" would be equally fitting, especially if we consider that reference is made here to a divine, spiritual domain out of which the whole universe emerged. If we can connect with this sphere, not only in our redeemed perception but also in our spiritually creative, moral capacities, the whole world is renewed through us—or through humanity as a tenth member of the ranks of the hierarchies, the developing "fourth hierarchy."[426] And then Ahriman is repulsed.

But this means nothing less than that Christ is identical with the primordial divine spirit in its "essence." This is of a different order of significance from other references to Christ as being, for instance, the "Sun Spirit of Wisdom" or the *Pleroma,* the totality of the six solar Elohim—who are all beings that belong to the spiritual–cosmic stream of evolution. Viewing Christ in his pure, divine-spiritual "essence," we could address the above-named entities as spiritual–cosmic sustainers. The divine "essence," by contrast, which precedes every "revelation," must be understood as being above and beyond even the spiritual cosmos of the hierarchies since the latter, after all, constitute the elaborated content of this revelation. This further sphere beyond them is, as such, a clear demonstration of the transcendence preceding and superordinate to all cosmic–hierarchical immanence;[427] at the same time it is proof of the eternity that existed even before time began, since time itself belongs also to the content of revelation.

Preparation for finding Christ, who belongs most profoundly to this eternity, lies, in accord with Michael, especially in cultivating knowledge-governed love for the outer world, so that human love does not become self-love. And so Steiner writes, "Once this love is present in affinity with Michael, love for the other will also be able to shine back into our own self—for we will be able to love without self-love. And on the paths of such love, Christ can be found through the human soul."[428]

In Christ or in "the Logos as Christ living on Earth among humankind,"[429] we can indeed find a connection with the eternal divine once more, from whose love we and all else emerged. Encountering Christ in the right way, we find in him the source and fount of revelation—the same source to which, ultimately, religious tradition (such as the Old and New Testament) returns. "With the right stance toward Christ, we can experience in living communication of the soul with him what we could otherwise only receive as the traditional revelations of faith."[430]

In the previous chapter, drawing on Rudolf Steiner's *Outline of Esoteric Science,* we saw how the manifestation—or revelation—of the universe was first accomplished in the creation of warmth (Old Saturn), to which air and light were later added (Old Sun). The revelation of Christ, of which Steiner now speaks in his letters on the *Michael Mystery*, can become for us an experience of "spiritual warmth" and "spiritual light." The same "spiritual warmth" in which divine and human love meet is something we can feel as penetrating us, "if we experience the 'Christ within,'" and, "This warmth leads you back again to your divine origin."[431] This corresponds to the reference above to the "Logos as Christ living on Earth among humankind," pointing to the connection with the original divine spirit that can be preserved through him. But here we must pause. For in the whole context of the letters on the *Michael Mystery*—and in particular in relation to Rudolf Steiner's comments on "essence," "revelation," "agency," and "works"—nothing less is being said than that the human being's primordial beginning was in, and emerging from, God.[432]

Of the "spiritual light" that can be experienced in the meeting with Christ, Steiner says further:

> In the light that the Christ brings to the human "I," the primordial light is present again. In such life in communion with Christ the following blessed thought can shine through our whole soul with sunlike brilliance: The glorious, primordial divine light is here once more; it shines although its shining is not of nature.[433]

It is within this light that we can experience the new revelation that was indicated in the previous quotation. And when, before that, we spoke of the being who will experience the divine spirit in its "passage through human nature" as a being who previously "did not reveal" this divine spirit, we can now assume that this being is nourished from the same "spiritual warmth," the same "spiritual light" that arises through the meeting with Christ, the eternal Logos.

The transcendence of God, as Steiner views it no later than the Liestal lecture through to the letters quoted here on the *Michael Mystery*, does not, it must be said, accord very well, for example, with the rejection of a "hypothetical" not experienced "Beyond," founded on a "borrowed" principles, as Steiner expresses it in his *Intuitive Thinking as a Spiritual Path: A Philosophy of Freedom.*[434] In his later work, however, this discord is reconciled and resolved through the figure of Christ, who introduces into the temporal world, into the realm of cosmic and earthly immanence, the eternal and transcendent as his own intrinsic being.[435]

The revealed spiritual and physical cosmos is accessible to reason and rational cognition—encompassing also the spheres of what is called "revelation" in the letters on the *Michael Mystery.* But the letters, at last, contain an acknowledgement by Steiner that we must assume the eternal existence of the divine "essence," the transcendent, which precedes all revelation, and which we can necessarily know only because it reveals itself, or has done so. And the source of this revelation of the divine essence is Christ: it was he two millennia ago, and can be so equally today also via paths that Anthroposophy seeks to show in the light of Michael.

Thus, at the end of his teaching work, Rudolf Steiner again picks up the esoteric comments that he made in his early period as a spiritual teacher.

In chapter 3 of this present work, "The Creative Word," we considered in detail the Logos and the tradition devoted to it. At the same time we also ascertained a striking convergence between Rudolf Steiner's comments on the Logos and those of Sri Aurobindo. The accounts by Steiner referred to from the early years of the twentieth century, made soon after he had taken up a leading role within the Theosophical Society, likewise focus on the Logos. Compared with the extraordinarily rich Christology that Steiner elaborated through many years thereafter, these comments on the Logos—or on the "three logoi"—initially appear somewhat abstract (though this may be due in part to the fact that they were preserved only in incomplete transcripts). But if we examine them in the light of his later comments on the divine "essence" and its "revelation" in the letters on the *Michael Mystery*, in retrospect they acquire more tangibility.

I would like to demonstrate this with a longer quotation, chosen by way of example, and of particular interest in this present work since Rudolf Steiner here connects Western and Eastern approaches:

> If we term the intrinsically absolute, which nothing we know possesses, as *over-being,* we have established an abstract concept for our thinking about the Logos: the inwardly contained, founded, resting and absolute Logos. Primal Logos—Sat—Father.
>
> If only this Logos is assumed, it rests within itself, is and is not present, over and above existence, never perceptible, since it is elevated above all perception, over all existence. From this it follows that this Logos is absolutely hidden, occult, since elevated above all revelation or manifestation. If it were not occult, it would inevitably be revealed; and then we are concerned with its reflection, the revealed Logos. Considering this we can immediately discover two concepts within this one, so that we have a Trinitarian quality—for a revealing or manifesting activity must be present in the revealer:
>
> 1. Logos: revealer
> 2. Logos: revelation, activity
> 3. Logos, revealed reflection
>
> [Indian] *Sat, Ananda, Chit*
> [Christian] Trinity:
>
> 1. Father
> 2. Son, Word
> 3. Holy Spirit

> These three are initially so sublime that we must again term them occult in relation to everything we ordinarily call revealed or perceptible. Thus three occult beings. They must first become manifest. There are only three of them, and so they can only reveal one another:
>
> The Father reveals himself to the Word,
> The Word reveals itself to the Holy Spirit,
> The Holy Spirit reveals itself back to the Father.
> These are the three kinds of revelation.[436]

These words largely accord with, and confirm, the previous thread of our reflections. But the last passage, on the three kinds of revelation, deserves particular attention: it shows that, in a first respect, revelation as such—in terms of both activity and content—is not yet a cosmic occurrence but unfolds as it were within the Trinity only. In other words, the eternal beginning of revelation itself is entirely intra-divine. But everything that can be revealed to human reason emerges from this first, unknown and primal revelation. This "emergence of the world from the Logos"[437] corresponds to what Rudolf Steiner also often terms "manifestation" in his early esoteric lessons.

The transition as such from the pre-cosmic, intra-divine revelatory process, from the unmanifest into the manifest—the "emergence of the world"—itself shows Trinitarian characteristics. In another private lesson Rudolf Steiner discourses on this, employing the Sanskrit terms *Akasha* and *Mahat* ("the Greatness," infinite vastness) as well as the names of high and highest hierarchical beings known in the Christian tradition. Alongside two further archangels, Michael also appears here, exactly as he will two decades later in the letters on the *Michael Mystery*, in the greatest proximity to Christ, the Son.

> The first, from which all else emerged, is the unmanifested godhead. From this the second then proceeded: Life or also the unmanifest creative substance. This Life then passes through the most manifold forms and is named *Akasha*, or *Mahat*.

> This Akasha, or Mahat, contains everything that exists as forms of life in the world. All the hierarchies of the Thrones, Cherubim, Seraphim, Powers, Principalities, archangels and angels emerged through Life and create the forms in which this one Life manifests. The first power, of unmanifest godhead, is also called the Father; the second is the Son, who is simultaneously life and creative substance; and the third is the spirit. Together these three original powers, thus Father, Son and Spirit, appear as consciousness, life and form. The power of life stands under the aegis of Michael, who belongs to the sun; that of form under the aegis of Samael, who belongs to Vulcan, where all life is transformed into living configurations. The power of consciousness stands under the aegis of Anael, who encompasses all that exists.[438]

This characterizes the transition from the unmanifest into manifestation; even Cherubim and Seraphim are "forms" coming forth from "Life," whereas the Father is to be regarded as the entirely "unmanifested godhead." And therewith begins a thread that will run through all anthroposophic cosmology and anthropology and concerns how the Trinity, thus Father, Son, and Holy Spirit, form the overall organization of its structure in their reflections in the cosmos. In the esoteric lesson from which we quote above a first example is then immediately given of what is meant: Rudolf Steiner shows how the Trinity is reflected in the future higher aspects of the human being—*atman, buddhi, manas*; or spirit body, life spirit, spirit self. The same basic Trinitarian structure also becomes apparent, furthermore, for the key spiritual or esoteric schooling that Rudolf Steiner will give his pupils, embodied in the key words of the Rosicrucian formula:

Ex deo nascimur
In Christo morimur
Per spiritum sanctum reviviscimus

This thread eventually leads—through many stages—to the grandiose expansion of this Trinitarian formula in the verses of the Foundation Stone meditation, given on the occasion of the refounding of the Anthroposophical Society at the Christmas Foundation Meeting 1923/24.[439] Whereas Rudolf Steiner's words on the Trinity between 1904 and 1924 often had a marked cosmic angle, concerned as they were primarily with structural traces of the divine three-in-one in human and world evolution and existence,[440] the survey offered here nevertheless shows that an underlying awareness of the transcendent reality of the divine must always have informed his lectures and books.

We conclude these thoughts on Rudolf Steiner's view of the divine with a brief note on him as a person and his own relationship to God. The spiritual teacher Rudolf Steiner was at the same time—albeit perhaps not at every stage of his life—someone who prayed a great deal. The most important prayer for him was the Lord's Prayer, which Christ Jesus himself taught the disciples to pray. From 1907 onward, Steiner devoted various reflections to this prayer, and prayed it himself.[441] He once expressed his extraordinarily high esteem for the Lord's Prayer during a question-and-answer session in June 1912:

> It is the most effective of prayers. The more respect and devotion one has for this prayer, the better it is for a consciousness soul. When we pray it—even if we know nothing of this—originating powers of the human being are at work in it. The one who taught human beings to pray this prayer, must have known these powers. If we use it we can have these powers unconsciously living in us. Our respect for it grows increasingly as we enter into it. Then times will come when, because of the sublimity of the Lord's Prayer, we do not dare to pray the whole of it on one day: we gain such a sense of grandeur from the interplay and concurrence of the seven petitions that we do not consider ourselves worthy to unfold this, the greatest initiation prayer, in our heart every day.[442]

What is said here about the "originating powers of the human being" relates directly to the letters on *The Michael Mystery* where Steiner speaks of the human being rediscovering a connection with the eternal divine through Christ (see above).

Ita Wegman, the physician who collaborated with Rudolf Steiner to bring anthroposophic medicine to birth, witnessed his acts of prayer. From October 1923 onward they worked early each evening on the foundations of this medicine.[443] Whenever possible, Ita Wegman visited Steiner for this purpose at around 6 p.m. But this was the hour when, each day he stood to pray aloud the Lord's Prayer—as well as expanded versions of it. Later, from his sickbed, their collaboration on the book continued, and she remained a witness of his praying until the very last days of his life. She prayed it with him.[444] In the end she had to help him to stand up in order to pray it. Those who passed the studio rooms of the joinery workshop at that time of day,[445] could hear the prayer resounding strongly through the wooden walls. Something very similar was reported of his early days in Berlin: "When he prayed at home in his room in Berlin, he spoke so loudly that you could hear the words in the adjoining room."[446]

To address the divine Father in person, in words that Christ Jesus gave during the Sermon on the Mount (cf. Matt. 6:5–15), is of enormous scope, especially if we consider that He himself, the Father, is the transcendental "essence" underlying what has been referred to now on many occasions as the "unrevealed," or "unmanifest"—the one who revealed himself to all humanity two millennia ago through his Son, in an unthinkable, unsurpassed demonstration of love. From all this, and in view of the high degree of consciousness of Steiner as spiritual teacher, we can here intimate the depth of his spiritual piety. It may well be that such piety, such prayer to a personal Father—in enactment of a responding divine love as it were objectified in Anthroposophy—formed the context for words about God such as these: "The all-encompassing quality of the godhead is not omnipotence, not omniscience, but love—the quality that cannot be further intensified. God is full of love, is pure love, is, as it were, born out of the substance of love."[447]

Already back in his time in Vienna or Weimar, in his "Credo—the Individual and the All," Steiner had formulated a kind of spiritual maxim about the human equivalent of God's love:

> Pious, truly spiritual love ennobles our being in its inmost fibers, enhancing all that lives in us. This pure, pious love transforms all soul life into something else that has an affinity with the world spirit. To love in this highest sense means to bear the breath of God to where usually only the most detestable egotism and irreverent passion is to be found. One has to know something of the sanctity of love, and only then can one speak of piety.[448]

The Divine in the Intuition of Sri Aurobindo

The place and significance of God in Integral Yoga developed organically from the fundamental experiences that accompanied Sri Aurobindo's reentry into the physical, emotional, and spiritual world of India. This included his first encounter with the "spirit of the place," when, as a twenty-one-year-old he placed his feet on Indian Soil again in Bombay for the first time in fourteen years.[449] This experience of immeasurable vastness, infinite stillness, came over him and remained with him for long months. It was to be followed in his outer life, starting with the period serving the Maharaja of Baroda, by the study of Sanskrit and Vedic and post-Vedic writings. This initial realization of 1893 was deepened decisively years later, at the start of 1908, after Sri Aurobindo had gone on a three-day yoga retreat in Baroda. All this was described in chapter 2 of this book. The meditation on which he now embarked enabled him, in a single tumultuous and comprehensive motion, to achieve all the stages of yoga that his guru could teach; and indeed to go beyond his teacher. What he first experienced in consequence corresponds—and this alone is astonishing—to the state of Nirvana for which Buddhism strives. Suddenly he found himself in a state of mind without thoughts, in fact above all thought, in which all mental and vital stirrings were extinguished. What he previously experienced as the world around him now showed itself to be illusion—empty, insubstantial, and completely silent, neither the One nor the Many.

The realization that began in this way, however, grew far beyond Nirvana. The illusory character of sense phenomena henceforth appears to Sri Aurobindo—as he passes from one state of realization to the next—at best as an insignificant "surface phenomenon," with an immense divine reality behind it, and preliminary only to this most sublime divine reality. This same intense divine reality now speaks to him from the core of everything he encounters. Peace, stillness, and infinite freedom—they remain with him; and later he intimated that at this point he began to perceive the world as a "continuous incident in the timeless eternity of the Divine."[450] During his imprisonment in Alipur between May 1908 and May 1909, as we heard earlier, this experience of the most sublime divine reality was to become concretized and personalized in unforeseen fashion when Sri Aurobindo entered into intimate discourse with Shri Krishna. Here in the prison Krishna showed himself to Sri Aurobindo as Vasudeva, that is, as Son of the Father,[451] but above all as Narayana, the all-indwelling *Ishvara,* or divine "Lord." In Alipur Prison Krishna himself gives Sri Aurobindo the *Bhagavad Gita*; and without delay he embarks on the yoga described there.

The *Bhagavad Gita* leads Prince Arjuna, and with him all who adopt the yoga contained there, to a series of peak experiences, including, in a special respect, the revelation of the Purushottama: Krishna as the divine person, as the sublime self of the Supreme Divine. For Sri Aurobindo this "sublime self" was to become indispensable when, in the coming twelve years, he wrote down his vision in the language of Integral Yoga philosophy.[452] In the *Gita*, Krisha reveals himself to Arjuna, repeatedly telling him of himself. Thus also here, in Song XV:

> Two are the *Purushas* in this world: *Kshara*, the Mutable, and *Akshara*, the Immutable; the *Kshara* is all the becomings; the *Kutastha*, seated on the summit of Immovability, is said to be the *Akshara*.
>
> The highest *Purusha* is yet another, called *Paramatman*, the supreme Self, who entering into the three worlds upbears them, the Lord Imperishable.
>
> Since I transcend the *Kshara* and am the Highest even above the *Akshara*, hence am I celebrated as the *Purushottama* in the world and in the Veda.[453]

Far-reaching questions are connected with these words about the Purushottama, and lead us deep into discussions about the older and younger Vedanta. But it is essential to trace this thread further if we are to begin to grasp Sri Aurobindo's view of the divine. Let us first clarify some necessary terms.

Whether the highest deity of Indian vision appears as an impersonal absolute, *nirguna brahman*, or as personal *ishvara*, the Lord, is a question to which no definitive answer is given within the Sanatana Dharma. In the Western world, there is insufficient clarity about this distinction. In European languages, therefore, the second of the two (*ishvara*) is often interpreted as subordinate to the first (*nirguna brahman*).

Around the time that Buddhism became more widely known in Europe and North America, the School of Advaita Vedanta likewise appeared in these regions as an original Indian form of spirituality.[454] In the twentieth century, both in India and the West, Shri Ramana Maharshi (1879–1950), the mahatma of Arunachala Mountain, gained special renown. He helped bring to new prominence and grandeur the teachings of Adi Shankaracharya (788–820)[455]—probably the most sublime form of the Advaita Vedanta. Whereas *Vedanta* means "the end of the Vedas," or in general the post-Vedic teachings that draw on and refer to the Vedas, primarily the Upanishads, *Advaita Vedanta* means roughly the Vedanta of non-duality. In this later doctrine, the oneness—or non-duality—of *atman* and *brahman* is taught and is the subject of meditation. For the adherents of this school, the liberation sought, *moksha*, consists in realizing this oneness, this non-duality, in meditative cognition. In his day, Shankara conveyed the furthest consequence of his Monist worldview—which is very hard to grasp—only at the level of a "higher knowledge" culminating in the insight and experience that the immutable *brahman* is the sole reality, and that all multiplicity, all evolution, and even the existence of diverse *atmans*, is simply *maya*.[456] This illusion is one in which the unenlightened are trapped, and from which one should irreversibly awaken. Shri Ramana Maharshi,[457] who brought Shankara's teachings to fulfillment, instructed his pupils according to the *atma vichara* method—implicit in which is the question of the self, of "who I am"—in order to lead them to *moksha:* I exist only insofar as *brahman* exists; outside of brahman, I do not exist, nor does anything else. Advaita Vedanta, as well as Buddhism, represent an ultimately radically impersonal spirituality that in the West is widely regarded—though with inadequate distinction—as the generally primary form of Indian spirituality.

Sri Aurobindo repeatedly took issue with the tendency (arising first with Buddha and later with Shankara) to see the highest and ultimate reality or divine nature in an impersonal existence—or, in Buddhism, nonexistence.[458] Already in the first chapters of his major work on yogic philosophy *The Life Divine* (chapters 2 and 3), he engaged with the problem of the "two negations": first the denial of the spirit in modern materialism, but then also the problem of denial of earthly-material reality by Eastern ascetics, the Advaitins (or Vedantic Monists) who strive solely for "the pure Self," the "inactive Brahman, the transcendent Silence." This study at the same time clarifies the terms of the other question relating to the personality or impersonality of God, to which we will return below. If this "transcendent Silence," seen as impersonal, is experienced in all its intensity, then, according to Sri Aurobindo, it is associated with an insistent "sense of the unreality of the world and the sole reality of the Silence." He continues:

> ...[this] is one of the most powerful and convincing experiences of which the human mind is capable. Here, in the perception of this pure Self or of the Non-Being behind it, we have the starting point for a second negation—parallel at the other pole to the materialistic, but more complete, more final, more perilous in its effects on the individuals or collectivities that hear its potent call to the wilderness—the refusal of the ascetic.[459]

Sri Aurobindo acknowledges that this ascetic spirit issued primarily from the non-Vedic movement of Gautama Buddha, yet nevertheless exerted a very powerful influence on Indian spirituality for over two millennia. And although the sense of the cosmos being an illusion did not fully express Indian thinking, this influence meant that, increasingly, "all...have lived in the shadow of the great Refusal." In his efforts, in turn, to overcome the "dangerous" limitations of Advaitic asceticism, Sri Aurobindo urged that alongside the great Advaitic formula the "One without a second," another assertion from the Upanishads, "All this is the Brahman," should also gain wider acceptance again; and this because of its positive inclusion of the whole world in the quest for God. The vehemence of the Indian Sannyasin's striving for the Divine, he said, must once more be fully incorporated into the descent of divine being into the earthly human world: "Its meaning [of the Divine] in Matter has not been so well understood as Its truth in the Spirit. The Reality which the Sannyasin seeks has been grasped in its full height, but not, as by the ancient Vedantins, in its full extent and comprehensiveness."[460]

It is clear that Advaitic rejection of the earthly material world, and Advaitic Impersonalism, are mutually determining. The exclusive and at the same time abstract singularity of a single, highest universal Self, which extinguishes all other true selves—since these, like all mundane multiplicity, would be only *maya*—cannot be the foundation of personality. Persons can only acquire tangible existence as a plurality of beings who can respond and enter into dialogue with one another. But irrespective of this, Sri Aurobindo repeatedly turns, in as emphatic a way as he deals with the problem of "materialism and spirituality," to the question of divine personality or impersonality. And he does so precisely by immersing himself in the mystery of the—both human and divine—self.

The gateway to the divine self is the realized human self. And this invites him to further reflections. True self-knowledge, for Sri Aurobindo, means insight into the self as being, quite simply, the pure principle of existence, connected in turn with realization of the self as one with all individual soul experience. This also signifies, for example, an overcoming of the apparent irreconcilable difference between the two poles of reality: of given existence on the one hand, and the idea on the other. Supramental experience, which for Sri Aurobindo, is primary, clearly shows that existence and idea are only "complementary aspects of the same Truth." This is associated in turn with the insight that unity and multiplicity are not mutually exclusive but that, in the true, transcendental self, both are raised to a higher synthesis. This higher unity is described as follows in *The Synthesis of Yoga*, "The Modes of the Self": "The accomplished sense of Unity is not that in which all are regarded as parts of one whole, waves of one sea, but that in which each as well as the All is regarded wholly as the Divine, wholly as our Self in a supreme identity."[461]

Thus individual selves are as eternal as divine being, though this does not mean they resolve into it and are subsumed entirely without separate distinction. Sri Aurobindo characterizes the condition of the realized individual self both as "immersion of ourselves in the Lord" through unity with the divine will or its conscious power, and as "the height of love," which is "rapturous immersion of ourselves in unity of ecstatic delight with the object of our love and adoration."[462]

On the other hand, however, the realized self of the sadhaka becomes a center of consciousness for divine working in the world, by means of which the divine will, united with divine love and light, can stream through the multiplicity of the universe. Thus the realized individual self, acting within nature—as "soul-form of the One"—maintains a special distinctiveness that "enables us to preserve relations of difference in Oneness with other beings and with the Supreme Himself."[463]

Doubtless the self must be distinguished from the transient personality subject to all temporal and cosmic mutability. While the personality is also Purusha and *brahman*, it is the "mutable Purusha." The soul can awaken in the "immutable Pususha," on the other hand, if it withdraws entirely from all cosmic and temporal activity. In accord with the *Bhagavad Gita*, this antithesis is resolved in turn and attains higher synthesis in the "supreme Purusha" already mentioned—the Purushottama. And this is of great significance not least for the individual self or soul:

> ...but the soul that can live in the Highest enjoys the eternal peace and power and delight and wideness of being, is not bound in its self-knowledge and self-power by character and personality or by forms of its force and habits of its consciousness and yet uses them all with a large freedom and power for the self-expression of the Divine in the world.[464]

The personal and the impersonal self, the constrained and unconstrained Purusha—or *kshara purusha* and *akshara purusha*—indicate a differentiation that also applies to the *brahman*. The Sanatana Dharma makes a very clear distinction between *nirguna brahman*, which is without qualities, and *saguna brahman*, which possesses them. It is true nevertheless that the sublime one employs both aspects of such polarities equally in order to express and demonstrate his unfathomability.

Sri Aurobindo calls "personality" and "impersonality" Western concepts, but at the same time he explains that they can certainly apply equally to coupled terms such as *saguna* and *nirguna*, active and passive *brahman*, or *kshara* and *akshara purusha*. Nevertheless he asserts that the European idea of, especially, the "personality" of God, is inadequate because it constrains supreme and sublime being with certain limiting qualities. Thus the benevolent, loving God of, say, Francis of Assisi, or the mercilessly strict God of Calvin are scarcely identical, but different in a way roughly comparable to the Indian deities Vishnu and Shiva. That the personal God is not limited by his qualities, that he is *ananta-guna*, or capable of infinite qualities, and that, nevertheless, he stands above and beyond all these so as to employ them in utter freedom as he desires—is something that is clearly very difficult for the "normal European mind" to grasp.[465]

Nevertheless, Sri Aurobindo's reflections culminate in striking words about God as the sole real person and the source of all personality. Here his view goes well beyond that of the schools of Advaita Vedanta and Sankhya, the first of which acknowledges only *nirguna brahman*, while the second claims countless spiritual monads or separate Purushas that can never enter into actual contact with Prakriti, the world of attributes.[466] True Sanatana Dharma, however, can integrate both approaches and lead them further. But this integrative power remains a huge challenge for all traditional linear thinking, and seemingly beyond its compass.

> It is for this reason that the normal European mind finds it so difficult to understand Indian religion as distinct from Vedantic or Sankhya philosophy, because it cannot easily conceive of a personal God with infinite qualities, a personal God who is not a Person, but the sole real Person and the source of all personality. Yet that is the only valid and complete truth of the divine Personality.[467]

In the chapter from which we have been quoting, "The Modes of the Self," Sri Aurobindo sums up his reflections by highlighting the need to consider three forms or degrees of approach to the personal deity:

> ...the first in which He is conceived with a particular form or particular qualities as the name and form of the Godhead which our nature and personality prefers, *ishta-devata*; a second in which He is the one real Person, the All-Personality, the Ananta-guna; a third in which we get back to the ultimate source of all idea and fact of personality in that which the Upanishad indicates by the single word *He* without fixing any attributes. It is there that our realisations of the personal and the impersonal Divine meet and become one in the utter Godhead.[468]

And furthermore:

> Through the realisation of higher and higher principles of being and states of conscious existence we arrive not at the annullation of all in a sort of positive zero or even an inexpressible state of existence, but at the transcendent Existence itself which is also the Existent who transcends all definition by personality and yet is always that which is the essence of personality.[469]

In the works of Sri Aurobindo we often encounter the term *sachchidananda* as a characterization of the deity. This word is a compound common in Sanskrit, formed of *sat*—pure, infinite being, *chit*—pure, infinite consciousness, and *ananada*—pure, infinite bliss. These three constitute the nature of *brahman* as intrinsically free of all attributes. Sri Aurobindo now expounds on how original, supreme, and eternal existence is not an empty existence, nor merely conscious being, but rather "a conscious existence the very term of whose being, the very term of whose consciousness is bliss."[470] He says that the absolute nature of supreme-being conscious existence is identical with the delight or bliss inherent in it. And he emphasizes that—even though absolute *brahman* is one with this bliss or delight—this does not mean the bliss is limited or constrained by the absolute. Rather, the divine can disclose and expend its self-bliss, as well as its self-being and its force of consciousness, in the infinite variations of the world of Creation, and continually does so: "It follows that all things that exist are what they are as terms of that existence, terms of that conscious force, terms of that delight of being."[471]

Sri Aurobindo replies to the question of why, in that case, suffering and pain exist in the world, since everything emerged from the conscious, divine bliss of being, by pointing out that—first—experiences of suffering and pain, as well as of joy and delight, are ultimately caused by the eternal self; and that—second—the self possesses the strength to accept such experiences so as, subsequently, to divest them of their character—of pain, suffering, joy, and delight—and eventually to transform them along with their underlying stances and habits. Thus they facilitate new ongoing experiences in which the deeper, broader human self, the bliss-being—*anandamaya*—can come to expression.

This transformation, and the term for bliss-being, *anandamaya*, have in turn a clear affinity with Sri Aurobindo's view of the divine, and the person of the deity. In the chapter "The Divine Personality," in Part III of *The Synthesis of Yoga*, which concerns divine love (Bhakti Yoga), he makes clear that we should understand *sachchidananda* as the fruit of a long-enduring process of abstraction set in motion by the philosophical intellect of ancient India.[472] The abstraction that began at that time, he says, was later taken still further by divesting *sat*—mere or pure existence—of both consciousness—*chit*—and bliss—*ananda*. Thus Indian tradition arrived at *sat* as the most abstract characterization of divine *brahman*. But the restless intellect was not yet satisfied by this and therefore—in the Buddha Dharma, outside of the Vedic tradition—it eventually came to dispute even existence itself; at which, according to Sri Aurobindo, nothing remained but "an infinite zero." However, "heart and life" could not live in such abstractions, and continually sought living development rather than abstract, apersonal being. Their intent was to experience the joy and activity of a finite or also an infinite person—*anandamaya purusha*—in relation to which the delights and forces of their own existence embody a reality:

> Therefore when the heart and life turn toward the Highest and the Infinite, they arrive not at an abstract existence or non-existence, a Sat or else a Nirvana, but at an existent, a Sat Purusha, not merely at a consciousness, but at a conscious Being, a Chaitanya Purusha, not merely at a purely impersonal delight of the Is, but at an infinite I Am of bliss, an anandamaya Purusha; nor can they immerge and lose his consciousness and bliss in featureless existence, but must insist on all three in one, for delight of existence is their highest power and without consciousness delight cannot be possessed. That is the sense of the supreme figure of the intensest Indian religion of love, Shri Krishna, the All-blissful and All-beautiful.[473]

But here again no final certainty is attained, for the Advaita Vedantin will invariably reply that this expresses only the mutable Purusha—or *saguna brahman*—which is defined by attributes, and as opposed to which *nirguna brahman* is infinitely supreme. In fact, Sri Aurobindo does accord this objection a certain justification, since the highest being is entirely free, in the fullest sense of retiring back into itself into that static condition which it cannot in truth ever lose. If, consequently, we were to consider only what remains after its self-withdrawal, we would, he says, find only the presence of "pure apersonality" or "empty nothing." But someone, on the other hand, who still retains awareness of what has withdrawn in this way into indistiguishability—that is, the person, the divine personality and everything that it manifested—could ultimately gain an intuition that leads beyond both modes of understanding. Whereas, for the mental intellect, supreme being becomes something undefinable through withdrawing into itself, the intuition underpinning integral vision of God could be summed up as follows: "But out of this unknowable the conscious Being, the divine Person, who has manifested himself here, still speaks, 'This, too, is "I"; even here beyond the view of mind, I am He, the Purushottama.'"[474]

The works of Sri Aurobindo testify to numerous engagements with the divine, and in a volume such as this, we can only convey an initial impression constrained by narrow limits. Yet the outline offered here would remain incomplete if we omitted Sri Aurobindo's enlargement of the idea of God to include the aspect of the feminine, on which he laid great value. This perspective was intimated already in chapters 1 and 3 of this book, in relation to the spiritual realities of Purusha and Prakriti—or Mula-Prakriti.[475] What was begun there must now be traced further.

Brahman as divine self-existence ensouls the entire universe, completely pervading it and essentially underlying it. *Brahman* as the only true reality—especially for the Mayavadins—contrasts in the perspective of the Advaita Vedanta with the universe as the realm of phenomenal multiplicity and continual change, in other words as maya. Sri Aurobindo, for his part, does not primarily regard maya as illusion but rather as the dynamic strength and consciousness of the self-existence of *brahman*. The *brahman* as the self of all existence, he says, relates to the universe as the atman does to an individual person in his development, his maya.[476] The self is experienced in the condition of silence, and felt as an immobile, unchanging existence, penetrating the whole universe and omnipresent: not dynamic and not active but rather elevated over the "mobile energy" of maya.[477] Purusha and Prakriti, as the pair is called above all in Sankhya philosophy, contrast similarly. Prakriti is to be understood as the agency and activity emerging from the Purusha, and intrinsically active by nature. We should note, though, that when Sri Aurobindo speaks of nature as such, he often means nothing other than the Prakriti, as the creatively producing principle giving birth from itself to the manifold phenomena of the cosmos and Earth, in which, however—among much else—unconsciousness dwells. A clearer distinction is as follows: classical Sankhya embodies the non-theist outlook in which the individual Purusha dwells in every separate being in a completely inactive and inwardly enclosed way; while not participating in what occurs in the cosmos, it is nevertheless a fully conscious witness of it all. But the Sankhya school rejects the idea of a supreme divine Purusha that is elevated above the multiplicity of Purushas. In contrast to this concept, Sri Aurobindo sees the Prakriti—with its three gunas *tamas, rajas,* and *sattva*—as the dynamic counterpole not only of the individual Purushas but, as we saw above, also of the Purushottama of the *Bhagavad Gita.*

> Prakriti presents itself as an inconscient Energy in the material world, but, as the scale of consciousness rises, she reveals herself more and more as a conscious force and we perceive that even her inconscience concealed a secret consciousness; so too conscious being is many in its individual souls, but in its self we can experience it as one in all and one in its own essential existence.[478]

He counters the position of the Sankhya with the clear critique that there cannot be any eternal, fundamental separation, no "dualism of Being and its Consciousness-Force, of the Soul and Nature."[479] Based on earlier reflections on the personal and impersonal in God, Sri Aurobindo then pursues his questions about male and female aspects of God, and eventually elaborates as supreme characterization of the divine couple the picture we encounter in tradition as *ishvara–shakti.* Ishvara (see above) is the "Lord," omniscient and omnipotent, all-loving and all-loved: at the same time he is both within and above the cosmos, encompassing within himself the dimensions of *brahman* and the supreme Purusha. He is one with them and yet he excels them: "the Eternal, the Infinite, the Ineffable, the Divine Transcendence."[480] And once again Sri Aurobindo affirms that the impersonal is not the highest manifestation of the divine:

> ...that what is impersonal is only a power of the Person: existence itself has no meaning without an Existent, consciousness

has no standing-place if there is none who is conscious, delight is useless and invalid without an enjoyer, love can have no foundation or fulfilment if there is no lover, all-power must be otiose if there is not an Almighty.[481]

The shakti, in turn, as the active, cosmic, creative force is the feminine, spiritual-divine counterpart of the "Lord." But it should not be conceived as mere "materia," simply the foundation for manifestation of divine resolves of will—which might lead to a one-sided understanding of "Prakriti." Just as an interplay of personal and impersonal aspects lives in the supreme being, so likewise *ishvara* and *shakti* cannot in reality be sundered. In her response to, and inmost connection with *ishvara*, in fact, *shakti* participates in the eternal nature of his personality and is itself also to be conceived in personal terms. If, as Sri Aurobindo puts it, we consider the "biune aspect of Self and Self-Power," then "in the Person Aspect a dual Person emerges, Ishvara–Shakti, the Divine Self and Creator and the Divine Mother and Creatrix of the universe."[482]

There becomes apparent to us the mystery of the masculine and feminine cosmic Principles whose play and interaction are necessary for all creation. In the superconscient truth of the Self-Existence these two are fused and implied in each other, one and indistinguishable, but in the spiritual-pragmatic truth of the dynamism of the universe, they emerge and become active; the Divine Mother-Energy as the universal creatrix, Maya, Para-Prakriti, Chit-Shakti, manifests the cosmic Self and Ishwara and her own self-power as a dual principle; it is through her that the Being, the Self, the Ishwara, acts and he does nothing except by her; though his Will is implicit in her, it is she who works out all as the supreme Consciousness-Force who holds all souls and beings within her and as executive Nature; all exists and acts according to Nature, all is the Consciousness-Force manifesting and playing with the Being in millions of forms and movements into which she casts his existence.[483]

And, in a nutshell: "One Being, one Reality as Self bases, supports, informs, as Purusha or Conscious Being experiences, as Ishwara wills, governs and possesses its world of manifestation created and kept in motion and action by its own Consciousness-Force or Self-Power—Maya, Prakriti, Shakti."[484]

For Integral Yoga and its sadhaka, divine nature, or *shakti*, is of great significance. Only by virtue of it, says Sri Aurobindo can one realize a higher level of being. Complete devotion is needed to divine being, *ishvara*, but ascent to the highest nature, or into it, can occur only through *shakti*: "[this] can only be done by the supramental Shakti taking up our mentality and transforming it into her supramentality."[485]

In chapter 2 we spoke of the descent of overmind that occurred on November 24, 1926, and of how, following this event, Sri Aurobindo withdrew from prominence in the life of the ashram, leaving responsibility for the yogic community entirely in the hands of Mirra Alfassa.[486] In the very first year of his seclusion, Sri Aurobindo composed four letters and an essay, which he published in Calcutta the following year, 1928, under the title *The Mother*. There we find a telling account of four cardinal aspects of *shakti* or *mahashakti—mahakali, mahalakshmi, mahasarasvati* and *mahesvari*—which we can easily recognize as related to the four principle branches of Integral Yoga: *mahakali* corresponds to the yoga of works, *mahalakshmi* to the yoga of loving devotion, *mahasarasvati* to the yoga of knowledge, while *mahesvari*, as integration of the three, represents the yoga of perfection.[487] And in relation to the realization of supermind, which is the overall intent of Integral Yoga, we read in the concluding passage of this short text on *The Mother*:

> The supramental change is a thing decreed and inevitable in the evolution of the earth-consciousness; for its upward ascent is not ended and mind is not its last summit. But that the change may arrive, take form and endure, there is needed the call from below with a will to recognise and not deny the Light when it

comes, and there is needed the sanction of the Supreme from above. The power that mediates between the sanction and the call is the presence and power of the Divine Mother.[488]

The Descent of the Supermind and the Second Coming of Christ

The motif of the descent of supermind makes its first appearance early on in the works of Sri Aurobindo—in 1912, fifteen years before the last-cited passage was written, in the essay *The Yoga and Its Objects*. In the introduction Sri Aurobindo writes:

> The Yoga we practise is not for ourselves alone, but for the Divine; its aim is to work out the will of the Divine in the world, to effect a spiritual transformation and to bring down a divine nature and a divine life into the mental, vital and physical nature and life of humanity. Its object is not personal Mukti, although Mukti is a necessary condition of the yoga, but the liberation and transformation of the human being. It is not personal ananda, but the bringing down of the divine ananda—Christ's kingdom of heaven, our Satya Yuga—upon the Earth.[489]

The more precise terminological usage of "descent" in connection with the "supramental" occurs from 1920 onward, and more frequently from 1927. This may lead us to presume that Sri Aurobindo thoroughly researched the corresponding realities over a long period. But in the passage above, one element above all is striking: the connection between that transformative "bringing down" of the divine will, divine nature, into the earthly world, and the reference to the kingdom of Christ, whose awaited and hoped-for return is one of the core messages of the New Testament. We will come back later to Sri Aurobindo's reference to Christ as the Son of Man and of God. Here, too, on the other hand, we should remark how this desired event is integrated into the context of the traditional Indian teaching of the yugas, or cyclical world epochs.

In the same book, *The Yoga and Its Objects*, Sri Aurobindo also goes into more detail on the yugas themselves, especially insofar as they are of interest for our modern era. Here he describes an increasing degeneration of the original purity and harmony of nature and world processes, as they were once optimally realized during the Satya Yuga; throughout the Treta Yuga and Dvapara Yuga, however, they continued to decline until eventually, in Kali Yuga, the "Dark Age," they succumbed to complete collapse and destruction.[490] In relation to Kali Yuga, Sri Aurobindo then writes:

> But the Kali is not merely evil; in it the necessary conditions are progressively built up for a new Satya, another harmony, a more advanced perfection. In the period of the Kali which has passed, still endures in its effects, but is now at an end, there has been a general destruction of the ancient knowledge and culture. Only a few fragments remain to us in the Vedas, Upanishads and other sacred works and in the world's confused traditions. But the time is at hand for a first movement upward, the first attempt to build up a new harmony and perfection.[491]

Entirely in accord with the Adesha, which he had received three years previously in Alipur Prison,[492] Sri Aurobindo sees a decisive role for India in relation to these new realizations, especially concerning the Purnayoga or Integral Yoga that is to be developed there. It must also be emphasized here that—in the same text of 1912—the Indian spiritual teacher still directly connects this forthcoming manifestation with the task of the Avatar:

> ...the reason for which the Avatars descend is to raise up man again and again, developing in him a higher and ever higher humanity, a greater and yet greater development of divine being, bringing more and more of heaven again and again upon the Earth until our toil is done, our work accomplished and *sachchidananda* fulfilled in all even here, even in this material universe. Small is his work, even if he succeeds, who labours for his own salvation or the salvation of a few; infinitely great is his, even if he fail or succeed only partially or for a season,

> who lives only to bring about peace of soul, joy, purity and perfection among all mankind.[493]

Reference to the Avatar, and thus initially Shri Krishna, is especially illuminating and palpable because he is most closely associated with the cycle of the yugas. For example, in the tradition of the Sanatana Dharma, the beginning of Kali Yuga—which according to Rudolf Steiner falls in the year 3101 BC—is defined by the "death" of Krishna in the same year.[494] Simplifying, we can say that the Kali Yuga is the period during which Krishna is absent. In the words quoted above, Sri Aurobindo tells us that the Kali Yuga has ended and that a new upward trend has been initiated toward a new Satya Yuga. He sees his own task as nothing less than furthering this new upward trajectory. Here we should remember his very profound relationship with the being of the Avatar, Krishna.

Rudolf Steiner also made it clear beyond doubt that the Kali Yuga was passing,[495] and he gives the date 1899. With the year 1900, he says, a new, "freer, brighter age" dawned.[496] Rudolf Steiner first spoke of the return of Christ in the etheric in early 1910. He had been giving lectures in Stockholm on the Gospel of St. John, which were not transcribed, and on January 12 also held a lecture out of sequence, of which only Marie von Sivers took personal notes, these not coming into wider circulation until 2009.[497] In his introductory words to this earliest account of the Second Coming in the etheric, Steiner already establishes a connection with the now expired Kali Yuga, and thus, indirectly with the being of Krishna:

> In 3000 BC, Kali Yug[a] began and lasted until 1899
> Transitional period
> 1933—human beings will again appear with clairvoyant
> capacities, which they will develop by nat[ural] means.
> In the time that is approaching, incip[ient] clairv.[oyant]
> capacities must come into their own
> experiencing how these should be employed:

> I am with you always even unto the end of the world
> Christ will appear in ether[ic] form[498]

Following this, Steiner speaks of how Christ became the spirit of the Earth, and henceforth is at the center of its evolution. Already in The Revelation of John, in the epistle to the fifth church (which represents our own era, the fifth cultural epoch) stands the prompting to be wakeful in order to recognize Christ in his reappearance (Rev. 3:3). The new clairvoyant faculties, says Steiner, would become ever more widespread in the coming two and a half millennia; and the year 1933 would be the first milestone of this development. Until then, groups of people should have begun to study the Gospels of the New Testament with new, spiritual understanding, of a kind deep enough to fittingly prepare for Christ's return. If not, there was a risk of great confusion, for in 1933 powers inspired by black magic would emerge, with the aim of announcing the appearance of a false "Christ" in physical form. By contrast it was true to say that each time Christ comes he will appear in a manner that addresses the most advanced capacities of perception at that time.[499]

The years 1910 and 1911 saw the most important communications by Steiner on Christ's reappearance in the etheric. The comments referred to above, from January 12, 1910, are repeated in similar form in most of the lectures given to members of the Theosophical Society held in various cities between January and May 1910.[500] Among other things, for instance, Steiner goes into more detail on these new capacities of perception in terms of a new vision of the natural world. In clairvoyant perception, the Christ will be especially apparent in nature forces, as the new spirit of Earth. The veil of illusion—which during Kali Yuga prevented people from truly seeing how spirit, in the form of etheric forces, gives rise to all life, all living phenomena on the Earth—will increasingly fall from human perception. Human beings will, at the same time, begin to survey the growth forces in the plant world, and this will enable them to perceive the Christ in a new way. The second kind of new clairvoyance can be termed "karmic vision," connected with our future progress as moral beings. This vision, says Steiner, will enable people to perceive, as an inner picture, the direct karmic consequences of any deed on which they embark. This will also lead people to a new perception of the Christ, who will not appear in the physical realm.

Rudolf Steiner, in particular, compares the way in which the being of Christ can be perceived in the etheric with the experience of Paul on the road to Damascus—as a unique form of initiation through Christ:

> [The being of the Christ] will no longer come in a physical body, since this was a unique event. But Christ will return in an etheric form at the period I have indicated. And people will learn to perceive the Christ by growing, through this etheric vision, up toward the one who no longer descends as far as physical incarnation but only into an etheric body. Thus human beings will have to grow upward to a perception of Christ. Christ's saying, you see, is true: "I am with you always, even unto the end of the world." He is present, is there in our world of spirit, and those especially graced and gifted can always perceive him in this spiritual–etheric world. One who was especially convinced by such perception was Paul at the event of Damascus. But this etheric vision is something that some people will develop as natural capacity. It will become ever more possible for people in future to have a Damascene experience as Paul did.[501]

The experience of Paul, which at that time was a highly individual one, will happen first to some individuals and then gradually become general human experience. But this Pauline experience should not be seen as separate from that most essentially human being who underwent the whole earthly path of Christ Jesus of Nazareth and was the bearer of the Christ spirit: the innocent Nathan Jesus soul. From 1912, Rudolf Steiner perceived this lofty being, who reunited humanity with its divine origins, as identical with the Avatar of humanity, Shri Krishna.[502] Only with this in mind—in relation to the reappearance of Christ in the etheric—can we understand the following words of Rudolf Steiner:

> Paul's vision near Damascus is of the Christ. The aura of light in which Christ is clothed, is Krishna. And because the Christ took Krishna as his own soul sheath, through whom he then continues working, all that was once the content of the sublime Gita is contained in what rays forth, is contained in Christ.[503]

This at the same time explains the fact, mentioned at the outset, that from the beginning Rudolf Steiner placed the mysteries of Christ's reappearance ("This is the greatest secret of our age: that of the reappearance of Christ")[504] in the context of the ending of the Kali Yuga and thus—as suggested above—connected it with a new dawn of Krishna's working. We should also remember that his words above about the "soul sheath" through which Christ "continues working" also contain an indication that in this sheath, in this "aura of light," which is Krishna himself, the Christ spirit will also be perceptible in his reappearance in the etheric.

We have already seen that Sri Aurobindo likewise perceived the new manifestation of the supramental in intimate connection with the working of the Avatar. And let us recall here, too, that Sri Aurobindo's special closeness to the being of Krishna originated in his experience at Alipur Prison, and thus began around 1909. The Adesha with which Krishna himself endowed Sri Aurobindo would of course eventually lead to elaboration of the whole of Integral Yoga. Insight into the future influx of divine life and divine nature into the earthly world, which he later spoke of as the descent of supermind, thus appears to have matured in the three years from 1909 to 1912: from the experience in Alipur to his authorship of essays on *The Yoga and Its Objects*.

What was happening during this period in Central Europe? In 1909, Rudolf Steiner first communicates knowledge about the innocent Nathan Jesus being, and three years later will acknowledge him—in his pre-Christian working—to be identical with Krishna. Thus understanding of the Nathan being can be regarded as a prelude to statements about the reappearance of Christ in the etheric. From this perspective, the year 1909 is a key year for both figures—Rudolf Steiner and Sri Aurobindo—in relation to spiritual realizations that seem to plumb the depths of the same mystery.

Rudolf Steiner confirms the significance of this year later too—toward the end of the Great War. In 1917, eight years after the key year 1909, he warns of the terrible loss it would mean for humanity if it overlooked Christ's reappearance in the etheric:

> And if humanity is not to commit a grave sin against the Earth's salvation, it must not pass by this event and ignore it; it must have the right attentiveness so that a sufficient number of people are prepared to really perceive the Christ, who will come at that time and who must be perceived.[505]

This, he said, would not be a sudden occurrence but something prepared over a period—similar to the way in which Christ only worked publicly and openly after this had been prepared through thirty years. The decisive moment, he said, was coming ever closer:

> This moment is already in preparation....And the occultist can show how, roughly since 1909, what is to come is being prepared in a clearly discernible manner; that, since 1909, we are living inwardly in a very particular time. And today it is possible, if only people seek this, to be very close to Christ, and to find him in a way quite different from how former eras found him.[506]

We should understand this new closeness to Christ Jesus in his form of manifestation in the etheric, initially perceptible to the spiritual researcher from 1909, and, from 1933, becoming available as an experience to wide circles of people. The years from

1900, the beginning of the "freer, brighter age," to 1909, can therefore be seen as a phase of preceding germination.[507]

Thus the accompanying circumstances make Christ's reappearance in the etheric and the descent of supermind, as Rudolf Steiner and Sri Aurobindo respectively describe them, a comparable event: as an occurrence at the beginning of a new age in the first half of the twentieth century, and in the intimate connection of this occurrence with a re-emergence of the Krishna or Jesus being. On the other hand there are also, clearly, important inner differences between the two occurrences, since the reappearance of Christ refers back to the original manifestation of the Christ spirit in Jesus of Nazareth two millennia earlier, whereas the descent of supermind is mostly described as an entirely new event, unfolding from the twentieth century onward.[508]

In this connection Sri Aurobindo saw his partner and companion Mirra Alfassa, "the Mother," as the one through whom supermind would first be realized. She was, he said, right into her physical body, the bearer of the divine *shakti* (see above), and identified with it.[509] This comment should be understood in terms of the fact that the descent of supermind is ascribed to the renewed working of the Avatar who emerged in the twentieth century, in intimate connection with the work of Sri Aurobindo.[510]

Unlike the reappearance of Christ in the etheric, the descent of supermind, as Sri Aurobindo describes it, consists very largely in realizations within human nature. These he believes will occur in consequence of yogic sadhana, which includes complete surrender to the divine, and arises through the divine workings of grace. The priority in Sri Aurobindo's seclusion from 1926 onward, in connection with realization of the overmind was also, as it were, to clear the way "from below upward" for the inraying descent of supermind. He therefore also speaks of "supramental yoga," although we should not forget that he expressly emphasizes, for instance in *The Synthesis of Yoga*, that the form of yoga he represents, unlike tantric yoga, starts consciously from the mental realm:

> Our synthesis takes man as a spirit in mind much more than a spirit in body and assumes in him the capacity to begin on that level, to spiritualize his being by the power of the soul in mind opening itself directly to a higher spiritual force and being.... For that reason our initial stress has fallen upon the utilisation of the powers of soul in mind...[511]

The ascending path to supermind—as precondition for its descent—therefore logically passes through the stages of the higher mind, the enlightened mind, the intuitive mind, and the overmind, to which then the cosmic and universal consciousness of the higher self, the *jiva*, becomes available. Here, finally—through engagement with the supermind—what is called the light mind can form, capable of living in supramental truth-consciousness and manifesting it individually as direct knowledge.[512] In this context we can understand why Sri Aurobindo refers to supermind simply by the Sanskrit term *Vijnana* and—translated into Greek—as *gnosis*. Gnostic, or supramental truth-consciousness, is thus synonymous concepts. But ascending through the various higher levels of the mental realm will, as previously stated, never lead on its own to the goal of his yoga:

> All human Yoga is done on the heights or levels of the mental nature; for man is a mental being in a living body. But mind if it is able to reflect some light of the divine Truth or even admit some emanations from her power, is incapable of embodying her. There is an eternal dynamic Truth-consciousness beyond mind; this is what we call supermind or gnosis. For mind is or can be a truth seeker, but not truth-conscious in its inherent nature; its original stuff is made not of knowledge, but of ignorance.[513]

The "original stuff" can of course only refer to a secondary condition—following separation of the human being from the fullness of the divine which precedes all life and existence. From this, notwithstanding, arises the following perspective which includes the question of nature's transformation:

> The supramental Yoga is at once an ascent of the soul toward God and a descent of the Godhead into the embodied nature. The ascent demands a one-centerd all-gathering aspiration of soul and mind and life and body upward, the descent a call of the whole being toward the infinite and eternal Divine. If this call and this aspiration are there, and if they grow constantly and seize all the nature, then and then only its supramental transformation becomes possible.[514]

However:

> In the end it will be found that this Yoga cannot be carried through to its end by any effort of mind, life and body, any human psychological or physical process but only by the action of the supreme Shakti. But her way is at once too mysteriously direct and outwardly intricate, too great, and too complete and subtle to be followed comprehensively, much more to be cut out and defined into a formula by our human intelligence.
>
> Man cannot by his own effort make himself more than man, but he can call down the divine Truth and its power to work in him. A descent of the Divine Nature can alone divinize the human receptacle. Self-surrender to a supreme transmuting Power is the key word of the Yoga.
>
> This divinisation of the nature of which we speak is a metamorphosis, not a mere growth into some kind of superhumanity, but a change from the falsehood of our ignorant nature into the truth of God-nature.[515]

Sri Aurobindo's comments on realization of the supermind are almost invariably concerned, either explicitly or implicitly, with the key place of human beings and their "surrender." Supermind will manifest on Earth only through human beings. If it seems that Sri Aurobindo gives less consideration to the natural world around us, nevertheless he is fully and clearly aware of it, as can be seen in the last passage. And accordingly he speaks at various places of how all nature, including the non-human world, awaits supramental transformation. For this reason he says of the highest goal of Integral Yoga that it is concerned "not to give up but to transform all world-nature and world-existence into a power of the Truth of the Divine Existence."[516]

What Rudolf Steiner expounds on the reappearance of Christ in the etheric likewise has great relevance for the realms of nature, even though, precisely like Integral Yoga, Anthroposophy unquestioningly places the human being in an all-important key role for future levels of evolution. We will return to this theme below.

The mind of light we have referred to seems to have been a late discovery by Sri Aurobindo—something which, like nothing else, can accomplish the mediation between upward-oriented efforts of the sadhaka and the downward-tending influx of the supermind seeking to manifest on Earth. The mind of light stands in a mysterious connection with the hidden capacity also of unconscious levels of matter to manifest supermind, and with the supermind itself, the Vijnana, the gnosis. Here it becomes apparent that the original divine substance slumbers in all levels of existence, and can be awoken through the descent of the supermind's truth-consciousness. Thus we can also assume a connection between the mind of light—in its diverse aspects—and the realms of nature for which, as indicated, the descent of supermind will have no less significance than for humanity on its evolutionary path. In his late essay on *The Supramental Manifestation,* Sri Aurobindo writes:

> Even this material world of existence is built upon a pattern of the truth in things that we call Law of Nature, a truth from which we climb to a greater truth until we emerge in the Light of the Supreme. This world is not really created by a blind force of Nature: even in the Inconscient the presence of the supreme Truth is at work; there is a seeing Power behind it which acts infallibly...; for what we call the Ignorance is a cloaked Knowledge, a Knowledge at work in a body not its own but moving toward its own supreme self-discovery. This Knowledge is the covert Supermind that is the support of the creation and is leading all toward itself and guides behind this multitude of minds and creatures and objects....[517]

As we saw earlier, Sri Aurobindo distinguishes an upper and lower hemisphere within the diverse worlds of the whole cosmos: the three lower worlds—up to the sphere of the "golden lid" which is to be seen as one with the pure Akasha; and then the worlds of the supramental gnosis, of the *sachchidananda* and of the absolute.[518] The mind of light still belongs to the lower hemisphere, but is fully connected with the upper. It originates in higher spheres and at the same time points to a mysterious latency within the unconscious and material levels. It is therefore of the greatest importance for the sadhana of Integral Yoga and the transformation of all human nature, which is its aim:

> The secret truth that emerges in Supermind has been there all the time, but now it manifests itself and the truth in things and the meaning of our existence. It is in this series of the order of existence and as the last word of the lower hemisphere of being, the first word of the higher hemisphere that we have to look at the Mind of Light and see what is its nature and the powers which characterise it and which it uses for its self-manifestation and workings, its connection with Supermind and its consequences and possibilities for the life of a new humanity.[519]

Mirra Alfassa's later work of penetrating down to the deeply unconscious realm of cellular life in the physical body can no doubt best be understood from these words by Sri Aurobindo, even if they only hint in this direction.

That the realms of nature participate in the fundamental occurrence of Christ's reappearance in the etheric, as Rudolf Steiner describes it for the primarily Western context, can turn our attention back to the earliest references to this return as already presented in the New Testament: it figures there in the language of striking elemental phenomena. In the Acts of the Apostles, following the account of the Ascension when, rising upon a cloud, Christ Jesus vanishes from the view of his disciples, two men dressed in white unexpectedly step forward and speak to those left behind (Acts 1:11):

> Ye men of Galilee, why stand ye gazing up into heaven? This same Jesus, which is taken up from you into heaven, shall so come in like manner as ye have seen him go into heaven.

In the *Revelation of Saint John*, therefore, it is said: "Behold, he cometh with clouds" (Rev. 1:17). Lightning is another image for the return of Christ. During his words about the end-time, he gives the disciples the earnest caution that, when the time comes, they should not lightly believe those who falsely proclaim his coming, saying, for instance, that he will be found in the desert. Quite at odds with this, Jesus says: "For as the lightning cometh out of the East, and shineth even unto the West; so shall also the coming of the Son of man be" (Matt. 24:27). In each instance, the reappearance of Christ is presented to the reader of the Holy Scriptures in connection with atmospheric phenomena. As we will see below, Rudolf Steiner takes this up in its full significance.

Just as, in Integral Yoga, an ascending movement toward supermind creates the conditions for its descent, so in the spiritual-scientific outlook of Rudolf Steiner, perception of the Christ who reappears in the etheric is preceded by characteristic changes in the nature of the human being. These lead, more or less like a natural law, to the new capacity of perception we spoke of earlier for the etheric realm—the "new clairvoyance." Rudolf Steiner—and this may seem surprising—sees these same changes as rooted in developments predominating since the Renaissance that have endowed us with capacities of intellectual thought. Such thinking, he says, calls forth within us a greater independence, and at the same time a permanent loosening of our life body, our etheric forces.

> Whereas on the one hand, the intellectual element grows stronger, on the other hand the etheric body becomes so much more independent that people will necessarily notice this. For a while after the Christ event, people did not yet think so intellectually as they do today. This thinking with the intellect leads to the

> etheric body becoming ever more autonomous, and also to it being used as an independent instrument. And in the process we can observe that it has passed through a secret development that makes it possible for us to perceive Christ in the etheric body. Just as Christ was seen physically back then, people will now be able to perceive him etherically. And thus, in this twentieth century, a capacity to perceive Christ, as Paul perceived him, will arise like a natural event. A number of people will become able to perceive Christ in the etheric.[520]

We must emphasize here that the etheric only represents the medium whereby the reappearing Christ can be experienced: in human beings it is the element that facilitates higher perception as the physical senses facilitate physical perception. For the Christ Jesus it is the carrier or substrate in which he clothes himself so as to be able to appear to humankind in their "new clairvoyance." He himself however is of incomparably higher nature. Rudolf Steiner distinguishes this natural evolution toward a higher capacity of perception from all knowledge that schooled clairvoyants can acquire. The latter were already able to find the Christ previously, albeit not in the manner in which he seeks to appear to human beings from the early twentieth century.

> It has always been possible to perceive the Christ clairvoyantly. But to encounter him because he now has a different relationship with humankind, in that he helps us from the etheric world, is a reality—outside us—that is independent of our development as a seer. From the twentieth century onward, and over the next three millennia, certain people will be able to meet him, meet him objectively as etheric figure.[521]

The new way in which Christ appears seems to lie in the gesture of repeatedly offering help and succor to individuals. At the same time, in the wake of the new etheric clairvoyance and the appearance of Christ Jesus in the etheric, our relationship with the surrounding world also profoundly alters. We begin to perceive the etheric world itself,[522] and thus also the beings who inhabit it.

However, these are not the only ones the human being encounters since, due to Christ arriving in the etheric realm, a new species of etheric being or "elemental being" arises. In relation to the Kali Yuga that has passed, and in a mysterious intimation of a new influx of the East into the Western world, Rudolf Steiner therefore speaks once more of an important new relationship of the human being to the natural world:

> And we have moved on into a year that is of great importance: 1899. The turn of the twentieth century is important for all cultural development due to the development working its way from Eastern into Western culture, mingling with it, enabling what can be drawn from natural life to dawn as something enlivening for our deepest life of soul. Those whose spirit is awoken will be able to perceive new entities within natural processes. Whereas someone who has not yet become clairvoyant will, despite all melancholy at the inexorable course of natural decline, increasingly experience something refreshing in nature, those whose clairvoyant powers awaken will see new elemental beings emerging from dying nature. While there will be relatively little to see in the coarser physical world of the great turnaround at the beginning of the twentieth century, the spiritually opened soul will feel that times are changing, and that we human beings have the duty to prepare spirit knowledge. It will become increasingly important to observe such things and to bear them in mind.[523]

These occurrences will also mean that the human being develops a new temporal relationship to the natural processes around him:

> Around the turn of the twentieth century, a new realm of natural beings will as it were be born, emerging from nature as a spiritual wellspring so that human beings perceive and experience them. Then there is something more. A human soul, of course, would be dull indeed if he could not recognize the resurgence of life in spring; but there is something else. Those who will become able to experience as a reality of nature what has just been described will retain such impressions in a way

> quite different from the ordinary workings of memory. In the same way that seeds survive through winter into the spring, such people will carry over into a different existence what flows toward them as new elemental spirits. Experiences they had in spring and fall in the past were separate from each other: this resurgence of nature in spring and this melancholy in the fall. What the cosmos now offers us of its memory means that we bear some of what we experience in the fall into the springtime. If we let the elemental forces of the fall work within us, then we can feel in a new way what will be given us in the future. In future everything will undergo renewal, and it is our duty to prepare our understanding of this through spiritual perception.[524]

And Rudolf Steiner stresses that those who experience all this—including "karmic clairvoyance" in relation to something specific one is in the process of accomplishing, as intimated earlier—will also gain vision of the Christ as etheric form. They will perceive "the one who will only intervene in the world's events from the etheric realm."[525] That the realms of nature are included in the new occurrence offers a prospect that ultimately not only a new perception of nature but also a new knowledge of it will develop as a "chemistry, a botany, and so forth that are pervaded by the Christ impulse."[526] And: "This is not founded on the unreality of molecules; everything present in nature comes from the spirit."[527]

As early as the spring of 1910, Rudolf Steiner had placed the reappearance of Christ in the etheric in a wider Eastern context—one we have not so far mentioned in this chapter but which it may be now easier to understand in the light of the last-quoted passage from late 1911. This concerns the connection of the new occurrence in the etheric with the spiritual reality that Eastern spirituality calls *Shambhala*. Steiner shows that the "mysterious land," Shambhala, had withdrawn from ordinary human vision during the Kali Yuga, although esoteric initiates were always able to find it. And again, as above, he speaks of the spiritual wellspring that issues from this reality of Shambhala.

> The original wellspring accessed by the clairvoyant gaze withdrew during Kali Yuga; it is described as a fairy-tale land that will return once more to the human realm. Shambhala will come into being again after the end of Kali Yuga. By normal human capacities humanity will once more grow into the land of Shambhala, from which initiates must draw their strength and wisdom for their mission. Shambhala exists, Shambhala once existed, and Shambhala will exist again for humanity. And Christ in his etheric form will be one of the first things that become apparent to human vision when Shambhala reveals itself again. There is no other guide for humanity to the land oriental writings tell us has vanished than the Christ. The Christ will lead human beings to Shambhala.[528]

All this is significant above all because it discloses the initially subterranean connection existing between the Eastern and Western mode of experiencing the "greatest mystery of our age." We encounter the spiritual reality of Shambhala primarily in the Buddhist context, but also, as we saw earlier, in the Sanatana Dharma—and there in intimate relationship with none other than the future, tenth Avatar, the Kalki Avatar. But it is he who advances the mission of Shri Krishna and thus—after all we have elaborated—stands in the greatest proximity to the Christ mystery.[529]

The etheric in which Christ Jesus appears is a new element in cosmic-terrestrial reality. It had been unfolding on the Earth since, nearly two millennia ago, the Son of God and Son of Man shed his blood on the Cross at Golgotha at his sacrificial death. This divine-human blood, says Rudolf Steiner, has been in ongoing transformation since that death, passing over into the condition of an entirely new etheric quality. In connection with the loosening of the human etheric body, mentioned earlier, through recent centuries a comparable "etherization of the blood" has increasingly occurred within individuals. In the corresponding lecture given to members of the Theosophical Society, Steiner says that this etherized blood rises in us from the heart to the head, and in its individual quality mediates efforts made in waking life to overcome our own ego nature. In the state of sleep at night, Steiner continues, in-streaming light qualities from without, from the macrocosm, connect with the etherized blood that has risen to the head. However, these macrocosmic qualities are of varying goodness, depending on the kind of efforts a person made while awake during the day. And then something else also depends on the quality of one's etherized blood; through true efforts in the domain of morality and knowledge it becomes possible for the terrestrial–cosmic stream of the etherized blood of Christ Jesus, rising from the Earth and permeating the Earth's atmosphere evermore strongly, to unite with the individual light stream of the etherized blood rising from the heart to the head. Indeed, Rudolf Steiner speaks of this ether atmosphere originating from the sacrificial blood of Jesus Christ as a "moral ether atmosphere"; he says that its forces—in contrast to all destructive powers continually increasing in the world—are "composing, cohering, positive forces." This condition, in which Christ Jesus arises and appears anew within an ever-growing "moral ether atmosphere," is something, he says, that the ancient Oriental mystics had already awaited and expected:

> Then a time will come over the Earth—which as so much else really is comprehended only in the grandeur of Oriental occultism, Oriental mysticism—when this moral atmosphere will have grown to a high degree. Oriental mysticism has been speaking of this moment for many millennia. And especially since the time of Buddha, it has spoken of the time when the Earth will be immersed in a moral ether atmosphere. And like a great future hope, Oriental mysticism since the days of the ancient Rishis envisaged a time when this impulse would come to the Earth and be intrinsic to the being of Vishva-Karman or, as Zarathustra said, of Ahura Mazda. This ancient mysticism already saw that this moral impulse, this moral Earth atmosphere would issue and emanate from the being whom we call Christ; and this Oriental mysticism set its hopes upon him, upon the Christ. The means available to Oriental mysticism

> were not adequate to picture this as such but these mystics could envisage what would come in consequence of it. They could perceive how pure Akasha figures immersed in the fire, the light of the Sun, would come within five millennia after the great Buddha's enlightenment as the consequence of something that Eastern mysticism alone could not discern. A wonderful thought indeed: something will come that, cleansing the moral atmosphere of the Earth, will make it possible for the sons of light and fire to dwell within the moral atmosphere of the Earth as pure Akasha figures rather than physically incarnated forms.[530]

It subsequently becomes clear that the "pure Akasha figures," the "sons of light and fire" are the "Agnishvattas" who, according to the *Vishnu Purana*, are the pre-earthly ancestors of the human race.[531] When Rudolf Steiner emphasizes, as here, that "Eastern mysticism alone" could not penetrate to full discernment of what, in its magnificent prophecy, it awaited as "intrinsic to the being of Vishva-Karman," this signifies in the context roughly that the pre-Christian, Indian sources could not yet comprehend the Christ mystery in the light in which it appeared through Christ Jesus' time on Earth: in the light of the Passion, Crucifixion, and Resurrection. At the same time, however, Steiner's accounts are full of reverent acknowledgement of that pre-Christian wisdom.

In relation to the whole of Anthroposophy, Rudolf Steiner never tires of saying that the "Mystery of Golgotha" encompasses a unique and all-decisive impulse for the Earth's future evolution. Yet in the major years of his Christological teachings, he also presents the workings of the Christ spirit as a recurring process, speaking for instance of "preparatory stages of the Mystery of Golgotha"[532] involving three stages in the Christ spirit's approach toward the Earth, and also prophetically describing future manifestations that are to follow the reappearance in the etheric.[533] Rudolf Steiner also regards the ongoing activity of the Christ spirit as the consequence of these rhythmic approaches, the most important of which is of course the one that stands at the central moment of Golgotha.

In connection with these reflections, we will reproduce below words of Sri Aurobindo from his epic *Savitri,* which concern the Mystery of Golgotha and endow it with the greatest conceivable gravity. In the context of Sri Aurobindo's collected works, we should remember also that elsewhere he characterizes Christ Jesus as one of the ranks of the Avatars, for instance speaking of "Christ, Krishna, Buddha" in one breath as it were.[534] No doubt, then, we find divergent perspectives. And Rudolf Steiner also has some severe words for Eastern spirituality: "For Eastern initiations inevitably fail to consider the *Christ principle* as central cosmic factor in evolution."[535] Just seven years later, by contrast, in a lecture in which Steiner refers to the removal of the Grail to the East, to the "three Indias" of Prester John, he speaks in far milder tones in response to a question connected with the above-mentioned pre-earthly preparatory stages of the Mystery of Golgotha:

> Ought we to expect, in accord with the old phrase *Ex oriente lux,* that, in contrast to what people think nowadays, the Christ forces still working unconsciously will complement in altered form what today has appeared as the light in the West? Should the light be able to unite with light? But for this to happen we will need to be prepared—we, whose karma has placed us upon the terrain of those geographical and cultural streams over which Christ passed as soon as his spirit had permeated Jesus of Nazareth in super-earthly regions, and was passing on toward the Orient. We can gaze upward and sense that Christ passed over us in the heights already in his pre-earthly manifestations. Let us render ourselves capable of understanding him, not failing to understand what he may perhaps be able to tell us when the time arrives: that other confessions of the Earth will be imbued by his impulses![536]

After many long years, the author of this book has come to see this as a task, to feel it as a burning impulse in the soul: in accordance with Rudolf Steiner's words above to be "prepared," and to render ourselves "capable" so that we do not "fail to understand" the new manifestations—a new utterance of Christ in a language to which we have not previously been accustomed; a new Christ light, though not, let us emphasize, a reflection of the light from the pre-Christian period; a new light which, coming from the East, seeks to unite itself with the light here in the West. The author regards this, still today, as the greatest imperative for the kind of dialogue between Veda and living Logos that this present work can perhaps help stimulate. In the long term, or even the medium term, the perspective of synthesis (as here, between Anthroposophy and Integral Yoga) may prove more vigorous—in relation, say, to the origins of human culture in ancient India, the creative Word and its emergence in East and West, in relation to a thinking that encompasses spiritual evolution and the true nature of the human "I," and in relation, finally, to the divine—than the old, well-worn and merely analytic determinism; and prove itself to be a more fruitful approach.

Sri Aurobindo's words about the descent of supermind do not point to a recapitulation of ancient, pre-Christian wisdom. Rather, he sees Integral Yoga in its totality as the expression of an evolutionary unfolding of humanity and spiritual history, which is of the greatest significance for people at their present stage of evolution. Sri Aurobindo's life companion Mirra Alfassa once remarked on his epic drama *Savitri* and on Sri Aurobindo himself, "*Savitri* is his whole Yoga of transformation, and this Yoga now comes for the first time to the earth consciousness."[537] And indeed, in this mighty epic we find perspectives that are also intimated in Sri Aurobindo's great elaborations of his yogic philosophy. There are communications about Christ Jesus in which, astonishingly, he refers to words from 1912 that we cited in the introduction to this section, "The Divine—the Second Coming of Christ and the Descent of Supermind": "It is not personal ananda, but the bringing down of the divine ananda—Christ's kingdom of heaven, our Satya Yuga—upon the Earth."[538]

The *Savitri* epic comprises around 24,000 lines of blank verse and is a unique accomplishment in India's English-language literature. Sri Aurobindo repeatedly revised it, a process that, after the initial composition, continued above all through the 1930s and 1940s. The poem refers to a legend in the Mahabharata, a great metaphor of married love triumphing over death: Savitri, the king's daughter, marries the prince of her choice, Satyavan, knowing that the gods have granted them only twelve months of shared happiness on the Earth. After this time expires, Satyavan must die. But Savitri is not willing to allow this to happen; and so, when the day of Satyavan's death arrives, a great and terrible battle begins with the god of death Yama to gain immortality for her beloved. Sri Aurobindo's epic demonstrates how this battle becomes an all-embracing initiation that will lead them to the furthest boundaries of the universe and to a vision of the highest divinity. When Savitri's mother first gets wind of the dire fate hanging over the pair and their marriage, she turns to the Rishi Narad who prophesies the death of Satyavan. And at her despairing insistence, Narad explains to the grieving mother why pain, suffering, and evil exist in the world, and why even a world savior must engage with the deepest core of suffering and death. Of the Redeemer, Narad then says:

> The Great who came to save this suffering world
> And rescue out of Time's shadow and the Law,
> Must pass beneath the yoke of grief and pain; . . .
> On their shoulders they must bear man's load of fate.
> Heaven's riches they bring, their sufferings count the price
> Or they pay the gift of knowledge with their lives.
> The Son of God born as the Son of man
> Has drunk the bitter cup, owned Godhead's debt,
> The debt the Eternal owes to the fallen kind
> His will has bound to death and struggling life
> That yearns in vain for rest and endless peace.

Now is the debt paid, wiped off the original score.
The Eternal suffers in a human form,
He has signed salvation's testament with his blood:
He has opened the doors of his undying peace.[539]

And:

It is finished, the dread mysterious sacrifice,
Offered by God's martyred body for the world;
Gethsemane and Calvary are his lot,
He carries the cross on which man's soul is nailed;...
He has trod with bleeding brow the Saviour's way.[540]

But later, in regard to the ongoing work of the "world-redeemer," Sri Aurobindo writes:

Hard is the world-redeemer's heavy task;
The world itself becomes his adversary,
Those he would save are his antagonists:
This world is in love with its own ignorance,
Its darkness turns away from the saviour light,
It gives the cross in payment for the crown....
A few are saved, the rest strive on and fail:
A Sun has passed, on Earth Night's shadow falls.
Yes, there are happy ways near to God's sun;
But few are they who tread the sunlit path;
Only the pure in soul can walk in light.[541]

In the subsequent passage, the redeemer again appears—and now perhaps as the tenth in the series of Avatars, the Avatar of supermind whose descent is hinted at in the words about a "truth-conscious world." We should recall that Sri Aurobindo often referred to supermind as the "truth-consciousness" of the upper hemisphere. In relation to the question of the interconnection that the Indian spiritual teacher sees among the Avatar, supermind, and Christ, let us recall that Sri Aurobindo strikingly identified the Logos, the creative universal Word, with the supermind as the living "inevitable word of the Truth of things."[542]

He [the world-redeemer] must enter the eternity of Night
And know God's darkness as he knows his Sun.
For this he must go down into the pit,
For this he must invade the dolorous Vasts.
Imperishable and wise and infinite,
He still must travel Hell the world to save.
Into the eternal Light he shall emerge
On borders of the meeting of all worlds;
There on the verge of Nature's summit steps
The secret Law of each thing is fulfilled,
All contraries heal their long dissidence.
There meet and clasp the eternal opposites,
There pain becomes a violent fiery joy;
Evil turns back to its original good,
And sorrow lies upon the breasts of Bliss:
She has learned to weep glad tears of happiness;
Her gaze is charged with a wistful ecstasy.
Then shall be ended here the Law of Pain.
Earth shall be made a home of Heaven's light,
A seer heaven-born shall lodge in human breasts;
The superconscient beam shall touch men's eyes
And the truth-conscious world come down to Earth
Invading Matter with the Spirit's ray,
Awaking its silence to immortal thoughts,
Awaking the dumb heart to the living Word.
This mortal life shall house Eternity's bliss,
The body's self taste immortality.
Then shall the world-redeemer's task be done.[543]

A reader familiar with the Revelation of Saint John may be vividly reminded by these words of the final cosmic scenes in that book.[544] This is surely not accidental. The reflections offered here on *Veda and Living Logos* thus come to a fitting conclusion, and do so in the future-oriented hope that our study will encourage people in both schools to go on exploring the parallels between Anthroposophy and Integral Yoga and to cultivate dialogue between them. It is left to future studies and encounters to extend the breadth, depth, and heights of these initial attempts.

And I saw a new heaven and a new Earth: for the first heaven and the first Earth were passed away; and there was no more sea. And I John saw the holy city, New Jerusalem, coming down from God out of heaven, prepared as a bride adorned for her husband. And I heard a great voice out of heaven saying, Behold, the tabernacle of God is with men, and he will dwell with them, and they shall be his people, and God himself shall be with them, and be their God. And God shall wipe away all tears from their eyes; and there shall be no more death, neither sorrow nor crying, neither shall there be any more pain: for the former things are passed away. (Rev. 21:1–5)

Appendix 1: Guru—a Modern View of an Ancient Concept

In Western spirituality and esotericism, especially in Rudolf Steiner's Anthroposophy, the figure of Christian Rosenkreutz is of outstanding importance. One of the two great masters of wisdom who inspire Western spiritual development in our era, he is an individuality at a very high level of self-realization who has worked on Earth in several incarnations since the late Middle Ages. In the past, in a way similar to Eastern mahatmas who inspired the theosophical movement, he was at risk of being heralded too eagerly as a miracle worker and healer. Measures to avoid this were taken by ensuring that only the very closest circle of his initiated pupils knew the identity of Christian Rosenkreutz, both during each lifetime and for a hundred years afterward. To all other contemporaries he appeared only as someone living, in most cases, an outwardly very ordinary life.

If he had met with mass acclaim, this would have signified only an immense pain, a real martyrdom for him. Rudolf Steiner speaks of this as follows:

> Now it is also very important to know that in every century Rosicrucian Inspiration is given without its bearer and instigator becoming publicly known. Only the highest initiates knew this. Today, for instance, we can only speak of matters of this kind that occurred a century ago, for that is the period that must elapse before they can be spoken of in public. There

> would otherwise be too great a temptation for people to give fanatic obeisance to such personally tinged authority—which is the worst thing imaginable. It is all too likely that this would happen. But this secrecy is not just necessary in regard to outward appeals to ambition and pride, which one might be able to fend off, but also above all against occult astral attacks to which such an individuality would continually be exposed. It is therefore necessary to preserve this condition according to which such a fact can only be spoken of after a century.[545]

This is why—although actively working—the master of wisdom Christian Rosenkreutz, one of whose best-known incarnations was the Count of Saint Germain (1696–1784), is not discernible to the seeker. Yet this should never stand in the way of true devotion. Rudolf Steiner speaks, rather, of "the right devotion to Christian Rosenkreutz."[546] Be that as it may, it is still incumbent on a pupil of higher knowledge to learn to travel new and more autonomous paths. Accordingly, the relationship of a pupil to his esoteric teacher changed in the Western Christian world in the late Middle Ages. As instance of this, Rudolf Steiner names Master Eckhardt (ca. 1260–1328) who developed his mysticism without ever being outwardly dependent on a spiritual teacher, a guru.

> A wholesome nature such as that of Master Eckhardt—like almost all the Christian mystics of the Middle Ages, who had no...guru—was protected by imbuing himself with a sense of no longer being himself, of having changed; and now being someone who no longer speaks, feels or wills as he did, but who allows himself to be entirely filled with Christ. He made the Pauline phrase—Not I but Christ in me—a reality. And this transformed him; in a sense he relinquished himself. He gave up his "I" and let himself be filled by another "I." To "unbecome," as the opposite of "to become," was a fine ideal of medieval Christian mystics. Rather than seeking to "become" an autonomous ego, these mystics sought to "unbecome," or in other words to relinquish their "I" entirely and to fill themselves with a different "I." This was how they countered the self-seeking claims of the "I," a means employed by mystics

> such as Master Eckhardt, or the mystic and author of the "Theologia Teutsch"; they sought not to speak out of themselves, but instead to give utterance to a higher man, a person within who can inwardly enliven and inspire us. This is why these mystics kept reiterating that they wished to devote themselves entirely to what they experienced within. Thus, as the new era approached, we see how the Christian mystics of the Middle Ages, already finding their way into the era of modern humanity, replaced an outer guru figure with an inner guru, with Christ.[547]

While Sri Aurobindo does not refer to Christ in this context but to the *jagad-guru* ("universal guru"), nevertheless he accords him a similar standing, thus demonstrating that he was by no means simply passing on traditional concepts but pursuing an ideal fitting for the modern era. He speaks of the possibility of securing as teacher and friend the Ishvara, thus the Lord, the Purushottama of the *Bhagavad Gita*. During his time in Alipur Prison (1908/1909) this is exactly what occurred for him. And later, too, certainly before 1920, this teacher–pupil relationship seems to have served as an example for the sadhana of those with whom he created the original yoga community in Pondicherry. Clearly, though, Sri Aurobindo subsequently came to the view that such realizations would only be possible for a very few sadhakas, and that he would therefore probably need to accept the role of outward teacher. Thus in Sri Aurobindo's *Synthesis of Yoga*, after showing how all teaching is a revealing of what already lies hidden in the soul of the learner, he writes:

> The usual agency of this revealing is the Word, the thing heard (*shruta*). The Word may come to us from within; it may come to us from without. But in either case, it is only an agency for setting the hidden knowledge to work. The word within may be the utterance of the inmost soul in us which is always open to the Divine; or it may be the word of the secret and universal Teacher who is seated in the hearts of all. There are rare cases in which none other is needed, for all the rest of the Yoga is an

> unfolding under that constant touch and guidance; the lotus of the knowledge discloses itself from within by the power of irradiating effulgence which proceeds from the Dweller in the lotus of the heart. Great indeed, but few are those to whom self-knowledge from within is thus sufficient and who do not need to pass under the dominant influence of a written book or a living teacher.[548]

Along with dedication to the highest divine nature, Integral Yoga is founded on the energetic work and individual intelligence of the sadhaka, with the aim of gradually spiritualizing this intelligence. It is for this reason that Jnana Yoga, the yoga of integral knowledge, is one of the three chief roots of the new Purna Yoga—or Integral Yoga. And this is also why Sri Aurobindo is firm in advising against awakening the lotus organs of higher development from below upward, as usual in traditional forms of yoga. He emphasizes that his new yoga starts from consciousness, and that the sadhana, if giving special attention to the chakras, should awaken them in descending order from above. This suggests the need for consistent, self-responsible effort in the course of which the "lotus of knowledge" with its seat in the heart, is awoken from above, and opens so that the inner guru becomes audible. Near the end of his life, in the fully revised version of Part I of *Synthesis of Yoga*, "The Yoga of Divine Works," which he published in book form in 1948, Sri Aurobindo writes in full accord with his original view of the inner guru as having priority and precedence over any outward teacher. The highest knowledge, the supreme shastra, or the loftiest teachings of Integral Yoga, he says, are "the eternal Veda secret in the heart of every thinking and living being." Ultimately this accords completely with what he says of the "supreme teacher":

> As the supreme Shastra of the integral Yoga is the eternal Veda secret in the heart of every man, so its supreme Guide and Teacher is the inner Guide, the World-Teacher, *jagad-guru*,

secret within us. It is he who destroys our darkness by the resplendent light of his knowledge; that light becomes within us the increasing glory of his own self-revelation. He discloses progressively in us his own nature of freedom, bliss, love, power, immortal being. He sets above us his divine example as our ideal and transforms the lower existence into a reflection of that which it contemplates.[549, 550]

Appendix 2: Mirra Alfassa, the "Mother," and the Beginnings of Auroville

In chapter 2 of this book we presented some salient aspects of Mirra Alfassa's biography. Besides what connects her with Sri Aurobindo, this also includes, not least, her important encounter with the "unknown occultist" Aia Aziz, also known as Max Théon. To illumine the relationship between these two exponents of a specifically European spirituality would be of great interest particularly in the context of anthroposophic Spiritual Science,[551] but exceeds the scope of the present book. By contrast, the later work of the founder of the Sri Aurobindo Ashram, following Sri Aurobindo's death, is an intrinsic part of these reflections, as is the ongoing influence connected with her other great work of founding Auroville.

After Sri Aurobindo died on December 5, 1950 (in all likelihood as a result of kidney failure), he lay in state for four days, something very unusual in southern India's hot, moist, subtropical climate, but possible in this case because the body did not decompose at all. Usually the deceased are cremated in India the day after death. During those days, around 60,000 people paid their final respects to Sri Aurobindo before the funeral on December 9, at nearly 5 p.m. in the inner court of the main building of the ashram—today's "Samadhi." Mirra Alfassa later reported that immediately after Sri Aurobindo's death she had an unmistakable experience of his powerful spiritual presence. And on the third day, December 7, she wrote:

> ...this morning Thou hast given me the assurance that Thou wouldst stay with us until Thy work is achieved, not only as a consciousness which guides and illumines but also as a dynamic Presence in action. In unmistakable terms Thou hast promised that all of Thyself would remain here and not leave the Earth atmosphere until Earth is transformed.[552]

On December 9 (and here, possibly because of the supramental transformation, there is a sense that Sri Aurobindo has literally been able to overcome death), she wrote in similar tone: "The lack of receptivity of the earth and men is mostly responsible for the decision Sri Aurobindo has taken regarding his body. But one thing is certain: what has happened on the physical plane affects in no way the truth of his teaching. All that he has said is perfectly true and remains so. Time and the course of events will prove it abundantly."[553]

It is said that for the rest of her life Mirra Alfassa maintained her hope in the possibility of vanquishing the seed of death strewn through the cells of the human body. As she sometimes expressed it, Sri Aurobindo had clearly entrusted her with realization of this task.

The descent of supermind "for earth consciousness" was not only thought to affect individual sadhakas in their inmost core but fundamentally transform the whole of earthly reality, including the forms of human social community. Mirra Alfassa now pursued this vision consistently, until the point when she founded the "city of the future," Auroville, in 1968. February 29, 1956 marked an important milestone toward its establishment. On this date, during the Wednesday evening meditation normal at the ashram, a spiritual event occurred that Mirra soon afterward formulated for those present in the following words:

> This evening the Divine Presence, concrete and material, was there present among you. I had a form of living gold, bigger than the universe, and I was facing a huge and massive golden door that separated the world from the Divine. As I looked at the door, I knew and willed, in a single movement of consciousness, that "*the time has come*", and lifting with both hands a mighty golden hammer I struck one blow, one single blow on the door and the door was shattered to pieces. Then the supramental Light and Force and Consciousness rushed down upon Earth in an uninterrupted flow.[554]

To access supramental light, strength, and consciousness in its descent "for earth consciousness" was something that people in the ashram had been working toward in a valuable preparatory way for many years. But a still more open and cosmopolitan manner of working had become necessary. The humanity of the twentieth century as a whole was to be addressed and engaged: Integral Yoga was to publicly demonstrate its transformative potential for all society. This motive was something apparent not least in comments by Sri Aurobindo in his collection of essays *The Ideal of Human Unity*, which he completed and published in book form in 1950, the last year of his life. In its penultimate chapter, "The Religion of Humanity," he once again considers the ideals of the French Revolution—freedom, equality, fraternity. And he writes that, since the eighteenth century, these ideals have been realized only in isolation from each other, and also only in entirely external approaches. According to Sri Aurobindo,[555] the reciprocal interplay of freedom and equality will only succeed if it begins from a fraternity that emerges when the dominance of the ego over the individual is replaced by the unfolding of the true soul in the human being.[556]

While Sri Aurobindo was still alive, probably around 1940, Mirra Alfassa had a vision of a future city—not necessarily in the vicinity of Pondichery, but perhaps in the region of the southern Indian city Hyderabad. In retrospect, she said, "For a long time, I'd had a plan for the 'ideal city,' but that was during Sri Aurobindo's lifetime, with Sri Aurobindo living at its center. Afterward...I was no longer interested."[557] Decades later she concretized her vision in a text that became known as "A Dream":

> There should be somewhere on Earth a place which no nation could claim as its own, where all human beings of goodwill who have a sincere aspiration could live freely as citizens of the world and obey one single authority, that of the supreme truth; a place of peace, concord and harmony where all the fighting instincts of man would be used exclusively to conquer the causes of his sufferings and miseries, to surmount his weaknesses and ignorance, to triumph over his limitations and incapacities; a place where the needs of the spirit and the concern for progress would take precedence over the satisfaction of desires and passions, the search for pleasure and material enjoyment. In this place, children would be able to grow and develop integrally without losing contact with their souls; education would be given not for passing examinations or obtaining certificates and posts but to enrich existing faculties and bring forth new ones. In this place, titles and positions would be replaced by opportunities to serve and organize; the bodily needs of each one would be equally provided for, and intellectual, moral, and spiritual superiority would be expressed in the general organization not by an increase in the pleasures and powers of life but by increased duties and responsibilities. Beauty in all its artistic forms, painting, sculpture, music, literature, would be equally accessible to all; the ability to share in the joy it brings would be limited only by the capacities of each one and not by social and financial position. For in this ideal place money would no longer be the sovereign lord; individual worth would have a far greater importance than that of material wealth and social standing. There, work would not be a way to earn one's living but a way to express oneself and to develop one's capacities and possibilities while being of service to the community as a whole, which, for its own part, would provide for each individual's subsistence and sphere of action. In short, it would be a place where human relationships, which are normally based almost exclusively on competition

and strife, would be replaced by relationships of emulation in doing well, of collaboration and real brotherhood.[558]

The "Charter" of the city of Auroville also accords with these ideals. As the city's founding document, Mirra Alfassa read it aloud on February 28, 1968, before a gathering of young people, representing twenty-three federal Indian states and 124 countries of the world, and who sealed earth from their homelands into a symbolic "urn." More than five thousand visitors were present for this occasion. The Charter states:

1. Auroville belongs to nobody in particular. Auroville belongs to humanity as a whole. But to live in Auroville one must be the willing servitor of the Divine Consciousness.
2. Auroville will be the place of an unending education, of constant progress, and a youth that never ages.
3. Auroville wants to be the bridge between the past and the future. Taking advantage of all discoveries from without and from within, Auroville will boldly spring toward future realisations.
4. Auroville will be a site of material and spiritual researches for a living embodiment of an actual human unity.[559]

From 1964 onward, Roger Anger, a Paris architect with whom Mirra Alfassa collaborated from the beginning, had been drafting the first designs for Auroville, initially to a rectangular plan. But these soon underwent rapid metamorphosis and culminated in a "Galaxy" spiral ground plan in 1967/68. But the terrain chosen for building the city is largely scorched red earth. The people of that region relate the *Irumbai* legend, according to which, many centuries ago, in one of the nearby Tamil villages, a great yogi had been mocked and disparaged. He punished the people of the region—north of today's Pondicherry—with a curse upon the land that made it entirely arid. All pleas for forgiveness proved futile. But the yogi prophesied that a time would eventually arrive when people would come from very faraway lands and make the country green again.

At the end of 1965 it was time to determine where the center of the city would lie. Roger Anger placed a map of the area in front of Mirra Alfassa and, after a period of concentration, she pointed to a point on the map which seemed of no particular significance. But when Roger Anger drove there in a jeep across the arid, pathless desert plateau, whose lack of any bushes or trees offered an open view to the Gulf of Bengal, he found one single, isolated but vigorous Banyan tree growing at the place Mirra Alfassa had indicated. The visionary was delighted when told of this, especially as Banyan trees are honored in India as divine, wish-granting trees; and she decided that this should be the center of the future city. People from faraway lands did indeed arrive, settling in the desert from 1967. In collaboration with the indigenous Tamils they planted forest—well over two million trees—and in the past fifty years have established the city of Auroville on an area covering twenty to twenty-five square kilometers. Mirra Alfassa referred to the inhabitants of the Tamil villages as "the first Aurovilians." More than 2,800 people now live there—still far short of the fifty thousand suggested in the 1960s.

Today a visitor to Auroville finds a very marked atmosphere of reverence toward Sri Aurobindo among its inhabitants, but especially also toward Mirra Alfassa, who is usually referred to simply as "the Mother." In some cases this goes so far as to identify Mirra Alfassa entirely with the divine mother. On the other hand, it should be noted in relation to Sri Aurobindo's great work of yogic philosophy, and his clear requirement that Integral Yoga must start above all from thinking, that this approach is often seen as too intellectual and altogether too strenuous. Mirra Alfassa based Auroville intentionally on the yoga of work, Karma Yoga, rather than on the yoga of knowledge. Big questions remain here, such as how far this can adequately address contemporary consciousness in a way fitting for our time.[560] The sense that all Auroville's inhabitants are "children of the Mother" ought, surely, to be complemented by energetic and conscious inner work in order to be fully contemporary. Mirra Alfassa herself left hints that she recalled three Egyptian incarnations, one of which she identified as "Queen Tiy," the mother of Amenhotep IV,[561] who later called himself Ekhnaton; and who, in the sixth year of his reign had a new city, Achet-aton (horizon of Aton) built in the desert region of Tell el-Armarna. Did the ancient Egyptian element resurface through Mirra?[562] Sri Aurobindo himself never made any references to his own former incarnations.[563]

Whatever the truth of it, Matrimandir, the "House of the Mother," was subsequently to be built in the immediate vicinity of the Banyan tree (a type of fig), in thirty-six years of building work after the foundation stone was laid in 1972. Mirra Alfassa called this place the "Soul of Auroville" and dedicated the "Inner Chamber" of the Martrimandir—a dodecagonal structure with twelve pillars—as a place of silence, deep meditation, and contemplation for the people of Auroville. It is certainly striking to see how the founder of Auroville, in just one session with her close disciple Satprem,[564] on January 3, 1970, designed this "Inner Chamber" in a single flow of images and ideas which were taken down in writing and can still be read; and that her blueprint was actually realized in the building that stands there today. At one place in this long discussion on January 3, these words appear: "Then people will be let in in order to concentrate—(*laughing*) to learn to concentrate! No fixed meditations, nothing of the sort, but they will have to stay there in silence—silence and concentration."[565]

Four huge concrete pillars that correspond to the four aspects of the divine mother[566] support the spherical shape of the Matrimandir. At the very minute the fourth of these pillars was completed in the center of Auroville on November 17, 1973, at seven twenty-five in the evening, Mirra Alfassa took her last breath in nearby Pondicherry.

Appendix 3: Johannes Hohlenberg

Translated by Shraddhavan

The author of this book knows of only one person who was a disciple of both Sri Aurobindo and Rudolf Steiner and in each case had direct personal contact with them—namely, Johannes Hohlenberg, a Danish artist, dedicated publisher and distinguished author, who was also the general secretary of the Anthroposophical Society in Denmark for eight years, from its inception in 1923 until 1931.

Johannes Hohlenberg (1881–1960) was born into the cultured family of a Copenhagen pastor. He enjoyed an early musical education at home, but as a young man he at first pursued the greater interest he felt for the arts. The study of Art led him to Paris in 1905, where he soon made the acquaintance of Mirra Alfassa (at that time Mirra Morisset) and her later husband Paul Richard. At that time, Mirra Alfassa was holding a regular salon, where artists and spiritual seekers from many different backgrounds met. Reminiscing, she once mentioned that, during his time in Paris, Johannes Hohlenberg "used to come and see me almost every evening."[567] The beginning of their acquaintance coincided with the time of Mirra Alfassa's most intense collaboration with the occultist Max Théon (alias Aia Aziz), whom she had visited twice by then (in 1906 and 1907) at his home in western Algeria, in the

Sufi-influenced city of Tlemcen, in order to get initiated into his methods and teachings.

Hohlenberg, too, must have engaged with the teachings of Théon, at least in their theoretical aspects, because Mirra Alfassa had the following to say about him: "He had read all of Théon's stuff and was well up on everything, and very earnest about it."[568] After she herself had decisive experiences of consciously leaving the body, Johannes Hohlenberg, following her return to Paris, seems to have been very eager for her to introduce him to these practices, too. She said, "He absolutely insisted.... So, I taught him how to do it, and what's more, I was there; he did it in my presence. And...the moment he went out of his body, he was thrown into such a panic! The man was no coward—he was very courageous—but it terrified him so! Sheer panic.... So I said, 'no, no, no.'"[569]

Johannes Hohlenberg's close contact with the Richards continued for about five years, until Hohlenberg traveled to Egypt to pursue his interest in the pyramids. His biographer writes, "Hohlenberg was fascinated by the mysterious and monumental architecture of the Pyramids. For six months he pursued intensive studies in Gizeh, which soon bore fruit in literary form."[570] That a strong connection must have existed not only to Richard but also to Mirra is evident from a postcard of September 21, 1911, sent from Cluses, in which Mirra enquires about his whereabouts:

> My dear Hohlenberg,
>
> Here, while awaiting a letter, is something to re-awaken in your memory our fine evenings in Paris and our long philosophical conversations.... I hope it will also evoke your enthusiasm and your hopes.... Never forget that you are always carrying them within you, and that they are waiting beneath your outer awareness for you to let them come to life outwardly, too.
>
> We send you our best thoughts, in all affection.
>
> M. P. Richard
>
> Don't be so silent. We would be happy to have news of you. We return to Paris in a few days.[571]

We may assume from this that, already in 1910, Johannes Hohlenberg must have taken an active interest in Paul Richard's reports from South India, where he had his first meeting with Sri Aurobindo. These had immediately inspired in Mirra the wish to go to Pondicherry herself as soon as possible.[572] It is also known that the Richards could not realize this plan until 1914, which then led within a few months of their arrival to the establishment of the monthly journal *The Arya,* which continued to appear for six and half years. In 1914, Johannes Hohlenberg received an invitation from the Richards to join them in Pondicherry and collaborate in editing the journal. But, "Then came the war, and therefore my departure was postponed for almost a year. I could not start until the spring of 1915."[573]

By this time, the Richards had already left India. "Nevertheless I made the journey and met Aurobindo,"[574] he wrote. His stay extended to only a little over a month, since, because of his regular contact with Sri Aurobindo, Hohlenberg soon became politically suspect and was deported back to Europe; such were the times of war. During those few weeks in Pondicherry however, he made a famous photograph of Sri Aurobindo—standing in profile—as well as sketches for an oil painting, which he would execute later in Denmark. In addition, Sri Aurobindo granted Hohlenberg daily evening interviews, which started with meditation, followed by intensive instruction in yogic philosophy.

In later years Mirra Alfassa reported Sri Aurobindo' s words about that time as follows: "A Danish painter also came and did a sketch of me. At the end of every meditation, he used to say, 'Let us now talk of the Ineffable!'"[575] After returning to his native country, Johannes Hohlenberg not only did the oil portrait,[576] but also wrote about his experiences of the yogic–philosophical evening talks with Sri Aurobindo. From these notes emerged his first literary work *Yoga I dens betydning for Europa,* which appeared simultaneously in 1916 in Copenhagen and Oslo (then Christiania). In the third edition of this book, in 1952 Hohlenberg added an informative new preface in which he emphasized the connection of the text to Sri Aurobindo, to whom he had also dedicated it. In this form the book was also eventually published in German translation in 1954:

> The preconditions for this book were created during my stay in India in 1915, in daily talks with a man to whom it is also dedicated: Sri Aurobindo Ghose. He was then about thirty years of age and already known all over India as a thinker and mystic.[577]

This book by Hohlenberg provides a revealing early insight into the contents of what Sri Aurobindo was writing during those years in the series of articles, later published as a book titled *The Synthesis of Yoga.* The subdivision of the Integral Yoga into Karma, Jnana, Bhakti, and Puma Yoga that characterizes this book also unmistakably appears in the major parts of Hohlenberg' s work. Toward the end of World War I, Johannes Hohlenberg first heard of Anthroposophy through the Copenhagen businessman Carl Vett (1871–1956), with whom he worked intensively to formulate the theory of Social Threefolding.[578]

In 1920, when he visited the first anthroposophical "High School Course" (*The Boundaries of Natural Science*[579]) in Dornach, Switzerland, he met Rudolf Steiner for the first time in person and became his disciple. When the international anthroposophic work was reorganized in 1923, and a national Anthroposophical Society was established in Denmark, Johannes Hohlenberg was elected as its first general secretary. In this capacity, he then also took part in the Christmas meeting of 1922/23 in Dornach for the establishment of the General Anthroposophical Society. As editor and publisher of the anthroposophic magazine *Vidar* (1926–1940), he revealed himself in the 1930s as a pointed critic of the lack of discrimination on the part of some officials of the Anthroposophical Society concerning the growing Nazi movement, which finally led him to resign all positions in the Society.

He concentrated entirely on his work as a publisher, from 1933 onward, of the Norwegian cultural magazine *Janus.* Impelled by his social interests, he became one of the first theorists in the anthroposophic sphere of universal basic income, two essays by him on this topic appearing in the magazine *Janus* in 1934 and 1937. Now less involved in anthroposophic work, Hohlenberg plunged into the existential philosophy of Søren Kierkegaard, on whom he published a much-acknowledged monograph in 1940.[580] Following World War II, he published a new magazine, which appeared in Copenhagen under the name *Øjeblikket* (Glimpse) from 1947 to 1954.[581] Just as he published in the last issues of *Vidar* the whole *Bhagavad Gita* serially in Danish translation, also in the final year of *Øjeblikket* he printed two essays by Sri Aurobindo and a selection of his work *The Life Divine,* obviously using his own Danish translation.[582] Both these actions may be interpreted as an indication of a conscious return to the beginning of his literary career. Even though, for more than twenty years, no hints of Eastern spirituality had appeared, these later references to the *Bhagavad Gita* and the work of Sri Aurobindo, as well as the later dedication of his book on Yoga to him, seem to show that the short but intense contact in 1915 had a stronger impact on him than had been supposed thus far.

The later General Secretary of the Anthroposophical Society in Denmark, Oskar Borgman Hansen (Chair Emeritus of Philosophy at the University of Aarhus) recalled a talk he had with Johannes Hohlenberg. In it, Hohlenberg mentioned a meeting with Rudolf Steiner, during which Hohlenberg's spiritual development before his contact with Anthroposophy had come up, along with other topics. Hansen reports that Hohlenberg was already undergoing a kind of occult training before he encountered Anthroposophy toward the end of World War I. In the talk, he had asked Rudolf Steiner whether, now that he had found Anthroposophy, he had to give up his earlier practices, to which Steiner replied that this was not necessary.[583] From this it is clear that the founder of

Anthroposophy must not only have been well aware of Hohlenberg's earlier practices and their origin, but also that in this spirituality—namely, that of Sri Aurobindo—he could not have seen anything that would have stood in the way of Hohlenberg's anthroposophic orientation.

A faint reflection of a mutual awareness of each other between Rudolf Steiner and Sri Aurobindo can possibly be discerned in the biography and work of the Indian spiritual teacher. In April 1920, Sri Aurobindo wrote a long letter in his native Bengali language addressed to his brother Barin, who at that time had just been released from political imprisonment. In this letter he gave an overview of his inner development since his own imprisonment in Alipore. But he also dwelled on "India's weakness" and stressed that he saw its cause neither in subjection and poverty nor in a lack of spirituality, but rather in the fact that one could deplore a "diminution of the power of thought, the spread of ignorance" everywhere in India, and this "in the birthplace of knowledge." In Europe, this would be different; for there existed a great culture and discipline of thought and striving after knowledge. He considered the revolutions and catastrophes in Europe not as heralds of destruction, but as "the first stages of a new creation."[584]

> But there is a fatal limitation to the power and thought of Europe. When she enters the field of spirituality, her thought-power stops working. There Europe sees everything as a riddle, nebulous metaphysics, yogic hallucination—"It rubs its eyes as in smoke and can see nothing clearly."[585]

But it need not remain so. Sri Aurobindo continued, "But now in Europe not a little effort is being made to surmount even this limitation."[586] Could Sri Aurobindo have had Rudolf Steiner in mind here? Numerous spiritual and esoteric movements were already in existence in early twentieth-century Europe. But only in the anthroposophic Spiritual Science (*Geisteswissenschaft*) of Rudolf Steiner was and is such unique and unmistakable stress laid on thought and striving after knowledge as might have been in the mind of the clear-sighted letter writer in Pondicherry, when he referred to "not a little effort." Sri Aurobindo's awareness of Rudolf Steiner's immense achievements in knowledge seems easy to explain if we assume that Johannes Hohlenberg remained in correspondence with the great Yogi for some time, even after the date when the Dane, approximately three years after he had left Pondicherry, discovered Anthroposophy in Central Europe.

This English translation by Shraddhavan was first published as an article in *Mother India: Monthly Review of Culture* (November 24, 2014).

Glossary

Sanskrit expressions, and terms (not exhaustive) used in the spiritual traditions of both Anthroposophy and Integral Yoga.

Adityas	Vedic deities of high status; according to the *Shatapatha Brahmana* the twelve sons of Aditi, the deity of the dawn and of unlimited, infinite space, representing the Akasha (see → akashic records).
Agni	Fire, the deva of fire. In the cosmos the Sun in the heavens, lightning in the atmosphere, and on Earth, visible fire. Over two hundred hymns of the → *Rig Veda* are dedicated to him. According to Sri Aurobindo, he mysteriously indwells matter, and at the same time governs consciousness and will. His habitation is the vast truth world where knowledge and will are one. Agni has a deep affinity with soul nature, and is also called the deity of → *psychic being.*
Ahriman	Also ahrimanic beings. According to Rudolf Steiner's spiritual research, these are adversarial powers that seek to corrupt regular human evolution by tempting us into premature realization of future evolutionary stages and too deep a connection with earthly–material reality. In ancient Iranian myth, Ahriman is the dark counterpart of the solar deity Ahura Mazda.

Akashic record	In Steiner's works, the cosmic chronicles imprinted in the boundary sphere between lower and upper devachan—that is, where spiritual configurations (*Rupa*) meet formless spiritual reality (*Arupa*). The Akasha that resides here is receptive to and permeable by form configurations and formative impulses arising in formlessness. Sri Aurobondo likewise speaks of the akashic script: *akasha lipi.*
Alaya vijnana	This Buddhist term from the Yogachara system refers to the "storage consciousness," which is the highest of eight levels of consciousness. It is distinguished from the other seven by the fact that it undergoes no alteration or evolution; it is comparable to the → akashic records or *akasha lipi.*
Archetypal plant	A discovery by Goethe: the archetypal image of a flowering plant, to which we—by means of *metamorphosis*—can relate the morphology of every particular blossoming plant species.
Astral body	The next higher suprasensory sheath of the human organization after the → etheric body; also called the sentient or consciousness body. It is the foundation for ensoulment of animal and human organisms.
Atman	The true being, or true self, of each human individual, but at the same time elevated far above the limits of individual personality. By its nature, *atman* is capable of experiencing unity with the → *brahman.* In Anthroposophy, *atman* is seen as the highest of the seven sheaths of our being, and at the same time seen as the fully spiritualized transformation of the physical body (as lowest sheath).
Avatar	A divine manifestation as in the ten classical, puranic Avatars—e.g., in the Lion Man, in Rama, Krishna, or in the → Kalki Avatar.

Bhakti, Bhakti Yoga	In Integral Yoga, devotion, love, reverent worship, and the longing of the soul to orient itself entirely toward the sublime. In *The Synthesis of Yoga*, bhakti yoga is "The Yoga of Divine Love."
Bhumi	Earth, world, place of manifestations.
Brahman	In the Vedanta, divine reality, the One apart from which nothing exists; the absolute, omnipresent reality, in which everything relative exists as *brahman's* forms or motions; its nature is *sachchidananda*: infinite existence (*sat*), infinite consciousness (*chit*) and infinite bliss (*ananda*).
Chaitya purusha	The individual human soul; synonym for → *psychic being*; not to be confused with *chaitanya purusha*, which refers to the consciousness of the divine → purusha.
Consciousness soul	The soul element becoming increasingly self-aware as the "I" evolves; it elevates itself far enough above desire, sympathy and antipathy, reason, and sensibility, to become capable of conscious contact with the spirit (in the spirit self or → Manas). It works in the closest, most intimate collaboration with the "I."
Deva	In Integral Yoga a cosmic deity presiding over the actions and influences of cosmic principles; thus the deva is a dynamic being, manifesting in → Prakriti so as to be able to accomplish works on the plane to which it belongs; however the term can also be used for the supreme Divine.
Ego	Lower self, arising through one-sided focus of self-reflective consciousness especially on the vital level or on astrality and the tissue of instinct, drive and desire residing there, or on the "desire soul." It is the source of egoistic possessiveness, envy, jealousy, etc. It causes lasting veiling and obscuring of our bright inner being, true "I"-being or → *psychic being.*

Elemental spirits	Also called elemental beings: suprasensory beings in the sphere of the spiritual world adjoining the physical world (the astral plane). In particular they animate and ensoul the four classical elements—earth, water, air, and fire. In accordance with the tradition going back to Paracelsus, Steiner speaks of gnomes, undines, sylphs, and salamanders.
Ether, Etheric body	In Anthroposophy, the ether or the etheric is the enlivening suprasensory principle that gives life to plants, animal, and humans. There are also cosmic ether qualities. In line with the four elements, four ether types are distinguished: the warmth, light, tone, and life ethers. It is comparable to the → Prana. The etheric body (also life body, or body of formative forces) is the suprasensory organization that causes and sustains all the life processes in an organism.
Eurythmy	Visible speech and visible music, rendered visible as movements, positions of the body, and gestures which use the physical body as instrument to reveal the inner nature and lawfulness of the → etheric body (i.e., the Logos nature of the human being).
Gayatri mantra	Still today in India one of the most important mantras, taken from the → *Rig Veda* (3,62).
Goetheanism	A term coined by Rudolf Steiner, following in particular his deep engagement with Johann Wolfgang Goethe's scientific writings. It is based on strict phenomenology and what Goethe called "beholding judgment" when observing the natural world, as well as based on organic laws such as that of metamorphosis.
Guna	The three gunas as the three fundamental properties of the → Prakriti are: *tamas, rajas and sattva. Tamas* represents torpidity, darkness and gravity—distance from God; *rajas* is the

dynamic principle, decomposition and composition, energetic and vehement contest; *sattva* is bright, conscious clarity and enlightenment in intense devotion to the divine.

Hierarchies — In Anthroposophy these are chiefly the three hierarchies of spirit beings connected with diverse spheres of the world of spirit. In accordance with Christian tradition (Dionysius the Areopagite) a distinction is made between Angels, Archangels, Principalities (3rd hierarchy); Exousiai, Dynameis, Kyriotetes (2nd hierarchy); and Thrones, Cherubim, Seraphim (1st hierarchy). Angels are closest to the human level, the Seraphim closest to the sight of God.

Idealism — Primarily, in philosophy, the school of German Idealism, represented chiefly by Johann Gottlieb Fichte, Georg Wilhelm Friedrich Hegel, and Friedrich Wilhelm Joseph Schelling, figures who were of decisive importance for the young Rudolf Steiner.

Indra — In the Vedas the king of the → devas, who sends lightning, thunder and rain. He overcomes evil with his thunderbolt. Like → Michael, he battles the dragon-like element. According to Sri Aurobindo, he governs the manasic, or mental, power.

Ishvara — The "Lord" of the universe, the highest being or the → Purushottama in the *Bhagavad Gita*; he manifests in time and sustains the cosmos. He possesses a universal consciousness in which he is aware of the truth of all things and entities; and he calls them forth into existence through his omniscience and in accordance with the laws indwelling them. He is both above yet within the cosmos: the most sublime and universal → *brahman*, the sublime self, the absolute.

Jiva	The individual soul; in Integral Yoga a partial manifestation of → Ishvara; at the same time it provides the stage where the → Purusha and the → Prakriti meet each other and are embodied in their cosmic activity.
Jnana Yoga	In Integral Yoga, the path of knowledge. On this path, the → mental is to be gradually illumined and led toward higher realizations such as the "intuitive mental" and the "light mental." In *Synthesis of Yoga,* it is called the "yoga of integral knowledge."
Kali Yuga	The dark age; in general it is said this began in 3101 BC, around the date when → Krishna withdrew from his physical manifestation. According to Rudolf Steiner, Kali Yuga ended in AD 1899. Sri Aurobindo held a similar view.
Kalki Avatar	The tenth of the ten Puranic → avatars.
Karma Yoga	In Integral Yoga—which is very close here to the teachings of the *Bhagavad Gita*—the yoga of action or deed. In *Synthesis of Yoga* it is called "The Yoga of Divine Works."
Krishna	The eighth of the ten Puranic avatars and the central figure in the *Bhagavad Gita*, where he initiates the Pandu prince Arjuna, whose divine father is → Indra, into all aspects of yoga. Rudolf Steiner identifies Krishna with the "innocent sister soul" of Adam: as his more heavenly aspect that was preserved from the Fall and only appeared in full incarnation again in the Nathan Jesus.
Krita Yuga	Roughly, the age of highest perfection; synonymous with the → Satya Yuga.
Logos	The divine Word that utters the world. Its power creates and elaborates all beings and resounds through them. In the West it is identified fully with the Son of God, the second

	person of the → Trinity, who became man in Jesus Christ.
Lucifer	Also, luciferic beings. According to Rudolf Steiner's spiritual research, adversarial powers that seek to corrupt the proper course of human evolution by tempting us back to former evolutionary stages and lifting us out of earthly reality.
Manas	In the works of Sri Aurobindo, this refers to the mental level; it is equivalent to the spirit self in Anthroposophy, the first truly spiritual aspect in the sequence of the human sheaths, achieved partly through cleansing and transforming the → astral body.
Mandala	Circle, curve, circumference; in this book especially, an expression for one of the ten song cycles of the → *Rig Veda*.
Manu	Oversees a cosmic era, a → *manvantara*. The last Manu, according to Rudolf Steiner, inspired the Seven Rishis to found ancient Indian culture. The human soul is called a "son of Manu" (Manuputra).
Manvantara	In Rudolf Steiner's works, the cosmic–evolutionary manifestation of a planetary condition. When a planetary manifestation withdraws into purely spiritual latency again, this is called → *pralaya*.
Mental, Mind	The mental level comprises our given human consciousness and its organization. In its subtler aspects it serves the → *psychic being* in its individual awakening. Higher levels of the mental are the "higher mind," the "enlightened mind" and the "intuitive mind." These stages lead on toward the "overmental Logos," to "overmind" as such, and to the "light mind" which forms the transition to "supermind." Mind in the

	works of Sri Aurobindo generally corresponds to → manas.
Michael	The archangel Michael. Of the seven archangels, he is assigned to the Sun. According to Rudolf Steiner he currently works as time spirit from the sphere of the Archai or Principalities (nineteenth to twenty-third centuries AD). Like → Indra, he stands in battle with the dragon forces. For Anthroposophy, he is a particularly inspiring figure.
Mitra	Vedic deity, the "friend of all beings"; one of the → Adityas.
Monism	Assumes the world as a whole to be an indivisible unity. In his *Intuitive Thinking as a Spiritual Path: A Philosophy of Freedom*, Rudolf Steiner sees Monism as the unity encompassing all actual and potential knowledge. To live or dwell in this, was, in this book, identical for him with "dwelling in God."
Planetary condition	In the view of Anthroposophy, the present stage of planetary condition evolution (Earth) was preceded by three previous stages: Old Saturn (warmth), Old Sun (warmth, light, and air), Old Moon (warmth, air and light ether, water and tone ether).
Post-Atlantean culture	Rudolf Steiner distinguishes seven post-Atlantean cultures following the catastrophe of the great flood in which Atlantis was submerged: those of ancient India, ancient Persia, Egypto–Chaldea, Greece and Rome, our present European culture, and two further cultural epochs still to come. Each of these epochs, in accord with a cosmic rhythm (the Platonic year), encompasses a period of around 2,160 years. Steiner places the beginning of the fourth cultural epoch (the Greco–Roman) in 747 BC, and the beginning of our current era in 1413.

Prajapati	"Lord of Creatures"; all creatures originate from him as his manifestations, as from the divine → Purusha. He is subordinate to Agni; and → Manu or the Manus proceed or emerge from him.
Prakriti	The active force of nature, divided into the three → gunas that it creates and sustains through its motions and which, as it passes over into rest, dissolves the phenomena of the cosmos. The universal energy which, in its activity at all levels of existence, delights the → Purusha. In yoga, Prakriti and → Purusha form a constant conceptual pairing.
Pralaya	In Steiner's works, the purely spiritual condition of latency into which the planetary manifestations (→ *manvantaras*) withdraw after their evolution has concluded.
Prana	Literally, the breath that flows in and out. The essential life force whose fivefold nature streams through the whole body.
Psychic being	For Sri Aurobindo, the individual human soul. The human being's threefold transformation is to start from psychic being and unfold through sustained successive ensouling or *psychicization* of the mental, vital, and physical levels.
Purusha	The human being, the person, the soul, the spirit, the self (→ *atman*) as originator, witness, supporter, lord, who delights in the forms and works of nature, → Prakriti. Conscious being, either universal or individual, which perceives the activity of nature on any of its planes. In yoga, purusha and → Prakriti form a constant conceptual pairing.
Purushottama	The most sublime being , the highest Purusha, as Krishna reveals himself to be in the *Bhagavad Gita* (xv,18); cf the entry on → Ishvara.

Rig Veda	The most ancient of the four Vedas, regarded as the primordial divine manifestation. In ten song cycles (→ mandalas) it comprises 1,028 hymns to the Vedic deities.
Rik	Verse, one of over 10,000 verses of the → *Rig Veda.*
Rishi	The poet seer of early Vedic civilization, author of Vedic hymns; the seven holy rishis, especially, governed that ancient culture through their connection with the deities.
Sadhaka	Pupil, aspirant, God-seeker; one who practices → sadhana.
Sadhana	Spiritual discipline, the practice of → yoga; literally, the instrument, the medium.
Sanatana Dharma	The eternal truth; the term used by Hinduism to designate itself and distinguish itself from the many sects and cults, as being the ongoing, original, transcendental background to Hinduism.
Sannyasin	An ascetic who lives in complete renunciation and divestment, and is focused only on *moksha*, or liberation from karma, birth, death, and rebirth.
Sanskrit	From *samskrita*, refined, ennobled, cultivated; as language, the refined form of speech used to express less material and more spiritual realities; the language of sacred written traditions and of priests and scholars. In contrast to Sanskrit is Prakrit, from *prakrita*, meaning ordinary, natural. Prakrit refers to a range of central Indian spoken languages, including Pali, the language in which the Buddhist canon was written, as well as Ardhamaghadi, the language probably spoken by the Buddha.
Saptarishis	The seven holy → Rishis.
Satya Yuga	The age of truth or also the "golden age"; in Puranic tradition a new Satya Yuga follows the

	current (or recently ended) → Kali Yuga. This new period begins with the emergence of the → Kalki Avatar. In divergence from this, at the end of the nineteenth century the West Bengali yogi and guru Shri Yukteshwar spoke of how the Kali Yuga will be followed by a gradual ascent through a new Dvapara Yuga and in the further future a Treta Yuga; only after this will a new Satya Yuga commence.
Triloka	The "three worlds"—Bhur–Bhuvar–Svar. They belong to the lower hemisphere and, according to Sri Aurobindo, are to be equated with the physical, vital, and mental worlds. In Rudolf Steiner's works, they correspond to the physical world, the astral plane, and lower devachan. Recitation of the → Gayatri mantra usually begins with an OM and an invocation of the "three worlds."
Trinity	In contrast to any other "triad," this refers explicitly to the threefold divinity of Christianity: Father, Son, and Holy Spirit, regarded as "three in one": as three personal aspects of one and the same being.
Varuna	Vedic deity, the "Lord of Wideness": one of the Adityas. Only in the post-Vedic period did he become the deity of seas and oceans.
Veda	Knowledge, wisdom, the revealed Word. The Vedas form the oldest stratum of religious literature in India: they are divided into the → *Rig Veda, Sama Veda, Tajur Veda,* and *Atharva Veda*. In a broader sense, *Veda* also refers to the later vedantic spirituality of the Upanishads. Sri Aurobindo's Integral Yoga can be seen as an attempt to awaken the Veda to a new life fitting for modern times.
Vedanta	Literally, the end of the Vedas: in the post-Vedic period it encompasses the schools of

	Vedic thought and comes to expression chiefly in the Upanishads; one of the six philosophical systems of Hinduism. The Advaita Vedanta, as the Vedanta of non-duality, refers to one of five schools of the Vedanta, and is the one best known in the West.
Vibhuti	A partial manifestation of Avatar realization, by contrast to the full → Avatar; responsible for smaller evolutionary transitions.
Yoga	Reunification of what was sundered in the course of world evolution—such as → *atman* and *param brahman*. Especially the various methods and practices for achieving this. The Integral Yoga of Sri Aurobindo especially creates a synthesis in purna yoga, the yoga of perfection, between Karma Yoga, the yoga of works, Jnana Yoga, the yoga of knowledge, and Bhakti Yoga, the yoga of loving devotion.

Endnotes

Introduction by D. Banerji and R. McDermott

1 The principal point Bracker seems to make is that extant scholarship dates the Veda to c.1500 BC, and sees it as the creation of Indo–European marauders who invaded the Indus Valley and established themselves in India. Against this, he posits two lines of difference: (1) the intuitions and akashic experiences of Rudolf Steiner and Sri Aurobindo, both of whom thought that the Veda as we know it was preceded by a much earlier phase belonging to an earlier layer of civilization; (2) modern, mostly Indian nationalist and pro-Indian-nationalist Western thinkers who are invested in the ideology of a pure Indian territoriality for the Vedas, see the Indus Valley as a Vedic civilization, and espouse an "Out-of-India Theory" to explain the philological family resemblance of the Indo–European (a.k.a. Aryan) languages and cultures. From this delineation Bracker argues for the development of the "inner science" of spiritual faculties combined with the "outer sciences" of archaeology and history to arrive at a better understanding of our past and its continuing legacy toward the future.

On the academic historical arguments fielded by Bracker, some of the sources he quotes, such as Koenraad Elst, are extremely questionable. None of them are established archaeologists or historians of ancient India. Moreover, his contention of the Aryan Invasion Theory (AIT) being the predominant academic view of the matter is outdated. Very few archaeologists, historians, or art historians today hold this view. It is true that Bracker also mentions the Aryan Immigration Theory in passing and dubs it as hardly different from the Invasion Theory, but this in fact is the more accepted theory in the field today and it would have been better for Bracker to have considered the nuances of its possibilities. Sri Aurobindo was not particularly invested in an ideology of racial purity for Vedic Indians or in Theosophical ideas of root races. It is regrettable that Bracker pushed a strong case for indigeneity of the Vedic poets. Fortunately, this issue is not central to his text.

2 One of the authors of this introduction, Debashish Banerji, opines that Sri Aurobindo does not speak of Kalki in *Savitri*. Though he speaks of Christ, it is not in the context of returning. He speaks of the "return" in more abstract terms. Klaus Bracker, in private responses to this comment, stated that "there is a significant connection between Christ (or: the mystery of Golgotha) and the tenth Avatar;" and further, "the view of Sri Aurobindo—the coming-down of Truth-Consciousness on earth (the mission of the 10th Avatar) karmically

is related to the sufferings and successions of the One who went his way onto Golgotha." It is fitting that this footnote should point to a divergence of opinion and spotlight the need for further research and reflection on Aurobindo's understanding of Christ.

3 The authors have pointed to the need for a fuller treatment of the Mother, particularly on her importance in the extension and implementation of Sri Aurobindo's Integral vision and Integral Yoga. It should be noted that Klaus Bracker is the author of an essay on Sophia in the journal *Novalis* (2004), currently available only in German and Dutch. A fuller exchange of perspectives would probably reveal that Bracker is affirmative of the reality and influence of Sophia for Steiner but does not emphasize the role of the Mother, either in the vision and work of Sri Aurobindo or as a manifestation of Sophia. Like the question of Sri Aurobindo's understanding of Christ in footnote 2, an understanding of both Sophia and the Mother is a profound topic requiring many perspectives reverently held and expressed. Readers interested in a deeper appreciation of the mission and teachings of the Mother would benefit from two volumes by George Van Vrekhem: *The Mother's Vision: Selections from Questions and Answers* (2000), and *The Mother: The Story of Her Life* (2002), both published by Sri Aurobindo Ashram Trust.

4 Thanks to this book and the entirely positive task of writing this introduction, Robert McDermott has learned more about Sri Aurobindo than he had known previously and Debashish Banerji, an advanced scholar of the Integral Yoga of Sri Aurobindo and the Mother, has opened a channel to the anthroposophic teachings and practices of Rudolf Steiner.

AUTHOR'S INTRODUCTION

5 Cf. the 2010 annual program of the Berlin Integral Forum. Integrales Forum Berlin, Rosenthalerstrasse 36, 10178 Berlin.

6 Cf. Rudolf Steiner's early epistemological and philosophical works—e.g., Rudolf Steiner, *Goethe's Theory of Knowledge: An Outline of the Epistemology of His Worldview,* SteinerBooks 2008; *Truth and Knowledge*, Anthroposophic Press 1981; *Intuitive Thinking as a Spiritual Path: A Philosophy of Freedom,* 1995.

7 The spiritual teacher and author Aurobindo Ghose (his given name) is generally known as Sri Aurobindo. In this book, he will be referred to as such throughout.

8 Like Gottfried Wilhelm Leibnitz two and a half centuries before, in the twentieth century such figures as Aldous Huxley regarded the "perennial philosophy" as a convergent religious wisdom of all cultures. Cf. Aldous Huxley, *The Perennial Philosophy,* Harper Perennial 2009. This idea of an eternal philosophy only apparently contradicts the concept of an evolving spirituality, since the latter in no way disputes the eternal as such. A concept of evolution without reference to eternal values would, rather, be at risk of inherent meaninglessness.

9 *Sanatana Dharma* (Sanskrit) means roughly "eternal truth." The term applies to the Indian high religion generally known as "Hinduism" in the West. In the further course of this book it will become clear that Sri Aurobindo regarded the traditional religion of India, with its many schools and cults, as a degenerate form of a purer religion of the past. He believed that the true Sanatana Dharma could look forward to a great, integral future. The Sanskrit terms used mainly in the context of Integral Yoga in this book will generally be given in their simplified form. Where necessary, the diacritic symbols otherwise normally also used will be given too. See also the glossary.

10 For this reason it will be necessary in this work to look back to humanity's past. The future evolution in preparation from our own time onward can then be described with all the more clarity.

11 In his "West–East Divan," Goethe wrote: He who cannot give account of three millennia history will stay in darkness close confined, compelled to live from day to day.

In connection with our enquiries in the present volume, it is interesting to consider the enlargement of perspective offered by Steiner in relation to the "three millennia" referred to by Goethe. In a lecture in 1912, Steiner summarizes this span with the names David, Homer, Dante, Shakespeare, and Goethe. These five, he says, embody everything that constitutes the three millennia of Western culture. But at the turn from the eighteenth to the nineteenth century in Europe, he suggests, these millennia concluded with the dawning of an "inner Orient": not solely through the translation of the Vedas or of the *Bhagavad Gita* into European languages, but also in a subtler respect. Cf. Rudolf Steiner, *The Gospel of St. Mark*, lecture of Sept. 15, 1912, Anthroposophic Press 1990.

12 Rudolf Steiner, *Anthroposophical Leading Thoughts: Anthroposophy as a Path of Knowledge.* Rudolf Steiner Press 1998.

13 Sri Aurobindo, *The Synthesis of Yoga*, page 783. Part IV, *The Yoga of Self-Perfection,* chap. 19 "The Nature of the Supermind." Vols. 23 and 24 of *The Complete Works of Sri Aurobindo.*

14 Ibid, p. 798.

15 The *Rig Veda* is one of humanity's most ancient religious texts. Veda (Sanskrit) means both knowledge and spiritual perception. The *Rig Veda* is the oldest of the four Vedas. Transcribed in ten song cycles (mandalas) it encompasses 1,028 hymns to the ancient Vedic divinities, and contains a total of 10,580 verses (rigs, or riks). The unadulterated collection of these hymns is called "Samhita." Cf. Martin Mittwede, *Spirituelles Wörterbuch. Sanskrit—Deutsch.* Dietzenbach 1999.

16 Sadhaka (Sanskrit) means, roughly, pupil, aspirant, god-seeker. His spiritual practice is termed Sadhana (Skr.).

17 The glossary in the appendix may be of some help with terminology.

18 The author also asks for understanding for the fact that in this book he offers a careful and detailed introduction to certain aspects of both Anthroposophy and Integral Yoga, for the sake of those readers who are, as it were, seeing the themes in question from the opposite shore. This too is part of the endeavor of reciprocal understanding.

Chapter 1

19 Rudolf Steiner, *Egyptian Myths and Mysteries,* Anthroposophic Press, 1971, lecture 2, Sept. 1908.

20 Rudolf Steiner, *Welt, Erde und Mensch,* Dornach 1983, lecture 13 Aug. 1908. In line with spiritual-scientific knowledge of the seven post-Atlantean cultural epochs and the cosmic rhythms that determine them, this culture is assigned to the period between 7227 and 5067 BC. Each cultural epoch lasts approximately 2,160 years, and the post-Atlantean eras can thus be dated as follows: 1) ancient India: 7227–5067 BC; 2) ancient Persia: 5067–2907 BC; 3) Egypt-Chaldea: 2907–747 BC; 4) Greco–Roman: 747 BC–AD 1413; 5) the modern era: 1413-3573.

21 Sri Aurobindo, *The Secret of the Veda*, page 12, chapter "A Retrospect of Vedic Theory." Volume 15 of *The Complete Works of Sri Aurobindo.* In a footnote he enlarges as follows on the "more ancient lyrical evangel": "The Veda itself speaks constantly of 'ancient' and 'modern' Rishis (*purvah . . . nutanah*), the former remote enough to be regarded as a kind of demigods, the first founders of knowledge." (Ibid).

22 To be accurate one should speak here of the Samhita (collection or anthology) of the *Rig Veda.* The *Rig Veda* Samhita is the earliest textual layer of the Rig-Vedic hymns. The *Rig Veda* as such also contains later texts that relate to it, the *Brahmanas,* the *Aranyakas* and the *Upanishads.*

23 Recent debate surrounds the fact that the Munda languages still spoken today, to which the mostly unwritten languages of the Adivasi tribal communities belong, may be older than the Dravidian languages. Accordingly, peoples of the Dravidian language group may, like the later arrival of Vedic Indo–Europeans, have been immigrants to the South-Asian subcontinent at a time when the Adivasi tribes had long been indigenous there.

24 Cf. Hermann Kulke, Dietmar Rothermund, *Geschichte Indiens. Von der Induskultur bis heute.* Munich 1998; Michael Witzel, *Das alte Indien,* Munich 2003; Harald Haarmann, *Die Indoeuropäer. Herkunft, Sprachen, Kulturen*, Munich 2010.

25 Cf. David Frawley, *The Myth of the Aryan Invasion*, Delhi 2005, the chapter "Harappan Civilization." Also, B.B. Lal (Braj Basi Lal), *The Earliest Civilization of South East Asia,* Delhi 1997, chap. 5.

26 Cf. Hermann Kulke, Dietmar Rothermund, *Geschichte Indiens. Von der Induskultur bis heute.* Op. cit., chap. 1, "Die frühen Kulturen im Nordwesten."

27 Cf. Harald Haarmann, *Die Indoeuropäer. Herkunft, Sprachen, Kulturen.* Op. cit., chap. 5, section on "Die Indo-Iranische Makrogruppierung."

28 Egbert Richter-Ushanas, *Der Herr der Tiere. Dreizehn Aufsätze zur Symbolik der Indus-Schrift und zur vergleichenden Kulturgeschichte.* Nordhausen 2010, chapter "Die Symbolik der Indus Schrift im Vergleich zum Rig Veda."

29 The *Rig Veda* refers only in one instance, in the late *Purusha Hymns*, to Brahmins and Kshatriyas as class or caste designations. On the other hand, it often speaks of the gods, too, as Kshatriyas or Brahmins.

30 This stands of course in crass contrast to the dire reinterpretation of this term (Skr., *arya;* Avest. *airija* = the noble one) in nationalism and Nazism in the nineteenth and twentieth centuries.

31 The expression "Arya" must certainly be understood here as having no racist connotation whatsoever.

32 Koenraad Elst, *Update on the Aryan Invasion*. New Delhi 1999.

33 David H. Osborn (ed.), *Science of the Sacred. Ancient Perspectives for Modern Science*. Rangapatna/Karnaka 2009.

34 David Frawley, *The* Rig Veda *and the History of India*. New Delhi 2003. The chapter, "Establishing a Time Line."

35 According to Indian accounts, Manu is the seventh of fourteen Manus, the Manu of the current world epoch. In the myth of his rescue by the horned fish Matsya, the fish incarnation of Vishnu (as related for instance in the *Matsya Purana*) he appears as King Satyavrata. This is the same figure as the son of the Sun god Vivasvan, who also bears the name Manu Vaivashvata.

36 Nowadays it is assumed that the glaciation of huge continental regions (ice covers with a depth of up to 3,000 meters) and the associated freezing of water masses, led during the Vistulian glacial period (Pleniglacial around 22,000–14,000 BC), to a lowering of sea levels by over 120 meters compared to today. Large coastal regions and island groups that were above sea level at that time (e.g., most of today's North Sea) were flooded again after the glaciers melted following a rise in sea levels. Cf. Jürgen Ehlers, *Das Eiszeitalter*. Heidelberg 2011, chap. 13, "Nord- und Ostsee in der Eiszeit."

37 It is worth noting how close these findings by Frawley coincide with Rudolf Steiner's statement that the 'primordial Indian cultural epoch' began around 7227 BC (see note 16).

38 In 1872/73, Sir Alexander Cunningham (1814–1893) made the first excavations that led to discovery of the Bronze Age city of Harappa (around 2600–1800 BC). In 1922, a group led by Sir John Marshall (1876–1958) came upon the foundations of the other Indus city of Mohenjo-Daro, which existed at the same period as Harappa. Only when the second discovery was made did it become apparent that the remains testified to a once widespread culture.

39 Sri Aurobindo, *The Synthesis of Yoga*, op. cit., chap. 25 "Toward the Supramental Time Vision." The terms *psychic self* and *supramental,*" characteristic in Integral Yoga, will be examined in more detail following. Sri Aurobindo speaks of the *trikaldrishti*, the perception of three ages or times. According to him, supramental consciousness is founded on "a total view of the three times as one movement singly and indivisibly seen even in their succession of stages, periods, cycles." And he goes on: "It [the supramental consciousness] will therefore have the knowledge of the three times, held of old to be a supreme sign of the seer and the Rishi." Ibid.

40 That Sri Aurobindo himself read the "akasha lipi" can be deduced from comments in his schooling diary that was first published in book

form in 2001 under the title *Record of Yoga*. In more than fifty entries of this diary of yoga practice, extending to 1,500 pages, he refers to the *trikaldrishti* and his practice-oriented research in this field. But one gathers from these notes that Sri Aurobindo was far more preoccupied with the future aspect of the *trikaldrishti* than with its past. Cf. Sri Aurobindo, *Record of Yoga*, Pondicherry 2001.

41 Rudolf Steiner, foreword to *Aus der Akasha-Chronik*. Andreas Neider has compiled a selection of profound texts by Steiner on the theme of the akashic records, with detailed commentaries. Cf. Rudolf Steiner (ed. Andreas Neider), *Lesen in der Akasha-Chronik,* Dornach 2008.

42 Cf. Rudolf Steiner, *Über die astrale Welt und das Devachan*, Dornach 1999, lecture on Jan. 28, 1904. In this lecture Steiner describes the sevenfold order of devachan. Four of its spheres belong to lower devachan, the fourth of these being the akashic sphere, the transition to the three upper domains of higher devachan.

43 Cf. Rudolf Steiner, *An Outline of Esoteric Science,* Anthroposophic Press 1997, the chapter "Cosmic Evolution and the Human Being." Here Steiner describes the akashic matrix also as "the spiritual foundation of the world."

44 Sri Aurobindo, *The Synthesis of Yoga*, op. cit., chap. 24, "The Supramental Sense." In the *Chandogya Upanishad*, the question is asked, "What is the essence of this world?" The reply given is: "Akasa [Akasha] said (Pravahana); "All these beings arise from Akasa alone and are finally dissolved into Akasa; because Akasa alone is greater than all these and Akasa is the support at all times." In: Swami Swadhananda (translator), *Chandogya Upanishad.* Chennai 2010. chapter I–IX–I.

45 In an earlier work, the author of this book provided a brief summary of Rudolf Steiner's view of this cosmic evolution. Cf. Klaus J. Bracker, *Grals-Initiation. Anthroposophische Esoterik und die künftige Jesus-Offenbarung.* Stuttgart 2009, chap. 1, in the sections "Weltenentwicklung in der Erkenntnis des Grals" and "Zukunft der Welt."

46 Traditionally, the "seven planets" refer to the five planets visible to the naked eye along with the Sun and Moon.

47 Rudolf Steiner, *Ägyptische Mythen und Mysterien.* Dornach 1992, CW 106, lecture 5, Sept. 1908. English: *Egyptian Myths and Mysteries,* Anthroposophic Press, 1971.

48 According to Steiner, these spiritual–cosmic secrets of the seven Rishis correspond fully to what he himself presented about the evolution of the cosmos in anthroposophic Spiritual Science. He says: "And this account is one we first find presented in the very ancient religion of the Indians, in what was called the 'Veda,' or, in German, the 'Word.'" Rudolf Steiner, *Egyptian Myths and Mysteries,* op. cit. Although *Veda* is usually translated as "knowledge," *Veda* and *Vac* (= voice or "word") have for a long time now been used almost as synonyms. Raimundo Panikkar writes about this as follows in his Veda anthology: "After the period of the Brahmanas the whole corpus of the Vedas is often designated by the name *vāc*, the Word, meaning

revelation." Raimundo Panikkar, *Vedic Experience. Mantramanjari.* Delhi 2006, chapter, "The Word."

49 Rudolf Steiner, *The Mission of the Folk-Souls,* lect 14, Rudolf Steiner Press 2005.

50 Cf. chapter 3 in the section of this book "Vak: The Word of the Sublime." In yogic philosophy *purusha* is the always transcendental, pure, spiritual self that rests eternally in itself above Creation, while *Prakriti* refers to this world of created things whose original substance, in its three basic conditions of *tamas, rajas,* and *sattva,* extends upward to very lofty suprasensory realms but is always subject and subordinate to *purusha.* The expression *maha-purusha* (great self, great soul) in particular designates Vishnu, while the expression *mula-Prakriti* designates the very earliest, most subtle and at the same time most all-encompassing germinal stage of *Prakriti.*

51 This future cultural epoch will, according to cosmic rhythms, fall in the period AD 5733–7893 (see note 20). The "axis of reflection" that establishes the center of the seven cultural epochs, arises through the qualitative midpoint of the fourth cultural epoch, and corresponds to the mystery of the death and resurrection of Christ Jesus of Nazareth. Cf. Klaus J. Bracker, *Grals-Initiation,* op. cit., chap. 5 in the section "Nördliche und südliche Mysterienströmung."

52 Sri Aurobindo, *The Secret of the Veda*, op. cit., p. 319, chap., "Brihaspati, Power of the Soul."

53 Ibid, p. 174, chap., "The Seven-Headed Thought, Swar, and the Dashagwas." The seven stars that form the Plough are part of Ursa Major. For the Indians, the Plough is connected with the Pole Star as an expression of the connection between the seven Rishis and Manu Vaivashvata.

54 Ibid, "The Angiras Rishis." Brihaspati is the giver, the Lord of the universal creative Word. In the post-Vedic period he metamorphosed into the God Brahma.

55 Sri Aurobindo, *The Secret of the Veda*, op. cit., chap., "The Herds of the Dawn."

56 Ibid, in the chap. "The Seven Rivers." In Vedic Sanskrit the terms *vāc* and *vāk* both figure; *vāc* (pronounced "vaach") is the root form, and *vāk* ("vaak") is the nominative singular as well as the vocative singular as form of address.

57 To commemorate the 100th anniversary of Sri Aurobindo's birth, anthroposophic author Heimo Rau wrote an essay outlining the life of this philosopher and yogi: "'Supramentale' Bewusstseinsentfaltung. Zum hundertsten Geburtstag von Shri Aurobindo." In: *Die Drei. Die anthroposophische Kulturzeitschrift*, Dec. 1972. In the anthroposophic context Dr. Julius Reubke also appraised Sri Aurobindo and Integral Yoga in a social science lecture on Oct. 9, 2004 at the Goetheanum, Dornach: "Tagore—Gandhi—Aurobindo. Ein Dreigestirn im Aufgang des 20. Jahrhunderts." This formed part of a conference entitled "Encounter Between Cultures: India—the Task of India in the World Organism. A Spiritual Legacy Between Illusion and reality." Archive of the section for Social Sciences at the School of Spiritual Science, Dornach.

58 Cf. Rudolf Steiner, *Autobiography*, SteinerBooks 2006; Christoph Lindenberg, *Rudolf Steiner, A Biography*, SteinerBooks 2012; Peter Selg, *Rudolf Steiner, Life and Work*, SteinerBooks 2016; Rudolf Meyer, *Wer war Rudolf Steiner?* Stuttgart 1961; Johannes Hemleben, *Rudolf Steiner: A Documentary Biography*, Henry Goulden, 1975; Gerhard Wehr, *Rudolf Steiner. Wirklichkeit, Erkenntnis und Kulturimpuls*, Freiburg i. Br. 1982.

CHAPTER 2

59 In Sanskrit the name Aravinda, which can also be written Aurobindo, originates in a name for the lotus. His father gave him this name due to a "sudden inspiration," as Sri Aurobindo later confided to his pupil Dilip Kumar Roy. Cf. Dilip K. Roy, *Sri Aurobindo Came to Me*. Pondicherry 1952.

60 For general biographical details insofar as they are not given here, see: Sri Aurobindo, *On Himself*. Sri Aurobindo Birth Centenary Library, volume 26, Pondicherry 1972; Satprem, *Sri Aurobindo ou l'Aventure de la Conscience*. Paris 1970 (translated into English: *Sri Aurobindo or the Adventure of Consciousness*. 2nd edition: New Delhi 2000); Peter Heehs, *The Lives of Sri Aurobindo*, New York 2008; Wilfried Huchzermeyer, *Sri Aurobindo.His Life and Work*, Karlsruhe 2012; Otto Wolff, *Sri Aurobindo*, Reinbek near Hamburg 1995.

61 Peter Heehs, *The Lives of Sri Aurobindo*, op. cit., in the chapter "Encountering India: Baroda 1893-1906."

62 Cf. Satprem, *Sri Aurobindo or the Adventure of Consciousness*, op. cit, chap. 3, "The End of the Intellect."

63 Sri Aurobindo distinguishes spiritual experiences based on memories from former lives from perceptions of the specific spiritual atmosphere of a particular place or region. He wrote of his arrival in India in Feb. 1893: "Then there was the experience when I came to India: as soon as I set my foot on Apollo Bunder, I felt a vastness and a tremendous calm coming over me. I did not know, of course, that it was an experience. It was a sense of calm and vastness pervading everywhere and I had not got it in the steamer. That is the atmosphere of the place." Ambalal B. Purani, *Evening Talks With Sri Aurobindo. Third Series*. Pondicherry 1966. Conversation 5. Feb. 1939.

64 As mentioned previously, this means "the eternal truth" or the "eternal religion," and is the term by which Hinduism refers to itself. For Sri Aurobindo, Sanatana Dharma is however something far more comprehensive than traditional Hinduism—that is, a spirituality deeply rooted in every true religion.

65 Svaraj means roughly "mastery of oneself." This term, adopted by the Bengal freedom movement, and soon afterward also by Mahatma Ghandi, is noteworthy for its second, esoteric meaning, which comes to the fore chiefly in theosophical literature. There Svaraj stands for the seventh ray, the synthesis of the seven solar logoi, or for Brahma.

66 Despite several later attempts by Ghandi at rapprochement between these two "great souls" (in Sanskrit *Mahatma,* or *Maha-Atma,* means "great soul"), the two never actually met.

67 Sri Aurobindo, *Bande Mataram. Political Writings and Speeches 1890–1908*. Pondicherry 2002.

68 Guru Lele's demand that Aurobindo should sit down and ensure that all thoughts approaching him from without (i.e., all thoughts) should not enter his consciousness, corresponds to the beginning of Patanjali's yoga sutras. There it is said that "*yogas citta-vritti-nirodhah*"—"yoga is the repulse of the functions (vritti) of the substance of thought (citta)." See Swami Vivekananda, *Raja-Yoga,* 2014, the chapter "Introduction to Patanjali's Yoga Aphorisms." That thoughts should be experienced as coming to us from without, and that we should simply let them pass by and not enter us, also corresponds to Buddhist approaches, especially as established in the Vipassana method of southern Buddhism, and in Zazen in Japan. This type of passive meditation does not really aim to "suppress" thoughts but cultivates instead a non-evaluating, non-attached attentiveness that enables the practitioner to allow thoughts as well as all other sensations or phenomena to pass before us. Thus we do not appropriate any mental object since doing so counts among the chief causes of suffering. By this means no thought can set our inner "thought factory" in motion, a term Sri Aurobindo also used. The reference to Vipassana is appropriate here since Sri Aurobindo himself places his 1908 experience in a Buddhist context when he speaks of the realization of Nirvana. Nor was Guru Lele himself speaking of the suppression of thoughts in its classical meaning but of not allowing them entry, which is an approach that comes close to Vipassana, and is fundamental to its forms of practice (Pali: the perception of the transience of all existence). Cf. Buddha (ed. Paul Dahlke), *Die Lehre des Erhabenen*, Munich 1979, the section "Maha-Satipatthana-Suttanta." Tibetan tantric Buddhism systematized the practice of Vipashyana (the same term in Sanskrit, meaning "distinguishing between the transience of existence and the true reality of Shunyata, the fundamental emptiness of all existence") and Shamatha (peace meditation). Commentaries on Vipashyana and Shamatha can help us to better understand these two "wings" of meditation both in their reciprocity and difference. Cf., for instance, Lama Sherab Gyaltsen Amipa, *The Opening of the Lotus: Developing Clarity and Kindness*. London 1987. ch. "Samatha and Vipassana.".

69 Sri Aurobindo, *Sri Aurobindo on Himself and The Mother*, Pondicherry 1953, vol. 35 of *The Complete Works of Sri Aurobindo*.

70 Ibid. Sri Aurobindo's expression "cinematic" is relevant here to the vision of the world he describes in his autobiography as a kind of filmic play of empty forms in the "impersonal universality of absolute Brahman." Cf. Sri Aurobindo, *On Himself,* op. cit.

71 Sri Aurobindo, *On Himself,* op. cit.

72 For a detailed discussion of this cf. Klaus J. Bracker, *Grals-Initiation*, op. cit., chap. 4, "Lebens-Umschwung als Wiedergeburt."

73 In support of the idea of going beyond Nirvana, or, more accurately, to be able to have experiences that transcend Nirvana, see the great Japanese philosopher of religion Keiji Nishitani (1900–1990) who, as a member of the famous Kyoto School, based his ideas firmly on Zen practice and the Mahayanan Buddha Dharma that corresponds to it. Familiar with modern existentialism, he also came into contact—for instance via Master Eckhart—with Christian thinking. In reference to the Gospel of St. Matthew, Nishitani speaks of the perfect love of God, of his *agape*, which equally embraces both evil and goodness; and he finds here an affinity with the Buddhist teaching of "non-distinguishing love beyond friend or foe." In the divine perfection of this love, he says, Jesus Christ divested himself of his nature, assuming the form of a human being and servant and showing the personal love of God, as Paul puts it in the second part of Epistle to the Philippians. The origin of this self-divestment or self-emptying by Christ, his *kenosis,* or "having become empty of himself," is, for Nishitani, founded in God from eternity and is "always contained in God's perfection." According to Nishitani, this is called *anatman* (no-self, or without self) in Buddhist terminology. In this view, he says, Christ's works of active love are personal, whereas the perfect *agape* of God allows this personal love to come forth from him, precedes it and is intrinsically *anatman*, thus transpersonal or impersonal, like the Buddhist Shunyata where friend and foe are not distinguished. However, there is a radical difference here from Shunyata (or in Japanese Buddhism the absolute nothingness or Mu), which a Buddhist analysis of existence finds simply to exist, in that this self-divestment or self-emptying of God is something actively accomplished. According to Keiji Nishitani, this act is one that someone must have accomplished throughout eternity. Who should do this if not the divine person or one of the three of the Trinity? At this point we can understand the Japanese philosopher only to mean that for him, through his questioning encounter with Christianity, an impersonal transcendence or immanence in the Zen experience of emptiness or absolute nothingness, penetrated by thinking, becomes "porous" or permeable for a hitherto unforeseen transcendent personality breaking through from beyond the Shunyata, from beyond the Mu. In the context of these philosophical experiences, Nishitani called himself a "Buddhist who has come into development" and a "still-developing Christian." Cf. Keiji Nishitani, *Was ist Religion?* Frankfurt a. M. 1982 (original Japanese edition: *Shūkyō-towa-nanika*, Kyoto 1961) in the chapter "Nihilismus und *sūnyatā*" ("Nihilism and *sūnyatā*").

74 Cf. also Klaus J. Bracker, "Das Jahr 1909. Die Wiederkunft Christi im Ätherischen und die Spiritualität des Orients." In: *Anthroposophie. Viertelsjahresschrift zur anthroposophischen Arbeit in Deutschland*, no. 248, vol. 2/2009.

75 "Dharma Rakshini Sabha," an organization of more local or regional importance.

76 Sri Aurobindo, *Uttarpara Speech.* Pondicherry 1999.

77 We should recall here that in the Krishna- or Vishnu-oriented schools of the Sanatana Dharma, Shri Krishna is seen as the highest

personality of God, more sublime even than the *brahman* of the Advaita Vedanta. The forms of address "Sri" in the case of Aurobindo, and "Shri" in the case of Shri Krishna, are more or less identical in meaning. The honorific aims to show that the bearer of the title possesses sanctity and higher knowledge. The Sanskrit letter श, or "Sha" (in academic texts rewritten as ś) is usually given as "sh" in this volume. In the name "Sri Aurobindo," the international form, without h or diacritic symbol, has become the norm, and is thus used here too. The name is always pronounced Shree Aurobindo.

78 Sri Aurobindo, *Uttarpara Speech*, op. cit.

79 Ibid.

80 Ibid.

81 Ibid.

82 In Sanskrit, *Adesha* has a very wide range of meanings: *dish*, corresponding to the word stem, means roughly "point of the compass" while the related *desha* means land or region. The prefix "a" here strengthens the meaning, an intensification of its inner significance as the receiving or obtaining of something. As verb, *adesh* can, for instance, mean pointing to something, determining, urging, instructing or giving (a task). In the context of Aurobindo's *Uttarpara Speech,* "giving Adesha" can be seen in terms of "giving a purpose or decision" and "urging one to go in a particular direction."

83 Sri Aurobindo, *Uttarpara Speech*, op. cit.

84 Ibid.

85 Sri Aurobindo, Karmayogin. *Political Writings and Speeches. 1909-1910.* Pondicherry 1997, in the address "The Ideal of the Karmayogin," June 19, 1909. Quoted in Peter Heehs, *The Lives of Sri Aurobindo*, op. cit, the chapter "In Jail and After: Bengal 1908-1910."

86 Peter Heehs, *The Lives of Sri Aurobindo*, op. cit., the chapter "In Jail and After: Bengal 1908–1910."

87 In an interview in *Hindu*, Jan. 4, 1915. Considering that Mohandas Karamchand Ghandi, who was three years older, would arrive in Bombay five days after publication of this interview, on Jan. 9, 1915, thus returning to his Indian homeland to pursue political campaigning there, and that Tagore welcomed him with the honorific "Mahatma," Sri Aurobindo's public declaration of his permanent withdrawal from political struggle on the one hand, and Tagore's greeting of Mahatma Ghandi on the other, can strike us like the transfer of the invisible torch of the Indian independence movement from one to the other across the subcontinent of southern Asia, or at least perhaps as if the one was giving up his place to the other. Of a later encounter between Tagore and Sri Aurobindo, Tagore wrote as follows: "The French steamer I was traveling on arrived in Pondicherry, and I met Aurobindo. At the very first sight I could realize that he had been seeking for the soul and had gained it, and through this long process of realization had accumulated within him a silent power of inspiration. His face was radiant with an inner light.... I felt that the utterance of the ancient Rishi spoke from him of the equanimity that gives the human soul its freedom of entrance into the All. I said to him,

'You have the Word and we are waiting to accept it from you. India will speak through your voice to the world, "Hearken to me."'"

88 In the early years because of the danger of political persecution, they stayed "under cover," often changing their address and suffering worsening conditions. They took it in turns to cook, often fish with curried rice (a Bengali dish) because it was cheapest. The only furniture they had was a couple of chairs, a desk and the suitcases they lived out of. There were times when they had to write begging letters, asking for a few rupees for their survival.

89 In fact, on the day he arrived in Pondicherry, Apr. 4, 1910, another warrant was issued for his arrest in Bengal.

90 Sri Aurobindo, *Sri Aurobindo: A Life-Sketch*. Pondicherry 1985. Aurobindo here writes about himself in the third person. Quoted in Peter Heehs, *The Lives of Sri Aurobindo*, op. cit., "A Laboratory Experiment: Pondicherry 1910–19."

91 Cf. Peter Heehs, *The Lives of Sri Aurobindo,* op. cit., the chapter "A Laboratory Experiment: Pondicherry, 1910-1915."

92 Alexandra David-Néel (1868–1969) visited Sri Aurobindo in Pondicherry in Nov. 1911. This visit belonged to the early stages of her fourteen-year journey through Asia, which was to lead her chiefly to Himalayan regions and Tibet, where she was ordained as a Buddhist nun.

93 Aia Aziz alias Max Théon, was probably born as Ludwig-Maximilian Bimstein, the son of a Warsaw rabbi, who was himself connected with the Cabbalistic traditions of the so-called Frankists.

94 Theodora and Eckhard Karnasch (eds), *Sri Aurobindo and The Mother* (bilingual edition), Pondicherry 2004.

95 For Sri Aurobindo, the name of the journal (synonymous with "Aryan") had nothing to do with racial characteristics, as it did later on for the Nazis. He sees the "Aryan" as someone who "accepted a particular type of self-culture, of inward and outward practice, of ideality, of inspiration." See Peter Heehs, *The Lives of Sri Aurobindo,* op. cit., "A Laboratory Experiment: Pondicherry 1910–1915." Cf. chap. 1.

96 Sri Aurobindo, *The Life Divine,* Lotus Press 1990, *The Ideal of Human Unity,* Lotus Press 1999, *The Human Cycle,* Lotus Press 1999, *Essays on the Gita,* Lotus Press 1995. Revisions and additions to essays that were first published in *The Arya* are in some instances very extensive. Important concepts such as the "Supermind" (from 1927 onward) were only formulated by Aurobindo in later years. His chief work, *The Life Divine*, was repeatedly revised by him over decades.

97 Further essays and shorter essay series that appeared in *The Arya*, are now compiled in vol. 13 of the complete works of Sri Aurobiondo, published in Pondicherry. Cf. Sri Aurobindo, *Essays in Philosophy and Yoga*. Pondicherry 1998, Part Three: "Writings from *The Arya* (1914–1921)."

98 From the perspective of the anthroposophic path of schooling this is especially significant since, according to comments by Rudolf Steiner, the new task of higher development from the twentieth century onward involves reintegrating and creating coherence between the

diverging soul faculties of thinking, feeling, and will by spiritual intensification of the individual I. Thinking corresponds to Jnana Yoga, feeling to Bhakti Yoga and the will to Karma Yoga. Thus the yoga of self-realization stands for awakening, developing, and strengthening of the higher self.

99 Cf. Sri Aurobindo, *Autobiographical Notes—and Other Writings of Historical Interest*. Pondicherry 2006, the section "Early Letters on Yoga and the Spiritual Life, 1911–1928."

100 Cf. Peter Heehs, *The Lives of Sri Aurobindo*, op. cit., chapter "The Ascent to Supermind: Pondicherry, 1915–1926)."

101 Mirra Alfassa (The Mother), *Questions and Answers. 1950–1951*. Pondicherry 2003. Discussion on March 17 1951.

102 Peter Heehs, *The Lives of Sri Aurobindo*, op. cit., the chapter "The Ascent to Supermind: Pondicherry 1915-1926."

103 Sri Aurobindo, *On Himself*, op. cit., quoted in: Otto Wolff, *Sri Aurobindo*, op. cit.

104 Since 1955, the ashram has been organized and run by the charitable "Sri Aurobindo Ashram Trust," led by a group of five "trustees." Currently the ashram in Puducherry (formally Pondicherry) has around 1,200 members, but the Ashram Trust states that the broader ashram community, with 400 students at the "Center of Education" and a similar number of permanent guests in the immediate proximity of the ashram, amounts to around 2,000 people altogether. Today there are over 400 houses across Puducherry that belong to the ashram. In the inner courtyard of the ashram's principal building in the Rue de la Marine lies the "Samadhi," a large shrine of white marble that is the last resting place of Sri Aurobindo and Mirra Alfassa. In Feb. 1956, in the Indian capital Delhi, the important "Delhi Branch" of the Sri Aurobindo Ashram was founded.

105 Cf. Wilfried Huchzermayer, *Sri Aurobindo.His Life and Work,* op. cit., the chapter "Pondicherry (1915-1926)."

106 Ambalal B. Purani, *The Life of Sri Aurobindo*. Pondicherry 2006, the chapter "Pondicherry: 1910–1926." Quoted in Wilfried Huchzermayer, *Sri Aurobindo.His Life and Work,* op. cit. Here it is very illuminating to consider a parallel with reminiscences of Rudolf Steiner. The important anthroposophic physician Willem Zeylmans van Emmichoven (1893–1961) described the experience he had in conversations with Rudolf Steiner. He writes: "I felt freer than ever, as if taken up into another world in which only the essential mattered; in which what we otherwise consider essential is discarded as unimportant. This gave a wonderful sense, a feeling of happiness and freedom. The fact we could sit next to one another, not facing each other, in physical space, and that he did not continually look at me, underpinned this feeling of freedom. His gaze was almost always directed forward, only turning round to me very suddenly at decisive moments—and then the whole sun power of his eyes met mine. There were moments when, without being noticeably impolite, nevertheless heard nothing of what I was saying but was clearly, rather, hearkening to something else in my soul." In: Maria Josepha Krück von Poturzyn (ed.), *A Man before Others: Rudolf Steiner Remembered,* Steiner Press

1993, quoted in: Peter Selg, *Rudolf Steiner, Life and Work. 1861–1925;* vols. 1–3, op. cit., vol. 1 (1861–1914), chap. 7, "Spiritual Community Building."

107 The word *sachchidananda* is composed of the three terms *Sat-Chit-Ananda,* and thus signifies divine being, divine consciousness and divine bliss.

108 Cf. Sri Aurobindo, *The Life Divine,* Book 1, op. cit., "The Divine Maya," Lotus Press 1990.

109 Sri Aurobindo, *Record of Yoga,* Pondicherrry 2001. Part Four: "Materials Written by Sri Aurobindo Related Directly to *Record of Yoga.*" The passage quoted here is part of a diagram for the "ladder of consciousness," dated 1931. Cf. also, Sri Aurobindo, *The Hour of God,* Pondicherry 1959.

110 The Sun god Vishvakarman is an instance of this. Rudolf Steiner describes him as a leading, divine-spiritual being of the solar system, the entity addressed as Ahura Mazda in the Persian Zend Avesta, and as part of the cosmic Christ being, the Logos becoming human. Vishvakarman, traditionally seen as an aspect of the Sun god Surya, and as the greatest creator ("the universal architect") among the devas, was indeed often represented in later Vedic texts as the highest godhead.

111 In the context of the Vedas, things become still more complex because here the rishis also often appear to have equal status with the devas—that is, the distinction between a human creature and a divine, spiritual being is erased. The reason for this is to be sought in the fact that, according to Rudolf Steiner, the Vedic rishis were the bearers of higher spiritual beings. Cf. Rudolf Steiner, *The Spiritual Guidance of the Individual and Humanity*, CW 15, lect. 7, June 7, 1911.

112 Sri Aurobindo, *The Life Divine*, p. 291, book 1, "Supermind, Mind and the Overmind Maya."

113 This demonstrates that Integral Yoga also encompasses Jnana Yoga within it, the yoga of knowledge. We could call one decisive path of development in sadhana practice the "spiritualization of the intellect," comparable to what Rudolf Steiner sought with his Anthroposophy under this same term.

114 Sri Aurobindo, *The Life Divine*, Book One, "Supermind, Mind and the Overmind Maya."

115 Ibid.

116 Ibid.

117 Cf. *The Isha Upanishad*, Sri Aurobindo Ashram Publications, 1986.

118 Sri Aurobindo, *The Life Divine*, op. cit., the chapter "Supermind, Mind and the Overmind Maya." "Existence-Consciousness-Bliss" here stands for the Sanskrit term *sachchidananda.*

119 Sri Aurobindo, *The Life Divine*, op. cit., the chapter "Supermind, Mind and the Overmind Maya." Here it seems appropriate to compare Sri Aurobindo's comments with those made by Rudolf Steiner in the context of anthroposophic Spiritual Science. They show the spiritual affinity between him and Sri Aurobindo, and also enable us to see how their concepts are related, although there is no intention here simply to "translate" the terms of Integral Yoga directly into those of

Anthroposophy. In what follows, Rudolf Steiner speaks of "spirit land" as the third of the three worlds (the world of physical corporeality, the soul world, and the world of spirit), and of the archetypes present in spirit land of all that exists in lower worlds: "You see, the archetypes in their true form are very different from their sensory copies; and they are likewise very dissimilar from their shadows, abstract thoughts. In the world of spirit everything is in continuous motion and activity, in ceaseless creative activity. There is no resting or dwelling in one place as occurs in the physical world. The archetypes are *creative beings*. They are the architects of everything that arises in the physical and soul world. Their forms change swiftly; and every archetype has the potential to assume countless different forms. We can say that they allow these distinctive forms to sprout from them, and scarcely has one been engendered than another begins to spring from the archetype. And the archetypes have reciprocal relationships of greater or lesser affinity. They do not work on their own, in isolation. The one requires the help of the other for its creative activity. Often, countless archetypes work together so as to give rise to this or that entity in the soul world or the physical world" (Rudolf Steiner, *Theosophy*, Anthroposophic Press 1994, "The Three Worlds"; this translation by Matthew Barton). This is very reminiscent of the last cited passage in which Sri Aurobindo describes the nature of overmind. But here only the three lower regions of spirit land, or of the lower plane of devachan referred to earlier, stand in direct relationship to the lower worlds. The fourth region has its distinctive quality, and above it connects with the upper plane of devachan, which encompasses the fifth, sixth and seventh regions of spirit land. Rudolf Steiner continues by describing the fourth region, that of pure Akasha, as follows: "The archetypes of the *fourth* region do not relate directly to the other worlds. In certain respects they are beings who rule over the archetypes of the three lower regions and mediate their interplay. They are therefore involved in ordering and grouping these subordinate archetypes. From this region, therefore, issues a more comprehensive activity than from the lower ones." (Ibid.)

The mental realm or plane according to Sri Aurobindo can perhaps be identified as Rudolf Steiner's three lower planes of spirit land. Beginning with the fourth region, of which Steiner speaks in the above passage, we find a great resemblance to Sri Aurobindo's account of the "original maya," the overmind. There is full accord between them in relation to the three regions of the higher spiritual world: "The *fifth, sixth,* and *seventh* regions are substantially different from the preceding ones. The beings that live there provide the archetypes of the lower regions with the *impulses* for their activities. There we find the creative powers at work in these archetypes. Someone who is able to ascend to these regions becomes acquainted with the *'intentions'* that underlie our world. Like living germinal points the archetypes here lie ready to assume the most diverse forms of thought beings. When these germinal points are led downward into the lower regions, they spring open as it were and reveal the most manifold forms. The creative ideas of the human spirit in the physical world are the reflection, the shadow, of these germinal thought beings in the higher world of spirit." (Ibid.)

Qualities of the supramental Vijnana also seem to play in here. The author of this book takes issue with the account by Udo Knipper, who produced a comparative study of Integral Yoga and Anthroposophy in the 1980s. Knipper draws parallels between Sri Aurobindo's mental plane and Rudolf Steiner's spirit land, and relates the overmind to all the planes described by Steiner as higher than those of spirit land, or the plane of devachan (the world of destiny, the planes of Nirvana, Parinirvana, and Mahaparinirvana). Some aspects of Udo Knipper's account give the impression that he does not wish to relate the two schools to each other in dialogic fashion but to establish a competitive rivalry between them. (Cf. Udo Knipper, *Anthroposophie im Lichte indischer Weisheit*, Gladenbach 1986.)

In more recent times, however, a further comparative study has been published of Anthroposophy and Integral Yoga (and Auroville). This was issued privately, and is less rigorously conducted, more strongly coloured by the author's personal experience and perspective. (Cf. Karl-Heinz Falkenburger, *Auroville ist überall. Die Bestimmung des Menschen im Lichte von Rudolf Steiner und Sri Aurobindo,* no publication data.)

120 *The Life Divine*, Book One, op. cit., "The Supermind as Creator."

121 Earth, air, and the heavenly Sun world. As the *triloka*, the three worlds, they signify the plane of physical corporeality, the vital plane, and the mental plane.

122 Datta, alias Dorothy Hodgson, an Englishwoman who had met Mirra Alfassa in France, went with her to Japan and moved with her to Pondicherry.

123 Ambalal B. Purani, *The Life of Sri Aurobindo*. Pondicherry 1958, "Pondicherry: 1910–1926," where this event is also summarized.

124 Sri Aurobindo, *On Himself*. Pondicherry 1958, "His Path and Other Paths."

125 For more on the concept of the guru in the works of both Sri Aurobindo and Rudolf Steiner, see also appendix 1 in this volume, "The Guru—a Modern View of an Ancient Concept."

126 Cf. Rudolf Steiner, *The Gospel of St. John*, June 24 1909.

127 Cf. Klaus J. Bracker, *Grals-Initiation*, op. cit.

128 Wilfried Huchzermeyer, *Sri Aurobindo. His Life and Work,* op. cit., "Pondicherry (1927–1938)." The words by Mirra Alfassa are published in the volume: Mirra Alfassa (The Mother), *Questions and Answers, 1957–1958*. Pondicherry 1973, 2003.

129 Cf. for example *Letters on Yoga*. Pondicherry 2012–2014 (4 volumes amounting to more than two thousand, four hundred pages).

130 Sri Aurobindo, *Savitri*, Pondicherry 1997.

131 Sri Aurobindo, *On Himself,* op. cit., the chapter "Sadhana for the Earth Consciousness," entry on Feb. 10, 1935. We explore the concept of supermind in more detail in a later chapter.

132 Sri Aurobindo, *On Himself,* op. cit., the chapter "Sadhana for the Earth Consciousness," in a letter of May 30, 1936.

133 Nirodbaran, *Correspondence with Sri Aurobindo*. Lodi, CA 1983. Quoted in Wilfried Huchzermeyer, *Sri Aurobindo. His Life and Work,* op. cit., the chapter "Pondicherry (1927–1938)."

134 Cf. Peter Heehs, *The Lives of Sri Aurobindo*, op. cit., "A Laboratory Experiment" (Pondicherry 1910–1915) and "The Ascent to Supermind (Pondicherry 1915–1926). See also Wilfried Huchzermeyer, *Sri Aurobindo. Leben und Werk,* op. cit., "Pondicherry (1910–1914)."

135 The seven-year rhythm is apparent in the first half of Sri Aurobindo's life: at the age of 7 he moved to England, returning to India at 21; at 28, he embarked on his political campaign; at 35, he experienced yogic realization in his encounter with Guru Lele (Nirvana and transcendence of it). During this sixth seven-year period of life, he had the experience at Alipur and moved to Pondicherry; at the age of 42 he met Mirra Alfassa and was inspired to begin writing (*The Arya* 1914–1921). But during the second half of his life, as he began to write, the twelve-year rhythm (the Jupiter rhythm) becomes apparent: in 1914 the first issue of *The Arya;* in 1926 the descent of overmind and the beginning of his strict seclusion; in 1938 the accident, which meant that some sadhakas gained regular access to Sri Aurobindo's rooms again. In the last twelve years of his life, from 1938 to 1950, Sri Aurobindo once more took a discernible interest in world affairs.

136 As representative of the wealth of literature produced by the ashramites during Sri Aurobindo's lifetime, I would refer here to Nirodbaran's reminiscences of the years 1938–1950: Nirodbaran, *Twelve Years with Sri Aurobindo*. Pondicherry 1972.

137 See the biographies cited in note 64 for more details about this period.

138 Sri Aurobindo, *On Himself,* op. cit., "Messages" The radio message was broadcast throughout India on Aug. 14, 1947.

139 Sri Aurobindo, *Essays in Philosophy and Yoga*, Part Five: *From the Bulletin of Physical Education* (1949–1950). "The Supramental Manifestation upon Earth, Supermind in the Evolution."

Chapter 3

140 Édouard Schuré (translated Rudolf Steiner), *Das heilige Drama von Eleusis*, Dornach 1939. Available in English as a reprint, in *The Genesis of Tragedy and the Sacred Drama of Eleusis,* Kessinger Publishing, 2010.

141 Édouard Schuré (translated Rudolf Steiner), *Die Kinder des Lucifer*, Available in English, in *East in the Light of the West /Children of Lucifer,* Garber Communications (U.S.), 1986.

142 Rudolf Steiner, *Four Mystery Dramas*, tr. R. and H. Pusch; rev. B. Renold, G. Williamson, J. Alexandra, Rudolf Steiner Press 2015. The first two of the four plays, *The Portal of Initiation* and *The Soul's Probation* are presented as "given *through* Rudolf Steiner," while the third and fourth, *The Guardian of the Threshold* and *The Souls' Awakening* are "*by* Rudolf Steiner" (translator's italics). The plays were first performed in Munich in the third or fourth week of August in, respectively, 1910, 1911, 1912, and 1913.

143 Cf. the "Vorbemerkung des Herausgebers" (editor's preface) in Rudolf Steiner, *Entwürfe, Fragmente und Paralipomena zu den vier Mysteriendramen*, Dornach 1985.

144 Édouard Schuré, *The Great Initiates, A Study of the Secret History of Religions,* Steiner Books 1992.

145 Ibid, from Rudolf Steiner's foreword to the third edition (1916). Elsewhere, speaking of the path upon which "the human being develops capacities of perception that slumber within him," the founder of modern anthroposophic schooling said that Schuré's book was "one of the best guides in the modern age" for discovering this path, since it "speaks of the deeds of the *illuminati* whom we can discern within the spiritual history of humanity, and it leads from these deeds back into the souls of these enlightened ones themselves." Ibid, from Rudolf Steiner's foreword to the first edition (1907).

146 Cf. Klaus J. Bracker, *Grals-Initiation*, op. cit., chap. 3 in the section "Anthropos—Der ur-adamische Krishna-Jesus." Here Shri Krishna's Avatar nature is thoroughly examined from the anthroposophic perspective.

147 Persia, with its Zarathustran religion, is mentioned here because Rudolf Steiner always accords it importance in his accounts. However, Schuré did not honor ancient Persia with its own chapter in *The Great Initiates*, but only refers occasionally to "Zoroaster."

148 Édouard Schuré, *The Great Initiates*, op. cit., in the chapter "Krishna" (this translation M. Barton).

149 Cf. Rudolf Steiner, *The Gospel of St. Mark.* SteinerBooks 1990. Lecture of Sept. 19, 1912.

150 Horace H. Wilson (ed.), *The Vishnu Purana: A System of Hindu Mythology and Tradition. Translated from the Original Sanskrit by H. H. Wilson.* London 1840. book 5, sect. 2. The book by Schuré mentioned contains in note 17 a comparable passage translated from the French by Marie von Sivers, which deviates in certain respects from the version given here. Cf. Édouard Schuré, *The Great Initiates, A Study of the Secret History of Religions,* op. cit., notes.

151 See note 50 in relation to "Purusha" and "Prakriti" (corresponding to "Maha-Purusha" and "Mula-Prakriti").

152 The practice of chanting, of speech-song, in the recitation of the Vedas, is traditionally known as *saman*, that is, sacred song; or also as *kirtana*, in the verbal form signifying praising, celebrating, recounting, or repeating.

153 *Rig Veda*, 3,62.10; quoted in Hermann Beckh, "Das Sonnen-Mantram des Rigveda und seine Bedeutung für die Entwicklungsaufgabe des Indischen Volkes." In *Die Drei. Zeitschrift für Anthroposophie in Wissenschaft, Kunst und sozialem Leben.* Year 1, no. 5/6, Stuttgart 1921.

154 Ibid.

155 Ibid. Cf. also Hermann Beckh, *Indische Weisheit und Christentum* (in the series *Theologie und Kultus*, volume 9), Stuttgart 1938, in the chapter "Der indische Yoga und Christus."

156 In Sanskrit, or in Devanagari, the most commonly used written form of Sanskrit, the spoken "o" is represented by a contraction of the sign for "a" and "u."

157 *Pranava* means roughly "vibrating sound," and signifies, at the same time, the "mystic syllable," or the "sacred syllable," which in India refers invariably and unmistakably to the OM.

158 This is the tradition of the Indian Veda schools, the *veda pathshala,* which however seem to be losing vigor increasingly in recent decades.

159 *The Principal Upanishads* (translated and edited by Sarvepalli Radhakrishnan), London 1953 (second impression 1968). The expression that figures here, *udgitha*, is sometimes explained as follows: *ut* is the heavens, *gi* the middle region, the atmosphere, *tha* the earth: this corresponds in turn to bhur–bhuvar–svar mentioned previously.

160 Maheshwar (ed.), *Bhagavad Gita: In the Light of Sri Aurobindo.* Pondicherry 1978, chap. 10.

161 Sri Aurobindo, *Kena and Other Upanishads.* Pondicherry 2001, "The Mandoukya Upanishad."

162 The fourth element of the AUM is expressed by the dot over the three curves of the OM symbol, hovering over and separated from the rest of the form by a semi-circle opening upward. In his *Speech and Drama Course*, Rudolf Steiner shows that the OM contains an essential passage from the "A" through the mediating "O" to the "U." Associated with the "A" is the tendency to fall asleep, with the "U" a tendency to awaken, and with the "O," however, the possibility of sustaining our consciousness in the tension between sleeping and waking. It is precisely this that is needed if we seek to accomplish the ascent through the four levels, as described by the *Upanishad.* Cf. Rudolf Steiner, *Speech and Drama,* SteinerBooks 2007, lecture on Sept. 5, 1924.

163 Cf. Rudolf Steiner, *How to Know Higher Worlds,* Anthroposophic Press 1994, "Continuity of Consciousness." In his book on esoteric schooling, *Knowledge of the Higher Worlds*, Rudolf Steiner takes his account of the continuity of consciousness only as far as the third level, that of deep sleep consciousness. But it is clear from his unfinished autobiography, that he also realized the fourth level in the course of his initiation. Cf. Rudolf Steiner, *Autobiography*, op. cit, chapter 22. More recently, Ken Wilber, in his spiritual journal of 1997, reported on his own experiences with continuity of consciousness. He speaks of "subject permanence" or "constant consciousness." Cf. Ken Wilber, *One Taste: The Journals of Ken Wilber*, 1999, rev. ed. 2000, journal entries for March 9, 23, and 24.

164 Cf. Sri Aurobindo, *The Hour of God,* op. cit., the "OM TAT SAT."

165 Cf. Rudolf Steiner, *The Influence of Spiritual Beings upon Man,* lecture of June 4, 1908, Anthroposophic Press 1961.

166 Rudolf Steiner, *Esoteric Lessons 1904–1909,* vol. 1, SteinerBooks 2007, lesson of Jan. 20, 1907. This text is not a full transcript but only a record by a participant in the class.

167 Cf. Ibid, esoteric lesson of Dec. 18, 1906.

168 Cf. Rudolf Steiner, *Menschenwerden, Weltenseele und Weltengeist,* Dornach 1987, the lecture of July 15, 1921. Here he pursues the theme further toward the higher stages of knowledge of Imagination, Inspiration, and Intuition.

169 Sri Aurobindo, *Kena and Other Upanishads*, op. cit., the chapter "The Mandoukya Upanishad."

170 *Shatapatha Brahmana,* I, 4,5.12. Quoted in Raimundo Panikkar, *The Vedic Experience—Mantramanjari*, op. cit, chapter, "The Word."

171 The expression "seemingly spiritual" does not mean to suggest that the wisdom imparted to humankind by luciferic beings is not drawn from the totality of truth and wisdom in the cosmos. It is problematic, rather, because it has been sundered from the true intention of the spirituality of the universe, according to which the entirety of material and spiritual evolution must be encompassed and penetrated. Only in this sense is it un- or anti-spiritual.

172 Rudolf Steiner describes the role of ahrimanic and luciferic beings in the evolution of the cosmos from many diverse perspectives, for instance in his magnum opus *An Outline of Esoteric Science.* Cf. Rudolf Steiner, *An Outline of Esoteric Science*, op. cit., "Cosmic Evolution and the Human Being."

173 Rudolf Steiner, *Kunst- und Lebensfragen im Lichte der Geisteswissenschaft*, Dornach 2000, lecture of July 18, 1915.

174 Rudolf Steiner, *Soziales Verständnis aus geisteswissenschaftlicher Erkenntnis,* Dornach 1989, lecture of Nov. 15, 1919.

175 Ibid.

176 As regards the last two lectures by Rudolf Steiner referred to above, both given to members of the Anthroposophical Society, it is important to remember that the first took place about a year after the start of World War I, and the second a few days after the first anniversary of Germany's capitulation. The motif Steiner addresses in these lectures, of distinctions and differentiations between languages, cannot be detached from virulent national conflicts raging in Europe and elsewhere at the time. It is a theme that still has great actuality today.

177 Cf. Sri Aurobindo, *The Renaissance in India and Other Essays on Indian Culture*. Pondicherry 1997, the chapter "Indian Literature."

178 Sri Aurobindo, *The Secret of the Veda*, op. cit., the chapter "The Philological method of the Veda." In relation to the phrase "this ancient psychology of the Word," it should be noted that in Sri Aurobindo's works the word "psychological" always signifies "related to the soul and spirit." His "psychological" interpretation of the Veda aims to be one that clearly conveys its soul-spiritual dimension.

179 See the introductory section in chap. 1.

180 Rudolf Steiner, *The Mission of the Folk-Souls,* op. cit., lecture of June 8,1910.

181 In the West today, *tantra* is often understood to mean special techniques for sublimating and spiritualizing the awoken libido between a man and woman. In fact this is only one of numerous branches of tantra, and perhaps for many the most sensational. In the oldest etymology, *tantra* means roughly "tissue, continuum,

context." It also has a Vedic origin, sometimes overlooked. In the context of rig-vedic worship, *tan* means, among other things, to "spread a fabric," while the related noun *tán* means "duration, continuation, uninterrupted sequence." There is a connection here with what was said above about reciprocal processes in Vedic practice, which constitute the "fabric of Vedic reality." Warp and weft in the unified tantric world view are reciprocal pairs like transcendence and immanence, Shiva and Shakti, divine Word and human word, macrocosm–microcosm, etc. In their interwoven nature they constitute the tissue of reality that is also continuous through time. For more on the roots *tan* and *tán* see Hermann Grassmann, *Wörterbuch zum Rig Veda*, Delhi 1999.

182 Sri Aurobindo, *The Future Poetry*, Pondicherry 1997, "The Word and the Spirit."

183 Cf. the last section of this chapter, "Ephesus and Eurythmy."

184 Cf. André Padoux, *Vac—The Concept of the Word in Selected Hindu-Tantras*, Delhi 1992, the chapter "Tantrism—The Texts of Kashmiri Shaivism."

185 *Rig Veda*, I,164.45; quoted in, Nishtha Müller, "Betrachtung zur Einführung in die Veden. Part VI: Vak, die Göttin des Wortes und Mutter der Veden." In: *Yoga aktuell. Magazin für Yoga, spirituellen Lifestyle und Gesundheit*, no. 56, 3/2009. Here *turiyam* is translated as "the fourth (plane)," due to counting from the lowest level up.

186 Sri Aurobindo, *The Future Poetry*, op. cit, "The Word and the Spirit."

187 Ibid.

188 Rudolf Steiner, *Materialism and the Task of Anthroposophy*, Anthroposophic Press 1987, lect. of Apr. 24, 1921. *Astral body* refers to the soul body that we have in common with animals.

189 In relation to Soma, Hermann Beckh writes: "This Soma however contains the enlivening powers of the universe; it encompasses the cosmic forces of the stars through to the ether forces of the plant world. The earthly Soma brewed from the milk sap of a certain plant was the cultic image of the heavenly Soma—of all that is not of earthly but of super-earthly and cosmic nature. These Soma forces become in the human being the priestly powers of seership. Soma has nothing to do with the lower clairvoyant powers of a dulled awareness, which the Indians saw, by contrast, in the lower intoxicant, the sura (which corresponds roughly to our alcohol). Soma, rather, is the awakener and, at the same time, the image of sublime and noble enthusiasm and ecstasy, of the true nature of higher consciousness." Hermann Beckh, *Indische Weisheit und Christentum*, op. cit., "Michael und die indische Vorzeit."

190 Rudolf Steiner, *The Arts and their Mission*, Anthroposophic Press 1967, Lecture of June 8, 1923.

191 Sri Aurobindo, The Secret of the Veda, op. cit., "Soma, Lord of Delight and Immortality." Brahmanaspati is another name for the better-known Brihaspati, of whom it is said in the Glossary to Records of Yoga: This deity is "a Vedic god, the 'Master of the Creative Word'; the universal deva as the 'self-expressive Soul,' giver of the supreme word, by which is effected the 'manifestation of the

different world-planes in the conscient human being' culminating in the manifestation of the superconscient, the Truth and the Bliss.'" Sri Aurobindo, *Record of Yoga,* appendix, vol. *Glossary to Records of Yoga,* op. cit.

192 In chapter 4, a thorough study of the question of the "I" will be undertaken. Here we will note only that the "I" constitutes a spiritual entity that undergoes emancipation by actively overcoming or integrating lower ego qualities. Thus *"I"* and *ego* are by no means synonymous terms.

193 Sri Aurobindo, *The Secret of the Veda*, op. cit., "Indra and the Thought-Forces."

194 *Tattiriya Brahmana* 3,10,8. Contained in the *Krishna Yajur Veda.* Quoted in David Frawley, *A Vedic Consecration to the Spiritual Heart* (www.vedanet.com). In contrast to the solar *Shukla Yajur Veda* (Shukla, the "white") the *Krishna Yajur Veda* (Krishna here signifying "the black") is regarded as having a lunar orientation. In southern India it is more widespread. The *Shukla Yajur Veda* is assigned to the Sun, and is more important in northern India.

195 *Rig Veda* X, 125,7,8. Quoted in Raimundo Panikaar, *The Vedic Experience. Mantramanjari,* op. cit, "The Word."

196 Raimundo Panikaar, *The Vedic Experience. Mantramanjari,* op. cit, "The Word."

197 Sri Aurobindo, *The Secret of the Veda*, op. cit, the chapter "Indra and the Thought-Forces."

198 *Kathaka Samkalana,* in the *Yajur Veda,* 12,5—quoted in André Padoux, *Vac: The Concept of the Word in Selected Hindu-Tantras*, op. cit., "Early Speculations about the Significance and the Powers of the Word." *Prajapati,* identical with *Vishvakarman,* figured at the beginning of the previous section, "Vak: the Word of the Rishis." Prajapati and Vak are seen in the last-cited passage—already in the Vedic and not yet the tantric context—in a clearly sexual image.

199 See note 50, chap. 1.

200 And yet this Aditi quality—which penetrates everything and sustains all forms—is intimately close and spiritually accessible to the world of human experience.

201 Sri Aurobindo, *The Secret of the Veda*, op. cit., the chapter "The Seven Rivers. Cf. also chap. 1, "Spiritual Insight into the Vedic World."

202 When speaking of the authentic human "I"-being, it should always be remembered that this must be distinguished, in an anthroposophic context, from the lower, empirical ego. In Integral Yoga, similarly, the *chaitya purusha* or "psychic being" should be distinguished from the ego.

203 Cf. chapter I, the section "Spiritual Insight into the Vedic World."

204 Rudolf Steiner, *An Outline of Esoteric Science*, op. cit., "World Evolution and the Human Being." Cf. also note 50.

205 Ibid, *Man in the Light of Occultism, Theosophy and Philosophy,* Steiner Press 1964, lecture of June 12, 1912.

206 This only seemingly contradicts the fact that Shri Krishna, for instance in connection with the events of Nov. 24 1926 (see chap. 2, "The overmind") is characterized as an overmental being. The overmental,

mula-Prakritic portrayal of Shri Krishna within original maya, is his cosmic manifestation. The revelation of his *svabhava*, his "self-creating being and becoming" nevertheless belongs to supermind, if not to the realm of *sachchidananda*.

207 Rudolf Steiner, *The Missions of the Folk Souls*, op. cit, lect. of June 14, 1910.

208 Rudolf Steiner, *Eurythmy as Visible Speech,* Dornach 1968, lect. of Aug. 26, 1923. According to Steiner the other group of speech sounds, the consonants, does not manifest human interiority, our spirit–soul, but instead they dynamically embody the external cosmos. They reveal the "world" in the elements of speech. And the world, according to spiritual-scientific knowledge, is constituted and configured through cosmic formative forces that shine in from the zodiac constellations in twelvefold diversity upon the earth. For this reason too the consonants have a twelvefold order, corresponding to the star signs of the zodiac. The relationship of the vowels to the consonants has always also been of interest to representatives of Kashmiri shivaitic tantrism. The following quotation from a book about *Vak* by André Padoux summarizes accounts from the *Malinivijayottaratantra,* a key text in the tradition founded on enquiries into the mysteries of language. There is a difficulty, however, in that very diverse classifications appear in tantrism of the 50 letters of the Sanskrit alphabet, one of which is presented here: "The initial twofold division—seed (*bija*) and womb (*yoni*)—is the basic one, for it corresponds to that of Shiva and Shakti: creation comes into being through their conjunction. Vowels (*svara*), which are aspects of Shiva, are the seeds or germs. Consonants (*vyanjana*) are energy and womb; as such they are held as inferior to vowels, which come before them and give them birth....With respect to the *tattvas*, the vowels are held as corresponding to Shiva, whereas consonants correspond to energy and to all of its contents, namely to all the other *tattvas* from *shakti* down to the earth." André Padoux, Vac—The *Concept of the Word in Selected Hindu-Tantras,* op. cit, the chapter, "Manifestation of Sound." This is illuminating if we consider that the 36 *tattvas* represent the formative forces of the universe. In Kashmiri tantrism, Shiva functions in fact as the Highest, beyond all duality, comparable to Shri Krishna as the Purushottama in the *Bhagavad Gita*.

209 Cf. Thomas Lehmann, *Sanskrit für Anfänger. Ein Lehr- und Übungsbuch*. Vol. 1: *Grammatik*. Heidelberg 2007. Lesson 1.2" "Das Vokalsystem." The sequence of the seven long vowels corresponds here to that of the Sanskrit alphabet. "Eh" and "oh" are experienced as pure vowels, but in Sanskrit they are "assigned to the composite vowels for philological reasons" (Thomas Lehmann, ibid).

210 Sri Aurobindo, *Kena and Other Upanishads*, op. cit., "Kena Upanishad: Commentary—II: The Question: What Godhead?"

211 David Frawley, *Agni and the Fire of Self-Inquiry*. In: *The Mountain Path Journal*. Tiruvannamalai / Tamil Nadu 2003. The expression "adhyatmic" refers to "adhyatma," meaning "inward" in the sense of "belonging to the eternal self."

212 Sri Aurobindo, *Kena and Other Upanishads*, op. cit, the chapter "Kena Upanishad: Commentary—V: The Supreme Word." This passage continues as follows: "The Word has its seed-sounds—suggesting the eternal syllable of the Veda, AUM, and the seed-sounds of the Tantriks—which carry in them the principles of things; it has its forms that stand behind the revelatory and inspired speech that comes to man's supreme faculties, and these compel the forms of things in the universe; it has its rhythms—for it is no disordered vibration, but moves out into great cosmic measures—and according to the rhythm is the law, arrangement, harmony, processes of the world it builds. Life itself is a rhythm of God." Ibid.

213 Rudolf Steiner, *Menschheitsentwicklung und Christus-Erkenntnis*, Dornach 1981, lecture of June 28, 1907.

214 Drawing on Anthroposophy and with an accent, respectively, on the history of religion, philosophy, and mystery practices, Wilhelm Kelber, Karl-Martin Dietz, and Frank Teichmann have authored groundbreaking studies on the Logos idea of Heraclitus and his successors. Cf. Wilhelm Kelber, *Die Logoslehre*, Stuttgart 1958; Karl-Martin Dietz, *Metamorphosen des Geistes,* Vol. III: *Heraklit von Ephesus und die Entwicklung der Individualität*, Stuttgart 1990; and Frank Teichmann, *Die griechischen Mysterien,* Stuttgart 2007.

215 Due to these qualities, a closer connection is suspected between Artemis and Demeter, and some people associate the Artemis mysteries with those of Eleusis.

216 Wilhelm Kelber here sees a clear accord with Rudolf Steiner's spiritual-scientific view and vision of the development of the four previous planetary conditions through warmth, air, water, and earth. Cf. Wilhelm Kelber, *Die Logoslehre,* op. cit., the chapter "Heraklit."

217 Karl-Martin Dietz, *Metamorphosen des Geistes,* vol. 3: *Heraklit von Ephesus und die Entwicklung der Individualität,* op. cit., "Das Werk Heraklits."

218 Heraclitus, *On Nature*, fragment 1, quoted in Wilhelm Kelber, *Die Logoslehre,* op. cit., "Heraklit."

219 Heraclitus, *On Nature*, Fragment 30, quoted by Karl-Martin Dietz in *Metamorphosen des Geistes,* vol. 3: *Heraklit von Ephesus und die Entwicklung der Individualität*, op. cit., "Das Werk Heraklits."

220 Heraclitus, *On Nature*, Fragment 64; quoted in Karl-Martin Dietz, ibid.

221 Ibid, Fragment 64a.

222 Heraclitus, *On Nature,* Fragment 46 (different numerical listing); quoted in William Harris, *Heraclitus: The Complete Fragments: Translation and Commentary and The Greek Text.* Middlebury, VT 1994.

223 Heraclitus, *On Nature*, Fragment 65; quoted in Karl-Martin Dietz, op. cit., "Das Werk Heraklits."

224 Ibid, Fragment 2.

225 Heraclitus, *On Nature,* Fragment 45, quoted in Frank Teichmann, *Die griechischen Mysterien,* op. cit., the chapter "Heraklit von Ephesos."

226 Cf. Karl-Martin Dietz, *Metamorphosen des Geistes,* vol. 3: *Heraklit von Ephesus und die Entwicklung der Individualität,* op. cit., "Das Werk Heraklits."

227 Rudolf Steiner, *Christianity as Mystical Fact,* the chapter, "Greek Sages before Plato in the Light of Mystery Wisdom."

228 Ibid.

229 Eusebius of Caesarea, *Praeparatio evangelica.* xv,14; quoted in: Wilhelm Kelber, *Die Logoslehre*, op. cit., "Der Ausbau der Logoslehre in der Stoa."

230 See also notes 208 and 212 (the latter with a passage by Sri Aurobindo). Kelber's view of the possibly unique character of the stoic concept of *logoi spermatikoi* is at odds, likewise, with the significance accorded to speech sounds and letters in the Jewish Kabbala. The latter is based specifically on the idea that God created the world through His Word, and that words and phonemes or letters constitute the founding elements of Creation; indeed, that every speech sound or letter embodies a "channel" for a specific creative energy that manifests divine will.

231 Cf. Johannes Hirschberger, *Geschichte der Philosophie.* vol. 1: *Altertum und Mittelalter,* Freiburg i. Br. 1981, "Neuplatonismus: Philosophie und Religion," section "Philon von Alexandrien." See also Wilhelm Kelber, *Die Logoslehre*, op. cit., "Die Logoslehre im Judentum."

232 In modern times the Logos was often interpreted in a one-sidedly spiritual or abstract way. The tangible aspect of its utterance and audibility faded increasingly from view. No less a writer than Martin Heidegger critically questioned this view (*logos* is "translated"—i.e., invariably interpreted—as reason, judgment, concept, definition, reason, relationship…"); he again emphasizes the tangible, sensory aspect of the Logos when he says that the *logos* is *phoneme*—a voiced utterance. Cf. Martin Heidegger, *Sein und Zeit*, Tübingen 1967, chapter 2, § 7, B—"Der Begriff des Logos."

233 In the wording of the King James Bible, from which all Bible passages will be taken.

234 Rudolf Steiner, *Christianity as Mystical Fact*, op. cit., "The Miracle of Lazarus." The reference to spiritual research on which Rudolf Steiner—like Sri Aurobindo—drew, is one the reader can relate to as, at least, working hypotheses whose plausibility arises from the overall context of what is presented. In chapter 1 of this book, in relation to the question of the dating of the proto-Indian, Vedic civilization, we examined the relationship between spiritual research of this kind and the prevailing academic findings. Recent studies on the New Testament—in contrast to the widespread assumption in the twentieth century that the Gospel of St. John was written by diverse authors—are in fact now once again supporting the thesis that both the Gospel of St. John and The Epistles of St. John originated with a single, brilliantly gifted author (cf. for instance Martin Hengel, *Die johanneische Frage. Ein Lösungsversuch*, Tübingen 1993; Klaus Berger, *Im Anfang war Johannes. Datierung und Theologie des vierten Evangeliums,* Stuttgart 1997).

235 Cf. Gerd-Klaus Kaltenbrunner, *Dionysius vom Areopag. Das Unergründliche, die Engel und das Eine*, Zug/Switzerland 1996, in "Die schwarze Schönheit als Sonnenfrau."

236 Cf. Eusebius of Caesarea, *Historia Ecclesiastica*, third book, chapters 23 and 31. Eusebius here cites as his authority, in particular, Irenaeus of Lyon (around AD 135–202) and Bishop Polycrates of Ephesus (AD 125–196).

237 Cf. Gerd-Klaus Kaltenbrunner, *Johannes ist sein Name. Priesterkönig, Gralshüter, Traumgestalt*, Zug/Switzerland 1993, the chapter "Vom Jünger, den Jesus liebte, zur mystischen Dynastie der Johanniden."

238 Clemens of Alexandria, *Teppiche: Wissenschaftliche Darlegungen entsprechend der wahren Philosophie (Stromateis)*, Munich 1936–1938; book one, chap. 1.

239 John Scotus Eriugena, *The Voice of the Eagle. Homily on the Prologue to the Gospel of St. John*. Hudson, NY 1990.

240 For an anthroposophic perspective on these sayings, see Friedrich Rittelmeyer, *Ich bin. Reden und Aufsätze über die sieben "Ich bin"-Worte des Johannesevangeliums*, Stuttgart 1951.

241 These comments touch on fundamental insights into the reciprocal nature of Christian worship, apparent most clearly in the words about "bread" and "wine." In the context of these observations, this can be compared especially with what was said earlier about the reciprocity inherent in the living, active nature of the Vedic Word. See the section "Om: The Pranava."

242 See the introductory passage of the fourth section of this chapter, "The Logos."

243 Rudolf Steiner, *Mysteriengestaltung*, Dornach 1998. Lecture of Dec. 2, 1923.

244 Here we can recall the comment by David Frawley about the Vak, which, as one of Agni's "three chiefly inward (*adhyatama*) forms," ensouls the human being in three levels of his nature, and is located between prana (life force) and buddhi (intelligence). See above, the relevant citation in the third section of this chapter, "Vak: The Word of the Sublime," and note 211.

245 Rudolf Steiner, *Mysteriengestaltung*, op. cit., lecture of Dec. 2, 1923.

246 Ibid.

247 Ibid.

248 For more on the importance of this collaboration, cf. J. Emanuel Zeylmans van Emmichoven, *Who Was Ita Wegman. A Documentation*, vols. 1–3; by the same author: *Strengthening the Heart. A Contemporary Mystery Schooling*, Mercury Press; also Peter Selg, *Ich bleibe bei Ihnen. Rudolf Steiner und Ita Wegman*, Stuttgart 2007.

249 For more on the fire that destroyed the Goetheanum building, see Klaus J. Bracker, *Grals-Initiation. Anthroposophische Esoterik und die künftige Jesus-Offenbarung*, op. cit., chap. 1, in the section "Grundsteinlegung für das 'Haus der Sprache.'"

250 Sri Aurobindo, *Essays in Philosophy and Yoga*, op. cit, in the section "Heraclitus."

251 Ibid.

252 Rudolf Steiner, *The Gospel of St. John*, Anthroposophic Press 1962, lect. of May 18, 1908.

253 Margarita Woloschin, *Die grüne Schlange. Lebenserinnerungen,* Stuttgart 1997, book 3, "Der Lehrling."

254 Later called Lory Maier-Smits. Cf. Rudolf Steiner, *Die Entstehung und Entwicklung der Eurythmie,* Dornach 1965; Magdalene Siegloch, *How the New Art of Eurythmy Began. Lory Maier-Smits, the First Eurythmist,* Temple Lodge 2015.

255 Rudolf Steiner, *Eurythmie, Die Offenbarung der sprechenden Seele,* address of June 2 1918, Dornach 1980. Also in, *An Introduction to Eurythmy: Talks Given before Sixteen Eurythmy Performances.* Anthroposophic Press 1984.

256 Rudolf Steiner, *Eurythmy as Visible Speech*, op. cit., lecture of June 25, 1924.

257 Cf. Sri Aurobindo, *Glossary to the Record of Yoga,* op. cit., entries on "vayu" and "Vayu." The later *prana* can be traced back to Vayu.

258 Cf. Rudolf Steiner, *Die Offenbarung der sprechenden Seele,* op. cit., address of Feb. 18, 1923. Also in *An Introduction to Eurythmy.* Anthroposophic Press 1984.

259 According to accounts by Rudolf Steiner, both eurythmy and Indian culture have very characteristic connections with the etheric body, first; and then also with the suprasensory body of the human being, called life spirit, and *buddhi* in Sanskrit, which will become significant only in the future. Eurythmy takes its point of departure, in a sense, from the movements and formative forces of the etheric body, but as an art form it relates to the life spirit, while poetry and speech relate to the spirit self, and music to the "I," etc. Regarding the latter, cf. Rudolf Steiner, *Art in the Light of Mystery Wisdom*, lecture of Dec. 29, 1914. This seems to illumine the "reflective" connection existing between the very ancient Indian cultural epoch and its future metamorphosis in the seventh cultural epoch (of which we spoke briefly in chapter 1, see note 51). This primordial Indian culture chiefly served to elaborate the human etheric body, whereas in the seventh cultural epoch initial work will be accomplished on the suprasensory body of the life spirit, which is eventually to embody a complete transformation of the etheric or life body. Cf. Rudolf Steiner, *Esoteric Christianity and the Spiritual Guidance of Humanity*, lect. of Jan. 9, 1912. Such a comparison is very enlightening in regard to the special status of the Ephesian mysteries, which on the one hand concentrated ancient Indian culture so as to offer the essence of the latter to a dawning Europe, and on the other prepared the seed from which eurythmy was able to emerge in the twentieth century.

260 Rudolf Steiner, *Mysterienstätten des Mittelalters. Rosenkreuzertum als modernes Einweihungsprinzip,* Dornach 1980, lect. of April 22, 1924.

261 Within earthly incarnation, eurythmists draw on a different sequence of sounds—I–A–O—which cultivates good interpenetration of the different bodies. Here we live, really, in the horizontality of both aspects of time—in the dynamic between past and future. In true "I"-being we thus form the vertical that connects physical existence in

the here and now with the sphere of eternity from which we originate. This indicates that the "A" [ah] of the etheric body (*pranamayakosha*) represents the past, whereas the "O" of the astral body (*manomayakosha)* represents the future. The "I" [ee], as expression of the individual, unsullied spirit–soul (*chaitya purusha*) embodies the vertical dimension. In relation to the Ephesian Artemis, and her connection with eurythmy, Thomas Göbel and Martin-Ingbert Heigl have offered important insights. Werner Barfod's work on the "I-A-O" in eurythmy also well repays study. Cf. Thomas Göbel, *Eurythmie als erlebte, gestaltete und wirksame Gebärde*, Dornach 1999, the chapter "Die Eurythmie als Erkenntnisaufgabe oder vom offenbaren Geheimnis des 'F' zur Ganzheit der Blaselaute." Martin-Ingbert Heigl, *Artemis—Eurythmie, Sprachgestaltung und Philosophie der Freiheit.* Norderstedt 2007. Werner Barfod, *I A O und die eurythmischen Meditationen,* Dornach 1999. Using the enlivening and soul-imbued expressive and representational movements of eurythmy, one task for the future would be to engage in groups with the hymns of the Veda, in ancient Vedic Sanskrit. If eurythmy and Vedic knowledge were to meet at a professional level, the outcomes would be all the more striking.

262 Rudolf Steiner, *Mysterienstätten des Mittelalters. Rosenkreuzertum als modernes Einweihungsprinzip,* Dornach 1980, lect. of April 22, 1924.

263 Friedrich Hölderlin, *Werke und Briefe,* Frankfurt/M., 1969.

CHAPTER 4

264 See the introductory section of chapter 2.

265 After Darwin refused the position, it was given instead to the philosopher Thomas H. Huxley, a famous friend of Darwin's and an energetic proponent of his theory of evolution ("Darwin's bulldog").

266 Cf. Ambalal B. Purani, quoted by Peter Heehs in *The Lives of Sri Aurobindo*, op. cit., "Early Years in India."

267 Between 1890 and 1897, Rudolf Steiner worked at the Goethe and Schiller Archive in Weimar. He was coeditor of Goethe's scientific writings, which were published between 1884 and 1896. Cf. Rudolf Steiner, *Goethean Science*, Mercury Press 1988; and *Goethe's Theory of Knowledge*, SteinerBooks 2008, op. cit.

268 The most commonly named distinction between the God of the Judeo-Christian tradition, who created the world and everything in it, and Plato's Demiurge, is that the latter found his primal material already to hand and formed his creatures from it, whereas the former called forth Creation from nothing.

269 We should also mention here Jean-Baptiste Lamarck (1744–1829) whose *Philosophie Zoologique*, published in Paris in 1809, was one of the earliest attempts to present a systematic (materialistic) theory of evolution. In the present enquiry, however, we will not focus specifically on his achievement since Charles Darwin and Johann Wolfgang von Goethe provided the more immediate background and

point of departure for, respectively, Sri Aurobindo and Rudolf Steiner. It is worth mentioning, however, that more recently—despite some dismissive remarks that Darwin made about Lamarck—it has been suspected that the Frenchman exerted a greater influence on Darwin than was long assumed.

270 Interestingly, Darwin adopted this term *survival of the fittest* from the philosopher Herbert Spencer (1820–1903) who formulated it in 1864 to designate social dynamics of a basic kind. Cf. Gerald Hartung (ed.), Eduard Zeller, *Philosophie- und Wissenschaftsgeschichte im 19. Jahrhundert*, Berlin 2010, in the chapter by Oliver Primavesi, "*Aristoteles oder Empedokles? Charles Darwin und Eduard Zeller über einen antiken Ansatz zur Evolutionstheorie.*"

271 Christoph Hueck, *Evolution im Doppelstrom der Zeit. Die Erweiterung der naturwissenschaftliche Entwicklungslehre durch die Selbstanschauung des Erkennens,* Dornach 2012, "Alle Gestalten sind ähnlich..."

272 It was also Richard Owen who formulated the term *dinosaur* for a largely extinct group of vertebrates.

273 Johann Wolfgang von Goethe, *Italian Journey*. Quoted in: Rudolf Steiner (ed.), *Goethean Science*, Mercury Press 1988.

274 Cf. Rudolf Steiner, "The Origin of the Idea of Metamorphosis," in Rudolf Steiner (ed.), *Goethean Science*, op. cit.

275 Johann Wolfgang Goethe, *The Metamorphosis of Plants*, in: Rudolf Steiner (ed.) *Goethean Science*, op. cit.

276 Ibid. In that volume, Johann Wolfgang Goethe, "On Morphology. Foreword to the Contents" (foreword also to *The Metamorphosis of Plants*).

277 Johann Wolfgang Goethe, "On Morphology. Introduction to the Aim" (Foreword also to *The Metamorphosis of Plants*). Quoted in Wolfgang H. Arnold, *Entwicklung. Interdisziplinäre Aspekte zur Evolutionsfrage*, Stuttgart 1989; the chapter by Frank Teichmann, "Die Entstehung des Entwicklungsgedankens in der Goethezeit."

278 Writing to Charles Darwin on Aug. 10, 1864, Ernst Haeckel said that Goethe, in his essays *On Morphology*, had shown himself to be the forerunner of the theory of descent. See: *The Correspondence of Charles Darwin*, eds. F. Burkhardt et al. 18 vols. to date (Cambridge: Cambridge University, 1985 onward), 12:299.

279 Cf. Marcus Andries, *Schellings Entwicklungsbegriff. Wandlungen und Konstanten in seiner Naturphilosophie*. PhD, Tübingen 2010, especially chap. 8, "Die Entstehung von Neuem—Prinzipien und Typus der Entwicklung in Schellings früher Naturphilosophie."

280 Friedrich Wilhelm Schelling, Die Weltalter (fragment, 1811). Quoted in: Wolfgang H. Arnold, *Entwicklung. Interdisziplinäre Aspekte zur Evolutionsfrage*, op. cit.; chapter by Frank Teichmann, "Die Entstehung des Entwicklungsgedankens in der Goethezeit."

281 Ibid.

282 Or, *vice versa*, to be able to incorporate one's consciousness into these motions.

283 What is known as the "synthetic theory of evolution," seen as standard today, integrates more recent insights drawn from genetics, paleontology and population biology into basic Darwinian ideas.

284 Not included in the Complete Works. Published in two parts, Berlin 1900–1901. Rudolf Steiner revised this work and republished it in 1914 as *Riddles of Philosophy: Presented in an Outline of Its History*. SteinerBooks 2009.

285 Cf. for instance, Ernst Haeckel, *Generelle Morphologie der Organismen*, Berlin 1866; *Natürliche Schöpfungsgeschichte*, Berlin 1868 (published in English as *The Natural History of Creation*); *Die Welträthsel. Gemeinverständliche Studien über monistische Philosophie*, Bonn 1899 (published in English as *The Riddle of the Universe at the Close of the Nineteenth Century*). Ernst Haeckel is also the originator of what is known as the "recapitulation theory," according to which the embryonic development of a single entity (ontogenesis) recapitulates the whole history of a species (phylogenesis).

286 Rudolf Steiner, *Autobiography*, op. cit., chap. 32.

287 Sri Aurobindo, *Essays in Philosophy and Yoga*. Pondicherry 1998, the section "Involution and Evolution."

288 Thomas H. Huxley, whom we mentioned as the proponent of Darwin, is considered the founder of epiphenomenalism; see note 265.

289 Back in 1902, Peter Kropotkin (1842–1921), the trailblazer of Communist anarchism, had already taken issue with Darwin's "survival of the fittest" position in his book *Mutual Aid: A Factor of Evolution*. Rudolf Steiner was full of praise for Kropotkin's idea of mutual support in the natural world. Cf. Rudolf Steiner, *Die Welträtsel und die Anthroposophie,* Dornach 1983, Oct. 12, 1905. More recently, something of Sri Aurobindo's vision seems also to dawn in the work of the medical theoretician Joachim Bauer on the "cooperative gene." Based on modern genetic research, he likewise comes to the conclusion that rather than a battle for survival determining evolution, the genes of living creatures communicate and cooperate with one another, and are engaged in reciprocal creative evolution. Cf. Joachim Bauer, *Das kooperative Gen. Abschied von Darwinismus,* Hamburg 2008.

290 Sri Aurobindo, *Essays in Philosophy and Yoga*, op. cit., the section "Evolution."

291 Here, for Sri Aurobindo, a variant of the same dualism plays an important role both in regard to the spirituality of the Sanatana Dharma on the one hand, and Western civilization on the other, in that Europe and America primarily show interest in the material world of the Prakriti, while India is chiefly oriented to the sublime spirituality of the Purusha. Accordingly, his ambition is also to bring the East and the West closer together.

292 The realms of nature embody the diverse levels of consciousness: the mineral kingdom is marked by a minimum level of consciousness, the plants by an awareness corresponding to deep sleep in the human being, the animal kingdom by a state corresponding to our dream consciousness. Only within human beings does consciousness become

wide awake and self-reflexive, internalizing itself into what Sri Aurobindo refers to as "psychic being," which is the soul proper.

293 See for instance Ken Wilber, *The Atman Project: A Transpersonal View of Human Development,* Quest Books 1996, chap. 18 "Involution." Here we read the following: "And the story of involution is simply the story of how the higher modes came to be lost in the lower—how they came to be enwrapped and enfolded in the lower states." It is questionable whether Wilber moved on from this view in his later works. Certainly there is no sign of it in his large study, *Sex, Ecology, Spirituality,* when he speaks of *holons,* levels, of Eros and Thanatos and of the emergence of the holons at respectively higher, evolutionary ascending levels. Nor is there any indication here of evolutive effects that stream in from superordinate spheres upon the process of evolution. Cf. Ken Wilber, *Sex, Ecology, Spirituality,* Shambhala, Boston 1995.

294 "But all our spiritual and psychic experience bears affirmative witness, brings us always a constant and, in its main principles, an invariable evidence of the existence of higher worlds, freer planes of existence.": "What we find is that these higher planes are actually at every moment acting upon and in communication with our own plane of being, although this action is naturally not present to our ordinary waking or outer consciousness, because that is for the most part limited to a reception and utilisation of the contacts of the physical world." "These worlds are not in their original creation subsequent in order to the physical universe but prior to it,—prior, if not in time, in their consequential sequence. For even if there is an ascending as well as a descending gradation, this ascending gradation must be in its first nature a provision for the evolutionary emergence in Matter." *The Life Divine,* book 2, part 2, op. cit., chap. 21, "The Order of the Worlds."

295 Sri Aurobindo, *The Life Divine,* Book 1, op. cit., chap. 14, "The Supermind as Creator."

296 Sri Aurobindo, *Essays in Philosophy and Yoga*, op. cit., the section "Involution and Evolution."

297 Sri Aurobindo, *The Life Divine*, op. cit, book 2, part 2, chap. 24, "The Evolution of the Spiritual Man." Sri Aurobindo uses initial capitals to accentuate the divine-spiritual nature of what he thus expresses, here for instance Maya and Shakti. In another passage in *The Life Divine* he writes that we cannot only have spiritual experiences as "silent witnesses" but also actively participate in the dynamic of spiritual reality. And: "we find that this Consciousness-Force, Maya, Shakti, is itself the power of the Being, the Self-Existent, the Ishwara," Sri Aurobindo, *The Life Divine*, op. cit., Book Two, Part I, chap. 2, "Brahman, Purusha, Ishwara—Maya, Prakriti, Shakti." *Ishwara* means the "Lord of the Universe," whom Sri Aurobindo identifies with Krishna or Vishnu. In relation to Brahman and Maya, or Purusha and Prakriti, in this book, see chapter 1, the section "Spiritual insight into the Vedic world," chap. 3, the section, "Vak: The Word of the Sublime," and chap. 5, the section "The Divine in the Intuition of Sri Aurobindo."

298 Sri Aurobindo, *Essays in Philosophy and Yoga*, op. cit., "Involution and Evolution."

299 Sri Aurobindo's literary production in *The Arya* (1914–1921) were, let us remember, later published in book form and constitute his major works. See chapter 2, the section "Pondicherry: Mirra, The Arya, and the Ashram."

300 Cf. Sri Aurobindo, *Record of Yoga*, op. cit., "Notes on Images Seen in March 1914—The Evolutionary Scale."

301 Since a comparison is interesting here with accounts of anthroposophic Spiritual Science, it is worth considering that, in terms of what is said here about Agni, Sri Aurobindo is certain too that the Creation emerges primarily from warmth, from fire. In Integral Yoga, Agni is characterized as the flame of divine strength, allied with divine knowledge. Sri Aurobindo writes of Agni as God that he is "the divine Consciousness formulating itself in universal energy." And: Agni's "divine birthplace and home—though he is born everywhere and dwells in all things—is the Truth, the Infinity, the vast cosmic Intelligence in which Knowledge and Force are unified." Cf. Sri Aurobindo, *Records of Yoga,* appendix vol. *Glossary to Records of Yoga*, op. cit.

302 Sri Aurobindo, *Record of Yoga*, op. cit., "Notes on Images Seen in March 1914—The Evolutionary Scale."

303 Rudolf Steiner, it is true, calls the previous manifestation of our present planet earth "Old Moon," yet he, too, speaks of a specific connection between the latter and the present Mars, such that today's Mars orbit marks the sphere that was to begin with occupied by Old Moon evolution. Later, he says, the Old Moon orbited a Sun of that time on the path that Mars takes today. See Rudolf Steiner, *The Spiritual Hierarchies and the Physical World,* SteinerBooks 2008, Apr. 14, 1909. Cf. also the account of cosmic evolution in this chapter, the section "Cosmic evolution—II."

304 Sri Aurobindo, *Record of Yoga*, op. cit., "Notes on Images Seen in March 1914—The Evolutionary scale—II."

305 Here I would like to attempt a "translation": the consciousness sheath, *manah-kosha*, corresponds both to what Rudolf Steiner calls the astral body and the human spiritual "body" of the spirit self that develops from it, which he also calls *manas*. The knowledge sheath, *vijnanakosha*, corresponds to the life spirit in Steiner, which he also terms "Buddhi." This stands for high intuitive intelligence, far exceeding our modern intellect. The bliss sheath, *anandakosha* should be assigned to spirit body. As expressed in the *Katha Upanishad*, this corresponds to *mahan atman*, the "Great Self," which is subordinate to the Unmanifest, *avyakta*, and finally—above the Unmanifest realm—to the Purusha. It is questionable whether the "dynamic" and "essential" planes, to which Sri Aurobindo refers in the previous quotation, correspond to the two dimensions of the Unmanifest and the Purusha. Traditionally, *Ahankara,* the "I"-maker, interposes itself between Buddhi and Manas. For Sri Aurobindo, the human soul indwells the inner nature of the human being, more precisely, the mental or *manahkosha*, as "inner being" or "psychic being." We will return to this context later in the chapter.

306 Sri Aurobindo, *Record of Yoga,* op. cit., "Notes on Images Seen in March 1914—The Evolutionary Scale." *Bhuvarloka* refers to the living world that belongs to the earth, roughly the "elemental world." See comments on the Gayatri Mantra and its introductory formula "OM—*bhur–bhuvar–svar,*" chap. 3, the section "Om: The Pranava."

307 Sri Aurobindo, *Record of Yoga*, op. cit., "Notes on Images Seen in March 1914—The Evolutionary Scale." [additions in square brackets by the author].

308 Ibid [additions in square brackets by the author]. The text continues thus: "called the Pashu, Vanara, Pishacha, Pramatha, Rakshasa, Asura, Deva, Sadhyadeva, Siddhadeva and the Satyadeva. The last three are known by other names that need not be written at present. The Pashu is mind concentrated entirely on the annam, the Vanara mind concentrated on the Prana, the Pishacha mind concentrated on the senses and the knowledge part of the chitta, the Pramatha mind concentrated on the heart and the emotional and aesthetic part of the chitta, the Rakshasa is mind concentrated on the thinking manas proper and taking up all the others into the manas itself; the Asura is mind concentrated on the buddhi and in the Asura Rakshasa making it serve the manas & chitta; the Deva is mind concentrated in vijnanam, exceeding itself, but in the Asura Deva or Devasura it makes the vijnana serve the buddhi. The others raise mind successively to the Ananda, Tapas and Sat and are, respectively, the supreme Rakshasa, the supreme Asura, the supreme Deva." According to Sri Aurobindo, Asura and Rakshasa also manifest as beings of demonic nature. Here their original, pure form is meant.

309 Rudolf Steiner, "The Nature and Importance of Goethe's Writings on Organic Development." In, Rudolf Steiner (ed.), *Goethean Science*, vol. 1, op. cit.

310 Chancellor Friederich von Müller, *Unterhaltungen mit Goethe*, May 7, 1830. Quoted in Ernst Lautenbach, *Lexikon Goethe Zitate. Auslese für das 21. Jahrhundert,* Munich 2004.

311 Rudolf Steiner, *Intuitive Thinking as a Spiritual Path*, op. cit., "The Consequences of Monism."

312 Rudolf Steiner, *Autobiography*, op. cit, chap. 3.

313 Rudolf Steiner, *An Outline of Esoteric Science,* op. cit., "World Evolution and the Human Being."

314 The account that follows is based especially on Rudolf Steiner's fundamental descriptions in his major work *An Outline of Esoteric Science.*

315 The "spirits of form" (Exousiai). In relation to these very lofty and sublime spirit beings, and the others referred to earlier, the following can be said: evolution of Old Saturn was chiefly determined and impelled by the beings of the first hierarchy, whom Rudolf Steiner calls the "spirits of will" (traditionally Thrones); evolution of Old Sun was governed by the "spirits of wisdom" (Kyriotetes) belonging to the second hierarchy; that of Old Moon by the "spirits of movement" (Dynameis) of the second hierarchy; and earth evolution was determined and instigated by the spirits of form (Exousiai, see above) who likewise belong to the second hierarchy. In Rudolf Steiner's

Outline of Esoteric Science and in numerous lectures to members of the Theosophical and later the Anthroposophical Society, Rudolf Steiner describes the hierarchies in accounts of much grandeur. In chapters 1 and 2, we already considered the Kyriotetes and Dynameis (cf. chap. 1, the section "Spiritual insight into the Vedic world"; and chap. 3, the section "Vak: The Word of the Sublime."

316 Rudolf Steiner, *An Outline of Esoteric Science*, op. cit., "World Evolution and the Human Being."

317 Sri Aurobindo, *Kena and Other Upanishads*, op. cit., "Kena Upanishad: Commentary—V: The Supreme Word."

318 Cf. Maheshwar (ed.) *Bhagavad Gita: In the Light of Sri Aurobindo.* Op. cit.

319 Cf. Klaus J. Bracker, *Grals-Initiation*, op. cit., chap. 3, in the section "Anthropos—Der ur-adamische Krishna–Jesus." In the section "Avatar und höheres Selbst—der Christus Jesus," the image and idea of the avatar is further traced in the works of Rudolf Steiner, who had Shri Krishna in mind in particular (though without using the term *avatar*). It is also worth recalling here that Rudolf Steiner, when founding the Anthroposophical Society in 1912/13, gave an associated lecture series on the *Bhagavad Gita*, that is, on Krishna. Cf. Rudolf Steiner, *The Bhagavad Gita and the West,* SteinerBooks 2008.

320 For further information, see The Bagavata Purana Research Project, University of Oxford, Oxford Center for Hindu Studies, 15 Magdalen Street, Oxford OX1 3AE, UK; Internet address: http://www.ochs.org .uk/research/bhagavata-purana-research-project.

321 Sri Aurobindo, *Letters on Yoga. Part One.* Birth Centenary Library, Pondicherry 1970; "Section Seven. The Purpose of Avatarhood." The letters reproduced in *Letters on Yoga* were largely written in the 1930s. The letter quoted here could not be more accurately dated. "*Vital rajasic*" and "*sattwic mental man*": these terms relate to the Sankhya concept discussed earlier of the three Gunas—Tamas (not named here), Rajas and Sattva. Sri Aurobindo wishes to indicate that the vital-emotional human type corresponds more to the Guna attribute of Rajas (fiery, passionate) whereas the mentally determined person has more of the quality of Sattva (calm, enlightened). "Nirguna Avatar" is to be understood as a manifestation that can represent the highest divine reality—*nirguna brahman*: without form, attribute or properties—within the created world.

322 This presumably should read not "from which" but "*with* which." In this and similar instances we should remember that it was often not possible for Steiner to check through transcripts of talks before they were published.

323 Rudolf Steiner, *Über die astrale Welt und das Devachan*, op. cit., private lesson, summer 1903, "The Sun Logos. The Ten Avatars." In this passage, *Dangma* (Tibetan) stands for a "purified soul," or someone whose higher eye has opened for clairvoyant vision. This corresponds to the Sanskrit term Mahatma or Jivanmukti.

324 There are only indirect indications of more esoteric nature with respect to the connection between Rosicrucianism and Indian tradition concerning the avatars, and in relation to questions of evolution. The

Count of Saint-Germain, who died in 1784, and in whom Rudolf Steiner recognized the Master Christian Rosenkreutz (i.e., a Mahatma) met with Rosicrucian alchemists in Vienna in 1790, six years after his death. At this period he is said to have told them that he would leave Europe toward the end of the eighteenth century in order to rest, removing to the region of the Himalayas. Eighty-five years after this, he said, he would be found again in Europe. Cf. Rudolf Steiner, *The Temple Legend,* Rudolf Steiner Press 1985, lect. of Dec. 16, 1904 (along with notes on the same lecture added by the editors). In addition, Steiner told his friend and esoteric pupil Édouard Schuré, in a confidential personal letter, that Christian Rosenkreutz only wished the esotericism he propounded to be made public (as Rudolf Steiner subsequently did) if mainstream science was willing to solve three problems of knowledge: "1) Discovery of spectral analysis, revealing the material constitution of the cosmos; 2) Introduction of material evolution into organic science; 3) Acknowledgement of the fact of other than a normal state of consciousness through recognition of hypnotism and suggestion." Rudolf Steiner, Marie Steiner-von Sivers, *Correspondence and Documents 1901-1925*, Anthroposophic Press 1988; in that volume: "Notes by Rudolf Steiner, written for Édouard Schuré in Barr, Alsace, Sept. 1907." Here we have hints that Christian Rosenkreutz's departure from Europe in the nineteenth century is related to his sojourn in India and Tibet, and also to the theme of natural evolution. The *Rosicrucian Chronicle* mentioned here seems likewise to shed characteristic light on this connection.

325 Rudolf Steiner, *Über die astrale Welt und das Devachan*, op. cit., private lesson, summer 1903, "The Sun Logos. The Ten Avatars." In this lesson, Rudolf Steiner lists the ten avatars as follows: 1. Fish; 2. Tortoise; 3. Beaver; 4. Man-lion. 5. Dwarf; 6. The warlike Parashurama; 7. Rama, the ideal king; 8. Krishna; 9. Buddha; 10. He who is to come: Kalki. Not all Sanskrit names reproduced in the relevant volume of the Collected Works of Rudolf Steiner (CW) are correct. In the *Bhagavat Purana* they are: 1. Matsya; 2. Kurma; 3. Varaha; 4. Narasimha; 5. Vamana; 6. Parashurama; 7. Rama; 8. Krishna; 9. Buddha; 10. Kalki.

326 The most pliable organic forms are fitted to the individuals representing this central line also insofar as they are least specialized within and to earthly conditions. The fact that we remain to a large degree free of organic specialization is also what distinguishes us as human beings today, by comparison to all other vertebrates. We can learn this for instance by considering the human hand in contrast to all animal hoofs, paws, claws, and talons, which in each case are fixed specializations. Our hands remain far more adaptable to, and capable of learning, many different functions.

327 A telling instance of such development of the human form from a soft, plastic "center" is known as "paedomorphosis" or "fetalization," for instance among the primates. This shows that juvenile features—such as the facial bones with their undeveloped, delicate chin form and high-arching forehead—stand as it were for a sign and forerunner of the species' future evolution and are most perfectly embodied in the

human form. Whereas primates fix and pass on the forms they develop in maturity, Homo sapiens shows in his evolution an ongoing tendency to rejuvenation.

328 The city and kingdom of Shambhala generally belong more to Tibetan Tantrayana Buddhism, in particular the Kalachakra tradition. Kali Yuga is the dark age or the age of iron, and Satya Yuga the succeeding age of truth, or also the new golden age.

329 Krita Yuga means, roughly, the age of greatest perfection. Cf. Stephen Knapp, *The Vedic Prophecies: A New Look into the Future. The Eastern Answers to the Mysteries of Life*. Charleston, SC 2011, "The Next Avatara of God: Lord Kalki and the End of Kali-Yuga."

330 At a suggestion from Rudolf Steiner, Emil Bock translated this passage as follows: "And the rider who sat upon him is the one who makes faith and knowledge true." Cf. *Das Neue Testament. In der Übersetzung von Emil Bock,* Stuttgart 1980; "Die Offenbarung des Johannes."

331 Sri Aurobindo, *Essays on the Gita*, op. cit., First Series, chap. 16, "The Process of Avatarhood." Sri Aurobindo's assessment of Christ as an avatar is not clear throughout his works. In a letter, for instance, he wrote to a Sadhaka, "Christ realized himself as the Son who is one with the Father—he must therefore be an *amsha avatara*, a partial incarnation." Sri Aurobindo, *Letters on Yoga*. Part One, op. cit., "Section Seven. The Purpose of Avatarhood." Christ as Son of God, in the Christian context a primary sign of his perfect divinity, is here interpreted in an opposite way by Sri Aurobindo. In the above-quoted passages from *Essays on the Gita*, by contrast, he does not speak of any such delimitation. In Rudolf Steiner's works, too, the concept and understanding of Christ undergoes marked changes and development, and we will return to this later. Christology and the teachings of yogic philosophy on the most sublime divinity, incarnation and descent, is the theme of chap. 5 in this book.

332 Sri Aurobindo, *Savitri. A Legend and Symbol*, op. cit., Book 6, Canto 2, "The Way of Fate and the Problem of Pain."

333 Idem, *Essays on the Gita,* op. cit., First Series, chap. 16, "The Process of Avatarhood."

334 These words heard by Moses from the burning bush—in Hebrew, *"ehyeh asher ehyeh"*—were for a long time translated as "I am the I am" in accord with the *Septuagint.* "I will be" can be interpreted in terms of the dynamic identity of existence, and the bringing forth of existence, in and through God. And this would at the same time be the bringing forth of the human "I"-being. We can also regard the answer to Moses, *"ehyeh asher ehyeh,"* as a refusal to speak his name. This would correspond to only Him knowing His own name. From this self-designation of God, *"ehyeh asher ehyeh,"* the name "Yahweh" was derived, meaning "He is." If we take existence in its identity with the bringing forth of existence, then the "He is" can also be understood as "I AM," as utterance in the first person.

335 Emil Bock, *The Apocalypse of St. John,* Floris Books 2005, "The Rider on the White Horse and the Thousand Years."

336 Ibid.

337 In relation to the second and third name of the white rider and Emil Bock's interpretation, see also Rudolf Steiner, *The Book of Revelation and the Work of the Priest*, 1988, Sept. 14, 1924.

338 The passage that follows once again summarizes accounts by Rudolf Steiner in his *Outline of Esoteric Science;* cf. the chapter "World Evolution and the Human Being."

339 Rudolf Steiner, *An Outline of Esoteric Science*, op. cit., "World Evolution and the Human Being."

340 Ibid.

341 On some occasions Rudolf Steiner describes the astral body also as "consciousness body." See for instance Rudolf Steiner, *The Christian Mystery*, Completion Press 2007, Mar. 17, 1907. This and the differentiation referred to into diverse aspects of the soul is enlightening for our present enquiry since Sri Aurobindo's term of "mind" or "mental" corresponds to this "consciousness body" and its more subtle structures.

342 See the introductory section of chapter 1 for more on the cultural epochs, where dates for each epoch are given. The current age of the consciousness soul began in AD 1413 and will last until approximately 3573.

343 This fact is of fundamental importance, for instance for anthroposophic pedagogy in Waldorf schools. This new "art of education," as Rudolf Steiner called it sees itself especially as aiding the "I"-being on its path toward a full, individual sense of self, something usually achieved around the age of 21. The close connection between healthy will development—through a young person's purposeful activity—and healthy incarnation of the "I" forms the context for the high value accorded to artistic, craft, and practical subjects in the anthroposophic art of education.

344 "As a human being as such possesses the 'I,' it is really entirely of will nature. But during the life between birth and death, as I have suggested, it develops by feeding impulses of will into human actions, yet only partially. Something remains behind. And this residue of will nature passes over into developing karma." In consequence one must "be fully aware that the I really only lives fully in our actions, only really awakens in human deed." Rudolf Steiner, *Cosmosophy*, Anthroposophic Press 1985, Oct. 2, 1921.

345 "The 'I' is only the baby." Rudolf Steiner, *Education for Special Needs: Curative Education Course*, July 7, 1924, Rudolf Steiner Press 2005.

346 Rudolf Steiner, *An Outline of Esoteric Science*, op. cit, "The Nature of Humanity."

347 Idem, *Theosophy,* op. cit., p. 49.

348 See the section in this chapter, "Cosmic Evolution I."

349 Cf. here Rudolf Steiner's reference, cited above, to the "I" as "baby"; also Grimm's fairytale "The Old Man Made Young Again," which is of particular interest not least in the context of questions of evolution. The Phoenix is a vivid mythological picture of this spiritual renascence, and one that connects Eastern and Western spirituality: periodically it consumes itself on a fire altar and is then reborn from its ashes. In

connection with the Egyptian mysteries, Rudolf Steiner speaks of the "Phoenix bird, that consumes itself in fire and then rises again from the ashes...It is the symbol of the soul." The soul, in turn, he says, has the task of "as it were redeeming the spirit again from nature." Cf. Rudolf Steiner, *Das Christentum und die Mysterien des Altertums 1. Ein Grundkurs in Geisteswissenschaft,* Bad Liebenzell 2005. Mar. 1, 1902.

350 Quoted in Nirodbaran, *Talks with Sri Aurobindo,* vol. 1, Pondicherry 2001. Conversation on Jan. 23, 1939.

351 Sri Aurobindo, *The Future Poetry and Letters on Poetry, Literature and Art,* Pondicherry 1970; "Source of Poetic Inspiration and Vision—Mystic and Spiritual Poetry."

352 Idem, *The Life Divine*, op. cit., "The Triple Transformation."

353 Ibid.

354 The fact that our superficial personality often overlays and conceals the psychic being can lead to an outlook and view among pupils of Integral Yoga that it must patiently await its release. Numerous pupils of Anthroposophy appear to have a much more self-evident relationship to the will nature of the "I" dwelling in them.

355 Sri Aurobindo, *The Life Divine,* book 2, op. cit., "The Triple Transformation."

356 "Between *psychisation* and *spiritualisation* there is a difference. The spiritual is the change that descends from above, the psychic is the change that comes from within by the psychic dominating mind, vital and physical." Sri Aurobindo, *Letters on Yoga. Part Four.* Pondicherry 1970; "Section One. The triple Transformation. Psychic—Spiritual—Supramental."

357 Sri Aurobindo, *The Life Divine.* book 1, "The Double Soul in Man."

358 Sri Aurobindo, *The Synthesis of Yoga,* op. cit., the chapter "The Ascent of the Sacrifice—'I.'"

359 Sri Aurobindo did not formally adopt these traditional yoga paths and simply incorporate them into a new system. Instead he takes up only the essential, living stances underlying traditional forms, synthesizing them and embedding them in a greater whole. The fact that, outside of Integral Yoga, they exist independently of, and alongside, each other, is for him an expression of a decadent development in the past, which he seeks to turn instead in a wholesome direction. Where this present volume speaks of "yoga" in general terms, or "yoga qualities" etc., this always refers to the Integral Yoga of Sri Aurobindo unless otherwise explicitly stated.

360 Cf. chap. 2, the section "Pondicherry: Mirra, the Arya, and the Ashram."

361 Sri Aurobindo, *The Synthesis of Yoga,* op. cit., "The Ascent of the Sacrifice—II."

362 Ibid.

363 Cf. Madhav P. Pandit (ed.), *Dictionary of Sri Aurobindo's Yoga,* Pondicherry 1992, the entry on "Love."

364 Rudolf Steiner, *Karmic Relationships,* vol. 3, Aug. 4, 1924. Rudolf Steiner Press 2002.

365 Ibid.

366 Sri Aurobindo usually refers to "rebirth." The expression "reincarnation," he says, invokes inappropriate associations, though he does occasionally employ the term. In anthroposophic literature, "reincarnation," "rebirth" and "repeating lives on earth" are all used. In Steiner's terminology, "rebirth" also refers to a certain high level attained on the path of initiation.

367 Sri Aurobindo, *The Life Divine,* book 2, part 2, op. cit.; in the chapter "The Philosophy of Rebirth." The account that follows here is based on the considerations expounded there. "Buddha Dharma" is Buddhism's own term for its practice; "Mayavadins" are adherents of the "Mayavada," the path of knowledge that sees nothing but "maya" or illusion in the whole of cosmic manifestation. Radical Advaita Vedanta, for instance as expounded by Shankaracharya (ca. 788–820), is regarded as Mayavada.

368 For more on the Buddhist concept of rebirth from an anthroposophic perspective, see Klaus J. Bracker, *Wiederverkörperung und die innere Natur des Menschen. Sankhya—Buddhismus—Anthroposophie*, Schaffhausen 1995. See in this volume reflections on the question of the "I," which take a different view from the one chosen in this work.

369 Sri Aurobindo, *The Life Divine,* book 2, part 2, op. cit., chap. 20, "The Philosophy of Rebirth."

370 Ibid.

371 Ibid.

372 Ibid.

373 Ibid.

374 Idem, *The Life Divine, Book Two, Part II,* op. cit., chapter 22, "Rebirth and Other Worlds: Karma, the Soul and Immortality."

375 Ibid.

376 Ibid.

377 Ibid.

378 Cf. Rudolf Steiner, *Lucifer-Gnosis. 1903–1908. Grundlegende Aufsätze zur Anthroposophie und Berichte*, op. cit.; "How Karma Works" (Dec. 1903); in English as *Reincarnation and Karma: How Karma Works,* Anthroposophic Press 1962.

379 Ibid.

380 In this connection see earlier in the chapter where, in line with Rudolf Steiner's Anthroposophy, an account was given of very early times in earth's evolution, in the section "'I'-being and Psychic Being."

381 It is noteworthy that in this context Rudolf Steiner refers once again to Ernst Haeckel.

382 Cf. Rudolf Steiner, *Lucifer-Gnosis. 1903–1908. Grundlegende Aufsätze zur Anthroposophie und Berichte*, op. cit.; "How Karma Works" (Dec. 1903); in English as *Reincarnation and Karma.*

383 Ibid.

384 Ibid.

385 See for instance Rudolf Steiner, *Theosophy*, op. cit., the chapter "Re-embodiment of the Spirit and Destiny (Reincarnation and Karma)." Our further account here follows the essay named above.

386 In numerous places Rudolf Steiner points out that the postmortem processing of these astral "residues" of our former life takes place over

a period roughly equal to a third of the life-span we lived. If we lived until the age of 75, for instance, this period in kamaloka will take around 25 years in earthly time.

387 Cf. Rudolf Steiner, *Lucifer-Gnosis. 1903–1908. Grundlegende Aufsätze zur Anthroposophie und Berichte*, op. cit.; "How Karma Works" (Dec. 1903); in English as *Reincarnation and Karma.*

388 Ibid.

389 In relation to the "free human spirit," Rudolf Steiner here points to his *Intuitive Thinking as a Spiritual Path: A Philosophy of Freedom,* op. cit.

390 Cf. Rudolf Steiner, *Lucifer-Gnosis. 1903–1908. Grundlegende Aufsätze zur Anthroposophie und Berichte*, op. cit.; "How Karma Works" (Dec. 1903).

391 Idem, *An Outline of Esoteric Science*, op. cit., the chapter "The Present and Future of the Evolution of Humanity and the World."

392 On questions of reincarnation and karma, besides *The Life Divine*, which has been frequently cited here, see also especially the collection of essays by Sri Aurobindo, *The Problem of Rebirth*, Pondicherry 2002.

393 On reincarnation and karma and the passage through the existence between death and a new birth, besides the works already referred to see, among others, the lecture cycles by Steiner, *Manifestations of Karma*, Rudolf Steiner Press 2011; *Okkulte Untersuchungen über das Leben zwischen Tod und neuer Geburt,* Dornach 2003; *Inner Nature of Man and the Life between Death and a New Birth,* Anthroposophical Publishing Company 1959; *Der übersinnliche Mensch, anthroposophisch erfasst*, Dornach 1999.

394 We can find something similar in C. G. Jung's "archetypes" as a multiplicity of different entities (in the broadest sense) rather than a single, overarching dimension from which all else emanates.

395 For more on the divinities or Devas as typal beings, see also Madhav P. Pandit (ed.), *Dictionary of Sri Aurobindo's Yoga,* op. cit, the entry "Gods." The non-evolving beings include the Asuras as well as the Devas, the former variously described as "hostile" beings.

396 Rudolf Steiner, *Karmic Relationships*, vol. 6, lect. of July 19, 1924. Rudolf Steiner Press 2002.

397 Drawing on the Christian tradition, and especially the esoteric school of the pupil of Paul, Dionysius the Areopagite, Rudolf Steiner speaks of three hierarchies, each of which is divided into three "choirs." The third hierarchy is composed of the choirs of angels, archangels, and principalities; the second of the spirits of form, the spirits of movement, and the spirits of wisdom; and the first of the spirits of will, the spirits of harmony and, finally, the spirits of love, who occupy the highest order. (The old names, in Greek and Hebrew, are, in the same sequence: III: Angeloi, Archangeloi, Archai; II: Exousiai, Dynameis, Kyriotetes; I: Thrones, Cherubim, Seraphim.) Behind the cosmic sway of these three hierarchies, according to Rudolf Steiner, lives the Trinity of the Father, Son, and Holy Spirit.

398 Quotations from Rudolf Steiner, *Karmic Relationships,* vol. 3, op. cit, July 4, 1924.

Chapter V

399 Subsequently we will also study Sri Aurobindo's view of God.

400 Between Sept. 5 and 28, 1924 alone, in the last weeks before the illness that led to his death, Rudolf Steiner gave four largely parallel lecture series: the ten lectures and an address contained in *Esoterische Betrachtungen karmischer Zusammenhänge* (*Karmic Relationships*), vol. 4, CW 238 (Dornach 1991); nineteen lectures on *Sprachgestaltung und Dramatische Kunst* (*Speech and Drama*), CW 282 (Dornach 1981); eleven lectures on *Zusammenwirken von Ärzten und Seelsorgern* (*Broken Vessels: The Spiritual Structure of Human Frailty*) CW 318 (Dornach 1994); eighteen lectures on *Apokalypse und Priesterwirken* (*The Book of Revelation and the Work of the Priest*) CW 346 (Dornach 2001). In addition, in the same period, he gave five lectures to the workers on the new Goetheanum building on "The Creation of the World and the Human Being."

401 Cf. Rudolf Steiner, *Autobiography,* SteinerBooks 2006 (which originally appeared in 70 instalments in *Das Goetheanum. Internationale Wochenschrift für Anthroposophie und Dreigliederung,* Dornach, Dec. 9, 1923 to Apr. 5, 1925); idem, *Anthroposophical Leading Thoughts: Anthroposophy as a Path of Knowledge: The Michael Mystery,* Rudolf Steiner Press 1998, op. cit. (likewise first published in a series in *Das Goetheanum* magazine, Dornach, from Feb. 17, 1924 to Apr. 12, 1925); idem and Ita Wegman, *Extending Practical Medicine,* Rudolf Steiner Press 2000.

402 Cf. chiefly, idem, *Karmic Relationships,* vols. 3, 4, 6.

403 Cf. Rudolf Steiner, *Goethe's Theory of Knowledge,* op. cit.; idem, *Truth and Knowledge*, op. cit; *Intuitive Thinking as a Spiritual Path: A Philosophy of Freedom,* Anthroposophic Press, 1994, op. cit.

404 See here the wide-ranging account and deep, persuasive analysis offered by Peter Selg in his 7-volume biography of Steiner, *Rudolf Steiner, Life and Work* (SteinerBooks 2015–2018). In relation to this question in particular, see vol. 1, *Childhood, Youth, and Study Years* (1861–1890).

405 Cf. for instance, *How to Know Higher Worlds*, op. cit.

406 The question remains as to whether these streams (and others with them) would come together and collaborate by the end of the twentieth century, or whether their souls would only *incarnate* then. In the latter case their common endeavor could only occur in the early twenty-first century. It is possible that the darkness and evil of the twentieth century led to corresponding changes to karmic configurations that deviated from the original "prophecy."

407 Cf. Plato, *Complete Works,* Hackett 1997: "Epistles. Seventh Epistle" (341 c-d).

408 For more on the spiritual history and spiritual context of the Platonic stream, see for instance Michael Frensch, *Wie öffnet sich das Grosse Portal. Betrachtungen zum Portail Royal der Kathedrale Notre Dame de Chartres.* Schaffhausen 2000.

409 Günther Röschert, *Metaphysik der Weltentwicklung. Rudolf Steiners Geheimwissenschaft im Umriss,* Stuttgart 2011.

410 Ibid, in the chapter "Metaphysik der Weltentwicklung."

411 In the Indian tradition, the Vedic divinity Indra, the dragon-queller, corresponds fully to Michael. Indra—whose brothers are Agni and Surya—is connected with the power of the higher, illumined intelligence in the universe (*buddhi*), which, with his spear and his lightning-hurling thunderbolt (*vajra*), he sends from the broad solar world (*svar*) into the earthly world—which is also the world of light that the demon has fettered in unconsciousness, and that must be liberated. The telling detail that this illumined intelligence (*buddhi*) is at home especially in the lofty sphere of the Sun world, and, interestingly, specifically in the Moon sphere of the Sun world (*chandraloka*), seems to be reflected in the fact that Ita Wegman—in the introduction to the compilation *Aus Michaels Wirken* ("On the Workings of Michael")—considers the as yet little understood Moon stream of Michael in clear relation to Indian tradition and, in particular, Indra. It is worth noting here that Sri Aurobindo accentuates the fact that the illumined intelligence mediated by Indra can only act within human nature in a body-free condition, independently of the rational consciousness connected with the nervous system. Cf. Nora von Baditz, *Aus Michaels Wirken*, Stuttgart 1988. Introduction by Ita Wegman; Klaus J. Bracker, *Grals-Initiation*, op. cit., chap. 3, in the section "Anthropos—Der ur-adamische Krishna-Jesus"; Sri Aurobindo, *The Secret of the Veda*, op. cit, the chapter "Indra, Giver of Light."

412 Rudolf Steiner, *Anthroposophical Leading Thoughts—Anthroposophy as a Path of Knowledge—The Michael Mystery*, op. cit, the chapter "The Future of Humanity and the Workings of Michael."

413 Rudolf Steiner, ibid, the chapter "Where is Man as a Being Who Thinks and Remembers [one's self]?"

414 The "world of rhythm" corresponds to the sphere of the world of spirit directly adjoining the physical plane, and is also called the "elemental world" or the "sublunary world."

415 Rudolf Steiner, *Philosophie und Anthroposophie. 1904–1918*, Dornach 1965: lect. of Oct. 16, 1916: "Human Life from the Perspective of Spiritual Science (Anthroposophy)."

416 Ibid.

417 Idem, *Die Philosophie des Thomas von Aquin*, Dornach 1993, lecture of May 24, 1920.

418 Ibid.

419 Cf. Klaus J. Bracker, *Grals-Initiation*, op. cit., chap. 4, in the section "Lebensumschwung als Wiedergeburt."

420 Rudolf Steiner (ed.), *Goethean Science*, vol. 5, Mercury Press 1988. "Proverbs in Prose" (section 10).

421 Idem, *Anthroposophical Leading Thoughts*, op. cit., "Michael's Task in the Sphere of Ahriman."

422 Ibid, the chapter "Michael's Experiences During Fulfillment of His Cosmic Mission."

423 Ibid, the chapter, "The Future of Humanity and the Work of Michael."

424 Ibid.

425 Ibid.

426 Cf. Rudolf Steiner's reference to the "fourth hierarchy": "The human being as the tenth in the whole series." Idem, *Grundelemente der Esoterik*, Dornach 1976, lect. of Oct. 8, 1905.

427 In contrast to "transcendent," "immanent" (Latin *immanere* = remaining within) describes all that remains within the entirety of the world's existence and is accessible to rational cognition. Strictly speaking, the cosmic hierarchies also belong to the realm of immanence. The transcendent, on the other hand is, based on Plato, the "above and beyond," the otherworldly, and entirely hidden. Plato sees "the good" as exceeding and superior even to "existence" (the absolute transcendence of the good). Transcendence and immanence form a conceptual pairing, however, that Rudolf Steiner scarcely ever used in this form.

428 Rudolf Steiner, *Anthroposophical Leading Thoughts: Anthroposophy as a Path of Knowledge: The Michael Mystery,* op. cit., "World Thoughts in the Working of Michael and in the Working of Ahriman."

429 Ibid, the chapter "The Future of Humanity and the Work of Michael."

430 Ibid, the chapter, "The Human Being's Experience of Michael–Christ."

431 Ibid, the chapter, "Michael's Mission in the World Age of Human Freedom."

432 It would be necessary to examine the consequences of this statement for the commonly held anthroposophic view of the cosmic origins of the human being, according to which the human being arose in a process leading from the first emergence of the physical on Old Saturn through to the predisposition for the "I" in the course of Earth evolution, instigated by the spiritual–cosmic working of hierarchical beings—from the Thrones down to the Exousiai. The primordial beginning of the human being in God appears, by contrast, to indicate a pre-cosmos reality.

433 Rudolf Steiner, *Anthroposophical Leading Thoughts,* op. cit., "Michael's Mission in the World Age of Human Freedom."

434 Cf. Rudolf Steiner, *Intuitive Thinking as a Spiritual Path: A Philosophy of Freedom* (Anthroposophic Press 1995), p. 237.

435 Rudolf Steiner did not fully examine the question of transcendence and immanence even in his *Outline of Esoteric Science*, as Günther Röschert shows in detail in his previously cited book. Steiner touches only briefly on this question there, in relation to his account of the first evolution on Old Saturn. He writes, "With this reference to early evolutionary conditions of Saturn, light is also shed on all further questions about the origin of these conditions. In purely rational terms, of course, it is possible to ask further as to the "origin of these origins." Yet the facts and realities themselves do not permit this." And: "It is not so easy to gain clear insight into the great questions about the universe. But if one looks at things with great care and exactitude, one finds that all questions about "origins" must end with the Saturn conditions described above; for here we arrive in a domain where the living entities and processes no longer explain themselves in terms of what they arise from, but only through themselves." *An Outline of Esoteric Science*, op. cit., "World Evolution and the Human Being."

436 Idem, *Bewusstsein, Leben, Form. Grundprinzipien der geisteswissenschaftliche Kosmologie,* Dornach 2001. Lesson of July 2, 1904.

437 Ibid, lecture of Nov. 10, 1904.

438 Ibid, private esoteric lesson, undated, probably 1904: "On the Logoi": "The Power of Life stands under the aegis of Michael." Regarding this outline and the following one, we must again recall the provisional character of the transcripts, which Steiner had no opportunity to look through before they were published.

439 Idem, *Die Weihnachtstagung zur Begründung der Allgemeinen Anthroposophischen Gesellschaft. 1923–1924,* Dornach 1963.

440 In a remarkable dissertation, the Catholic scholar and educator Carlo Willmann traced the Trinitarian structure informing anthroposophic pedagogy in Waldorf schools. Cf. Carlo Willmann, *Waldorfpädagogik. Theologische und religionspädagogische Befunde.* Cologne / Weimar / Vienna 1998.

441 Cf. Peter Selg, *The Lord's Prayer and Rudolf Steiner,* Floris Books 2014.

442 Rudolf Steiner, in: *Beiträge zur Rudolf Steiner Gesamtausgabe. Veröffentlichungen aus dem Archiv der Rudolf Steiner-Nachlassverwaltung, Dornach,* no. 110: *Die Erneuerung des religiösen Lebens.* Dornach 1993, therein: "Fragenbeantwortungen."

443 Idem and Ita Wegman, *Extending Practical Medicine,* op. cit.

444 Peter Selg, *Rudolf Steiner and the Lord's Prayer,* op. cit, chap. 1.

445 Rudolf Steiner remarked on several occasions that from an esoteric perspective the new day begins at 6:00 p.m.

446 J. Emanuel Zeylmans van Emmichoven, *Who Was Ita Wegman.* vol. 4. "Strengthening the Heart," "Ita Wegman's Schooling Sep. – Dec. 1923." Mercury Press 2013.

447 Rudolf Steiner, *Erfahrungen des Übersinnlichen. Die drei Wege der Seele zu Christus,* Dornach 1994, lecture of Dec. 17, 1912, which also includes these words: "Love is for the world what the Sun is for outward life. No soul could thrive any longer if love disappeared from the world. Love is the moral sun of the world."

448 Idem, *Start Now! A Book of Soul and Spiritual Exercises,* SteinerBooks 2004. "Credo: The Individual and the All."

449 Cf. chap. 2, especially note 67.

450 Sri Aurobindo, *Sri Aurobindo on Himself and The Mother,* op. cit. Quoted in: Sri Aurobindo, *Integral Yoga,* (ed. Otto Wolff), op. cit. See here also Sri Aurobindo's account of his own experiences, which are only summarized in this chap. 5. The full passages are contained in the first section of chap. 2.

451 The father of the eighth Avatar manifestation, thus of the child Krishna, was called Vasudeva. In calling himself Vasudeva (or rather Vāsudeva, which indicates the lineage) Krishna makes clear that in that manifestation he had chosen the earthly-human form of existence.

452 After some preparatory work, the fundamental works of Sri Aurobindo's yogic philosophy were written down in the years 1914-1921. Cf. chap. 2, the section "Pondicherry—Mirra, *The Arya,* and the Ashram," especially note 102.

453 Maheshwar (ed.) *Bhagavad Gita: In the Light of Sri Aurobindo.* Op. cit., chap. 15, 16–18 The Sanskrit words *kshara* and *akshara* mean respectively "what is mutable" and "what is immutable." The reference to the "three worlds (*bhur, bhuvar, svar*) was explained in chap. 3 of this book, cf. the section "Om: The Pranava."

454 One of the first proponents of this school, the Bengali Swami Vivekananda (1863–1902) is regarded as the most important pupil of the realized master Ramakrishna Paramahamsa (1836–1886). The latter, in turn, had an experience of enlightenment that led him to seek a synthesis of world religions, especially Hinduism, Christianity, and Islam. Swami Vivekananda became very widely known in the West for his much-acclaimed appearance at the "World Parliament of Religions" held in Chicago in 1893. Today he is acknowledged as the chief figure in this Chicago congress.

455 In his previous work, the author of this book addressed the theme of Adi Shankaracharya (or simply Shankara) and his teachings, and the response to this Advaita Vedanta formulated centuries after him by the southern Indian master Ramanuja (ca. 1050–1137). Cf. Klaus J. Bracker, *Grals-Initiation*, op. cit., chap. 5, the section "Fichte und die östliche Spiritualität."

456 This is why the Advaita Vedantins, the adherents of Shankaracharya, are also called Mayavadins.

457 Cf. Klaus J. Bracker, *Das Jahr 1909. Die Wiederkunft Christi im Ätherischen und die Spiritualität des Orients*, op. cit., in relation to the encounter of anthroposophist Hans-Hasso von Veltheim-Ostrau with Shri Ramana Maharshi in 1909, a year of spiritual importance in the development both of Sri Aurobindo and Rudolf Steiner.

458 Like his talk on Buddhism, Sri Aurobindo's account of Advaita Vedanta must be seen in the context of his own experiences. An expedition with the Maharaja of Baroda to Kashmir took him, in early summer 1903, to, among other places, the cliffs of Takht-i-Sulaiman near Srinagar. While looking at the surroundings of the Shankaracharya temple there, he was unexpectedly overcome by a sense of "formless solitude," an experience he formulated years later in the following words: "All had become one strange Unnameable, | An unborn sole Reality world-nude, | Topless and fathomless, forever still." In retrospect he said of this experience that it gave him insight into the Absolute, *brahman.* Quoted in Peter Heehs, *The Life of Sri Aurobindo*, op. cit.; "Encountering India: Baroda 1893–1906."

459 Sri Aurobindo, *The Life Divine.* Book I, op. cit.—chapter 3, "The Two Negations. 2. The Refusal of the Ascetic." This also includes the short phrases quoted above.

460 Ibid. Author's addition in square brackets.

461 Sri Aurobindo, *The Synthesis of Yoga*, op. cit., part 2, *The Yoga of Integral Knowledge* (Jnana Yoga), chap. 2, "The Modes of the Self."

462 Ibid.

463 Ibid.

464 Ibid.

465 But here we must ask whether Sri Aurobindo was perhaps unaware of the Christian tradition of "apophatic" knowledge of God, also

called "negative theology." This states that positive attribution of qualities to the being of God, however sublime, can never come close to his entirely transcendental reality. Dionysus the Areopagite, Master Eckhart and Nikolaus of Kues, are among the best-known representatives of apophatic thinking. Sri Aurobindo's argument in relation to Saint Francis and Calvin does not stand up in relation to these thinkers.

466 See in relation to the Hindu school of Sankhya, Klaus J. Bracker, *Wiederverkörperunhg und die innere Natur des Menschen. Sankhya—Buddhismus—Anthroposophie,* Schaffhausen 1995.

467 Sri Aurobindo, *The Synthesis of Yoga*, op. cit., part 2, chap. 2, "The Modes of the Self."

468 Ibid.

469 Ibid.

470 Sri Aurobindo, *The Life Divine*, Book One, chap. 11, "Delight of Existence: The Problem."

471 Ibid.

472 Here he is referring to the middle and to more recent periods of the Upanishads.

473 Sri Aurobindo, *The Synthesis of Yoga*, op. cit, sect. 3, chap. 5, "The Divine Personality."

474 Ibid. In direct reference to the passage in Song 15 of the *Bhagavad Gita*, on which these reflections were based, Sri Aurobindo elsewhere also formulated his vision as follows: "This then is the integral truth, the highest and widest knowledge. The Divine is supracosmic, the eternal Parabrahman who supports with his timeless and spaceless existence all this cosmic manifestation of his own being and nature in Space and Time. He is the supreme spirit who ensouls the forms and movements of the universe, Paramatman. He is the supernal Person of whom all self and nature, all being and becoming in this or any universe are the self-conception and the self-energising, Purushottama." Sri Aurobindo, *Essays on the Gita*, op. cit., Second Series, chapter 6, "Works, Devotion and Knowledge."

475 Cf. chap. 1, in the section "Spiritual Insight into the Vedic World" (especially also note 51) and chap. 3, the section "Vak: The Word of the Sublime."

476 The Advaita Vedanta characteristically calls the five sheaths of the human organization *maya-koshas*, or sheaths of appearance: *anna-maya-kosha*—the nutrition sheath; *prana-maya-kosha*—the sheath of breathing and life force; *mano-maya-kosha*—the sheath of mental consciousness; *vijnana-maya-kosha*—the sheath of higher intelligence and wisdom; *ananda-maya-kosha*—the sheath of felicity.

477 Cf. Sri Aurobindo, *The Life Divine*, Book 2 (part 1), op. cit., chap. 2, "Brahman, Purusha, Ishvara—Maya, Prakriti, Shakti."

478 Ibid.

479 Ibid.

480 Ibid.

481 Ibid.

482 Ibid.

483 Ibid. *Para-Prakriti* stands for the supreme Prakriti; *Chit-Shakti* for the creative consciousness force.

484 Sri Aurobindo, *The Life Divine,* book 2 (part 1), op. cit, chap. 2, "Brahman, Purusha, Ishvara—Maya, Prakriti, Shakti."

485 Ibid.

486 Cf. chap. 2, the section "Overmind."

487 This equates with the three soul faculties of will, feeling, and thinking, and the over-arching human "I." At the same time this is an example of how we should regard popular deities within Hinduism in terms of Integral Yoga, specifically the goddesses Kali, Lakshmi, and Sarasvati—as diverse aspects of an earlier, comprehensive divine being, in this case *shakti.*

488 Sri Aurobindo, *The Mother: With Letters on the Mother*, Pondicherry 2012, chapter 6. The spelling "supermental" was here adjusted to bring it into line with the term *supramental* as the usual usage.

489 Sri Aurobindo, *The Yoga and Its Objects*, Pondicherry 2002.

490 Enumeration of the world epochs starts from the Kali Yuga, the "Age of Kali," as the goddess of time who brings destruction with her (Kali means "the dark" or "the black." Kali Yuga is therefore the "Dark Age" or also the "Iron Age"). Then follows the Dvapara Yuga, the "Second Age" (also known as the "Bronze"). The Treta Yuga is the "Third Age" (also the "Silver"). Satya Yuga, finally, is the "Age of Truth" (also called the "Golden"). Satya Yuga also equates with the Krita Yuga, the "Age of Perfection and Completion."

491 Sri Aurobindo, *The Yoga and Its Objects*, op. cit. Here "Kali" and "Satya" are abbreviations for "Kali Yuga" and "Satya Yuga."

492 Cf. chap. 2, the section "Alipur."

493 Sri Aurobindo, *The Yoga and Its Objects*, op. cit.

494 The author is aware that Rudolf Steiner speaks of the "death" of Krishna in relation to a second date, which he places at the end of the third post-Atlantean epoch (and thus roughly 750 BC). In this context, Indian calculations are of interest, according to which the Kali Yuga only began in 701 BC. See next note.

495 In harmony with this, Indian tradition speaks of the year 3100 BC as the beginning of Kali Yuga. Current ideas about its duration, however, comprise quite different periods than the 5000 years ending in 1899: in this tradition the Satya Yuga is said to last 1,728,000 human years; the Treta Yuga 1,296,000 human years; the Dvapara Yiga 864,000 human years; and the Kali Yuga, finally, 432,000 human years (note the ratio 4:3:2:1). But the guru of Yogi Paramahansa Yogananda, who became famous in the West, Sri Yukteswar, seeks to show that such huge periods are based on serious errors of calculation made by Indian astrologers over two and a half millennia ago. His efforts are directed at relating the four yugas (descending and ascending in turn) to the Great Platonic Year. Unlike the 25,920 years familiar to us from Steiner, Sri Yukteswar gives a figure of only 24,000 years, although this is of a comparable magnitude. He retains the ratio given above and thus arrives at 2 x 4,800 years (descending and ascending), 2 x 3,600 years, 2 x 2,400 years and 2 x 1,200 years. He sees the Kali Yuga as beginning in the year 701 BC and ending in 1699. After a

200-year "twilight" period, he says, the actual new Dvapara Yuga began in 1899; and thus he more or less exactly confirms Rudolf Steiner's calculations, as well as those of Sri Aurobindo, although the latter did not give a precise date. Cf. Sri Yukteswar, *The Holy Science*, Self-Realization Fellowship 1990. See also Klaus J. Bracker, "Die Yugas. Aspekte zu ihrem Verständnis." In: *Novalis. Zeitschrift für spirituelles Denken*. Schaffhausen 2001, no. 5/6, 2001.

496 Rudolf Steiner, *The Reappearance of Christ in the Etheric,* Anthroposophic Press 1983. Lect. of May 10, 1910.

497 Cf. Thomas Meyer, "Rudolf Steiner eröffnet in Stockholm die Vorträge über die Wiederkunft Christi im Ätherischen." In: *Der Europäer. Monatsschrift auf der Grundlage der Geisteswissenschaft Rudolf Steiners*. Year 14, nos. 2/3, Basel 2009.

498 Rudolf Steiner, quoted in: Rudolf Steiner Archive (ed.), *Archivmagazin. Beiträge zur Rudolf Steiner Gesamtausgabe,* no. 1, June 2012: Roland Halfen, "Notizen von Marie von Sivers zum Vortrag Rudolf Steiners in Stockholm am 12. Jan. 1910 über das Wiedererscheinen des Christus im Ätherischen." The date 3000 BC is probably a rounding down of the date given earlier (3101 BC). The Biblical quote, "I am with you always... " is the last saying of Christ in the *Gospel of St. Matthew* (Matt. 28,20).

499 See note 498 above.

500 Cf. Rudolf Steiner, *The Christ Impulse and the development of the Ego Consciousness,* Anthroposophic Press 1976; idem, *The Reappearance of Christ in the Etheric,* op. cit.

501 Idem, *The Reappearance of Christ in the Etheric,* op. cit.

502 Cf. the detailed accounts in Klaus J. Bracker, *Grals-Initiation*, op. cit., especially chap. 2, "Das Sonnenkreuz des Jahres 1909."

503 Rudolf Steiner, *The Bhagavad Gita and the West*, op. cit., lect. of Jan. 1, 1913.

504 Idem, *The Reappearance of Christ in the Etheric,* op. cit., lect. of Jan. 25, 1910.

505 Idem, *Building Stones for an Understanding of the Mystery of Golgotha*, Rudolf Steiner Press 2015, lect. of Feb. 6, 1917.

506 Ibid.

507 This indication from the year 1917 also hints at a connection with the year 1879, when the archangel Michael became the time spirit. Corresponding to the analogy given with the life of Jesus of Nazareth—lasting for 30 years, until, with the Jordan baptism, Christ Jesus worked openly for three years—there seems also to have been a 30-year preparation period (1879–1909) of the "greatest mystery of our age," followed by three and a third years centered especially on Christ Jesus (June 1909 to Sept. 1912), who thereafter is to be expected in his etheric manifestation. These three years mark the high-point in Steiner's work of his spiritual-scientific Christology (if one thinks only of the great lecture cycles in these three years on each of the four Gospels of the New Testament). These three years are as it were sealed into one by publication of the *Calendar of the Soul* (1912/13), which in 52 weekly verses offers the human soul an entirely new kind of access to the working of the cosmic Word (the Christ) in the life of

nature through the four seasons; then also by the emergence of the new art of movement, eurythmy (cf. chap. 2, the section "Ephesus and Eurythmy").

508 In a letter, Sri Aurobindo gave the date of May 4, 1967 as an important moment for the descent of supermind and its unfolding work. Cf. Michael Klostermann, *Auroville. Stadt des Zukunftsmenschen.* Frankfurt a. M., 1976, chap. 5, sect. 3, "1962–1967."

509 Cf. Sri Aurobindo, *Letter of Sri Aurobindo on The Mother*, Bombay 1951, Section One, "Who is The Mother?"

510 Cf. Nirodbaran, *Twelve Years with Sri Aurobindo*, op. cit. chap. "Conclusion: 'He is here.'"

511 Sri Aurobindo, *The Synthesis of Yoga*, op. cit., the chap. "The Principle of the Integral Yoga."

512 Cf. Jyoti and Prem Sobel (eds.), *The Hierarchy of Minds. The Mind Levels,* Pondicherry 2011.

513 Sri Aurobindo, *Essays Divine and Human*, Pondicherry 1997, part 2, sect. 3, "Integral Yoga."

514 Ibid.

515 Ibid.

516 Ibid. This quotation, in fact, relates also to the human individuality, and thus for Integral Yoga the object is "not to lose oneself altogether in some ineffable featurelessness..., but to renounce ego for our true divine person one with the universal and infinite." Idem, ibid.

517 Sri Aurobindo, *The Supramental Manifestation on Earth*, quoted in Michael Klostermann, *Auroville. Stadt des Zukunftsmenschen,* op. cit., the chapter "Das Jahr 1970."

518 Cf. chap. 2 in the section "Overmind."

519 Sri Aurobindo, *The Supramental Manifestation upon Earth*, in the section "Supermind and Mind of Light." Quoted in Michael Klostermann, *Auroville. Stadt des Zukunftsmenschen*, op. cit., the chapter "Das Jahr 1970."

520 Rudolf Steiner, *Das esoterische Christentum und die geistige Führung des Menschheit,* op. cit., lecture of Sept. 17 1911.

521 Ibid.

522 Sri Aurobindo would probably speak of the *subtle bhu*, as a sphere, a *loka*, in which the spirit bases its manifestation "on a subtler and more plastic, more conscious principle of Matter." Sri Aurobindo, *Record of Yoga*. Appendix volume: *Glossary to Records of Yoga*, op. cit., the entry "subtle bhu."

523 Rudolf Steiner, *Das esoterische Christentum und die geistige Führung der Menschheit,* op. cit., lect. of Sept. 19, 1911.

524 Ibid.

525 Ibid.

526 Ibid.

527 Ibid.

528 Rudolf Steiner, Das *Ereignis der Christus-Erscheinung in der ätherischen Welt,* op. cit., lect. of Mar. 6, 1910.

529 In chapter 4 of this book we already focused on "Shambhala" in relation to the Puranic texts and the future Kalki Avatar. Cf. chapter 4, the section "Avatar and Evolution"; especially note 356.

530 Rudolf Steiner, *Esoteric Christianity and the Spiritual Guidance of Humanity*, op. cit., lecture of Oct. 1, 1911. Rudolf Steiner foresees expected further manifestations of the returning Christ for future millennia: today Christ Jesus is appearing, to be precise, in etheric form on the astral plane. In two to three millennia he will appear in astral form—in the world of lower Devachan; then millennia later again "as the spiritualized 'I'-Self...in higher Devachan." Rudolf Steiner, *Esoteric Christianity and the Mission of Christian Rosenkreutz*, op. cit., lect. of Nov. 4, 1911.

531 Cf. Horace H. Wilson (ed.), *The Vishnu Purana. A System of Hindu Mythology and Tradition. Translated from the original Sanscrit by H.H. Wilson,* op. cit., book 1, chap. 10; book 2, chap. 12.

532 Rudolf Steiner, *Approaching the Mystery of Golgotha*, SteinerBooks 2006.

533 See note 530.

534 Sri Aurobindo, *Essays on the Gita*, op. cit., chap. 16, "The Process of Avatarhood."

535 Rudolf Steiner, Marie Steiner-von Sivers, *Correspondence and Documents 1901–1925*, Anthroposophic Press 1998: "Introduction. Notes by Rudolf Steiner written for Édouard Schuré in Barr, Alsace, Sept. 1907."

536 Rudolf Steiner, *Christ and the Spiritual World*, Rudolf Steiner Press 1963, lect. of Jan. 2, 1914.

537 Mirra Alfassa, quoted in Mangesh Nadkarni, *Savitri—A Brief Introduction*, Pondicherry 1999.

538 Sri Aurobindo, *The Yoga and Its Objects*, op. cit., see note 489.

539 Idem, *Savitri, a Legend and a Symbol,* op. cit., book 6, canto 2: "The Way of Fate and the Problem of Pain."

540 Ibid.

541 Ibid.

542 See chap. 3, the section "Vak: The Word of the Sublime."

543 Sri Aurobindo, *Savitri, a Legend and a Symbol,* op. cit., book 6, canto 2. As here in *Savitri*, Sri Aurobindo writes similarly in *Essays on the Gita*: "The rationalist who would have cried to Christ, 'If thou art the Son of God, come down from the cross,' or points out sagely that the Avatar was not divine because he died and died, too, by disease,—as a dog dieth,—knows not what he is saying: for he has missed the root of the whole matter. Even, the Avatar of sorrow and suffering must come before there can be the Avatar of divine joy...." op. cit., ch. 16, "The Process of Avatarhood." The words about dying "as a dog" relate to Gautama Buddha, who was also regarded as an Avatar.

544 At the beginning of the '80s, a study on Integral Yoga and esoteric Christianity reached a similar conclusion. See Rainer Püschel, *Selbst-Transformation. Integraler Yoga nach Sri Aurobindo und esoterisches Christentum.* Gladenbach 1981.

Appendix 1

545 Rudolf Steiner, *Esoteric Christianity and the Spiritual Guidance of Humanity*, op. cit., lecture of Sept. 27, 1911.

546 Ibid, lecture of Sept. 28, 1911. For more on Christian Rosenkreutz from an anthroposophic perspective, see Paul Regenstreif (ed.), *Christian Rosenkreutz und seine Mission*, Freiburg i. Br. 1980; Karl Heyer, *Geschichtsimpulse des Rosenkreuzertums. Aus dem Jahrhundert der Französischen Revolution*, Basel 2004; and Peter Selg, *Rudolf Steiner and Christian Rosenkreutz,* SteinerBooks 2012. The work by Regenstreif offers a helpful survey of the numerous comments by Rudolf Steiner on Christian Rosenkreutz.

547 Rudolf Steiner, *Macrocosm and Microcosm*, Rudolf Steiner Press 1968, lecture of March 25, 1910. But here we must also consider that another, somewhat younger mystic of the late Middle Ages, Johannes Tauler—of whom Master Eckhardt approved—did, according to Steiner, have a teacher, master or guru. This teacher was the "unknown friend of God from Oberland," who helped Tauler pursue the inner path to his inner awakening or rebirth. Cf. Rudolf Steiner, *Eleven European Mystics,* Rudolf Steiner Publications Inc., 1971; the chapter "The Friendship with God." Cf. also Klaus J. Bracker, *Grals-Initiation. Anthroposophische Esoterik und die künftige Jesus-Offenbarung,* op. cit., the chapter "Seelen-Umschwung."

548 Sri Aurobindo, *Synthesis of Yoga*, op. cit., "The Four Aids."

549 Sri Aurobindo, *The Synthesis of Yoga. Part I:* "The Yoga of Divine Works." Madras 1948.

550 Hermann Beckh refers to the secret center of the heart mentioned by Sri Aurobindo, in comments that likewise relate to the World Teacher, in which he accentuates the proximity of this teacher to Christ: "Between the twelve-petalled and ten-petalled lotus lies the eight-petalled lotus flower, which Dr. Steiner also mentions on a few occasions....In Indian tradition, as the true and deeper heart lotus, this has an independent position alongside the twelve-petalled lotus. Nor is it, like the others, connected with the elementary spine but really with the heart. It is described and represented in diverse ways.... The imaginative language of India terms it a 'jeweled isle,' thus hinting at secrets of consciousness; or as a 'jewel throne' upon which the World Teacher is perceived. Here, more so than elsewhere in Indian tradition, we find ourselves in close proximity to mysteries of the Christ." Hermann Beckh, "Der übersinnliche Organismus im indischen Yoga (Lotosblumen, Kundalini) im Lichte der Erkenntnis der ätherischen Bildekräfte." In *Gäa Sophia. Jahrbuch der naturwissenschaftlichen Sektion der Freien Hochschule für Geisteswissenschaft am Goetheanum Dornach,* vol. 3. Dornach 1929.

APPENDIX 2

551 Or in an anthroposophic appraisal of the history of European esotericism.

552 Mirra Alfassa, *Words of the Mother—I*. Pondicherry 1980, 2003. The section, "Mahasamadhi."

553 Ibid.

554 Mirra Alfassa (Satprem, ed.), *Mother's Agenda. 1951–1960*, vol. 1, Paris 1978; Mère, 29 février 1956, *l'Agenda de Mère*, Volume I, 1951–1960, editions and copyright Institut de Recherches Evolutives, Lion, Mer, France. Entry for Feb. 29, 1956.

555 Cf. Sri Aurobindo, *The Human Cycle*, Pondicherry 1997; *The Ideal of Human Unity*, chap. 34, "The Religion of Humanity." There, for example, he writes: "Freedom, equality, brotherhood are three godheads of the soul; they cannot be really achieved through the external machinery of society or by man so long as he lives only in the individual and the communal ego."

556 Rudolf Steiner solved the problem of the initially abstract nature of the demand for "freedom, equality, fraternity" by showing that freedom must hold sway especially in the human being's mental and spiritual life, equality in the regulation of all legal matters, and fraternity in all shared economic activity. In this respect he spoke of the "threefold social organism." Cf. Rudolf Steiner, *Towards Social Renewal*, Rudolf Steiner Press 2000; idem, *Aufsätze* über *die Dreigliederung des sozialen Organismus und zur Zeitlage 1915–1921*, Dornach 1982. In Auroville recently a certain interest in Steiner's ideas on the threefold social order has become apparent here and there. They are regarded as compatible with Sri Aurobindo's comments.

557 Mirra Alfassa (Satprem. ed.), *Mother's Agenda*, 1965, vol. 6, Op cit. 1977, entry for June 23, 1965.

558 Mirra Alfassa, *Collected Works of The Mother, vol. 12. On Education*. Pondicherry 1978, 2002; the section, "A Dream."

559 Mirra Alfassa, *Words of the Mother—I*. Pondicherry 1980, 2003, the section, "Auroville Charter."

560 As anthroposophic Spiritual Science sees it, the consciousness soul has an intrinsic orientation to freedom and to self-determination founded on thinking and self-knowledge.

561 Cf. Anurag Banerjee, *The Former Incarnations of Sri Aurobindo and the Mother*. See: http://savitri.in/blogs/light-of-supreme/the-former-incarnations-of-sri-aurobindo-and-the-mother-by-anurag-banerjee.

562 The influential Dutch anthroposophist Daniel J. van Bemmelen, who traveled widely in India, remarked skeptically after visting the ashram in Pondicherry in 1969, and the city of Auroville that had just been founded, that his impression of the relationship between Sri Aurobindo and Mirra Alfassa was that "Aurobindo has succumbed entirely to her power." Daniel J. van Bemmelen, Reisverlag uit India. II. In: *Mededelingen van de Antroposofische Vereniging in Nederland*, year 24 (1969), no. 3. This critical view was not one, however, that Bemmelen explained in any more detail.

563 Cf. Anurag Banerjee, *The former Incarnations of Sri Aurobindo and the Mother,* op. cit.
564 Bernard Enginger (1923–2007).
565 Satprem (ed.), *Agenda of the Supramental Action upon Earth.* Volume 11. Entry, Jan. 3, 1970. Mysore 2000.
566 Cf. chapter 5, in the section "The divine—in the Intuition of Sri Aurobindo."

Appendix 3

567 Sujata Nahar, *Mother's Chronicles,* book 3, *Mirra—the Occultist.* Paris, 1989, chap. 25 "Hohlenberg."
568 Ibid.
569 Ibid.
570 Terje Christensen, "Hohlenberg, Johannes," in Bodo von Plato (ed.), *Anthroposophie im 20. Jahrhundert. Ein Kulturimpuls in biografischen Portraits.* (Anthroposophy in the twentieth century: A cultural impulse in biographical portraits), Dornach 2003.
571 "Two Postcards," in Sri Aurobindo, *Archives and Research,* vol. 13, no. 1, Apr. 1989. Pondicherry. The formulation "...something to re-awaken in your memory..." relates to a portrait of Paul Richard on the front of the postcard. "M. P. Richard" signifies both Mirra and Paul Richard.
572 Cf. Sujata Nahar, *Mother's Chronicles,* book 3, chap. 2, "Mirra, *The Arya,* and the Ashram."
573 Hohlenberg, "Letter to Judith Tyberg," July 21, 1948. From the archive of Terje Christensen, the Norwegian biographer of Johannes Hohlenberg, which was kindly made available to the author.
574 Ibid.
575 Nahar, *Mother's Chronicles,* book 3, chap. 25, "Hohlenberg."
576 With the assistance of Hohlenberg's widow Eli, this oil painting reached the Sri Aurobindo Ashram in Pondicherry many years later. This can be seen in her letter of 1978 to a prominent Ashram member, Jayantilal Parekh, who in 1973 had initiated the Sri Aurobindo Archives. She wrote, "I hope the portrait and the pencil sketches will reach you safely, and I would be grateful to receive a few words informing me of their arrival." The portrait—which had been purchased from Eli Hohlenberg by German friends of Integral Yoga—was restored in Germany and then later brought to Pondicherry.
577 Johannes Hohlenberg, *Der atmende Gott. Yoga und der europäische Mensch* [The living God: Yoga and the Europeans], Hamburg 1954. "Vorwort zur dritten Auflage" [preface to the 3rd ed.]. In fact, Sri Aurobindo was then 42 years old. In 1920 in Sweden, Selma Lagerlöf had important yogic experiences inspired by Hohlenberg's book, which also soon appeared in Swedish.
578 For more on this anthroposophic theory, see Wikipedia, "social threefolding."

579 Steiner, *Grenzen der Naturerkenntnis* (*The Boundaries of Natural Science*), Dornach 1981; lectures of Sept. 27 to Oct. 3, 1920. In addition to the specific "high school" course, two lectures were added on Oct. 2 and 3, 1920, in which Rudolf Steiner dealt on the one hand with the meaning of Eastern mantras, and on the other with traditional yoga. Here one could justifiably wonder whether in these lectures Steiner specifically intended to refer to Hohlenberg's experiences in South India.

580 Hohlenberg, *Søren Kierkegaard. Eine philosophische Biographie* (Søren Kierkegaard: A philosophical biography), Basel 2011.

581 Reference: Bodo von Plato (ed.), *Anthroposophie im 20. Jahrhundert. Ein Kulturimpuls in biografischen Portrdts* (Anthroposophy in the 20th Century: A cultural impulse in biographical portraits) Dornach 2003; (op. cit. Terje Christensen "Hohlenberg, Johannes").

582 "Naturen og Udviklingslreren," in Øjeblikket, 7. no. 1, Jan. 1, 1954; in the English original: Selection from "Man and the Evolution," in Sri Aurobindo, The Life Divine. Op. cit.; "Overmenneskets Ide" in Øjeblikket, 7, no. 2, Apr. 1, 1954; in the English original: "The Superman," in Sri Aurobindo, *Essays in Philosophy and Yoga,* op. cit.; "Om Menneskets Frie Villie," in Øjeblikket, 7, no. 3, Jul. 1, 1954; in the English original: "All-Will and Free-Will," in Sri Aurobindo, *Essays in Philosophy and Yoga.*

583 Letter from Oskar Borgman Hansen to the author, Skagen, Jul. 15, 2012.

584 Sri Aurobindo, *Bengali Writings: Translated Into English.* Pondicherry 1991, ch. 10, 2, "A Letter to Barin."

585 Ibid.

586 Ibid. There is a strong agreement with Sri Aurobindo's stand on the importance of thought and knowledge for spiritual development, in what the anthroposophic Waldorf teacher, as well as founder and first head of the Max Mueller Bhavan (Goethe) Institute in Mumbai, Heimo Rau, wrote on the Indian, "Thus Sri Aurobindo sees in the development of thinking consciousness the path of humanity toward the spirit and to further evolution. He agrees in this with Rudolf Steiner, who pointed out and presented the training of thought toward knowledge of higher worlds as the path that suits the present state of human consciousness. Aurobindo has taken up the heritage of India and transmuted it for modern-thinking humanity" (Heimo Rau, *Indiens Erbe—Illusion und Wirklichkeit heute* (India's heritage: Illusion and reality today, Stuttgart 1982).

Index